D1478271

The World through Soccer

The World through Soccer

The Cultural Impact of a Global Sport

Tamir Bar-On

ROWMAN & LITTLEFIELD
Lanham • Boulder • New York • Toronto • Plymouth, UK

Published by Rowman & Littlefield
4501 Forbes Boulevard, Suite 200, Lanham, Maryland 20706
www.rowman.com

10 Thornbury Road, Plymouth PL6 7PP, United Kingdom

British Library Cataloguing in Publication Information Available

Library of Congress Cataloging-in-Publication Data

Bar-On, Tamir.
The world through soccer : the cultural impact of a global sport / Tamir Bar-On.
pages cm
Includes bibliographical references and index.
ISBN 978-1-4422-3473-4 (cloth : alk. paper) — ISBN 978-1-4422-3474-1 (ebook)
1. Soccer—Social aspects. 2. Sports and globalization. I. Title.
GV943.9.S64B37 2014
796.334—dc23
2013049800

Printed in the United States of America

Contents

Preface

There is nothing like soccer. Nothing beats playing a soccer game on a hot summer afternoon. It feels really liberating. There is no rush like going to the soccer stadium. The forest of flags, the exalted songs, and the crowd feel like a combination of freedom and ritual communion. When the World Cup comes around, real fans don't want to miss even one game. The cafés, bars, and restaurants showing the games feel electric. The human bonding is intoxicating—minus the alcohol and drugs. After the World Cup, you follow your favorite clubs, as well as various regional and international tournaments. It seems that you can never get enough of the game: the millions of fans worldwide who form one transnational soccer tribe. You get the soccer virus early in life and it never leaves you. I got injected by the soccer virus. Dad injected me and mom let me play with reckless abandon.

For all that this beautiful game has given me, this book is my debt of gratitude. I dedicate this book to all those who have been involved with "the beautiful game" since it was first institutionalized in England in the latter part of the nineteenth century. These fans learn many lessons from soccer. The love billions of us feel for soccer adds spice, passion, and beauty to the world.

As a North American, I call the game soccer throughout the book but recognize that it is called football or variations of football in most of the world. In Spanish the game is known as *fútbol*, in French *football* (or *le foot*), in Dutch *voetbal*, in Czech *fotbal*, in Portuguese *futebol*, in Filipino *futbol*, and in Esperanto *futbalo*. In Mexico, the game is sometimes called *fútbol-soccer*. When I quote others or use official titles such as the International Federation of Association Football, I maintain the original usage of the word football.

Acknowledgments

Most of all, I thank my mom, dad, and brother Saggy for their generosity, love, and wisdom. I thank Christen Karniski, Kellie Hagan, and the people at Rowman & Littlefield for believing in this project.

Lots of other people have been most kind in assisting me. I thank Ale, Maddy, and Darko Campa for their kindness. I thank Silvia Rivera, her mother, and family for providing me with an inviting environment and delicious meals on game days for Querétaro FC. I thank Oswaldo for suggesting player choices, in particular Xavi and Iniesta. I thank Fernando Arriaga Cervantes for informing me about the philosopher Mauricio Beuchot and the "Sacred Flock," the fans of *Club Deportivo Guadalajara*. I thank William Coffin for kindly giving me his copy of *Foul! The Secret World of FIFA: Bribes, Vote-Rigging and Ticket Scandals*. I thank Jay Pence for lending me his copy of *My Life and the Beautiful Game: The Autobiography of Pelé*. I thank Mario Vázquez for providing me with a few important Spanish-language sources about soccer. I thank my university, *Tecnológico de Monterrey* (Campus Querétaro), in particular Angélica Camacho and Dr. Gabriel Morelos, for giving me the time to write this book. I thank Nereo Sanchez and Leslie Ortega for taking me around Pachuca and Real del Monte, the birthplace of soccer in Mexico. I thank Manuel Mancilla for generously sharing his passion for soccer and his unique paintings. I thank Andréia Michels for her inspirational soccer paintings. I thank Nebojša Vasović for alerting me to the genius of Dragan Džajić. I thank two assistants, Sophie St-Onge and Fernanda Martínez, for helping me with the bibliography and index. I thank my favorite teams, its players, and soccer fans in general as they have all inspired me. In particular, I thank my former teammates at Maccabi Toronto FC, FK Sarajevo, the McGill Redmen, and Armourdale Soccer Club. I thank my friends and teachers. I thank Mexico and its people.

They are blessed with a shining, warm, and welcoming spirit. As the famous song and saying goes, "*Como México no hay dos*" ("There are no two countries like Mexico"). Indeed, Mexico is unique and deep in my heart. I thank the game of soccer, which is precious like the oxygen we breathe.

Introduction

The World through Soccer combines my passion for politics and culture with a love of soccer. I am a politics professor and neo-fascism scholar,[1] as well as an insatiable soccer fan. I had an amateur soccer career that spanned more than twenty years and a website, footofgod.com, that was the largest soccer video clip archive worldwide until it was unceremoniously shut down in February 2001 by FIFA (Fédération Internationale de Football Association/ International Federation of Association Football), the world's soccer governing body. In the *New York Times* on February 13, 2001, Jack Bell wrote about footofgod.com shortly after its launch:

> More than 10,000 people a day have discovered the Internet delight of www.footofgod.com. This independent Web site is the brainchild of TAMIR BAR-ON and KADIMA LONJI, soccer fanatics who offer more than 3,000 video clips of classic goals from around the world.
>
> The site was launched in December and now has about 1,000 subscribers who get daily clips of great goals by e-mail messages.
>
> GEORGE BEST's incredible dribbling exhibition that was voted the North American Soccer League's Goal of the Year when he played in San Jose in 1981? Got it. DIEGO MARADONA's 70-yard run against England in the 1986 World Cup (not to mention the infamous hand of God goal)? Got it (both). JOHAN CRUYFF? GIORGIO CHINAGLIA? PAOLO ROSSI? Got them all.[2]

Two days after the appearance of the *New York Times* piece, the guardian.co.uk reported that footofgod.com "has been forced to shut down after threats of legal action from FIFA and other copyright holders."[3] Cahal Milmo of *The Independent* used more colorful imagery to describe the tribulations of footofgod.com:

> If it wasn't already over, it is now. A football website showing free video clips
> of famous goals submitted by fans paid the penalty yesterday after the govern-
> ing body of world football shut it down.
>
> The site, FootofGod.com, removed itself from the internet after lawyers
> acting for FIFA served its owners with a notice requiring them to take the
> cyber equivalent of an early shower.[4]

As Sam Green aptly put in *Soccer America*, footofgod.com was not interested in confronting "the big-wigs at FIFA" but being "to soccer fans what
Napster was to music lovers."[5] Napster was initially the free music file-
sharing site, while footofgod.com acted as a free soccer video clip file-
sharing site. Footofgod.com had not only video clips and accompanying
commentaries of sensational soccer goals, tackles, and saves from around the
globe, but also bloopers, commercials, tragedies, hooliganism, and even Jamaican reggae star Bob Marley showing off his soccer skills! When footof-
god.com was given its "red card" by FIFA, an e-mail campaign consisting of
more than 320,000 fans worldwide urged FIFA and other copyright owners
to reverse their legal decision.[6] With some sadness in my heart, I left footof-
god.com behind and returned to teaching and writing about politics, but I
vowed to one day write a book uniting three of my principal passions: soccer,
politics, and culture. *The World through Soccer* is the book I yearned to write
many years ago.

Politics is about the struggle for power and ideas among individuals,
communities, classes, states, and other actors—from corporations to civil
society and non-governmental organizations. Soccer, on the other hand, is
undoubtedly the world's most popular sport and evokes widespread and fren-
zied passion. As a political scientist, I am constantly struck by the intersec-
tion between soccer and politics. Pelé, whose real name is Edison "Edson"
Arantes do Nascimento, is perhaps the most recognizable soccer player of all
time. Born in Três Corações, Brazil in 1940, Pelé was known as *O Rei do
Futebol* (The King of Soccer) for his remarkable exploits, including his role
as the only soccer player in history to win three World Cups. In 1999, he was
rated Soccer Player of the Century by the International Federation of Football History and Statistics (IFFHS) and prestigious French soccer magazine
France-Football. In the same year, the International Olympic Committee
named Pelé Athlete of the Century. In a career spanning from 1956 to 1977,
Pelé scored a whopping 1,281 goals in 1,363 games. Pelé's popularity in his
native Brazil was so breathtaking that in 1995 Brazilian president Fernando
Henrique Cardoso dubbed him "Extraordinary Minister for Sport." World
leaders longed to be photographed with Pelé; the former Shah of Iran waited
for three hours at an international airport to speak with him, and Nigeria
declared a two-day truce in its war with Biafra to allow the combatants to see
him play.[7]

Soccer is no ordinary game. According to Brazilian scholars Ricardo dos Santos and Francisco Teixeira of the Federal University of Rio de Janeiro, soccer is "like the secular religion of this era with all its myths, rules and revered heroes."[8] One might add pre-match, match, and post-match rituals (supporters' songs, players clapping for their supporters when they are substituted, or players exchanging jerseys with their opponents at the end of the match); sacred commandments (never refusing to play for your national team or refusing to play for your cross-town club rivals); and places of worship (soccer "shrines," "temples," or stadiums such as the majestic Azteca in Mexico City or the Maracanã in Rio de Janeiro). There is even an *Iglesia Maradoniana* (Maradonian Church), with its eleven commandments, in Rosario, Argentina, which was created by fans of retired Argentinean soccer legend Diego Maradona.[9]

Bill Shankly, the legendary Scottish manager of Liverpool FC between 1959 and 1974, went further than Maradona worshippers in a 1981 television interview: "Some people believe football is a matter of life and death, I am very disappointed with that attitude. I can assure you it is much, much more important than that."[10] Shankly was commenting on the intensity of the cross-town rivalry between Liverpool FC and Everton FC. Yet Shankly's insight that soccer is "much more important" than "life and death" is true for millions of people in the countries where I have lived: soccer-mad Mexico, Israel, and even hockey-fixated Canada. In Italy, France, Spain, Russia, Brazil, Argentina, Morocco, South Africa, Senegal, Qatar, South Korea, and many other countries around the globe, the status of soccer eclipses "life and death." Shankly's statement also applies to "nations" without their own states that have qualified or attempted to qualify for the World Cup, including Scotland, Wales, Northern Ireland, Tahiti, and Palestine.

Demonstrating that soccer is "a matter of life and death" is easier than showing that it is "much more important" than life and death. Countless Brazilians have committed suicide after painful national team losses, including the shocking 2–1 defeat to Uruguay on home soil in the finals of the 1950 World Cup.

In Toronto, Canada, some gravesites are adorned with shirts, flags, pendants, shot glasses, and other assorted paraphernalia of the favorite soccer clubs of the deceased: Porto FC (Portugal), Benfica FC (Portugal), and Boca Juniors (Argentina). In death, as in life, these men and their families celebrated loyalty to their clubs.

Colombia's twenty-seven-year-old defender Andrés Escobar was tragically gunned down in Medellin after scoring on his own net against the USA in the 1994 World Cup. He was murdered one month before he was to marry his girlfriend, Pamela Cascardo. Escobar was an adored player for his clean and elegant style, which earned him the nickname *El Caballero del Fútbol* (The Gentleman of Soccer). It was widely rumored that powerful Colombian drug lords incurred major gambling losses due to the USA's 2–1 upset win against Colombia. The Colombian loss meant that the South Americans exited the 1994 World Cup in the first round of the competition. A staggering 120,000 fans attended Escobar's funeral. As part of his legacy, Escobar's family founded the Andrés Escobar Project, which assists disadvantaged kids in learning to play soccer.[11]

Numerous soccer players have died while playing the game. Lightning strikes have killed scores of amateur and professional players in Mexico, the United States, South Africa, and other countries. In the Democratic Republic of Congo in 1998, eleven players from the same club were killed by lightning, while the other side's players left the pitch miraculously unscathed. Thirty other people received burns from the lightning bolts. BBC News stated that "Kinshasa daily newspaper *L'Avenir* said local opinion—known to believe in charms and spells—was divided over whether someone had cursed the team."[12] On August 29, 2007, the twenty-eight-year-old Zambian international striker Chaswe Nsofwa died of sudden heart failure while playing in a training match for Israeli team Hapoel Beersheba. In that same year, Ivan Karačić (NK Široki Brijeg, Bosnia-Herzegovina), Antonio Puerta (Sevilla FC, Spain), and Phil O'Donnell (Motherwell, Scotland) all died during or shortly after soccer matches. During the 2003 Confederations Cup semifinals between Cameroon and Colombia, the Cameroonian international Marc-Vivien Foé collapsed and died shortly later in a hospital of hypertrophic cardiomyopathy, a disease caused by the thickening of the muscle of the heart. These deaths ignited debates about how modern professional soccer, which is increasingly driven by commercial imperatives and a win-at-all-costs philosophy (including the use of drugs and sophisticated doping techniques), contributes to such tragedies.

Famous soccer clubs faced tragedies that touched their respective nations. In what became known as the Munich air disaster of February 6, 1958, a plane carrying Manchester United and their supporters crashed from a wet runway in Munich. The team was returning from a European Cup match in Belgrade, Yugoslavia, against Red Star Belgrade. Out of the forty-four passengers on the plane, twenty died, including eight Manchester United players and three staff members, as well as journalists, fans, and friends. Manchester United goalkeeper Harry Gregg, a crash survivor, was conspicuous for his bravery as he stoically remained behind to pull survivors from the wreckage. Johnny Berry and Jackie Blanchflower, two other survivors, never played again and died in 1994 and 1998, respectively. Bobby Charlton, another fortunate survivor, was a member of the only English team to win a World Cup in 1966 and that year also won the prestigious European Footballer of the Year award. Geoff Bent, Roger Byrne, Eddie Colman, Duncan Edwards, Mark Jones, David Pegg, Tommy Taylor, and Liam Whelan were not as lucky and are immortalized in Manchester United club history.

On December 8, 1987, the entire Alianza Lima soccer club was killed in a crash off the Pacific Ocean near the port city of Callao, Peru. Forty-three players, managers, staff, cheerleaders, and crew died, the pilot being the lone survivor. The Peruvian Navy concealed the nature of the accident until 2006 when it was revealed that the pilot lacked night flying experience and training in emergency procedures, while poor mechanical conditions also played a role in the crash.[13] The lone survivor was Peruvian Navy Lieutenant Edilberto Villar, whom the Peruvian Navy was "protecting," while also saving face in the context of the country's "war on terror" against the Maoist *Sendero Luminoso* (Shining Path) guerrillas.

Generally viewed as the best player Austria has ever produced, Matthias Sindelar (1903–1939) was an extraordinary forward "with skills so subtle that he became famous for dribbling the ball into the net rather than shooting."[14] Sindelar played for the famous Austrian *Wunderteam* that dominated European soccer in the 1930s. He scored twenty-seven goals in forty-three appearances for Austria, but also made countless other goals through his guile and cunning. As a Jew, Sindelar was followed by Nazi authorities and this harassment increased when he opened a Vienna coffee house (named Café Annahof, in honor of his wife) after his retirement.[15] Sindelar grew increasingly depressed, disappeared, and it is suspected that he committed suicide. After his tragic disappearance, the small street in which Café Annahof is located was named Sindelar.

The World through Soccer advances the argument that soccer is a pedagogical tool that can teach us about life and death, as well as the world, irrespective of one's nationality, culture, faith, age, gender, or sexual orientation.[16] Soccer is a mirror of our world and an expression of our greatest tragedies and hopes. Soccer can open our eyes and hearts to new ways of seeing and being, perhaps toward greater knowledge and even wisdom. If we examine the world through soccer, we learn lessons about human nature, leadership, discipline and hard work, talent, luck, time, rules, values, ethics, passion and reason, individuality and teamwork, winning and losing, friendship, childhood, love, culture, politics, business and marketing, violence, spirituality, life meaning, joy, philosophy, art and literature, and social struggle.

The first part of Eccelesiastes 1:14 states "I have seen everything that is done under the sun."[17] If one searches hard enough in soccer, one can find "everything that is done under the sun"; everything about the story of the human condition from its longings and joys to its horrors. Contrary to the second part of the quote from Ecclesiastes, "and behold, all is vanity and a striving after wind,"[18] everything is not meaningless or fleeting and from soccer we can gain invaluable lessons about almost "everything that is done under the sun."

The World through Soccer is an outgrowth of both my joy and mild dissatisfaction with the literature on soccer. Renowned thinkers from Eduardo Galeano[19] to Jean Baudrillard[20] have written about soccer, while esteemed literary giants from Albert Camus to Vladimir Nabokov[21] were both soccer practitioners (goalkeepers) and commentators. Mexican, Argentinean, Uruguayan, and Brazilian writers have been particularly moved to write about soccer and they combined to pen a special issue of *Foreign Affairs En Español* (Foreign Affairs in Spanish) in the context of the 2006 World Cup in Germany.[22] Increasingly there is a vast body of literature on the sociology of sport,[23] as well as soccer and politics. While the sociology of sport and soccer literature is impressive, it is often too narrowly focused on the politics or culture of sport;[24] what soccer means to a particular country or region;[25] memoirs and autobiographies of players, managers, and even hooligans;[26] the relationships between soccer, capitalism, neo-liberalism, and globalization;[27] sport as a civilizing safety valve of controlled excitement and ritualized aggression;[28] or soccer as a tool of support for or resistance against empire, authoritarianism, or the nation-state.[29] *The World through Soccer* expands and deepens the focus of writers, sociologists, anthropologists, cultural and political theorists, journalists, players, managers, and fans who have written about soccer. It argues that soccer is not merely about politics, culture, entertainment, or business, but is also a great educational tool for all of humanity and billions of soccer fans worldwide.

The plan of *The World through Soccer* is rather straightforward. Each chapter is devoted to a lesson we can learn when we examine the world through soccer. The eleven chapters (lessons) are related to a brilliant player or several great players, who wore the number of the lesson and embody the essence of the lesson in question. Traditionally, English soccer assigns numbers based on a player's position on the field, with the starting eleven players wearing numbers 1 through 11, and substitutes wearing numbers higher than 11. The goalkeeper will generally wear number 1, while the defenders, midfield players, and forwards follow in ascending order.

In many leagues around the world now, even starting players wear numbers higher than 11, with the classic example being David Beckham's number 23 when he played for the Los Angeles Galaxy. The brilliant French strike force of Just Fontaine and Raymond Kopa wore numbers 17 and 18 respectively during the 1958 World Cup. At the 1974 World Cup, Poland's breathtaking winger Lato wore number 16 as he won the Golden Shoe for the tournament's highest scorer—seven goals—and led his country to a third place finish. The retired French international defender Lillian Thuram played as a central defender or right full-back, but wore the number 15. Johan Cruyff, the Dutch master of the 1970s and one of the greatest soccer stars of all time, was an attacking midfielder or forward who wore the number 14.

I attempted to be fair by avoiding the trap of Eurocentrism. I picked European, South American, North and Central American, African, Asian, and Oceania players because soccer is a truly global game and soccer geniuses are found on all continents. I chose both contemporary and retired players.

As with most Brazilian national team coaches, I could have picked many talented teams! *The World through Soccer* does not claim that we can learn merely eleven lessons about soccer, but that the game is a useful educational tool for all people from all cultures and for all times. The number eleven is symbolic and represents the eleven players selected to start a soccer match for the respective teams. Eleven is also the name of a well-known French soccer magazine, *Onze*. I adored reading *Onze* in my early twenties when I would visit my French relatives and make trips to the grounds of AS Nancy. AS Nancy was the club of French soccer legend Michel Platini from 1972 to 1979. Eleven was also the number worn by my father when he played in Morocco, France, and Israel. I urge my readers to use the basic pedagogical insights of *The World through Soccer* to come up with other lessons, whether in public policy,[30] management,[31] law, sexuality, fashion, communications, or psychology.

The book is divided into two parts.[32] Chapters 1 through 7 are topics often discussed in the classroom and broadly related to politics, society, and religion, including the relationships between soccer and politics, religion, ethics, and business and marketing. Part 2 includes chapters 8 through 11, which are related to the identity and character of the game. These chapters examine the relationships between soccer and leadership, childhood dreams, the meaning of life (philosophy), and fine arts. The first five chapters of the book are an outgrowth of an article I wrote in *Sociological Research Online* in 1997.[33] I am proud of that piece because it was my first peer-reviewed academic article. In that article, I never presented the argument of soccer as an educational tool. This framework is new to *The World through Soccer*. Rather, I highlighted the five functions of soccer listed below, which were heavily biased toward the relationship between soccer and politics and the hope that soccer could be a vehicle for social transformation. I use these five functions of soccer as my first five chapter lessons:

1. Soccer and competing discourses of national identity.
2. Soccer as an instrument of authoritarian and totalitarian governments.
3. Soccer as an arena for ideological hegemony and "class warfare."
4. Soccer as a vehicle for social change.
5. Soccer as a secular or pagan religion.

Let me explain the first five lessons. Chapter 1 is about how soccer is used to advance differing discourses of national identity. Soccer is a site for reflec-

tion and contestation with respect to different conceptions of national identity. When France won its only World Cup in 1998 under its talisman captain
Zinedine Zidane, a Marseille-born superstar of Berber Algerian roots, it was
imagined that France could become a more multicultural, inclusive, and egalitarian society. According to this logic, change in the soccer stadium could
precipitate changes in values and practices in government, business, media,
and civil society in general.

Chapter 2 examines the way authoritarian and totalitarian regimes have
used soccer as an instrument of political and ideological control. The lesson
of chapter 2 is the way soccer is commandeered to maintain existing power
elites, even authoritarian forms of governance. It should nonetheless be
pointed out that soccer has its limits. Chapter 2 asks the question of whether
authoritarian and totalitarian regimes have been successful in their extreme
efforts at politicizing soccer.

Chapter 3 argues that soccer is a terrain for ideological hegemony and
"class warfare." Today billions of the world's global poor long for human
security and social justice, while soccer for some has promoted a global
circus to divert attention away from real problems such as extreme poverty.
Historically, soccer has been used as a weapon of socio-economic and political elites in order to undermine broadly leftist or democratic political tendencies: Marxist, anarchist, social democratic, or the organization of working
people. The real reasons for the Soccer War in 1969 had little to do with
soccer. Nationalist discourses, the desire to maintain authoritarian military
regimes, and "class warfare" united in a deadly cocktail to unleash the Soccer
War between Honduras and El Salvador. In more recent times, we examine
the increasingly commercial nature of professional soccer and the way it
helps to conserve the status quo.

Chapter 4 examines soccer as a medium of social transformation. Del
Burgo argues that soccer is a "social phenomenon in its own right, which
may in turn have implications for the world beyond the game."[34] Soccer can
be used as a tool to "enter into a dialogue with society at large";[35] heal
divided societies; promote anti-racism; tackle neglected societal issues (for
example, rampant authoritarianism and militarism, sexism, homophobia,
poverty, environmental disasters, or ethnic and religious sectarianism); and
conceivably transform the hearts and minds of billions of followers worldwide. In 2013, nation-wide Brazilian protests against government corruption,
excessive World Cup and Olympic Games spending (for the public, this
meant less spending on education, welfare, and poverty reduction), and high
transportation prices during the Confederations Cup won the hearts of numerous Brazilian national team players and fans. In the same year, rival
Turkish fans from Istanbul (that is, Galatasaray SK, Fenerbahçe SK, and
Beşiktaş JK) put aside their differences to unite in street protests against the

authoritarian tendencies and religious conservatism of Prime Minister Recep Tayyip Erdoğan.

If FK Sarajevo soccer matches fell on or around Valentine's Day, the hard-core fans held up a banner that stated "FK Sarajevo, my love, my only love."[36] Whether one agrees or disagrees with the banner's message, soccer does not merely have to be the terrain for all that is ugly in our society. Some incidents that have stained "the beautiful game" include: the Heysel Stadium tragedy in Belgium in 1985, which killed thirty-nine Juventus FC fans before the European Clubs' Cup final between Juventus FC of Turin and Liverpool FC; Paolo Di Canio's infamous fascist salute in 2005, which led to a hefty fine by the Italian soccer authorities;[37] despicable racial taunting and anti-Semitism, which reduced professionals such as Ivory Coast's Marc Zoro to tears in one Italian league match; the aforementioned Soccer War; or Mussolini's promotion of fascist ultra-nationalism when Italy won two World Cups in 1934 and 1938. Yet soccer can also be about love and humor, as exemplified by FK Sarajevo's Valentine Day's banner, or even joy, hope, life meaning, social solidarity, resistance against corporate or colonial and state domination, and longings for societal transformation.

Chapter 5 analyzes soccer as a secular or pagan religion. Following Marshall McLuhan, soccer is a medium of communication, as well as an extension and amplification of our psychic and social selves.[38] McLuhan insists that the spectator's role in premodern societies was religious or spiritual in nature: the game was a direct replica of the struggles of the gods and the drama of the cosmos.[39] In the twenty-first century, soccer satisfies numerous human cravings and longings (some rather ugly such as hooliganism and racism), including the physical and psychic needs for personal relations and leisure in an excessively commercial age; the mystical experience of communion in soccer "temples"; what ethnologist Konrad Lorenz called "ritualized aggression"; and the mysteries of the game's events, rituals, and outcomes compared to the routinized, linear materialism of modern life.

Chapter 6 is broadly about ethics. The French existentialist writer Albert Camus, the author of such classics as *The Outsider* and *The Plague*, once said "After many years during which I saw many things, what I know most surely about morality and the duty of man I owe to sport and learned it in the RUA."[40] The RUA was the *Racing Universitaire Algérios* (RUA) junior team Camus played for as goalkeeper before contracting tuberculosis. I use this aforementioned Camus insight to draw life lessons about soccer and rules, morals, values, social responsibility, and ethics.

Chapter 7 is about business and marketing. Soccer is today increasingly a global business consisting of fans, players, clubs, corporate sponsors, advertisers, national soccer federations, and FIFA. Soccer marketing might have had its origins with the Northern Ireland international and Manchester United star George Best in the late 1960s and 1970s and Brazilian mega-star Pelé, but with modern stars such as Cristiano Ronaldo, Neymar, and Lionel Messi, soccer is today a global marketing and business tool hitherto unseen in the history of the game.

Chapter 8 is about leadership. In this chapter, I utilize leadership insights, which break down the static conception between leaders and followers, to argue that soccer is a leadership opportunity for all of us. In soccer, it does not matter whether we are young or old, men or women, players, coaches, referees, journalists, administrators, or fans. Soccer is a terrain to exercise our leadership skills, whether we are amateurs or professionals; whether we are in official positions of leadership, or far from official leadership roles.

Chapter 9 is about childhood and the notion of soccer as a dream. This chapter offers the reader meditations about soccer, childhood, and friendship. For most soccer fans around the globe, it is in childhood that we learn our love for the game. It is from childhood that we learn differing styles of play, or nostalgia for a more "pure soccer" based on the ludic qualities of the game. From soccer we make our friends. The bonds of camaraderie from soccer are profound. These bonds can last from childhood into adulthood. With our soccer teammates we laugh and joke around. Our teammates can make us upset and even angry, but we hopefully forgive and forget. From our teammates, we might learn to respect a diversity of worldviews and life-styles. From soccer we surprisingly learn about love. We are often told that love is reserved for your wife or girlfriend, mom and dad, brothers and sisters, relatives, or best friends. Don't get me wrong, but I love all those people! But what if love is also the spirit of giving everything you have for club, country, or your mates? What if love is continuing to fight on "with hope in your heart," as Liverpool FC's anthem states, even when you are down 3–0 at halftime? What if love is knowing "you'll never walk alone" even after a miserable season? What if love is sadly scoring on your own net in one half and finding the courage to score the tying goal in the next half? What if love is making up for a teammate's grave error with a game-saving defensive tackle? What if love is love of soccer and all that it teaches us about this momentary life?

Chapter 10 is about philosophy, the human quests for knowledge, spirituality, and life meaning. In this chapter, I examine soccer, the human condition, and the human longings for immortality. There is this stereotype in North America about the "dumb jock," the great athlete (perhaps a sexy athlete as well!) with absolutely no brains. I played as a defender and mid-fielder with the McGill University Redmen for three seasons. As I was completing my courses, working on my Ph.D. dissertation, doing my duties as a teaching assistant, and marking papers, I was also playing for the Redmen. Numerous Redmen teammates were also graduate students. Those Redmen players went on to become an award-winning writer and journalist, a cardiologist, a doctor, a tenured professor, and numerous other professions. They still all love their soccer and they are certainly not "dumb jocks." Soccer and other sports are unfairly denigrated in some intellectual circles. Yet people who put down soccer as a mere "opiate of the masses" fail to recognize that soccer players and their fans are not "dumb," but are rather in a privileged position to gain knowledge, wisdom, and life lessons about the world through an activity that is pleasurable.

Chapter 11 is about soccer and fine arts. *The World through Soccer* is a contribution to the growing body of literature connected to soccer. Famous writers have opined about soccer. Artists, sculptors, and architects have created pieces associated with the sport, while soccer players use the pitch as their canvas to create masterpieces. Songs and films have immortalized soccer stars. This lesson examines how we might appreciate the similarities between soccer and the arts.

In the conclusion, I link together the eleven chapters (lessons) of soccer with Shankly's insight that soccer is more important than life and death. The player choice for the conclusion will surprise many of my readers!

When Shankly uttered his famous remark in 1981, he got to the heart of what soccer means for billions of fans and players around the world. I have been to American football, hockey (ice and field), baseball, volleyball, basketball, and lacrosse matches, but never have I witnessed such levels of passion and love as at soccer stadiums around the world. I have been privileged to see thrilling soccer games in stadiums around the world: in Israel, Canada, the United States, Mexico, Italy, France, Spain, England, and Sweden. I have visited veritable soccer shrines around the world such as *Guiseppe Meazza* or *San Siro* (the homes of both Inter Milan and AC Milan) and *Delle Alpi* (the home of Juventus FC) where for ninety minutes I felt transported to a magical realm; a festive space where time was no longer the existential heaviness of linear time. Seeing *Il Divin Codino* (The Divine Ponytail), the Italian superstar Roberto Baggio, scoring twice against Bulgaria at Giants Stadium during the 1994 World Cup semi-finals was a fan's ultimate dream. When the brilliant Pelé retired in a final tribute match between the New York Cosmos and Santos FC in 1977, he ended his speech to his adoring fans with the words "Love, Love, Love!" While my favorite clubs, save Liverpool FC, are obscure by most standards (Hapoel Beersheba FC, Hapoel Tel-Aviv FC, Toronto FC, FK Sarajevo, Querétaro FC, and Liverpool FC),[41] the passion of their fans still leaves me with goosebumps. I am in my forties. Yet on match days, going to the stadium feels like I am a young child again being carried on my father's shoulders to see his modest Ashdod FC, a port town south of Tel-Aviv, Israel. The often electric atmosphere, large crowds, colorful banners, innovative, humorous, and touching supporters' songs, visiting fans' section, and aura of expectation are the same for young and old, manual laborer or professor, man or woman, Israeli,

Palestinian, Mexican, Moroccan, Spaniard, Japanese, South African, American, or Canadian.

Yet soccer also evokes the kind of explosive passions that no other game does. It has precipitated ugly displays of ultra-nationalism and racism, violent hooliganism, a Soccer War, has further divided divisive nations, united divided nations (for example, within nations or former colonial powers and colonies such as Portugal and Brazil),[42] and also given billions of people joy, meaning, and hope for a better world. In 2001, soccer was nominated for the Nobel Peace prize by Swedish parliamentarian Lars Gustafsson. "Soccer has and will continue to play an important role in the global arena, when it comes to creating understanding between people," opined Gustafsson in his nomination letter to the Norwegian Nobel Committee in Oslo.[43] Furthermore, Gustafsson argued that soccer had survived two world wars and numerous ethnic and regional conflicts, while "hostile nations" could meet on the pitch when other contact would be impossible.[44] Despite their profound mutual hostility since the 1979 Islamic Revolution, Iran and the USA met as opponents on the soccer pitch for the 1998 World Cup.

Despite soccer's nomination for a Nobel Prize, soccer has a history of violence both on and off the field. In the mid-1960s soccer hooliganism was seen as an "English" or "British disease," but it has since spread like wildfire with neo-Nazi supporters in soccer stadiums in eastern Germany, Croat-Serb hooligan soccer violence acting as a harbinger for the breakup of Yugoslavia in the early 1990s, and heightened violence at Italian, Dutch, Turkish, Russian, Argentinean, and other domestic leagues around the world. In the 1960s and 1970s, soccer was utilized to advance nefarious political goals such as the boycotting of soccer games against Israeli clubs and its national team by Arab and Muslim states, as well as some Communist states. Communist North Korea refused to play Israel in the qualification matches for the 1970 World Cup in Mexico. An Asian soccer champion and powerhouse in the 1960s, Israel qualified for its only World Cup in 1970. To avoid political entanglements, Israel switched regions for its World Cup qualifiers from Asia to Oceania and later Europe.

The World through Soccer expands on Shankly's statement and seeks to use soccer as a tool for learning about politics, religion, economics, culture, society, philosophy, spirituality, art, literature, and the human condition. While I make no excuses for soccer's drift in recent years toward a materialist, win-at-all-costs philosophy, its ugly episodes of violence, and its sometimes unnecessary mixture of soccer and political imperatives, I hope to vindicate the silent majority of decent and honest soccer fans worldwide. Institutionalized soccer is a relatively simple game born in the England of the late nineteenth century that teaches us lessons both related and unrelated to the classroom. *The World through Soccer* seeks to pass on those lessons to my readers and the billions of fans of "the beautiful game." These are the fans that continue to pay homage to the technical wizardry of Zinedine Zidane at the 1998 World Cup, Diego Maradona's breathtaking dribbling display against England on the second goal (overshadowed by the infamous first goal known as "the hand of God") at the 1986 World Cup, Pelé's goalscoring artistry in three World Cup triumphs, and the genius of Northern Irish international George Best as he terrorized defenders by making them eat dirt, or to the new soccer "gods" from Colombia's Radamel Falcao to Argentina's Lionel Messi, as well as the ones still to be born on a dusty street in Abidjan or perhaps some sleepy *barrio* (neighborhood) in a hitherto unknown Mexican town. This book is dedicated to all those fans that love soccer. It is also an invitation for people from around the world that want to examine and learn about the world through soccer.

Chapter One

Saving the Nation

Soccer and National Identity

Nationalism is a modern idea with ancient roots; it is a "state of mind," writes Hans Kohn.[1] Based on the unity of strangers, its group solidarity is linked by a common language, territory, attachment to the native soil, and traditions.[2] It finds its highest expression in the destiny of the nation and a sovereign state.[3] For the renowned English writer George Orwell, international soccer matches enhanced existing nationalistic tensions: "If you want to add to the vast fund of ill-will existing in the world at the moment, you could hardly do it better than by a series of football matches between Jews and Arabs, Germans and Czechs, Indians and British, Russians and Poles, and Italians and Yugoslavs."[4]

While this perspective is still valid today, as there has been no official soccer match between Israel and any Arab state, Orwell did not point to how national soccer teams can also be sites for inclusion within states. So, for example, the monarchy and national soccer team are two of the few symbols that unite an ethically and linguistically divided Belgium. Or, against Orwell's perspective, the former president of South Africa Nelson Mandela could declare that the national soccer team united blacks and whites in the post-apartheid era: "Soccer is one of the most unifying activities amongst us."[5] When Afghanistan defeated India 2–0 in the final of the South Asian Soccer Federation Championship in 2013, it won its first international soccer trophy, united a nation divided by years of civil strife, and sent Afghans into the streets waving the country's flag.[6] "The youth of Afghanistan showed that our nation, our people have the ability to make progress and succeed," stated a choked-up President Hamid Karzai in a message posted on YouTube after Afghanistan's historic victory.[7]

This chapter will explain how soccer advances differing discourses about national identity. Soccer is a site for reflection and debate in respect to different conceptions of national identity. As Armstrong and Testa point out in relation to Italian soccer, "[many people,] ranging from liberals to a multitude of right and left organizations and even those promoting pro-Catholic sentiment, have valued the game, and the arena in which it is enacted, as both a tool and locale for their proselytizing."[8]

National soccer teams are ideally representative of their respective states. National teams theoretically unite nations and nation-states but can sometimes divide them if there is a perception that some players are not selected because they represent historically marginalized ethnic or cultural communities. National soccer teams can also exclude not merely because one needs to be a citizen of the country to play for it but also as a result of societal pressures to field ethnically or religiously homogeneous squads. This latter perspective is known as *ethnic nationalism*, which stresses the predominance of tribal solidarity, an emotional and mystical connection to an idealized past, and national development.[9] In contrast, civic nationalism focuses on liberal universalism, rationality, individual rights and self-transcendence, and a community of numerous sovereign states living in harmony.[10] This type of nationalism is, in theory, more cosmopolitan and colorless than ethnic nationalism and based on shared republican values. Hence, civic nationalists would want players not just from the dominant ethnic group on the pitch, but all citizens of the state (irrespective of their ethnic or biological origins) united by merit and shared liberal values.

Despite this opposition between civic and ethnic variants of nationalism, one nationalism scholar warned that we should not be "too complacent" and posit a simplistic dichotomy between our "good" liberal nationalism in the West and "bad" ethnic nationalism in Russia today or Germany in the Nazi era.[11] We might also rightly ask why we continue to base our political communities on nationalist distinctions between "us" and "them," which unites ethnic and civic nationalisms. We also underestimate how even civic liberal forms of nationalism, which have their origins in the American and French Revolutions, are in part based on ethnic forms of belonging rather than merely commitment to shared liberal ideals, values, and constitutional principles.

JERSEY #1: THE LAST DEFENDER

The Russian writer Vladimir Nabokov was a goalkeeper at Trinity College in Cambridge, England, in the 1920s. He was "crazy" about the art of goalkeeping. Nabokov neatly described the mystique of his position: "The goalkeeper is the lone eagle, the man of mystery, the last defender."[12] Nabokov could also see the goalkeeper as the "keeper of a dream," whether for club or country. In chapter 9, I further explore the notion of soccer as a dream that begins in childhood.

Picking a goalkeeper, who traditionally wears the number 1 jersey, was no easy task. The goalkeeper in question must have "saved the nation" in a double sense. That is, he needed to make key saves in important international matches, which allowed the nation to achieve victories and recognition. In addition, this goalkeeper "saved the nation" in a larger metaphorical sense by giving joy and hope to the nation through his feats and uniting a potentially divided nation composed of different linguistic, ethnic, cultural, or religious groups. Moreover, our goalkeeping choice needs to be an exceptional goalkeeper recognized by the larger soccer community of administrators, managers, coaches, players, and fans.

That honor of world's greatest goalkeeper would probably go to one of the following: Ricardo Zamora (Spain), Lev Yashin and Rinat Dasaev (both USSR), Gordon Banks and Peter Shilton (both England), Josef Maier (West Germany), Dino Zoff (Italy), František Plánicka (Czechoslovakia), Gilmar dos Santos Neves (Brazil), Pat Jennings (Northern Ireland), Vladimir Beara (Yugoslavia), Jean-Marie Pfaff (Belgium), Peter Schmeichel (Denmark), Thomas Ravelli (Sweden), Rüştü Reçber (Turkey), Oliver Khan (Germany), Amadeo Raúl Carrizo (Argentina), Ladislao Mazurkiewicz (Uruguay), Antonio Carbajal (Mexico), Joseph Antonio Bell and Thomas N'Kono (both Cameroon), José René Higuita (Colombia), Naser Hejazi (Iran), Badou Zaki (Morocco), Sadok Attouga (Tunisia), or Iker Casillas (Spain).

Against all these great goalkeeping options, my choices for the number 1 jersey are the retired Paraguayan international José Luis Félix Chilavert González and the contemporary Italian international Gianluigi ("Gigi") Buffon. Buffon is the current captain of both the Italian national team and Juventus, the famous Turin-based club playing in Italy's *Serie A*.

Saving and Scoring for the Nation

José Luis Félix Chilavert was wildly passionate, fiery, eccentric, and an incredible competitor. He was unique among goalkeepers in world soccer history because he could make spectacular, outlandish saves and also score goals! He would "save the nation" when he scored for his country. Chilavert mostly scored goals from the penalty spot and set pieces with his majestic left foot. A regular free-kick taker, Chilavert could delicately chip the opposing goalkeeper, or unleash a thunderous drive from long distance. For many years, Chilavert had the record for most goals by a goalkeeper. The Paraguayan goalie had a whopping 62 goals in 737 professional matches for country and various clubs.

Chilavert's record was broken by the Brazilian goalkeeper Rogério Mücke Ceni (b. 1973), who played for São Paulo FC for most of his professional career. In about two decades of professional soccer, Ceni won fourteen major titles, including three Brazilian League trophies and two *Copa Libertadores* titles. He also scored more than one hundred goals during his career, all of them coming from penalties and free kicks. Ceni became the first and only player in his position to reach that milestone. In 2006, Ceni surpassed Chilavert's record goal tally.

Why choose Chilavert? Why not Ceni? Although Ceni has the goalscoring record for goalies and is a decent shot stopper, he contributed less to the Brazilian national team than Chilavert did for the Paraguayan national team. Ceni was a Brazilian international for nine years and garnered sixteen caps for his country. He was selected to the Brazilian squad that won the 1997 Confederations Cup and was picked for the 2002 and 2006 World Cups. Yet Ceni was never Brazil's first choice goalie. He only appeared in two games in major tournaments for his country.

In contrast, Chilavert was Paraguay's first choice goalkeeper for many years. Chilavert played for the national team from 1989 until the year before his retirement in 2003. He played in seventy-four matches and scored eight goals for Paraguay. In his first game for Paraguay in a qualifying match for the 1990 World Cup in 1989, Chilavert scored a penalty in a famous 2–1 win against rival Colombia. Chilavert brilliantly represented Paraguay at the 1998 and 2002 World Cups, in France and South Korea-Japan (joint hosts), respectively. At the 1998 World Cup, Paraguay was eliminated in the second round on a golden goal by Laurent Blanc. France won the 1998 World Cup and its gravest test was the stellar defense of Paraguay and the goalkeeping heroics of Chilavert. At the 1998 World Cup, Chilavert also became the first goalkeeper ever to take a direct free kick in a World Cup match against Bulgaria. He came within inches of scoring!

José Luis Chilavert was born on July 27, 1965, in the Paraguayan city of Luque. It is located in the smallest province in Paraguay (Central Department), yet it is the most populated and economically prosperous province in the entire country. Luque was the capital of the Paraguayan Republic in 1868 during the Triple Alliance War in which Paraguay faced off against Brazil, Uruguay, and Argentina. Luque is also the host city for the *Confederación Sudamericana de Fútbol*, the South American Soccer Confederation.

In 1980, Chilavert made his debut for Sportivo Luqueño in the Paraguayan First Division at the tender age of fifteen. He played with the club until 1983. In 1984, Chilavert moved to one of the bigger clubs in the Paraguayan capital city Asunción, Club Guaraní, where he won the First Division championship.

In 1985, Chilavert caught the eyes of Argentinean club San Lorenzo de Almagro. In 1988, he was transferred to Spanish club Real Zaragoza, where he played until 1991. It was at Real Zaragoza that Chilavert scored his first club goal in 1990.

The club that was probably closest to Chilavert's heart was an Argentinean outfit, Buenos-Aires-based Club Atlético Vélez Sarsfield, where the Paraguayan goalkeeper reached the apogee of his soccer accomplishments. Chilavert remained with the Argentinean team from 1992 to 2000, the longest of any of his seven clubs in two continents. It was at Vélez Sarsfield that Chilavert perfected his techniques in shot stopping and scoring. He scored an incredible forty-eight out of his sixty-two goals for Vélez Sarsfield. Moreover, it was at his beloved Argentinean club that Chilavert won four domestic titles (1993, 1995, 1996, and 1998) and five international titles, including both the South American Club Championship and Intercontinental Cup in 1994.

After his long career in Argentina, Chilavert moved to French team *Racing Club de Strasbourg* from 2000 to 2003. At the French club, Chilavert scored one goal and won the French Cup in 2001.

South America called again in 2003 and this time Chilavert joined the famous Montevideo-based outfit Peñarol, where he scored four goals. Peñarol won the Uruguayan First Division title in Chilavert's only season with the club.

In 2004, Chilavert retired and in his final year returned to play one last campaign for his beloved Vélez Sarsfield. On November 15, 2004, in front of a packed *Estadio José Amalfitani* stadium in Buenos Aires, Chilavert played in his spectacular farewell match. The great South American players of the generation were all on hand: Iván Zamorano, Carlos Valderrama, René Higuita, Enzo Francescoli, Alex Aguinaga, Celso Ayala, Daniel Cáceres, Claudio Morel, Celso Esquivel, and Marco Etcheverry.

Representing the Nation

Chilavert "saved" Paraguay with his shot-stopping abilities and goals. After his retirement, Chilavert said the following about his potential market value: "I don't know what a Chilavert would be worth at today's prices, but I'm sure it'd be a lot of money. There aren't many keepers who can go forward and score goals."[13] Yet Chilavert was interested in more than financial gain. He was immensely proud of representing Paraguay, a landlocked South American country of about 6.5 million people, bordering Argentina, Brazil, and Bolivia. After Paraguay's heroic performances at the 1998 World Cup, Chilavert could say that the national team put an unknown South American country on the map of world consciousness: "Nobody had heard of us when we arrived in France. They couldn't even place Paraguay on the map. The whole world knew about us after the tournament though."[14]

The World Cup offers an international stage for little-heard-of nations. Paraguay's stellar defensive performances and Chilavert's brilliant saves in 1998 led many soccer fans to search for more information about the country. Spanish and the indigenous Guaraní are the official languages of Paraguay, with more than 90 percent of the population speaking both languages. Paraguay's history has not been an easy one. Following Paraguay's independence from Spain, the South American state was ruled by a series of dictators. The disastrous Paraguayan War (1864–1870) saw the country lose 60 to 70 percent of its population and large amounts of territory. Paraguay faced the Triple Alliance of Argentina, Brazil, and Uruguay in the Paraguayan War.

Thus, given its history, Paraguay has always been touchy about its sovereignty and territorial integrity. Chilavert was fond of pointing out that the Republic of Paraguay is "for always" a "free and sovereign nation," which is independent of any "foreign power."[15] He could tell Bolivian, Argentinean, and Brazilian leaders Morales, Cristina Fernández, and Rousseff not to interfere in Paraguayan internal affairs after they called the impeachment of former Paraguayan president Fernando Lugo in 2012 a "coup d'état."[16]

During large chunks of the twentieth century, Paraguay was ruled by the military strongman Alfredo Stroessner (1919–2006), who led one of South America's longest surviving military dictatorships from 1954 to 1989. In line with a wave of democratizing processes throughout Latin America, in 1989 Stroessner was ousted and free elections were held in 1993. Chilavert responded positively to the new changes in his country, arguing that he was "proud" of the "democratic and constitutional" changes in Paraguay.[17]

In 1991, Paraguay joined Mercosur (or *Mercado Común del Sur*—Southern Common Market) along with Argentina, Brazil, and Uruguay. Venezuela and Bolivia later joined the organization. Note that this Mercosur agreement was with three states that historically waged war against Paraguay, thus creating a new chapter in Paraguayan history. Chilavert was not shy about linking Mercosur to a more subtle project led by the old Triple Alliance nations Argentina, Uruguay, and Brazil, designed to "stab" Paraguay "in the back." He was thus a Paraguayan nationalist both on and off the field. In 2012, Paraguay was suspended from Mercosur over the Lugo "coup d'état." In 2013, the country's suspension was lifted.

"GIGI": A NEO-FASCIST IN DISGUISE?

If Chilavert was a devoted Paraguayan nationalist, Gianluigi "Gigi" Buffon was possibly an Italian ultra-nationalist and neo-fascist in disguise. He is undoubtedly one of the greatest contemporary goalkeepers and the most consistent from the mid-1990s until today. Born on January 28, 1978, in Carrara, Italy, Buffon has also been hailed as one of the legendary goalkeepers of all time. The diving and acrobatic save Buffon made on a thumping Zinedine Zidane header in extra time of the 2006 World Cup was one of the most brilliant saves of all time and gave Italy the opportunity to win the competition in a penalty shootout. France was denied its second World Cup triumph and Italy won its fourth World Cup title.

An Italian international since 1997 (more than 135 appearances until 2013), Buffon was selected by Pelé as one of the 125 greatest living soccer players in the world. He has been named the *Serie A* Goalkeeper of the Year a record nine times and was the winner of the 2006 Yashin Award for best goalkeeper after Italy won the World Cup in 2006. In 2003, Buffon became the only goalkeeper to have won the UEFA Club Soccer Player of the Year Award. He also won the award for best goalkeeper that year and was voted into the UEFA Team of the Year in 2003, 2004, and 2006. In 2006, Buffon was runner-up for the prestigious *Ballon d'Or* as the world's greatest player. The IFFHS has named him the goalkeeper of the year four times, goalkeeper of the last quarter century (1987–2011), and goalkeeper of the decade.

There are few doubts about Buffon's shot-blocking skills and his ability to commandeer defenses with Parma, Juventus, and the Italian national team. Buffon's problems are off the field. In May 2006, along with other Juventus players, Buffon was accused of participating in illegal betting on *Serie A* matches. Buffon cooperated with authorities, but insisted that he never placed bets on Italian soccer matches. Buffon was cleared of all charges in 2007; his club was found guilty. Juventus was stripped of two *Serie A* titles and relegated to *Serie B*. Many fans questioned Buffon's moral compass. Keep Buffon's actions in mind when I examine the relationship between soccer and ethics in chapter 6.

Buffon was not new to the controversy business. He first stirred controversy while establishing himself as one of the world's greatest goalkeepers with Parma from 1995 to 2001. Buffon has worn the number 1 jersey with Juventus since 2001 and also wears the same number with the Italian national team. Yet in the 2000 to 2001 season Buffon caused outrage throughout Italy when he chose to wear the number 88 jersey. For those people familiar with neo-fascist and neo-Nazi symbolism, number 88 is not a benign number. Writing in *The Guardian*, Jon Brodkin explained Buffon's choice of shirt number, the reactions in Italy, and Buffon's less than sincere responses to the controversy:

> The goalkeeper's decision to wear 88 caused consternation among Italy's Jewish community, which pointed out that the figure is a neo-Nazi symbol. "H" is the eighth letter of the alphabet, so 88 equates to HH, or Heil Hitler.
> Buffon has previously worn a shirt bearing the slogan "*Boia chi molla*"— "Death to cowards"—which was used by fascists in Benito Mussolini's day. But he called a press conference yesterday to explain that people had the

wrong impression. After his mother had said her son's accusers "should be ashamed of thinking such things," that is.

"I have chosen 88 because it reminds me of four balls and in Italy we all know what it means to have balls: strength and determination," he said. "And this season I will have to have balls to get back my place in the Italy team."

The plot, though, thickens. "At first I didn't choose 88," he explained. "I wanted 00 but the league told me that was impossible. I also considered 01 but that was not considered a proper number. I liked 01 because it was the number on the General Lee car in the TV series the Dukes of Hazzard."

Buffon, who said the Holocaust disgusted him and the "Nazi slur" had hurt him, added that he was willing to heed a call from the Jewish community, which asked him to switch shirts "out of respect for Jews, *tziganes* [gyspies] and homosexuals."

"I am ready to change numbers if that will help," he explained. "I didn't know the hidden meaning of 88."[18]

Buffon took the path of supposed ignorance. This was hard to believe in a country that brought the world the first fascist movement in 1919 under a radical former socialist firebrand named Benito Mussolini, who mixed ultra-nationalism with Marxist revisionism to create a potent, revolutionary, and new ideology.[19] The controversy ended when Buffon offered to wear the number 77 jersey and the following year he went to Juventus, where he has worn the number 1 shirt and been the first choice goalkeeper since 2001.

It is interesting to note that Buffon's reaction was mirrored by the retired Italian soccer player and former Sunderland manager Paolo Di Canio. Di Canio and some members of the neo-fascist National Alliance insisted that there should be no "drama" after the Italian national soccer federation fined him in 2005 for his fascist salute while playing for Lazio. Yet Di Canio was candid enough to say the following about his fascist salute, which former Italian prime minister Silvio Berlusconi justified as an act of a mere "exhibitionist": "I will always salute as I did yesterday because it gives me a sense of belonging to my people."[20]

As the Sunderland manager, Di Canio sought to focus on his "managerial skills" rather than his pro-fascist sympathies, even earning the disdain of an anti-fascist miners' association in Durham. The miners' welfare group protesting Di Canio's appointment as Sunderland manager stated "it will end its opposition only if the club agrees to join it in an anti-fascist campaign."[21] After being hired as Sunderland manager in 2013, Di Canio set perfect professional and marketing tones and changed his tune about fascism: "I am not political, I do not affiliate myself to any organisation. I am not a racist. I do not support the ideology of fascism. I respect everyone. I am a football man. This and my family are my focus."[22] In chapter 4, I point to the possibilities for social transformation through anti-racism campaigns, while in chapter 7, I highlight the marketing logic of such initiatives.

It is important to underscore that Di Canio forgot to mention his pro-fascist sympathies, as well as that Lazio (the club where he gave the fascist salute) was the team of Italian fascist leader Benito Mussolini and that he has an obsession with the infamous dictator. He has a tattoo with the word *Dux*, the Latin word for *Duce* and the nickname of Benito Mussolini.[23] On match day outside the Olympic Stadium in Rome, home to both Lazio and Roma, "the stadium stands sell not only football-related merchandise but busts of Mussolini and other fascist regalia."[24] Moreover, in a 1999 match against cross-town rivals Roma—a team widely supported by the city's small Jewish community—Lazio's hardcore fans "reached dizzying anti-Semitic heights when they unfurled a 50-metre banner around their section of Rome's Olympic Stadium that read: 'Auschwitz is your town, the ovens are your houses.'"[25]

Di Canio's and Buffon's messages are more veiled in a "post-fascist age" where it is no longer acceptable to say that you want to re-open the gas chambers or Auschwitz.[26] Like most fascists in a "post-fascist age," Buffon and Di Canio play "a clever double-game."[27] On the one hand, they provoke with the fascist salute or the choice of the number 88 jersey, symbols that represent ultra-nationalism, race laws, anti-Semitism, imperial expansionism, colonialism, militarism, the exaltation of violence, the cult of the leader, and the aim of totalitarianism.[28] On the other hand, the two soccer idols claim that their symbols are innocent, "normal, banal, and apolitical."[29]

Some of Di Canio's and Buffon's supporters also insist that left-wing symbols at soccer stadiums produce no reactions from the authorities, while fascist symbolism is severely sanctioned. The same complaints could be heard from Italian neo-fascist soccer fans. These fans do not always represent the views of official neo-fascist movements and parties, but reflect the general right-wing tide in Italian society since the mid-1990s and the rise of Silvio Berlusconi, who served three times as Italian prime minister. Rather, they use the soccer stadium to articulate their non-conformist ideas since, as one neo-fascist supporter from Rome argued, "The state does not allow the individual to freely speak out because of rampant political correctness."[30]

The change in rhetorical strategies on the part of neo-fascist soccer players and fans is mirrored by extreme right-wing political parties such as the French National Front (*Front National*) and the allegedly "post-fascist" Italian National Alliance (created out of the ashes of the neo-fascist Italian Social Movement), which joined national coalition governments in 1994 and several times in the twenty-first century under Prime Minister Silvio Berlusconi. The rhetorical strategies are borrowed from the French or European New Right (*nouvelle droite*) intellectuals such as Alain de Benoist and Guillaume Faye. These intellectuals have sought to create a fascism with "another name, another face."[31] These intellectuals insist that they are anti-fascist, anti-racist, anti-totalitarian, and pro-multiculturalism, yet long for ethically pure states cleansed of immigrants and official multiculturalism.[32]

The pro-fascist views of Buffon and Di Canio were not new for professional soccer. Tragically, numerous soccer players, managers, or referees were involved or killed during World War II, or due to the Holocaust and Nazi collaborationism. Southampton and Arsenal lost numerous soccer players during World War II: Norman Catlin, Sid Gueran, and Charlie Sillett (all Southampton), as well as Bobby Daniel, Leslie Lack, and Herbie Roberts (all Arsenal).

In the introduction, I pointed to the best soccer player Austria has ever produced, Matthias Sindelar, a national team star in the 1920s and 1930s. Sindelar was a Jew harassed by Nazi authorities and probably committed suicide as a result of his mistreatment.

More ominously, Alexandre Villaplane, the Algerian-born midfielder and captain of the French national side at the inaugural World Cup in Uruguay in 1930, became one of the leaders of a North African Brigade during World War II that collaborated with the Nazi SS against resistance organizations.[33] On December 1, 1944, Villaplane was sentenced to death for his direct involvement in at least ten killings. He was executed by firing squad on December 26, 1944.

Furthermore, the Simon Wiesenthal Centre accused Estonian international goalkeeper Evald Mikson of war crimes against Jews during World War II because he acted as deputy head of police in Tallinn.[34] The Estonian Historical Commission for the Investigation of Crimes Against Humanity accepted that Mikson was guilty of war crimes. Mikson eventually moved to Iceland. In 1993, the Icelandic government began a war crimes investigation against Mikson, but he died in Reykjavík that year before coming before the court.

Soccer players and managers also perished in the Holocaust. The Hungarian manager Árpád Weisz died at Auschwitz in 1944. Julius Hirsch, the first Jew to represent the German national soccer team, died at Auschwitz in May 1945.[35] Decorated with the Iron Cross for his four years of service to the German Army in World War I, Hirsch was a German patriot who could not believe that Germany would be so cruel as to devour its own heroes.

SOCCER AND DISCOURSES OF NATIONALISM

At this juncture, I will demonstrate how Buffon and Chilavert are good representatives of lesson one, namely, soccer and competing discourses of nationalism. Let us begin with some general comments about soccer and discourses of nationalism and statehood in Latin America, as well as about nationalism in general. These comments will be especially useful in relation to Chilavert, while the general comments about nationalism help us better understand the political engagements of both Buffon and Chilavert.

After having largely broken the legacy of colonial rule in the nineteenth century, the idea of nationhood was consolidated throughout Latin American in the twentieth century.[36] Across the region, the idea of the nation was "imagined, created, and constructed" by Latin American political and cultural elites in speeches, literature, museums, various art forms from painting and theater to dance and folk traditions, and a plethora of national and political institutions.[37] Within this general awakening of Latin American nationalism, soccer became intertwined with discourses of statehood and the search for national identity.

The use of soccer as an instrument to construct national identity was not lost on the Marxist historian Eric Hobsbawm: "The imagined community of millions seems more real as a team of eleven named people."[38] For Hobsbawm, soccer is able to seize the popular imagination and arouse both nationalistic and chauvinistic tendencies more concretely than other realms of cultural and political production. As Argentinean intellectual Beatriz Sarlo neatly put it, soccer is the "favorite glue" used to salvage a country's national identity.[39] Furthermore, as a mass appeal sport, which is not considered discriminatory along class lines like more "snobbish" and expensive games from rugby and golf to tennis and cycling, soccer in the Latin American context is considered a more legitimate "national game" as it can encompass and unify all social classes. Or, for Markovits and Rensmann, soccer can both "construct and deconstruct national identity," while trends associated with "postindustrialization" and "second globalization" enhance cosmopolitan inclusiveness ("people love good players" on the national team, "no matter their origins") and reinforce "frozen sports spaces" connected to traditional conceptions of collective, nationalist identity.[40] In short, the national soccer team can be a site for inclusion or exclusion.

Yet soccer has historically been wedded to national teams that are exclusively male. The Women's World Cup is a recent event, its first competition taking place in China in 1991. By contrast, the Men's World Cup was first inaugurated in Uruguay in 1930. At the 2007 Women's World Cup, U.S. captain Kristine Lilly competed in her fifth and final World Cup, making her the first woman and one of three players in history to appear in five World Cups. Bente Nordby (Norway), Formiga (Brazil), Brirgit Prinz (Germany), and Homare Sawa (Japan) have also participated in five World Cups. The only two male players to represent their nations at five World Cups were the Mexican goalkeeper Antonio Carbajal, known as *El Cinco Copas* (The Five Cups), and the legendary German midfielder and sweeper Lothar Matthäus (1982, 1986, 1990, 1994, and 1998), who won the prestigious FIFA World Player of the Year in 1991.

The 1999 Women's World Cup final between the USA and China, held on July 10 at the Rose Bowl in Pasadena, California, was the most attended women's sports event in history with an official attendance of 90,185. Despite the professionalization of the women's game, state and corporate funds have tended to favor the men's game. It is rather interesting that as late as 1979 Chilavert's Paraguay banned women from playing soccer, declaring it contrary to their "natural femininity."[41]

In countries that face stark economic and political problems from extreme poverty to a "war on drugs," soccer acts as the great societal equalizer as it provides popular expressions of celebration and pride for national team victories. Before heading off to Chile for the 1962 World Cup in an attempt to repeat as World Cup champions, Brazilian players were received by President Goulart who told them "We must keep this Cup because it is the pride of the entire nation; it makes us forget the economic difficulties of our compatriots and is worth more than any riches."[42] When Mexico surprisingly won the soccer gold medal at the 2012 Olympic Games in Britain by defeating the favorite Brazilians in the finals, there was hardly a city in Mexico that did not witness spontaneous mass celebrations. Alternatively, national gloom, mourning, and occasional suicides are not uncommon after national team losses. While it is true that there are different conceptions of national identity from more inclusive to exclusivist forms of belonging, the visceral emotions elicited by the national colors, the chanting of the national anthem, and the anticipation of match day generally leads toward a united front on behalf of the collective national entity.

In the mirror of the national soccer team, one finds expressions of national identity and national pride, perhaps even of national style. In all the chapters, I pay homage to players that were not selected, but that nonetheless help us to understand the lesson in question. For this chapter, those two players are Colombian-born goalkeepers Miguel Calero Rodriguez and José René Higuita. A naturalized Mexican goalkeeper, Miguel Calero Rodriguez (1971–2012) played fifty times for Colombia from 1995 to 2007. Calero was a member of the Colombian national team at the 1998 World Cup. In 2001, he had his greatest moment as a member of the Colombian national team when they won their first ever Copa América (South American) championship. Known for wearing a distinctive baseball cap while he played, Calero had his most stunning club performances with CF Pachuca in the Mexican first division. From 2000 to 2011, Calero made 395 appearances for Pachuca and even managed to score two goals. In honor of his excellent goalkeeping abilities, Pachuca retired his number 1 jersey after he played his last game with the club in 2011. Calero won an impressive ten domestic and international titles with Pachuca.

While I was writing *The World through Soccer*, Miguel Calero tragically died at the age of forty-one after suffering a stroke caused by a blood clot in his arm. About five thousand faithful supporters attended a chillingly beautiful wake in his honor in Pachuca, with fans chanting "Tuzo forever" (Tuzo is the nickname of the Pachuca club and means gopher) and "Calero, we will always remember you."[43] Calero had retired merely one year before his death. After his death, Calero's number 1 Pachuca jersey was permanently retired.

There are different conceptions of the nation in states and civil societies. Calero had dual citizenship (Colombian and Mexican). He was loved by Colombians and Mexicans alike. FIFA, the world's soccer governing body, does not allow players to play for different senior national teams. Yet soccer authorities did allow players to play for different national teams in another epoch. Alfredo Di Stéfano (b. 1926), one of the greatest soccer players of all time and a legend in his native Argentina, played internationally for Argentina in 1947, Colombia in 1949, and Spain from 1957 to 1961. In a globalized world of fluid and multiple identities, as well as double and triple citizenship, should FIFA allow players to switch national teams? However, there are fans and voices in society who insist that naturalized players should not be allowed to play for the national team and thus advance an ethnically exclusivist and homogeneous notion of national identity.

The Colombian goalkeeper Higuita was a real character. He loved to play with his feet, long before it was fashionable or necessary. He tended to dangerously drift out of his net and dribble with the ball. Known as *El Loco* (The Madman), Higuita is immortalized in soccer history for his famous "The Scorpion" clearance against England at Wembley Stadium in a 0–0 draw on September 7, 1995. What Higuita did that September day at Wembley was appreciated by all those that love "the beautiful game." Jamie Redknapp's shot could have been easily caught or punched. Instead Higuita invented a maneuver that came to be called *El Escorpión* (The Scorpion), an acrobatic and risky technique that left fans worldwide in awe and the Colombian manager sweating! "The Scorpion" entails the goalkeeper arching his body backward and letting the ball drop behind his head. The goalkeeper then clears the ball with the outside of his heels, while elevating both of his feet above his back. In 2008, Higuita's "The Scorpion" was elected as the greatest moment in soccer history by the English website Footy-Boots.com.[44] About 20 percent of those participating in the voting opted for "The Scorpion" as the best moment in soccer history, thus lending some credence to the notion that people love soccer for its aesthetic qualities. Fans can love the game intrinsically, irrespective of the final results.

Higuita was known as "The Madman" for other reasons too. As a goalkeeper, he scored forty-one goals, fourth on the all time list, several places behind one of the representatives of lesson one: Chilavert. The Medellín-born Higuita was imprisoned in 1993 due to his mediation role in a kidnapping. He acted as an intermediary between the drug lords Pablo Escobar and

Carlos Molina, eventually helping secure the release of Molina's daughter by delivering the ransom money. He received a handsome payment and thus violated Colombian law. He was sent to prison and released without charge after seven months. While "The Scorpion" was one of the great aesthetic moments of soccer history, Higuita was also responsible for one of the most embarrassing moments in Colombian soccer history. Known for coming way too far out of his net and dribbling excessively, Higuita was dispossessed at the halfway line by Cameroon forward Roger Milla and the latter scored to send Cameroon to the quarterfinals of the 1990 World Cup. Higuita colorfully described the error as "a mistake as big as a house."[45]

The question we might ask here is whether Higuita represented the Colombian nation through his eccentric character. Did his eccentric, risky, and imaginative style of play represent the aspirations of the Colombian nation? Or was Higuita for most Colombians a caricature of the nation? Did his "The Scorpion" clearance embody the joie de vivre of all Colombians? Was the craziness of "The Madman" laughed at or lauded? What is more important for the Colombian nation: winning or playing with style? Or winning with style?

* * *

Paraguay is a relatively unknown South American nation compared to Colombia, Brazil, and Argentina, but it fills Chilavert and Paraguayans with pride that they have participated in eight World Cups, including the inaugural World Cup in 1930. The Paraguayan national team, locally known as *Los Guaraníes* in homage to the indigenous language or *La Albirroja* (The White and Red), has reached the second round of the World Cup four times: 1986, 1998, 2002, and 2010. The 2010 World Cup saw Paraguay make their first appearance in the quarterfinals. Paraguay's only major tournament victories have come in the *Copa América*, when they triumphed in 1953 and 1979.

Soccer triumphs for small nations such as Paraguay become popular national symbols of unity, resolve, and national character. Soccer for Paraguay, or other small nations from Costa Rica to the Ivory Coast, confirms national existence to the international community. Eduardo Galeano argues that tiny Uruguay built many soccer fields and participated in international soccer tournaments as early as the 1920s as part of a positive nation-building scheme.[46] The strategy has paid off for Uruguay with greater international recognition as a result of its overachieving performances at major soccer tournaments. Uruguay is the smallest country in the world to have won a World Cup: it had less than two million people when it won the first World Cup in 1930. The UN Secretary-General Kofi Annan put best what participating in the World Cup means to smaller nations like his native Ghana:

> For any country, playing in the World Cup is a matter of profound national pride. For countries qualifying for the first time, such as my native Ghana, it is

a badge of honor. For those who are doing so after years of adversity, such as Angola, it provides a sense of national renewal. And for those who are currently riven by conflict, like Côte d'Ivoire, but whose World Cup team is a unique and powerful symbol of national unity, it inspires nothing less than the hope of national rebirth. [47]

For others, in the face of worldwide capitalist globalization and cultural homogenization, soccer is a national symbol of enduring loyalty. Indeed, Pablo Alabarces has gone so far as to suggest that the notion of national unity represented by the national soccer team is a "mere illusion" in a postmodern age based on multiple identities where television revenues, rampant capitalist consumerism, and a weak citizenry reign. [48] In this respect, for Alabarces Buffon's betting charges and the commercialization of the game rather than his pro-fascist sympathies are fundamentally more important.

For still others, in the euphoria of national soccer matches, the divisions of left versus right, environmentalists versus pro-business activists, or bourgeoisie versus proletariat all melt into air. Del Burgo argues that while the diversity of social, cultural, religious, and ethnic origins that comprise the citizenship of any nation can be problematic and divisive, soccer is one means of "imagining" national unity within the national consciousness. [49] In diverse multi-ethnic societies, Hecht insisted in the late 1960s that soccer is "without doubt one of the principal factors in bridging the gap between the white and colored races." [50] National soccer aspirations create a common purpose in order to stunt potential or actual internal divisions and exaggerate external ones. When the national team is not very successful, it is leading club teams that act as catalysts for the crystallization of popular nation-wide support. Before Chilavert's Paraguay began its great run of entering successive World Cups from 1998 to 2010, it was club team Olimpia that provided Paraguayans with national joy when they won the coveted South American *Copa Libertadores* in 1979 and 1990 and the World Club championship in 1979.

It is also true that soccer has been used to advance racist, chauvinist conceptions of the nation. Markovits and Rensmann insist that while soccer increasingly acts as a cosmopolitan force for inclusiveness through the principle of merit at both club and country, they point out that in Europe, in contrast to North America, racist ultra-nationalism, chauvinism, and skinhead violence at stadiums against foreigners are examples of "strong antimodern reactions that reflect generalized cultural opposition to globalization and cosmopolitanism, especially in traditionally ethnically exclusive societies." [51] Before a 2012 "friendly" game played in Budapest between Hungary and Israel, the Israeli newspaper *Haaretz* reported that Hungarian fans chanted "stinking Jews," "Heil Benito Mussolini," and "Palestine, Palestine" during the singing of *Hatikvah*, Israel's national anthem. [52] In a chilling You-

Tube video, the racist fans are seen holding Hezbollah and Islamic Republic of Iran flags, turning their backs, and booing as the Israeli anthem is being played. Hezbollah and the Islamic Republic of Iran are united by a genocidal anti-Semitism and have both called for the elimination of the state of Israel.

Hardcore neo-fascist soccer fans known as *Ultras* can be found in various clubs throughout Europe and they tend to cultivate transnational ties: Roma (Italy), Benfica (Portugal), Hammarby (Sweden), Real Madrid (Spain), Werder Bremen and Lokomotiv Leipzig (Germany), Panathinaikos (Greece), and Paris St. Germain (France).[53] The Boys Roma, a neo-fascist supporters' group based in the Italian capital, puts out a monthly fanzine titled "The Honor of Rome" and regularly publishes the following poem:

> I walk along the streets bold and proud. I am the son of an ancient EMPIRE
> I serve my fatherland, I am Italian
> I am proud to give the Roman SALUTE
> Attached to affections and to the religion [Catholic]
> Never will I bend my will in front of the "master" [Italian authorities]
> The motto that I follow is
> Will, Power and Freedom
> I do not love the weak and promiscuity
> I am not violent
> I do not wish to repress
> But I wish that everyone remains in their nations
> People respect me
> Because they know I am a perfect citizen
> I wait for the Celtic Sun to rise
> In the hope that everything will improve.[54]

A charismatic French extreme right-wing leader from 1972 until 2011, Jean-Marie Le Pen stressed the idea that he was supposedly not racist and that the ideal form of globalization is that "everyone remains in their nations." The former French *Front National* leader was an anti-immigrant politician and an inspiration for ultra-nationalist politicians throughout Europe. He protested that French national soccer team players did not chant the French national anthem with enough vigor. It mattered little to Le Pen that France won its only World Cup in 1998. The implication of Le Pen's assertion was that France's national team was too black, brown, and Arab, or not "French French" (white, Catholic, and biologically French) enough. He thus longed for a French national identity that was based on the principal of *jus sanguinis* (birth by blood) rather than *jus soli* (birth by soil) and attachment to liberal, republican values. Presumably Zinedine Zidane, Thierry Henry, Lilian Thuram, Patrick Vieira, Marcel Desailly, and Christian Karembeu, all black or Berber members of the 1998 World Cup-winning squad, were not "French French." For Pablo Alabarces, wearing the national colors are code words for representing the "blood and soil."[55]

Liberals and leftists in France, on the other hand, praised the French national team when they won the 1998 World Cup. Its talisman Zinedine Zidane was of Berber Algerian origins and did not fit Le Pen's definition of "French French." For liberals and leftists, the systematic racism of French society and the state could be overcome if only we followed the meritocratic, colorless ethos of the French national soccer team and the principles of the 1789 French Revolution: liberty, equality, and fraternity. Or as Laurent Dubois, the author of *Soccer Empire: The World Cup and the Future of France*, commented, "the mass communion that took place in the streets in 1998" after France won the World Cup liberated "many from the shackles of their own uncertainty about their place in French society" and "should serve as a charter for a different way of being French." [56]

When France won the World Cup in 1998, soccer became a site of contestation for different conceptions of national identity, what it means to be French, and competing models of statehood. Nations and states around the world have faced similar struggles in respect to their national soccer teams and competing discourses of national identity.

Manuel Gameros insists that soccer can be "converted" into a "national aspiration": it demonstrates the virtues of national political discourses; projects the image of the state abroad; generates mechanisms of social consensus; and channels the interests of politicians in power. [57] Indeed, Gameros is correct when he argues that soccer acts to advance a "national aspiration." FIFA has 209 member associations, more members than the United Nations. It is a more "democratic" organization than the United Nations because Scotland, Wales, Northern Ireland, Palestine, Hong Kong, Guadeloupe, Tahiti, and the Faroe Islands all have "national teams," despite the fact that they are not fully sovereign states. In addition, the Catalans have played international friendlies, despite the fact that the Catalan region of Spain is a de facto part of Spain. These nations or regions without a state use soccer as a marker of their identity; to differentiate themselves from the perceived assimilationist thrust of their nation-states; and to keep alive the dreams of independence, autonomy, or cultural distinctiveness.

At times, club sides such as Cardiff City FC and Swansea City AFC (Wales) or Bnei Sakhnin FC (Israel) galvanize nationalist or regionalist identities, or act as sites of protest against England and Israel by the Welsh or Palestinian Arab (Israeli Arab) citizens of Israel. [58] So, for example, Martin Johnes, a lecturer in history at Swansea University, points out that Swansea City, which played in 2013 in England's top professional soccer league, has a fan culture impregnated with nationalistic anti-English songs, including "We hate England, we hate England" and "We'll never be mastered by no English bastard, Wales, Wales, Wales." [59] Conversely, these aforementioned club sides can act to integrate politically, culturally, and economically marginalized groups into the national body politic, thus demonstrating the virtues of an "equal opportunity" state.[60] Tamir Sorek points out the high number of Palestinian Arabs (Israeli Arabs) playing professional soccer and even on the national soccer team, insisting that sport is "the only public sphere in which Arab excellence is tolerated by the Jewish majority."[61] The Israeli government, on the other hand, argues that Palestinian Arab citizens of Israel have equal opportunities and the proof is that they are populated in the world beyond the soccer pitch as parliamentarians, mayors, judges, diplomats, university professors, and business owners.

Joseph Arbena argues that soccer has been used to advance nationalism on three fronts: 1) the establishment of domestic physical education programs, soccer competitions, and the permanent institutions necessary to run programs; 2) the preparation of individuals and teams capable of competing successfully internationally; and 3) the hosting of international soccer events.[62] According to Arbena, soccer has been utilized by political elites in order to build the nation from within and gain respect and legitimacy from without.[63]

However, the use of soccer to foster nationalism has its critics. First, the national selection process and the holding of national soccer matches may heighten regional alienation and perceived and real socio-economic inequities between the central metropolitan and peripheral regions. Second, some national soccer institutions are chronically underfunded, thus possibly dampening nationalistic sentiments. Third, the hosting of the World Cup reflects the geopolitical imbalance of world politics as few countries can host World Cup events. In 2010, South Africa became the first African nation to host the World Cup. In Latin America, Uruguay (1930), Brazil (1950 and 2014), Chile (1962), Argentina (1978), and Mexico (1970 and 1986) have used the World Cup to win international favor, garner quick profits, and achieve an aura of advanced modernization in the eyes of domestic and international audiences. Yet Brian Glanville correctly maintains that despite Argentina's triumph on home soil in the 1978 World Cup, the tournament brought neither lasting economic prosperity nor social peace as the military generals still ruled the country.[64] The victory was short lived as the military junta did fall in the 1980s, in conjunction with a broader wave of democratization throughout Latin America. I return to the question of soccer and authoritarian regimes in chapter 2.

While a cross-section of social classes can celebrate national soccer victories, the reality is that you can use soccer to construct competing nationalist discourses (that is, from the Italian goalkeeper Gianluigi Buffon's embrace of a coded Italian neo-fascism to the USA national soccer team as a reflection of the country's multicultural "melting pot"), but after the victories or losses come the bitter existential struggles of the majority of the world's poor. As Fausto Pretelin Muñoz de Cote astutely points out, "soccer cannot create miracles."[65] When Mexico won the gold medal at the 2012 London

Olympic Games, the Mexican coach Luis Fernando Tena was deliberately sanguine when he argued that the victory "gave Mexicans joy," but it could not change the realities of the thousands of dead in a "war on drugs" since 2006, or the biting poverty of many of his compatriots. In short, while soccer is used to advance competing discourses of national identity, it no doubt has its limits.

José Luis Chilavert "saved" his nation with spectacular saves and was instrumental in leading Paraguay in World Cup qualification campaigns with timely goals. At the 1998 World Cup, in a second round match the talented goalkeeper of the Paraguayan team heroically kept the World Cup winners France at bay in a double-overtime game before surrendering a solitary, losing goal. He won accolades from his compatriots and soccer fans world-wide.

Writing in the *Washington Post*, Jim Hoagland said that Chilavert's heroism extended to the period after the match between Paraguay and France: "Then, in his most manly act of the day, Chilavert consoled his grief-stricken teammates like a father comforting children at a family funeral."[66] In the same piece entitled "The Game of Nations," Hoagland also made this trenchant remark: "Character is the bedrock of sports as it is national survival. It surfaces under the most trying and demanding of circumstances."[67] Indeed, Chilavert oozed character, life, spice, vitality, and love for the game. He was outspoken, larger than life, and a lover of his beloved Paraguay. He did Paraguay proud in historical circumstances that were undoubtedly different from the Triple Alliance War. He led them out of the wilderness of national obscurity. Yet along with his teammates, Chilavert and Paraguay showed the world that the country exists, that it is a hard-working nation, and that what it does not have in size it compensates with grit, determination, talent, organization, and a never-say-die national character.

Hoagland completed his aforementioned article with an astute comment with respect to citizenship and World Cup competitions: "In the World Cup you are chosen to play on the team of your country of citizenship, not of residence or employment. You reach the height of your career because of national identity and skills."[68] Some politicians like Jean-Marie Le Pen and pro-fascist Italian players such as Paolo Di Canio, Christian Abbiati, and Gianluigi Buffon are keen to use soccer as a vehicle for an exclusivist, soldierly, and ethnically defined view of national identity.[69] Others such as José Luis Chilavert remind us that soccer is also an expression of national sovereignty and national survival. Winning on the soccer pitch and merely competing against the giants of international soccer in major tournaments spawns historical memories of national glories and defeats.

According to the Mexican writer Juan Villoro, the national soccer team is akin to a "tribe" and the players on the pitch represent "us," "defend" what "defines us" and what is "ours," and carry in their boots both "our hopes" and "our scars."[70] Mexican national soccer teams often qualify for World Cup competitions (fourteen), but have never fulfilled the country's expectations. As a result, Mexico looked to individual heroes to carry the banner of the nation abroad. Antonio Carbajal, a Mexican goalkeeper who played in five World Cups from 1950 to 1966, is a national legend. He is the only goalkeeper to play in five World Cups. Paraguay's Chilavert could sometimes make outlandish statements, or clash with opponents on the pitch. He once stated: "I've had a lot of fights on the pitch, but what did people expect? With the face I've got I have to play the bad guy. It's a lot easier that way. Being the good guy just isn't me."[71] Yet all was forgiven because he was a Paraguayan national idol. Did Italians forgive Buffon's pro-fascist leanings when he was heroic in goal in the 2006 World Cup and led the nation to its fourth World Cup title? Diego Maradona was even more controversial than Chilavert with his pro-leftist leanings, friendship with former Cuban Communist leader Fidel Castro, and drug problems. However, León Krauze points out that despite what Maradona said or did all was "forgiven" because he "cleansed" and "saved" the nation through the national jersey in moments when the nation most needed him.[72] Maradona was the star of Argentina's World Cup triumph in 1986.

Whether stopping a penalty shot in scintillating form, or scoring a thunderous goal with his trusted left foot, Chilavert was similarly seen as the "savior" of the Paraguayan nation. The Paraguayan goalkeeper was idolized by his compatriots, yet this did not mean that discourses of nationalism in Paraguay slavishly replicated those posited by their idol. Nationalist discourses with respect to soccer are as diverse as the discourses in civil society. They run the gamut from Buffon's crypto-fascism and Chilavert's more standard defense of Paraguayan nationalism to Calero or Higuita's unique conceptions of representing the nation(s).

* * *

This chapter raises a number of questions with respect to nationalism. Does soccer contribute to the formation of national identities, or does it merely reflect those identities? Do Chilavert and Buffon contribute to the construction of various national identities, or are they merely reflecting the differing identities in their respective societies?

As the German political scientist Michael Minkenberg points out in his university course entitled "Soccer and the Politics of Identity," collective identities today are multiple: territorial (local and regional), ethnic and racial, religious-cultural, national, and post-national.[73] He points out that those loyalties to national soccer teams are "situated between, but not necessarily competing with, local and transnational identities." If this is the case, should Calero have been allowed to play for Mexico after he was granted citizenship in the country and had represented Colombia earlier? Soccer is both inclusive of "others" regardless of class, creed, or color and simultaneously exclusive (that is, the discourse of the neo-fascists, which insist that the national team should be ethnically or biologically "pure").

However, the truly best national soccer teams understand that merit, strength of character, love for country, and talent matter more than the color of your skin or your country of origin. Or, as former UN Secretary-General Kofi Annan put it, "only two commodities matter" in soccer: talent and team work.[74] This is the civic nationalist perspective. In this respect, Mario Balotelli, an Italian national soccer team star with African and Jewish roots, represents the changing and more inclusive face of Italy. In contrast, Balotelli's teammate Buffon, who subtly pines for the Italy of the Fascist past (the Italy that won two World Cups under Mussolini's reign in 1934 and 1938), assures us that the past has not passed. He promotes an ethnic variant of nationalism based on "monuments and graveyards, even harking back to the mysteries of ancient times and of tribal solidarity."[75] Yet Anan insists that the Balotelli vision of soccer will triumph above Buffon's perspective because it promotes economic, social, and cultural development, allows us to "open and broaden minds," and "illustrates the benefits of cross-pollination between peoples and countries."[76]

Chapter Two

"Believe, Obey, and Fight"

Soccer and Dictators

This chapter examines the history of the politicization of soccer by dictators. As Markovits and Rensmann argue, "Throughout the twentieth century, dictatorships of various kinds utilized the charismatic power of sports for their own, often nefarious, causes."[1] Hitler, Mussolini, Stalin, and Franco explicitly used sport to serve the nation, dominant ideology, party, and leader. Dictators-in-waiting could also engage in extreme cruelty to advance their political cause. The radical Somali Islamist group Al-Shabaab, which controlled large areas in the southern part of the country and harshly imposed *Sharia* law, killed seventy-six people in Uganda who gathered to watch the World Cup finals on television in July 2010.

Despite the use of soccer by dictators throughout history, Eduardo Galeano points out how some brave soccer players in the Ukraine resisted Nazism and paid with their lives:

> A monument in the Ukraine commemorates the players of the 1942 Kiev Dynamo team. . . . During the German occupation they committed the insane act of defeating Hitler's squad in the local stadium. When the game was over all eleven were shot with their shirts on at the edge of a cliff.[2]

This chapter highlights the numerous ways in which authoritarian and totalitarian regimes have used soccer to teach "constructive values" such as improving health, morals, and discipline, reducing crime, assisting developing economies, enhancing notions of community and cooperation, and promoting patriotism and extreme forms of nationalism.[3] The lesson of this chapter is the way soccer has been used to maintain existing power elites, even authori-

23

tarian forms of governance. In this chapter, I travel from the Latin American military dictatorships of the 1970s to Franco's Spain (1939–1974) and Fascist Italy (1922–1943) to underscore the ways soccer has been used to advance the imperatives of dictators. It should be noted that it is not merely authoritarian and totalitarian regimes that have utilized soccer in order to maintain the status quo. Politicians and generals of all political stripes have used soccer in order to promote the maintenance of existing regimes. Today it is almost ritualistic to see presidents, prime ministers, or monarchs at important international soccer matches.

Nonetheless, it should be pointed out that soccer has its limits in terms of conserving the status quo. Today military governments are a thing of the past in most of Latin America. Moreover, political elites might seek to construct and mold identities through soccer, but it does not mean that that they are always successful; that their politicization schemes are durable in the long term; or that ordinary people and soccer fans do not resist naked displays of the politicization of soccer. Chapter 4 explores the various ways movements in civil society have sought to use soccer as a vehicle to transform individuals and communities.

JERSEY #2: THE DEFENSE

Picking a great number 2 was a difficult task. There are many excellent defenders who wore the number 2 shirt. The best number 2s are known for their galloping and overlapping runs from the back, as well as their dangerous crosses into the penalty area.

"Don" Elias Figueroa

While Brazilian stars Djalma Santos and Carlos Alberto, or El Salvador's Roberto Rivas could have been good choices for the number 2 shirt, I chose the retired Chilean international defender Don (Sir) Elias Figueroa. He played professional soccer in Chile, Uruguay, Brazil, and the United States from the late 1960s until the early 1980s. Figueroa wore the jersey numbers 2, 3, 5, and 7. Figueroa had exceptional defending skills, which led the great Pelé to call him one of the greatest defenders of all time and the best in Latin America.[4] Pelé also included Figueroa in his list of the 125 best living soccer stars of all time. Franz Beckenbauer, one of the greatest sweepers of all time, paid a fitting tribute to Figueroa when he called himself "Europe's Figueroa."[5] Thus, there is no doubt that Figueroa was one of the greatest defenders in soccer history.

Figueroa approved of the military dictatorship, or remained silent during the Augusto Pinochet regime, even as some star players from the Chilean national team were being harassed by the dictator. Along with the rest of the

Chilean political right, as well as other famous Chilean athletes such as former tennis stars Patricio Cornejo and Hans Gildemeister, Figueroa openly campaigned for the pro-Pinochet "Yes" side in the 1988 referendum on the military regime.[6] Pinochet was commander-in-chief of the Chilean army from 1973 to 1998 and president of the military government junta of Chile from 1973 to 1981. The referendum took place on October 5, 1988, but was defeated and meant that the transition to Chile began and constitutionally Pinochet could not stay in power until 1997.

The soccer website *Ferplei* points out that the Chilean soccer idol Figueroa would have been all too willing to be an "executioner" in the service of the Pinochet regime and would be marked by his open support for the authoritarian regime.[7] Writing in *Marca.com*, Miguel Ángel Iara points out that Figueroa was ideologically "close to the military regime," while another Chilean international Carlos Caszely openly campaigned against the Pinochet regime in the 1988 referendum and could declare that Pinochet's leftist predecessor Salvador Allende had his "defects," but was a "good person" that "wanted to make Chile a great nation."[8] As a result of his leftist ideals, Caszely's mother was arrested by the Pinochet regime and tortured.[9] Alberto Quintano, an international defender on the Chilean national team who played with Figueroa and Caszely, insisted that Caszely was left off of Chile's 1978 World Cup team for his political views, and afterward the players even refused to talk about Caszely because of fear of the authoritarian regime.[10]

It is rather instructive that in 1970 Pelé was investigated by the Brazilian military dictatorship for suspected leftist sympathies and his support for the release of political prisoners. Yet Pelé did not really get seriously involved in political resistance struggles against the Brazilian military regime. In chapter 4, I explore the case of Brazilian soccer star Sócrates and his bold democratization campaign against his country's military regime in the 1980s.

Refusing to get politically involved is the rule for most soccer players under dictatorships. Military regimes invoke a climate of fear and silence, thus weakening the possibilities of political resistance through sport. Some Chileans might rightfully criticize Figueroa for remaining silent while even professional soccer players and their families were being tortured. At other times in the transition to democracy during and after the 1988 referendum, Figueroa blatantly appeared a supporter of the Pinochet regime.[11] One Santiago-based newspaper called Figueroa one of the "100 most famous figures" to support the pro-Pinochet "Yes" side in the 1988 referendum.[12] Osvaldo "Arica" Hurtado was another soccer player that openly backed the dictatorship in the 1988 referendum.[13] The aforementioned paper also asked whether the two Chilean soccer players, in conjunction with famous politicians, actors, singers, and businessmen, were "passive accomplices" to the horrors of the Pinochet regime.[14] In any case, by maintaining a low profile politically during the Pinochet regime, Figueroa was able to receive national honors and international awards. It is true that in the context of a more democratic Chile, he has not received the same recognition as he did during the dark years of the military junta. After his retirement, Figueroa also became a FIFA Player for Peace. For a player that certainly did not promote the peace and well-being of his Chilean compatriots that were being tortured and "disappeared" under the military junta, is this really an appropriate honor?

Elías Ricardo Figueroa Brander was born on October 25, 1946, in the Chilean Pacific port city of Valparaíso. Built upon numerous steep hillsides overlooking the Pacific Ocean, it is called "the Jewel of the Pacific." The city's unique labyrinth of streets and cobblestone alleyways allowed it to gain UNESCO World Heritage Site status in 2003. Valparaíso is ironically the birthplace of both Chilean dictator Augusto Pinochet and Salvador Allende, the democratically elected Marxist leader ousted by Pinochet and the military junta on September 11, 1973.

Figueroa is considered the best Chilean soccer player of all time. At an early age, his doctor told him that he would not be able to play any sports because of breathing problems and polio, but this only made Figueroa more determined to become a world-class player.[15] After his polio diagnosis, the young Figueroa even had to learn to walk again. Along with Bobby Moore, Franz Beckenbauer, Daniel Passarella, Gaetano Scirea, and Franco Baresi, Figueroa is perhaps the greatest modern defender ever to play the game. He could play with ease as a commanding sweeper, or as a right-sided defender.

Figueroa played for many clubs during his long, illustrious career, including his hometown Santiago Wanderers, Brazil's Internacional, and Uruguay's Peñarol. Figueroa made forty-seven appearances for Chile, including a record three World Cups in non-successive tournaments: 1966, 1974, and 1982. The selection of an ageing Figueroa for the 1982 World Cup was criticized by sectors of the Chilean media.

Figueroa was known for his elegant style of play. He was certainly an uncompromising defender, yet his playing style was generally clean. Looking back at the footage of the 1974 and 1982 World Cups, what is striking about Figueroa is his calmness on the ball coming out from the back. Those that know and play the game understand that it is not always easy to know how much time we have on the ball, especially when opposing players are breathing down your neck and looking to pounce on an error! Figueroa was calm, able to cleanly win a ball from a decisive tackle and then start a menacing counterattack. Despite his pro-Pinochet support, Figueroa was a gentleman on and off the pitch.

Figueroa began his long career with Chile's Santiago Wanderers in 1964. Yet his best soccer moments were as foreigner in Brazil, which was then ruled by a military dictatorship. He is a hero to SC Internacional (Porto Alegre) fans in Brazil. While playing for SC Internacional, he twice won the *Bola de Ouro*, the Brazilian Player of the Year award, in 1972 and 1976. He was also the winner of the prestigious South American Footballer of the Year award three times in a row in 1974, 1975, and 1976. In his tenure with SC Internacional, the team won a stunning seven domestic titles. Figueroa was also named Best Player in Uruguay in 1967 and 1968 while playing with Peñarol. Near the end of his career with club side Palestino, he was even voted Best Player in Chile in 1977 and 1978. Everywhere Figueroa went he touched gold. He won domestic titles with every team he played for in various countries. Figueroa played his final season with Santiago-based Colo-Colo in 1982. He also retired from the Chilean national team in 1982. Figueroa spent the 1981 season with the Fort Lauderdale Strikers of the now defunct North American Soccer League.

SOCCER AND DICTATORSHIPS

Let us open this section with the sad story of Joe Gaetjens (1924–1964), a Haitian immigrant to the United States on a scholarship at Columbia University in the 1940s. Gaetjens would make soccer history. Gaetjens played for Brookhattan in the American Soccer League, where his performances first caught the eyes of U.S. soccer officials. Although Gaetjens never received U.S. citizenship, he played all three games for the USA in the 1950 World Cup in Brazil and was the goalscorer in the USA's stunning 1–0 upset against England in Belo Horizonte. There is a famous photograph of Gaetjens with a beaming smile being paraded around the field by joyous Brazilian fans. After the World Cup, Gaetjens moved to France, where he played with Racing Club de Paris and Olympique Alès. Gaetjens then moved back to Haiti and even played for Haiti in a World Cup qualifier against Mexico in 1953. He continued to play domestically with Etoile Haïtienne.

Although Gaetjens was not interested in politics, he would soon discover the cruel realities of military dictatorships. Gaetjens had the bad luck to be a relative of Louis Déjoie, who lost the 1957 Haitian presidential election to the dictator François "Papa Doc" Duvalier. Some of Gaetjens's brothers were also associated with a group of exiles in the Dominican Republic who wanted to stage a coup d'état.[16]

Duvalier declared himself Haiti's "president for life" on July 7, 1964. While most of the Gaetjens family fled the country, Joe Gaetjens stayed behind. He did not think that the new dictatorship would care about an athlete. He was wrong and he paid the heaviest price: arrested by the *Tonton Macoutes* secret police, Gaetjens was presumably killed by the regime. His body has never been found or recovered.

As the Gaetjens story demonstrates, authoritarian and totalitarian regimes are indeed brutal vis-à-vis the politicized and non-politicized alike. In addition, these regimes have openly manipulated soccer and sport in general in order to maintain the status quo, project a positive regime image (even as they were systematically jailing, torturing, or killing citizens), or to demonstrate a sense of superiority vis-à-vis other ideological systems and nations.

John R. Tunis recognized the way dictators used sport as an instrument of policy a long time ago in a piece he wrote for *Foreign Affairs* in 1936.[17] Tunis posited that dictators use sports for three main purposes: 1) to keep people (the young in particular) "occupied" and "happy"; 2) for propaganda purposes (that is, to demonstrate a superior race, nation, or ideological system); and 3) to create men who are capable of defending "the fatherland."[18] Joseph Stalin, the general secretary of the Communist Party of the Soviet Union from 1922 to 1952, was the first dictator to "discover" the importance of sports. Stalin argued that physical conditioning was a duty of all Soviet citizens in order to "repel external attacks." For Italian Fascist leader Benito Mussolini, sports could be used in order to "militarize the nation," create "good soldiers," and demonstrate "the superiority of the race" and sanctity of Fascist principles.[19] Under Mussolini, sports and soccer ceased to be mere leisure activities and became government functions. Mussolini made it obligatory to join a national sport, leisure, and cultural organization called *Opera Nazionale Dopolavoro* (National Recreational Club).[20] As early as 1926, the Fascist Party controlled the Italian Olympic Committee. In this way, Mussolini was able to transform all sporting activities into a "grand national industry."

Dictatorships have also touched contemporary soccer players. One case is instructive. He was a right-sided defender for both Arsenal and Cameroon's national soccer team. His name is Laureano Bisan-Etame Mayer (b. 1977), but he is commonly known as Lauren. He is a retired defender who was born in Equatorial Guinea. He played for Arsenal from 2000 to 2006, making 159 appearances for the club. He was part of the great Arsenal team of the 2003 to 2004 season, which went undefeated and won the Premier League title. In 2000, he played for Cameroon and won the Olympic gold medal in Sydney, Australia. Lauren not only faced great adversity due to political circumstances under a dictatorship, but he was fortunate to even be born:

His father, Valentin Bisan-Etame, was a politician in Equatorial Guinea and dared to speak out against the country's psychotic dictator, Francisco Macías, in 1977. It was a brave thing to do: Macías impaled his enemies' heads on poles, banned the use of the word "intellectual" and hailed Hitler as "the savior of Africa." His crimes were so bad he was given 101 death sentences when brought to trial in 1979. Valentin was imprisoned and sentenced to death for his comments but managed to escape to Cameroon with several of his children and his wife, who was pregnant with Lauren. "If our family hadn't escaped, I probably wouldn't have been born," Lauren said. His trials were not over though: his family moved to Spain where he and his 14 siblings had to survive in Seville's tough Montequinto district.[21]

Authoritarian Spain under Franco

Writing in a 1985 issue of *History Today*, Duncan Shaw explains how the Spanish dictator Francisco Franco was on hand to watch Spain's national soccer triumph in 1964:

> On June 21st, 1964, an ecstatic crowd of 120,000, awash in a sea of red and yellow, cheered and applauded Generalissimo Francisco Franco as he stood up to leave the Madrid summer evening gathering. This was no mass rally of political affirmation that the dictator was leaving, but a football match. Spain had just beaten the Soviet Union in the Final of the European Nations' Cup; so much more than just a football victory: a triumph for international co-operation over Cold War hostility, but, conversely, perhaps also a triumph over the old Red enemies of the Civil War. [22]

Shaw also points out that the mainstream Spanish press was giddy with national enthusiasm after beating their ideological enemy, the Marxist-Leninist Soviet Union:

> The conservative ABC newspaper was moved to comment the following day: After twenty-five years of peace, behind the applause could be heard an authentic support for the Spirit of July 18th. In this quarter of a century there has never been displayed a greater popular enthusiasm for the State born out of the victory over Communism and its fellow-travellers. . . . Spain is a nation every day more orderly, mature and unified, and which is steadfastly marching down the path of economic, social and institutional development. It is a national adventure. [23]

Spain today is a soccer powerhouse. They were World Cup winners for the first time in their history in 2010, while also capturing successive victories in the 2008 and 2012 European Nations' tournaments. However, Spain's only other notable soccer victory came in 1964. From 1938, when he became prime minister, until his death in 1975, Franco skillfully politicized soccer after many international triumphs achieved by Spanish teams. Franco was a loyal fan of Real Madrid CF, which won the European Cup numerous times under his reign: 1955–1956, 1956–1957, 1957–1958, 1958–1959, 1959–1960, and 1965–1966. Between 1953 and 1964, Real Madrid's legendary player was the Argentinean-born Alfredo Di Stéfano, who scored a remarkable 246 goals in 302 appearances for Real Madrid. King Alfonso XIII, the Spanish monarch from 1886 to 1931, also realized the political importance of Spanish soccer. In 1920, King Alfonso XIII bestowed the title *Real* (Royal) to the Madrid-based soccer club. Real Madrid is today one of the most famous and richest soccer clubs in the world.

The 1964 triumph against the Soviet Union was important for the Franco regime as Spain was "regarded as the last bastion of fascism by a hostile outside world."[24] In short, the 1964 Spanish victory provided Franco with "a means of purifying his foreign image, of painting a lighter picture of Spain to replace that of a brutal dictatorship," writes Shaw.[25]

During his reign, Franco received backing from Juan Antonio Samaranch, a major Spanish and Catalan sports administrator and diplomat. Samaranch was the president of the International Olympic Committee from 1981 until 2001, "had been a career fascist," and "a minister in the government of the murderous Spanish dictator Franco."[26] When he passed away in 2010, his funeral was attended by members of the Spanish royal family. They had forgotten that as a sports journalist for *La Prensa* he was dismissed in 1943 for criticizing the supporters of Real Madrid CF after its 11–1 drubbing of FC Barcelona.[27] Samaranch later joined his family's lucrative textile business and would become the second longest-serving president of the International Olympic Committee.

It is rather interesting that while Franco could have some success in improving the image of Spain as a result of the national team and Real Madrid victories, his politicization of soccer did not help him domestically. Franco clearly identified with Real Madrid, a team he portrayed as popular and the "pride of the nation" after it won six European titles during his reign. It was no accident that Santiago Bernabeu, the president of Real Madrid, was a soldier in the Francoist military forces during the civil war. Shaw points out that politicians close to Real Madrid could win political favor with the regime: "In order to make progress in their careers, ambitious junior ministers and army officers jostled to get themselves noticed at Real's magnificent Bernabeu stadium, cheering on Madrid against some provincial also-rans."[28]

Franco's support for Real Madrid fit well within his authoritarian structure of governance and centralism, which concentrated all power in the capital city. As the Catalans and Basques rejected the authoritarian centralism of Franco and remembered his harsh military policies against the regions in the context of the Spanish civil war (1936–1939), they used soccer as a way to express animus for Franco's Real Madrid. CF Barcelona and Athletic Bilbao became the de facto clubs of Catalan and Basque nationalisms, respectively.

Under the Franco regime, it was forbidden to speak any other language but Castilian Spanish, to fly a regional flag, or even to hold a meeting with more than seven people.[29] Flying the Basque or Catalan flags could get you imprisoned or tortured. As a result, the home matches of Barcelona and Athletic Bilbao "became regular expressions of anti-Franco regionalist sentiment."[30] Every Spanish soccer fan knew that wearing the red and blue colors of Barcelona, or red and white of Athletic Bilbao, meant support for Catalan and Basque regionalism, autonomy, or even outright separatism. They also knew that if you put on those jerseys, you were expressing popular protest against the Franco dictatorship. Shaw points out that Athletic Bilbao "became a pole of resistance to Francoism right across the country."[31] Bucking the trend of signing rich superstars from around the world, Athletic Club Bilbao players today are all Spanish citizens and largely of Basque origins. The English first name for the club, Athletic, rather than the Spanish Club Atlético (like Atlético de Madrid), also highlights the English roots of the club and its disdain for the Spanish.

Owing to their shared political ideology and cultural backgrounds, the Latin American military generals of the 1970s also utilized soccer in order to maintain the status quo, strengthen national loyalties, and cleanse their reputations as authoritarian brutes. It was in Argentina and Chile in the 1970s that the right-wing military dictatorships became infamous for their "disappearances," in which thousands of leftists, liberals, and other "anti-national traitors" were taken from their homes or from the streets and never seen again. The torture techniques of these regimes were cruel and unusual, as political dissidents could be dropped from planes into the ocean. It is estimated that about 30,000 people disappeared in Argentina under the reign of the military dictatorship from 1976 to 1983, while Chile's Pinochet, after a 1973 CIA-assisted coup, saw close to 3,000 disappearances and over 30,000 torture victims. As a result of the excesses of the Pinochet regime and the coup against leftist leader Salvador Allende, the Soviet Union broke relations with Chile. They also refused to play in Chile's national stadium in a qualifier for the 1974 World Cup, insisting that the stadium was used as a "concentration camp" during and after Pinochet's military coup.[32]

Ryszard Kapuściński, the author of *The Soccer War*, highlighted the politicization of soccer by a collection of different Latin American military regimes from the 1960s until the early 1980s. In a sardonic tone, Kapuściński quotes an exiled Brazilian colleague after Brazil's third World Cup victory in 1970: "The military right-wing can be assured of at least five more years of peaceful rule."[33] Markovits and Rensmann correctly point out that the Argentinean military junta gained "much-needed legitimacy" after the national team triumph in the 1978 World Cup.[34] More ominously, Kapuściński underscores the dual use of some Latin American soccer stadiums: "In peacetime they are sports venues; in war they turn into concentration camps."[35] He also points out that in El Salvador the national stadium has been used to carry out televised, nation-wide assassinations against political opponents. Roberto Rivas (1941–1972) was a right back from El Salvador. He played for Alianza (San Salvador) in El Salvador, where he won two domestic titles in the 1960s. He was a member of El Salvador's national team at the 1970 World Cup in Mexico. Alianza retired his number 2 jersey after Rivas died in unusual circumstances, either an accident or a suicide.[36] Rivas was an excellent defender and he lived under a military dictatorship that was involved in the infamous "Soccer War" in 1969. Keep Rivas in mind when I discuss the Soccer War in chapter 3.

Janet Lever highlighted how the Brazilian military government of the 1960s used the national game of soccer (or is it the national religion?) in order to instill in its inhabitants a notion of the nation's vast geographical terrain.[37] Since many remote regions of Brazil were unknown to its citizens, the 1969 Sports Lottery was implemented by the military regime in order to enhance national consciousness, raise funds for social projects, and include soccer results from distant provinces. Some commentators have also suggested that in the early 1980s the Brazilian military regime sought to "whiten" the image of the distinctively multi-racial national soccer team in order to win favor with the West. The Brazilian national teams of 1982 and 1986 were two of the most talented teams in the history of soccer not to win the World Cup. They were certainly not fully "whitened"—a near impossibility in multi-racial Brazil. Any attempts to completely "whiten" Brazilian national teams would have meant the loss of soccer legends such as Didi, Djalma Santos, Pelé, Jairzinho, Cafu, Roberto Carlos, and many more black or mixed players.

Some of the greatest number 2s in the history of the game have played for the Brazilian national team, including Djalma Santos and Carlos Alberto. These two Brazilian legends won World Cup trophies in different decades. Both Brazilian number 2s played under military dictatorships. Djalma Pereira Dias dos Santos (b. 1929) was known by his legions of fans as Djalma Santos. Santos had incredible longevity as he started for the Brazilian national team in four World Cups in 1954, 1958, 1962, and 1966. He was thirty-seven when he was chosen for the 1966 World Cup, ahead of the highly rated and younger Carlos Alberto. He won two World Cups in 1958 and 1962. He is undoubtedly one of the greatest right backs the game has ever known. In 2004, Santos made Pelé's list of the top 125 living soccer players of all time. In defense, Santos could also support the midfield and forwards with surging runs down the flank. As the Brazilian military dictatorship began in 1964, Santos lived under the regime for six years of his playing career as he retired in 1970.

Carlos Alberto Torres (b. 1944) is a retired Brazilian international and one of the most highly rated defenders of all time. He was the captain of the Brazilian national team when they won the 1970 World Cup. He scored one of the greatest team goals in World Cup history in the finals against Italy. He had the honor to be selected to the World Team of the Twentieth Century, despite only appearing in one World Cup. Alberto did not participate in the 1974 World Cup due to a knee injury and played several qualifiers for the 1978 World Cup, but retired before the tournament began. He ended his career with the New York Cosmos in 1982. Carlos Alberto was also selected by Pelé as one of the top 125 greatest living soccer players of all time. I could have selected Carlos Alberto since his playing days from 1963 to 1982 coincides almost exactly with the Brazilian military dictatorship.

In Argentina, military generals were notorious for their politicization of soccer. Long before the policy of disappearances practiced by the military junta in the 1970s and 1980s, General Juan Peron's largely working-class supporters would rally around Buenos Aires-based Boca Juniors with spontaneous chants: *"Boca y Peron, un solo corazon"* (Boca and Peron, one single heart).[38] Peron was later exiled in a bloody military coup in 1955 and his supporters were prevented from seeking public office. His wife, Isabel Peron, was also unseated by military generals on March 24, 1976. Led by General Jorge Videla, the man credited with the term "disappearances," the military junta would remain in power until 1983.

In 1978, the military junta led by General Videla staged the World Cup and was rewarded with a brilliant 3–1 triumph against the Netherlands in the decisive final game. On July 5, 1978, Videla received the Argentinean coach Luis Menotti at the national residence to celebrate the World Cup victory. A few days earlier he would disingenuously tell the BBC that it is true that he attended eight World Cup matches (admittedly a "high number" of matches), but that he did not attend the matches for "political motives" because "it would be wrong to capitalize on a triumph that belonged to all."[39]

The hero of the 1978 World Cup victory was the long-haired Mario Kempes, nicknamed *El Toro* (The Bull), the leading goalscorer of the tournament with six goals, including two in the finals. In a prolific career, Kempes scored twenty times for his country and represented Argentina in three World Cups in 1974, 1978, and 1982.

While Kempes was the star on the pitch for Argentina in 1978, off the pitch it was the military generals that were orchestrating the show. While the Argentinean economy was in shambles with high unemployment, weakened manufacturing and agricultural sectors, and the banning of major labor unions, the junta was spending money on trying to win the World Cup for the first time ever for Argentina. It is estimated that the military generals used 10 percent of their budget to stage the 1978 World Cup,[40] the implication being that no less than victory was satisfactory for the junta.

Brian Glanville points out that winning the World Cup allowed Argentina's generals to obfuscate the regime's horrific record of disappearances, systematic torture, and widespread human rights violations.[41] However, the scripted control of the 1978 World Cup in order to legitimize the military junta and the nation had its share of critics. Argentina reached the finals only after a dubious 6–0 victory against Peru. They needed to win by a large margin of four goals in order to advance to the finals against the Netherlands. A margin of four goals in World Cup soccer is indeed substantial. Peru was not a shabby national team. There were popular feelings that Argentina and Peru colluded in order to get the desired result. Conspiracy theories insisted that the Peruvian goalkeeper was born in Argentina, Peru was dependent on Argentinian grain shipments, and there were allegations that the Peruvian and Argentinean militaries conspired. Although nothing has been proven, many Latin Americans cried foul play and insisted that the Argentinean military junta needed the World Cup win in order to "clean" their image both at home and abroad.

Italian Fascist leader Benito Mussolini ruled Italy with an iron fist from 1922 to 1943, until he was ousted by the Fascist Grand Council. His motto was the chilling "Believe, obey, and fight," which meant "Believe, obey, and fight" for Mussolini, the Fascist Party, and a militaristic conception of the Italian nation. He helped create a new ideology called fascism in 1919, which was revolutionary, totalitarian, ultra-nationalistic, expansionist, and by 1938 virulently anti-Semitic. While the Fascist regime lasted just over twenty years, it will be forever associated with racism, chauvinism, colonialism, war, totalitarianism, and the silencing of political opponents.

Like the Argentinean military junta and the authoritarian Franco regime, Fascist Italy politicized national soccer matches. Fascist Italy was even more politicized than these aforementioned authoritarian military regimes. A distinction needs to be made between authoritarians like Videla, Pinochet, and Franco, on the one hand, and totalitarians such as Mussolini, Hitler, Stalin, and Mao.[42] Both authoritarian and totalitarian regimes were brutal toward their political opponents, while in some phases of their regimes some authoritarians like Franco engaged in more systematic terror than totalitarians such as Mussolini. Mussolini inaugurated a new totalitarian ideology, which did not exist in previous historical epochs. Totalitarianism implies the complete control of civil society by the state, including sporting activities. Authoritarians leave some areas of civil society free of the state such as church and business elites, which might find favor with the regime. Authoritarians are in general more conservative and less radical than totalitarians, who want to create "new men," a revolutionary new society, and believe that all state forces should be marshaled in the service of the nation or race. Totalitarians generally erect a new, secular "political religion,"[43] while authoritarians pay more respect to traditional religion. In terms of managing the economy, totalitarians are, in theory, more revolutionary than authoritarians, insisting that a "developmental dictatorship" is good for the nation and that capitalism must be restrained for the public welfare.[44] Fascist totalitarians rejected traditional models of politics and longed for a revolutionary "third way" beyond capitalism and communism, as well as liberalism and socialism.

Given the totalitarian character of fascism, it was within the DNA of the Italian Fascist regime to utilize soccer as a way to highlight the glories of the Italian nation. Unfortunately, the Italians, who won the World Cup in 1934 and 1938 under the reign of Benito Mussolini, could count on important moral support from the father of the World Cup, the Frenchman Jules Rimet.[45] Mussolini's interventionism in soccer was blatant. He followed the rule of dictatorships as "monopolies of thought" and often action. Shortly before the 1938 finals in France, the Italian dictator sent an ominous telegram to the Italian coach: "Win or die."[46] Following Juan Villoro's insight that the eleven named players in the starting lineup represent a "tribe" distinct from their eleven opponents, what mattered for the Italian "tribe" and Mussolini was winning at all costs.[47] Playing against the Brazilians in the finals, the Fascist Italian press saw the World Cup victory in racial terms as the triumph of the "genius" of the "Italian race" against the "brute force of the Negros."

Cruyff, Figueroa, and Authoritarian Regimes

For Mussolini, Hitler, Franco, and the Latin American military generals, soccer was used as a blatant political tool. Although they had less state control than Mussolini or Hitler, the military generals in Argentina prevented journalists from speaking negatively about the 1978 World Cup or criticizing the national team coach Cesar Luis Menotti.[48] In holding the 1978 World Cup, the military regime received full support from then-FIFA president João Havelange.

An exponent of the "total soccer" of Dutch manager Rinus Michels in the 1970s, Johan Cruyff won the prestigious *Ballon d'Or* three times in 1971, 1973, and 1974. In 1999, the IFFHS named Cruyff the European Player of the Century and he finished just behind Pelé in the World Player of the Century poll. One of the greatest players in the history of soccer, Cruyff missed the 1978 World Cup after guiding the Netherlands to a second place finish at the 1974 World Cup. Cruyff refused to participate in the 1978 World Cup because he insisted that Argentina's military junta was systematically torturing people and making its own citizens "disappear." This is what Cruyff claimed back in 1978. The human rights situation under the Argentinean military junta was grave, as U.S. president Jimmy Carter gave his support to the Inter-American Commission of Human Rights to travel to Buenos Aires in 1979 in order to investigate the military regime. In 2008, however, Cruyff's initial reason for missing the World Cup and retiring from international play were thrown into doubt when he told the Catalunya Ràdio journalist Antoni Bassas that his family was involved in a kidnapping attempt in Barcelona a year before the tournament.[49]

Many people admired Cruyff's stance against the military dictatorship until his 2008 interview with Antoni Bassas. Then admiration turned to doubt. Cruyff had used the military dictatorship in Argentina as an excuse to miss the World Cup, when in reality he could have been more honest about the kidnapping attempt on his family and stated that he was fearful of a similar incident in Argentina.

The Cruyff story highlights how soccer players both within and outside military regimes find it difficult to swim against the tide of the politics of the day. Living under the ambit of military regimes is another story. Elias Figueroa lived under the military dictatorship in Chile during a part of his playing days. He also lived under the Brazilian military dictatorship while turning SC Internacional into a household name in Brazil. While the majority of Chilean players found it difficult to speak out against the horrors of the military junta (including Figueroa), there were other players that risked far more than Cruyff by speaking out against the regime. These included Chamaco Valdes, Chamuyo Ampuero Lepe (imprisoned by the regime), and the brilliant forward Carlos Caszely, who played in the 1974 and 1982 World Cups. Caszely openly criticized a military regime that could be so cruel as to threaten his mother and friends with death. He was a Communist supporter of the democratically elected Salvador Allende government, which was ousted by the military junta in 1973. Caszely was the only Chilean player that refused to salute the Chilean dictator.[50] In reference to the beginning of the Pinochet military regime, Caszely remembers "a sad country," a "silent" country, a country "without laughter," and the feeling of "darkness."[51] Why Caszely was not killed is an interesting question, but one assumes that Pinochet had begrudging admiration for the Chilean forward because he was a national icon. In forty-nine international appearances for his country between 1969 and 1985, Caszely turned in many dazzling performances and scored an impressive twenty-nine goals.

Without a doubt, Figueroa remained silent during the Pinochet military regime in order to survive and maintain his privileges as a player. Yet what he did during Chile's transition to democracy is more instructive and demonstrates his pro-authoritarian leanings. On May 27, 2005, Chile's *La nación* reported that Figueroa gave his support for the referendum held on October 5, 1988, which was a mandate on whether the Chilean population wanted the continuation of Pinochet's military regime.[52] Recall that Figueroa's international teammate Carlos Caszely campaigned for the "No" forces. In the referendum on whether Pinochet could stay in power until 1997, 44 percent of Chileans said "Yes" and nearly 56 percent said "No." The referendum and its result were historic because they began the transition toward Chilean democracy. It is rather interesting that in the aforementioned *La nación* piece, the claim is made that Figueroa was less recognized in his own country in the democratic age after the fall of the military dictatorship.[53]

Figueroa was not alone in lending his support to the military regime. Ivo Basay, the Chilean coach of the famous Colo-Colo club and later Santiago Wanderers, could opine that "Pinochet was a very necessary man in a certain moment in the history of Chile."[54] Basay was expressing a common sentiment among those on the right (including one held by Elias Figueroa) that by coming to power the anti-Communist Pinochet regime had prevented worse horrors akin to the *gulag* system of the Marxist-Leninist Soviet Union. The great Russian dissident writer Aleksandr Solzhenitysn argued that the gulag was a systematic and state-led system of "corrective labour camps" that saw

50 million people pass through its brutal conditions from 1918 until 1956 when Soviet leader Nikita Khrushchev denounced Stalin's Reign of Terror.[55] Thus, it was no surprise that in an interview long after his retirement Elias Figueroa gave the following answer to this question: "How can sport assist in the creation of a world in peace?"[56] Figueroa's answer is telling because it could have been voiced by the generals associated with the Pinochet regime: "Sports is the best recipe against drugs, alcohol, and all those things. A sporting nation spends 25 per cent less on health."[57] As Figueroa expressed interest in becoming a Chilean parliamentarian in 2013, he was undoubtedly conscious of his pro-Pinochet past and thus stated: "What interests me more than politics is the social and sports."[58]

In contrast to Figueroa, one would assume that world peace includes both "negative peace" (that is, the absence of violence or war) and "positive peace" (that is, "the integration of human society," including the abolition of poverty and racial discrimination).[59] Pincohet's Chile saw neither "negative peace," nor "positive peace." A more comprehensive peace might be assisted by ending the monopoly of violence of authoritarian military regimes, feeding the hungry and poor, undermining violence against women, fixing our profound environmental problems, or reconceptualizing an economic system based on greed rather than the common good. Politics did not take away from the genius of Figueroa on the soccer field. Yet lesson two attempted to highlight that given the politicization of soccer from Mussolini and Franco to the Latin American military generals, soccer is following Shankly's insight a "matter of life and death."

As a footnote to our story about Elias Figueroa, the retired Chilean soccer star was chosen as ChangeFIFA's candidate to clean up FIFA following the scandal-hit 2018 and 2022 World Cup bids.[60] Figueroa claimed that he wanted to change professional soccer, particularly the perception of deep corruption in the FIFA hierarchy. In a somewhat surprising move on March 31, 2011, Figueroa decided that he was not ready for the job to replace Sepp Blatter at the helm of FIFA in such a "short period of time."[61] Did this decision have anything to do with the futile sense that FIFA's corruption woes were too big to handle? Or Blatter's authoritarian tendencies? Or perhaps with fear that Figueroa's brilliant soccer career would be overshadowed by focus on his dark past as a supporter of Augusto Pinochet's military junta?

Chapter Three

Winning Hearts and Minds

Soccer, Ideological Hegemony, and "Class Warfare"

The lesson of this chapter is that soccer is one of many cultural terrains in which the dominant political and economic classes attempt to achieve ideological hegemony and promote "class warfare." From this perspective, professional soccer clubs and national teams are part of the larger cultural battle in liberal capitalist societies designed to win hearts and minds.

In this chapter, the notion of "class warfare" is used in its Marxist and Frankfurt School (that is, Theodor Adorno, Max Horkheimer, and Herbert Marcuse, among others) connotations. "Class warfare" is waged by dominant states, classes, politicians, and even soccer clubs. It is waged through both the battle of ideas in the cultural realm and the hard powers of the state, such as the army, police, or judiciary. "Class warfare" is designed to maintain the capitalist system, its attendant inequalities, and the privileges of existing political and economic elites.

For Karl Marx and Friedrich Engels, the bourgeoisie and proletariat are pitted in a titanic class struggle, which will lead to the eventual elimination of capitalism and the erection of a classless, egalitarian, and socialist order.[1] Or as Marx wrote in *The Eighteenth Brumaire of Louis Bonaparte*, "Men make their own history, but they do not make it just as they please; they do not make it under circumstances chosen by themselves, but under circumstances directly encountered, given and transmitted from the past."[2] In short, Marxists insist that historical materialism gave humanity a new and invaluable tool to understand the changing circumstances of history and thus allowed the masses of men and women "to make history knowingly and intentionally."[3] This meant that humanity was free to forge profound political and economic change through collective action, but that its freedom was restricted by the existing economic structures and its attendant belief systems.

Western Marxists included the Italian communist Antonio Gramsci (1891–1937) and the Frankfurt School, which was associated with the Institute for Social Research at the University of Frankfurt am Main and the tenure of its director Max Horkheimer beginning in 1930. These Western Marxists "accepted in broad outline Marx's analysis of the structure and dynamics of capitalism," but were less dogmatic than orthodox Marxists who thought that capitalism would fall from its own contradictions.[4] Progressive social change, insisted Gramsci, "would not follow in train behind economic developments."[5]

Unlike the orthodox Marxists who saw culture as a direct reflection of dominant socio-economic relations, Gramscians view culture as a critical terrain of social struggle. Gramsci insisted that liberal capitalism is cemented as the ruling ideology in the West because of the "common sense" support it receives from the masses in civil society, rather than the "repressive state apparatus" (for example, the police and army).[6] One of the gravest errors that we make as human beings, insisted Gramsci, "is the belief about everything that exists, that it is 'natural' that it should exist, that it could not do otherwise than exist."[7] For Gramsci, "common sense" is informed by "everyday experience" and is the "traditional popular conception of the world."[8] In short, common sense is an uncritical and "largely unconscious way of perceiving and understanding the world" that has become "common" in any historical epoch.[9] Ultimately, common sense limits our mental horizons and thus stunts the creation of alternative political futures. Common sense is forged in relation to our ideas about the state, market, culture, and even soccer matches.

JERSEY #3: GIFTED DEFENDERS

I now select the representatives for lesson three. In selecting the number 3 shirt, one retired Italian number 3, Paolo Maldini (AC Milan), stands out among the pack. Founded in 1899, AC Milan is one of the famous soccer clubs in Italian history. Maldini is a recently retired defender (2009) who had an illustrious career and saw his number 3 jersey retired. (Maldini has two sons playing in the AC Milan youth system and he thus consented to the use of the number 3 shirt at some time in the future should his children make the jump to the AC Milan first team.)

Paolo Cesare Maldini was born in Milan, Italy on June 26, 1968. The Italian defender could play in the heart of the defense or as a left back. He was adept with either foot, although he was naturally right footed. He spent twenty-four seasons playing for Serie A club AC Milan before retiring at the advanced age of forty-one in 2009. He is the longest-serving AC Milan player in its history. During his illustrious career, Maldini won numerous honors: the European Cup/Champions League five times, seven Serie A titles, one Coppa Italia, five Supercoppa Italiana, five European Super Cups, and two Intercontinental Cup titles.

Tall, handsome, and elegant, Maldini became the youngest first team player for AC Milan. He was sixteen when he made his debut in 1985. In a career that spanned from 1985 until his retirement in 2009, Maldini set records in appearances for the club (902 in all competitions and 647 Serie A appearances). Equally impressive was that he played at the top level of domestic European soccer for more than two decades. At thirty-nine, Maldini won the Best Defender trophy at the UEFA Club Soccer Awards. He holds the record for most UEFA club competition appearances: 175. In 1995, Maldini came second to the Liberian international and his teammate George Weah for the FIFA World Player of the Year award. He was also the AC Milan and Italy captain for most of his career and was considered a genuine leader, hence his nickname *Il Capitano* (The Captain).

The Maldinis are an AC Milan institution. Cesare Maldini, Paolo's father, played and captained AC Milan in the 1950s and 1960s, as well as represented Italy at the 1962 and 1966 World Cups. His two sons, Christian (b. 1996) and Daniel (b. 2001), have already been signed by AC Milan and currently play in the youth teams. We might think of this as the perpetuation of an intergenerational system of ideological hegemony, as AC Milan remains one of the richest and most powerful clubs in the world.

Maldini played for fourteen years on the Italian national team, making his debut in 1988, before retiring in 2002 with 126 caps, seven goals, and four World Cup participations (1990, 1994, 1998, and 2002). Although he was a stalwart with the Italian national team, he never won a major trophy for his country. He was a runner-up twice for Italy in major competitions: the World Cup in 1994 and the European Championship in 2000. In recognition of his defensive qualities, Maldini was selected for the World Cup All-Star teams in 1990 and 1994.

Maldini is one of my picks for the number 3 jersey because his club AC Milan and its owner Silvio Berlusconi allow us to better understand the notions of ideological hegemony and "class warfare." In liberal societies, "class warfare" is not waged through open violence. Instead, liberal societies attempt to attain ideological hegemony in civil society through sporting contests and other cultural activities. The aim of ideological hegemony, argued Gramsci, was to defend capitalism and liberalism through the support of the masses. As a famous soccer star with AC Milan (owned by the three-time prime minister of Italy Silvio Berlusconi and one of the richest clubs in the world), Maldini unwittingly became the public face of a club that contributed to the creation of ideological hegemony in civil society. Silvio Berlusconi, the team's owner since 1986, was engaged in a project of "class warfare" as he used his AC Milan connections to run for public office and, as prime minister, was later accused of cutting state funding for the most disadvantaged sectors of society.

Salvador Mariona

The other choice for the number 3 jersey is a retired soccer star from El Salvador named Salvador Mariona.[10] Most of you have probably never heard of Salvador Mariona. You are not alone, as I did not know about the retired El Salvadoran international until undertaking my research for *The World through Soccer*. He certainly did not have as accomplished a career as Paolo Maldini. Yet in his native El Salvador, Mariona was a star and a hero for the tiny Central American nation. He was the captain of El Salvador's national team at the 1970 World Cup in Mexico, one year before the infamous Soccer War between El Salvador and Honduras. Mariona was also the captain of the El Salvador national team in its six qualification matches for the 1970 World Cup, including the matches leading up to the Soccer War. He played in three bitter qualification matches against Honduras in 1969, which precipitated the one hundred-hour Soccer War. El Salvador won the final match 3–2 in extra time in the famed Azteca Stadium in Mexico City. It was the first time that the El Salvador national soccer team qualified for the World Cup. The only other World Cup appearance for El Salvador came in 1982 in Spain. The Soccer War took place on the battlefield for about one hundred hours between July 14 and July 18, 1969. The tensions between El Salvador and Honduras were exacerbated by extreme nationalism and the World Cup qualifying soccer matches pitting the two Central American nations against each other. Mariona also played in three humbling defeats in the 1970 World Cup against the hosts Mexico, the Soviet Union, and Belgium.

Salvador Antonio Mariona Rivera was born on December 27, 1943, in Santa Tecla, El Salvador. Mariona had an eight-year career with El Salvador's national soccer team in the 1960s and 1970s. He was a gifted defender, who began his career in the 1960s with obscure second and third division sides in his country. Mariona was also a star with club side Alianza FC from 1964 until 1977, one of the most fancied sides in El Salvador's soccer history. Founded in 1960, San Salvador-based Alianza won its first championships in the 1965–1966 and 1966–1967 seasons. More significantly, Alianza was the first Central American and Salvadoran club to win the CONCACAF Champions' Cup in 1967. Mariona played on all those championship-winning teams. When he retired, Mariona founded a company named *AIG Unión y Desarrollo, SA*. Today, he is the chief executive of his old soccer club, Alianza.

Mariona helps us see "class warfare" in a more conspicuous manner than Maldini. Whereas in liberal societies, "class warfare" is waged through sporting contests, the media, or the education system, in authoritarian states, "class warfare" is waged more openly and violently, as highlighted by the Soccer War. As the captain of El Salvador's national team in the qualifying matches for the 1970 World Cup, Mariona was the public face of a state that used a nationalistic Soccer War in order to allow the military regime to remain in power.

SOCCER AND THE "REVOLT OF THE MASSES"

The Frankfurt School and Antonio Gramsci had their critics in the ideological uncertainty of the interwar years, which produced the totalitarian horrors of Fascist Italy (1919–1943), Nazi Germany (1933–1945), and the Stalinist Soviet Union (1922–1953). It was a Spanish philosopher Ortega y Gasset who in an article entitled "*El Espectador*" (The Spectator), written in 1934, criticized the rapid rise of mass soccer.[11] Also the author of a famous political tract *La rebelión de las masas* (*The Revolt of the Masses*), Ortega y Gasset saw mass soccer, like the mass politics of the Communists and Fascists, as examples of "bad taste," the degeneration of a "noble life" based on effort, the denigration of a spirit of critical reflection, and a harbinger of the politics of vindictive violence.[12] While Ortega y Gasset heavily criticized the extremists of both the right and left, he shared with the Frankfurt School luminaries the notion that culture and sports could be harnessed to uncritically support those in power or the reigning ideology of the day. While culture was historically identified with "refined" elites and "barbarism" with the masses, Ortega y Gasset and the Frankfurt School demonstrated how culture and sporting contests such as soccer were increasingly mass activities that would revolutionize the way politics was conducted.

A German social psychologist, Gerhard Vinnai, wrote a fascinating small book in 1970, *Fussballsport als Ideologie*, about soccer as an ideology and its mass psychology. The book was translated into English as *Football Mania* (1973), while the Spanish translation stayed true to the original German meaning and is called *El fútbol como ideología* (Soccer as ideology).[13] In this work, Vinnai interpreted soccer as a game in which the goals are scored "against the dominant." For the renowned cultural theorist Stuart Hall, culture (including soccer) is a "critical site of social action and intervention, where power relations are both established and potentially unsettled."[14] In chapter 4, I examine soccer as a medium of social transformation and return to the insights of Hall and Vinnai. For now, I argue that soccer is a site of contestation between different class interests and that on numerous occasions soccer goals have more often been scored on behalf of the dominant soccer continents, nations, clubs, and social classes. From this perspective, Maldini's Italy and AC Milan and Mariona's El Salvador and Alianza advance the interests of capitalism and serve to legitimize and recreate the inequalities of their respective societies.

Marxist and neo-Marxist scholars argue that historically soccer has been utilized as a weapon of dominant socio-economic and political elites. As institutionalized soccer was created in the latter part of the nineteenth century in England, it was inevitable that the game become associated with mass industrialization and the growth of an organized labor movement. The first Communist International, or International Working People's Association, saw its creation in London in 1864, its first meeting in Geneva in 1866, and its culmination in 1876. At its peak, the First International had five to eight million members, including the two most famous members, German-born Communist Karl Marx and the Russian anarchist Mikhail Bakunin, who were bitter rivals. The Football Association was also created in London in 1863, one year before the erection of the First Communist International. The Football Association was formed in an attempt to standardize the rules of the game. The universal spread of the rules of the game would eventually allow for the growth of international matches between nations and club teams from different countries.

Soccer spread universally in a manner that conformed to Gramsci's insight, namely, through spontaneous, "informal" support among common people rather than the imposition of what Louis Althusser called the "repressive state apparatus." Yet the spread of institutionalized soccer could also be linked to the "repressive state apparatus" because it coincided with the rise of British imperialism in the late nineteenth and early twentieth centuries. English soldiers, businessmen, and sailors backed by British imperial might played a key role in "informally" spreading institutionalized soccer worldwide. Little did the British know that one day mass soccer would be used to resist the colonialist enterprise:

> For many former British colonies sport has a history of serving the colonized people in resisting British rule. Often it was used by the colonizers to foster a sense of discipline and hard work, but mostly it was meant to help control. However, this control was often flipped on its head and used against the colonizer. Sport in the British Empire served as a unifying force, often imbibing nationalist rhetoric, with matches serving as focused representations of the climate of social and political struggle. Football was the most popular sport in the empire and it often unified the colonized across economic and social classes. Once adopted, football matches would be opportunities for indigenous people to resist. [15]

British imperialists were not alone in fearing the democratizing impulses of soccer. There were problems closer to home. Concerned with the mass mobilization of socialist ideas through factories and the Communist International, socio-economic and political elites were keen to keep the workers busy and relatively happy. The oldest English soccer clubs, including Sheffield Football Club (1857), Hallam Football Club (1860), Cray Wanderers (1860), Worksop Town Football Club (1861), Notts County Football Club (1862), Stoke City Football Club (1863), Nottingham Forrest (1865), and Sheffield Wednesday (1867), were created around the same time as the foundation of the Football Association and the First Communist International, in 1863 and 1864 respectively.

Numerous clubs were formed in England through factories and mills in the second half of the nineteenth century. So, for example, Millwall Football Club was founded as Millwall Rovers by the workers of J. T. Morton's canning and preserve factory in the Millwall area of London's East End in 1885. One team even had the name of the factory attached to it: Royal Ordnance Factories Football Club was a soccer club from southeast London that was founded in the late nineteenth century. In 1893, the former workers' team at the Royal Arsenal in Woolwich, Woolwich Arsenal FC, joined the Football League. The workers at the Royal Arsenal, some of who still played as amateurs for Woolwich Arsenal, sought to create a new workers' team to fill the void, thus in the same year they founded Royal Ordnance Factories FC. The company bosses and politicians of an anti-Communist hue were all too pleased to channel the energies of their youthful workers toward productivity and soccer rather than a class struggle, which threatened their entrenched interests.

It is rather fascinating how many Latin American club sides saw their creation as a result of the tireless efforts of upper- and middle-class elements from England, whether businessmen, soldiers, or sailors. Institutionalized soccer clubs were born throughout Latin America as early as the late nineteenth century and mostly in the first half of the twentieth century. For example, current professional club names such as Newell's Old Boys (Argentina), Liverpool (Uruguay), The Strongest (Bolivia), and Wanderers (Chile) reflect the distinctively English origins of the Latin American game. Some of the oldest Latin American club sides date to the rise of mass industrialization near the end of the nineteenth century: Gimnasia y Esgrima (La Plata) and Quilmes (both Argentina, 1887), Rosario Central (Argentina, 1889), Peñarol (Uruguay, 1891), Santiago Wanderers (Chile, 1892), Flamengo (Brazil, 1895), and Nacional (Uruguay, 1899).

Men from Cornwall, England introduced institutionalized soccer to Mexico. Cornish miners in the picturesque, mountainous town of Real del Monte, Pachuca played the first soccer game in Mexico in 1900 on a field adjacent to the mine. The first soccer team in Mexico, Pachuca Athletic Club, was created in 1901. The first team consisted of Cornish immigrants to Mexico, who also introduced Cornish pastes (a delicious baked pastry) to the region. Pachuca today remains a Mexican soccer hotbed with CF Pachuca playing in Mexico's first division and receiving widespread regional support. Pachuca remains "the cradle of Mexican soccer" and thus it was fitting that in 2011 the city became home to the first Hall of Fame of global and domestic soccer figures.[16]

In contrast to the developing institutionalized variant of soccer, the streets, fields, beaches, and ports of urban settings offered spaces for spontaneous soccer and social interaction for the dispossessed social classes facing new industrial, capitalist realities that engendered their share of social injustices. In the late nineteenth and early twentieth centuries, essentially the transition from a raw "street soccer" to the institutionalized codified game, Latin America witnessed soccer matches with distinctively class-oriented and ethnic flavors. Competitive matches were held between mostly white elite clubs against workers and black slave descendants (Brazil), rural indigenous migrants to the city (Bolivia and Mexico), and the region's *mestizo* (mixed-race) population.[17] The institutionalized clubs were largely white and European, while the non-institutionalized sides were predominantly black, mestizo, and indigenous. Del Burgo insists that it is from the earlier origins at the borders of the institutionalized and non-institutionalized games that is born the exhilarating brand of Latin American soccer: the encoded way of life and *joie de vivre*; the myth of spontaneity against the jackboot of authority and discipline; the individual style that rejects the structured institutionalized formations and produces soccer geniuses; and the sharp contrast with the regularity and drudgery of Latin American mass poverty.[18] Soccer geniuses from the region such as Garrincha, Pelé, Carlos Alberto, Falcao, Sócrates, Romario, Teofillo Cubillas, Maradona, Juan Ramon Riquelme, Enzo Francescoli, Lionel Messi, and Neymar are, no doubt, in part products of non-institutionalized street soccer. The Beach Soccer World Cup, which was held in Tahiti in 2013, is a professional competition mimicking the raw excitement of street soccer.

Latin American businessmen, politicians, and families with large land holdings feared the non-institutionalized, spontaneous, and socially marginalized non-white sides. They thus created efforts designed to direct the popular classes toward the institutionalized game. The institutionalized game could better control the burgeoning working classes, whether white or non-white.

Del Burgo further points out that non-institutionalized soccer has the feel of a carnival atmosphere in Latin America. This carnival feeling was transplanted to many contemporary Latin American soccer stadiums, although with the rise of hooliganism from Argentina to Mexico, a more militaristic atmosphere with an excess of security and police officials pervades some stadiums. Is hooliganism, whether in Latin America or Europe, a violent expression of the anguish of the declining industrial classes? A violent protest against established authority and "civilized societies"? A tendency of human beings to behave less responsibly toward "them" in collective situations where the self is lost in the higher collective calling of the team ("us")? An expression of the nihilism of contemporary culture? An aggressive display of passions more tolerated by established authorities than revolutionary working-class struggle? As the French philosopher Jean Baudrillard pointed out, hooliganism is often not about the game of soccer itself, but social, psychological, political, economic, and cultural problems that have their roots outside the soccer stadiums.[19]

While institutionalized soccer led to the institutionalization of hooliganism among hardcore, violent fans in soccer stadiums worldwide, Del Burgo is convinced that soccer historically served as an inconspicuous agent of mass social control. A pamphlet published by the anarcho-syndicalist Free Workers' Union Germany movement saw soccer as a "counterrevolutionary phenomenon" and insisted that young soccer players have "no time for the revolution" when they play soccer.[20] In 1917, an Argentinean leftist anarchist newspaper *La Protesta* could denounce soccer as "pernicious idiotization caused by the running after a round object."[21] Soccer became, to crudely paraphrase Marx, an "opiate of the masses"; a "drug" that prevented the emerging industrial workers from seeing their real conditions as exploited economic producers in a "heartless" capitalist world. Del Burgo writes the following in reference to Latin America's soccer history:

> In the early years of the century, many old style establishments—not only football clubs but also factory management boards and the like-representatives of Latin America's elite, made attempts to form relationships with working-class teams. At times, this took the form of patronage, with an established club funding an affiliated local team. At other times, it took on other dimensions—managers encouraging the creation of football sides among the workers to engender company loyalty and, perhaps more importantly, to divert employees' attentions away from the more damaging spectre of industrial unrest. In these early relationships formed between the elite and the masses in football, can be seen the origins of the most compelling arguments in the analysis of football in Latin America; that football serves as an opiate of the masses, an instrument of mass control, a social adhesive binding the most volatile and precarious of ethnic and political mixes.[22]

Whereas Marx had in his *Communist Manifesto* (1848) exhorted "Workers of the World Unite! You have nothing but your chains to lose!" soccer of the late nineteenth and early twentieth centuries was for some a powerful weapon used to divide, pacify, distract, and co-opt the masses of newly industrialized workers. As conditions in the early twenty-first century are vastly different from the late nineteenth century, the question remains: Is soccer still "an instrument of mass control"?

THE SOCCER WAR

We have thus examined the rise of soccer clubs in England and South America as agents of social control in an age of greater worker consciousness. I now turn to the way the 1969 Soccer War between Honduras and El Salvador was related to class struggle and ideological hegemony. The Soccer War was also sometimes called *La Guerra de cien horas* (The 100-Hour War) because it lasted approximately one hundred hours. In this case, soccer became a pretext for the use of the "repressive state apparatus" by two Central American states. Jingoistic nationalism in civil society and the states in El Salvador and Honduras, as well as soccer matches between the two countries, were utilized to advance hegemony in the "ideological state apparatus."

Although the soccer star Salvador Mariona is one of the representatives of lesson three, the Soccer War was undoubtedly not caused by soccer. Soccer acted as the instrument and trigger that launched a bitter war between two poor Central American states with a history of militarism, authoritarianism, and deep-seated class divisions.[23] When the guns of war were silenced after less than one week, 6,000 people tragically lost their lives, 12,000 more people were wounded, and 50,000 individuals lost their homes, fields, or villages.[24]

Let us revisit the facts of the Soccer War in order to better understand this unusual event in soccer history. The Soccer War occurred precisely because sectors of the mainstream media and cultural milieux in both countries promoted extreme nationalism, jingoism, and war. The "repressive state apparatus" was necessary because Honduras and El Salvador were then military dictatorships, not liberal democratic states. Hence, those states did not have the same refined mechanisms for ideological control in civil society as liberal states.

Here are some of the key events leading to the Soccer War. El Salvador and Honduras were drawn in the final round of qualifying for the 1970 World Cup in Mexico. We must recall that at the time the World Cup was an elite tournament with only sixteen countries, which then increased to twenty-four countries in the 1982 World Cup and later to today's thirty-two nations. It was a big deal for two relatively unknown Central American states to have the opportunity to qualify for the most important global soccer tournament. El Salvador and Honduras had never qualified for the World Cup before 1970. Thus, soccer was an opportunity for both countries to positively project their states to the world. After two tense matches in El Salvador and Honduras, a final deciding match was held at the famed Azteca in Mexico City. Mariona played in these matches.

There was sporadic fighting between fans in conjunction with the first game in the Honduran capital of Tegucigalpa on June 8, 1969, a 1–0 triumph for Honduras. The second game, on June 15, 1969 in San Salvador, saw El

Salvador gain an emphatic 3–0 victory. There was more violence. The final playoff match took place in Mexico City on June 26, 1969. El Salvador dramatically won 3–2 after extra time. This meant that El Salvador qualified for the World Cup. There is a famous, touching photograph of an El Salvadoran player consoling his Honduran opponent after the match, but the good will did not last very long. Given the war that took place off the field, how did Mariona and other teammates feel after the victory? On the field, Mariona was acknowledged as a "giant" and one of the greatest players in the history of El Salvadoran soccer; he was praised in national team songs, and his club side Alianza once defeated Pelé's mighty Santos.[25] One blogger points out that the Salvadoran players must have felt great pride in qualifying for a tournament that was punctuated by the trials and tribulations of a Soccer War and voodoo ceremonies against the national team before a qualifying match against Haiti.[26] Mariona's teammate Mauricio Alonso Rodríguez Lindo, the goal scorer that put El Salvador into the 1970 World Cup, declared: "We gave the country joy in difficult times (in times of war)."[27] In an interview with the radio station *La Kaliente*, Mariona pointed out that while the players were paid very little by today's standards, they had a dream of playing in the World Cup and played the qualification matches with feelings of great national pride, honor, and heart.[28]

At the matches in San Salvador and Tegucigalpa, the respective capital cities of El Salvador and Honduras, opposing national team players and officials were faced with hostile crowds and even feared for their lives. Concentrating on the soccer matches became nearly impossible as rival fans camped outside the hotel rooms of the opposing national team, ensuring that they would have a terrible sleep and not be fully alert for the key match. The El Salvadoran team was not allowed to sleep the night before their key match in Honduras because of the noise of Honduran fans outside their hotel and the local food that had made some players ill with diarrhea.[29] Local police or military could do little to halt such a hostile atmosphere. The mass media outlets in the respective countries, or the "ideological state apparatus," contributed to the tense atmosphere between the two countries with crude, jingoistic nationalism—the stock and trade of Latin American military regimes. Both El Salvador and Honduras were ruled by right-wing military juntas, which were not shy about using the "repressive state apparatus": army and police.

Soccer was only part of the story. The most significant events of the Soccer War took place off of the soccer field. The roots of the Soccer War lie in a deadly cocktail of authoritarian, military governments, nationalism, geopolitics, issues over land reform (class conflict), and immigration and demographic problems.

Basic geopolitics played a key role in the Soccer War. It is generally acknowledged that countries with bigger territories, larger populations, and better demographic growth rates outperform smaller countries in terms of Gross Domestic Product.[30] Yet this was not completely true for El Salvador and Honduras. El Salvador is much smaller than Honduras in terms of territory, but in 1969 at the outbreak of the Soccer War, El Salvador had a population that doubled that of Honduras. By 1969, more than 300,000 Salvadorans were living in Honduras, looking for a better life in a country that had lots of land and very few people. The Salvadorans made up a sizeable percentage of the peasant population of Honduras.

Throughout its history, land in Central America has been badly distributed. Land reform schemes were rare. In Honduras, a large majority of the land was owned by large landowners or big corporations. The United Fruit Company, a U.S. multinational, owned a sizeable amount of the land. The United Fruit Company allied itself with the Honduran National Federation of Farmers and Livestock-Farmers of Honduras, which sought to defend wealthy landowners and was radically anti-small farmers and anti-Salvadoran.

A land reform law was passed in Honduras in 1962 and more forcefully enforced by 1967. It set the stage for class conflict and tensions between Honduras and El Salvador. The effect of the land reform law was that the Honduran government turned over land occupied legally or illegally by Salvadoran immigrants and redistributed this land to native-born Hondurans. Thousands of Salvadorans were left homeless.

In both Honduras and El Salvador, the tensions were intense and nationalistic sentiments increased. Salvadoran civil society claimed that atrocities were being committed against Salvadorans in Honduras by the military and paramilitary groups, as well as ultra-nationalist thugs. In the press, the most ultra-nationalistic elements in both countries even called for war.

As El Salvador and Honduras were military regimes, both respective governments stressed anti-communism, the protection of large rural landowners, an exalted nationalism, and war as the ultimate crucible of national unity. The Soccer War is a classic example of a "diversionary war": a war instigated by a leader or leaders of country in order to distract the population from domestic problems at home.[31] In a "diversionary war," national unity is engendered through extreme nationalism and a shared enemy, which focuses problems on the external conflict and the war rather than domestic problems. According to this "diversionary war" theory, wars are manipulated in order to keep leaders in power that have a tenuous grip. Authoritarian regimes, which often have little support in civil society, can more easily engage in a "diversionary war" because they do not face the scrutiny of the people in regular and democratic elections.

It is no doubt true that both the El Salvadoran and Honduran military regimes of the period were authoritarian and anti-democratic. Economic opportunities and upward mobility were limited by large companies and rural landowners. Popular dissent was limited, while government harassment of small farmers' organizations seeking land reform was widespread. Outside pressure from the United States in the rabidly anti-Communist context of the Cold War and large companies such as the United Fruit Company ensured "class warfare" and maintained wealth in the hands of the few: foreign companies and wealthy landowners at the expense of the many. Once the order to expel the Salvadorans from Honduras accelerated after the implementation of the land reform law in 1967, the two military governments' interests converged. That is, El Salvador feared a Marxist-inspired revolution as a result of the displaced 300,000 peasants returning home, while Honduras feared a backlash from its own people and perhaps a revolution should they continue to privilege the El Salvadoran peasants above their own landless poor. Nationalism, negative mirror images of the "other," conflict, and ultimately war masked common class interests, which united the two military regimes, key corporate elites, and established landed families in both El Salvador and Honduras.

The Soccer War ended on July 18, 1969. The ceasefire between the two countries was organized by the Organization of American States. The war resulted in a twenty-two-year suspension of the Central American Common Market, a regional integration project that had been set up by the United States in order to counteract the effects of the Cuban Revolution. The military regimes of both El Salvador and Honduras were reinforced. Mariona continued to play with his club side until 1977 and ended his career with Platense Zacatecoluca in 1978. He later became the assistant coach of El Salvador's national team in the 1982 World Cup. He also managed both Alianza and Platense Zacatecoluca for one-year spells. As a key El Salvadoran defender and captain during the infamous Soccer War, Mariona helps one understand the linkages between soccer, class warfare, and authoritarian military regimes. As a former national team star and the current chief executive of his beloved Alianza FC, Mariona also contributed toward cementing ideological hegemony in civil society.

MARIONA, MALDINI, AND IDEOLOGICAL HEGEMONY

Writing in *Avanti!* on August 27, 1918, Gramsci noted that soccer is "a model of individualistic society. It demands initiative, competition and conflict. But it is regulated by the unwritten rule of fair play."[32] Gramsci also advanced the notion that soccer was an "open-air kingdom of human loyalty."[33] In chapter 7, I explore how the crass commercialism of the game is eroding "human loyalty." In chapter 6, I return to the notion of "fair play," when I discuss the relationship between soccer and ethics. Note how, for Gramsci, soccer is a reflection of the values of liberal capitalist societies. On the one hand, capitalism demands "initiative, competition and conflict," as a few capitalists own the means of production and the vast majority of workers (including professional soccer players) worldwide must sell their labor in order to earn a wage and survive. On the other hand, there is the ideal of "human loyalty" to club and country. In addition, laws are created by the liberal state to protect capitalism, the bourgeoisie, and private property. These laws also ensure equal rights for all ("fair play") in the public sphere as a consequence of the legacies of the American and French revolutions in the late eighteenth century (for example, citizenship laws, periodic elections, equality before the law, and later equality between the sexes and various ethnic groups).

In what amounted to a perspective keenly aware of ideological hegemony, Cesar Luis Menotti, the coach of Argentina's World Cup-winning squad in 1978, stated the following: "Our football belongs to the working class and has the size, nobility and generosity to allow everyone to enjoy it as a spectacle."[34] In contrast to Menotti, Adorno and Horkheimer insisted in 1944 that cultural activities, including professional soccer matches, are more about the "entertainment business" than the sport itself: "The culture industry perpetually cheats its consumers of what it perpetually promises."[35] Or the German-born thinkers could pessimistically write "Amusement under late capitalism is the prolongation of work."[36]

Thus, following Gramsci, Menotti, and Adorno and Horkheimer, professional soccer embodies: 1) the terrain for working-class inclusiveness and "generosity"; 2) a deceptive realm in which the matches are boring and predictable and perpetuate capitalism's fixation on work and profits; 3) a reflection of the individualistic (even egoistic) and competitive nature of liberal capitalist societies, but also its ethos of "fair play"; and 4) the end of "authentic" leisure and the acceleration of a Protestant work ethic.

For Gramsci and Frankfurt School thinkers, civil society, including culture, music, film, literature, folk traditions, and even sporting contests such as soccer matches, is the site of contestation designed to overturn the "hegemonic" (dominant) conception of the world, which ideologically legitimizes and supports capitalism. Gramsci understood that liberal capitalist societies are relatively stable and receive a high degree of mass support because they do not generally rely on the "repressive state apparatus." Even the "repressive status apparatus," argued Gramsci, is premised on the consent it receives from sectors of the state and civil society. Gramsci called for a tactical "war of position" in the cultural realm in contrast to the orthodox "Bolshevik strategy of frontal assault on the state."[37] As a result, Gramsci argued that sports and other cultural activities could be used to create "counter-hegemonic" discourses in civil society, which challenge liberal capitalism's "hegemonic" appraisal of reality. With this in mind, lesson three advances the notion that soccer is a rich cultural terrain and a site of contestation between "hegemonic" and "counter-hegemonic" discourses of the world. Hegemony here is understood as a form of rule "premised more upon consensual aspects of power rather than direct coercion."[38] Moreover, this chapter demonstrates how soccer has, at times, been a milieu in which "class warfare" has been practiced by dominant classes in order to maintain the existing inequalities associated with capitalism.

In order to better understand the notion of ideological hegemony, Markovits and Hellerman point to the United States's soccer "exceptionalism."[39] Soccer is not the "hegemonic" or number one sport in the United States in terms of ordinary peoples' "emotional attachments," but it is the most popular sport in most countries around the world.[40] The "hegemonic" sports in the United States are American football, baseball, and basketball. In contrast, soccer is the "hegemonic" sport in the majority of countries around the world. Thus, soccer has the potential ability to influence billions of fans around the world. In chapter 4, I examine how soccer can positively transform individuals and communities. This perspective can be contrasted with the pessimistic view of some Marxists and Frankfurt School scholars such as Adorno and Horkheimer, who view culture and sporting activities as governed by a crude and singular worldview: "Business is their ideology."[41]

The French Marxist Louis Althusser (1918–1990) made a distinction between the "repressive state apparatus" and the "ideological state apparatus," both of which serve the ruling economic class.[42] This distinction is important for our two player choices for this lesson: Maldini and Mariona. The "repressive state apparatus" is based on violence and the logic of obey and command: the heads of state, government, police, courts, and the army. The "ideological state apparatus," on the other hand, includes all of civil society outside the ambit of the state: the family, the media, religious organizations, the education system, culture, and sporting contests. According to Althusser, the "repressive state apparatus" acts in favor of the ruling class through covert and overt forms of violence. In this chapter, the 1969 Soccer War between Honduras and El Salvador and by extension Mariona's El Salvador is used as an example of the use of the "repressive state apparatus." Yet the "repressive state apparatus," insisted Althusser, also functions through ideology and it heavily favors dominant social classes. The "ideological state apparatus" functions principally through a dominant ideology and the intimation of symbolic violence as it can call for the support of the "repressive state apparatus."[43] As the club is located in a liberal society, Madini's AC Milan highlights the subtle nature of the "ideological state apparatus." In addition, the Italian and El Salvadoran national soccer teams, as well as professional club sides AC Milan (Italy) and FC Alianza (El Salvador), highlight the "ideological state apparatus."

Salvador Mariona and Paolo Maldini are the representatives of lesson three. Both number 3s allow us to understand how ideological hegemony is used through soccer. Maldini and his club AC Milan help us see linkages with the "ideological state apparatus," and Mariona allows us to reflect on the extraordinary powers of the "repressive state apparatus." Remember that Althusser pointed out that the "ideological state apparatus" supports the "repressive state apparatus" in liberal and illiberal societies alike. In the Soccer War, the "ideological state apparatus" (including national soccer teams in both countries) reinforced the imperatives of the "repressive state apparatus" (that is, the military regimes in El Salvador and Honduras).

Gramsci understood that a "war of position" might tactically necessitate both the use of violent and non-violent cultural struggle in order to defeat capitalism and create a socialist society. Gramsci and the Frankfurt School thinkers highlighted the way culture, including sporting contests, were integral to maintaining the capitalist system and upholding class inequalities. These intellectuals could also insist that culture and sports might also be a space to challenge capitalism and the class-based realities of our world. In the cases of both Mariona and Maldini, soccer clubs and national teams acted to reinforce support for capitalism, extreme nationalism, and the status quo.

Maldini and Mariona lived in very different societies, cultures, regimes, and epochs. Both were captains of their national teams and major soccer clubs in their respective countries, AC Milan and FC Alianza. As part of the "ideological state apparatus," the Italian and El Salvadoran national teams and their respective clubs acted to enhance mass support for localism, nationalism, and capitalism. Both players were "pawns" in what Adorno and Horkheimer called a "culture industry," which merely acted to reinforce the competitive values of capitalism. Maldini might have been bothered by the way AC Milan's owner mixed politics with soccer, or perhaps Mariona and other players were deeply troubled by the Soccer War and the fact that it took place in the context of World Cup qualification matches between El Salvador and Honduras. Yet Adorno and Horkheimer would have insisted there was little that Mariona and Maldini could do to challenge a structurally inhumane capitalist system.

West German international Paul Breitner was another brilliant number 3. He was admired worldwide because he had a roaming style and is one of only four soccer players to have scored in two different World Cup final matches, sharing the distinctive honor with Pelé, Vavá, and Zinedine Zidane. He scored in the 1974 finals against the Netherlands when West Germany won 2–1 and in the 1982 finals against Italy in a 3–1 loss. Recall that Gramsci thought that sport was an important arena of ideological struggle designed to win hearts and minds. Breitner tended to voice revolutionary, leftist opinions on the political and social issues of the day. He thus had the ability to influence the hearts and minds of his legions of fans and create what Gramsci called "counter-hegemonic" conceptions of the world, which might assist in capitalism's demise.

Against the view posited in relation to Breitner, Alan G. Ingham is adamant that soccer matches "serve as rites and representations that reproduce
liberal democratic society in hegemonic terms."[44] Soccer games and their
clubs such as AC Milan and FC Alianza (the clubs of Maldini and Mariona),
argues Ingham, also provide us with

> *serialized civic rituals* that mask the differences between dominant and subor-
> dinate groups in both class and community terms. They are part of the renewal,
> recreational, defensive, and modificational processes through which the hege-
> mony fends off its challengers. I argue, then, that the organic intellectuals of
> the capitalist classes (the public relations, media relations, advertising and
> marketing specialists) are spin merchants who dream up euphoric rites/rituals
> to reaffirm the moral authority of liberal democratic societies as the capitalist
> classes and the functionaries of the State have envisioned it on their terms.[45]

For Ingham, the civic is "the new domain which blurs the distinction between
the public and the private, the State and civil society, and self-interested
ideologies with the 'common good' or the 'commonwealth.'"[46] The matches,
clubs, national teams, and players, whether it was FC Alianza in the 1960s
and 1970s or AC Milan in the Berlusconi era, promote "serialized civic
rituals" in order to fend off ideological challenges to the status quo. The
rituals of the matches serve a legitimizing function with respect to cementing
the inequalities and hierarchies associated with global capitalism and state
structures. In chapter 7, I further explore the "spin merchants" when I discuss
the relationships between soccer, business, and marketing.

The case of Paolo Maldini is instructive in this respect. Whereas Mariona
contributed to creating ideological hegemony in an authoritarian context,
Maldini helps to cement ideological hegemony in a liberal context. His club
AC Milan and its owner, Silvio Berlusconi, use the cultural capital of soccer
in order to forge ideological consensus. Maldini was a real professional for
his entire career for both club and country. He rarely complained. Instead, he
honorably and stoically served his club AC Milan for almost twenty-five
years, as well as the Italian national team. Maldini's skill, character, tenacity,
and loyalty were his admirable traits. In an age when more money and
adventures in foreign lands are tempting, Maldini was the rare player that
played his entire career for one club. Yet the club that he played for is an
important part of the story. AC Milan is owned by Silvio Berlusconi, the
media magnate and three-time Italian prime minister: 1994–1995,
2001–2006, and 2008–2011. Berlusconi was the longest serving post-war
prime minister of Italy, as well as the third-longest serving since Italian
unification, after Benito Mussolini and Giovanni Giolitti.

Silvio Berlusconi used his successes with AC Milan to create a new
political party, *Forza Italia!* (a soccer rallying cry for Italy's national team),
which catapulted him to the highest political office of the country. As Italian

prime minister, Berlusconi applied the lessons of AC Milan: the power of money, media image, populism, and the state as an instrument of "class warfare." Markovits and Rensmann point out how Berlusconi used soccer's "symbolic capital," more than its commercial pull, to attract and mobilize millions of Italians:

> Silvio Berlusconi, Italian prime minister on multiple occasions, used his success as president and principal owner of AC Milan to convince the Italian public that he could govern the country with similar results, bringing to Italy the same fame and pride that his club "Milan" attained. Berlusconi's "soccer power" was crucial on his road to attaining the pinnacle of Italy's political power. In addition, Berlusconi's party *Forza Italia* was named after the soccer slogan "Go Italy." With this slogan Berlusconi successfully used the appeal of Italian national soccer to gain political support for his populist one-man party in a time of highly divisive and collapsing party politics. [47]

Not all Italians were impressed by Berlusconi's use of soccer for the symbolic and cultural capital that it generates. Italian liberals or leftists complained that Berlusconi made the Italian state more corrupt, gutted social welfare programs for the poor, rigged taxes in favor of the rich, and invited anti-immigrant and neo-fascist political parties into his coalition governments such as the *Lega Nord* (Northern League), the *Movimento Sociale Italiano* (MSI—Italian Social Movement), and *Alleanza Nazionale* (AN—National Alliance).

The MSI was an openly neo-fascist political party until 1995 when, under Gianfranco Fini, it turned "post-fascist." As deputy prime minister, Fini even visited Israel and apologized for the "absolute horrors" of the Fascist race laws under Benito Mussolini after 1938. Although the leader of the LN, Umberto Bossi, came out of an anti-fascist tradition, his political party railed against Muslims immigrants from the Global South, arguing disingenuously that Northern Italian regional cultures were threatened with extinction like the Native Indians of North America under the weight of colonialism. Under Berlusconi, Italian politics drifted right, with Berlusconi waving the mantle of anti-welfare state populism and his coalition partners making Italy more anti-immigrant and xenophobic.

Recall that early English and Latin American soccer clubs used the game as a tool of worker social control. AC Milan is one of the best supported soccer clubs throughout Italy, as well as one of the most successful European clubs in history. It has won eighteen Italian *Serie A* championships, five *Coppa Italia* titles, six Supercoppa Italiana tophies, seven UEFA Champions League titles, two UEFA Cup Winners' Cups, three Intercontinental Cups, and one FIFA Club World Cup trophy. In line with soccer as a co-optation tool, AC Milan was supported by the city's working-class and trade unionists, while cross-town rivals Inter Milan were mainly supported by the more prosperous Milanese middle class. Yet the AC Milan hardcore fans are of various ideological stripes. Given AC Milan's historical support in the working classes, one would expect a more left-wing fan base. Yet since Silvio Berlusconi is the president of AC Milan, the club was often associated with Berlusconi's right-wing politics, corporate gigantism, and corruption. AC Milan's deep pockets and success meant that it could count on about 20 million fans throughout Europe, thus rivaling European giants such as FC Barcelona, Real Madrid, Manchester United, Arsenal, Bayern Munich, and Borussia Dortmund.

For Terry Eagleton, the British literary theorist and distinguished professor of English at Lancaster University, soccer is a useful tool for conserving the class privileges of rich soccer clubs, their owners, and maintaining the gross inequalities of the capitalist system. During the 2010 World Cup, Eagleton went so far as to suggest that the mass following associated with soccer is a real impediment to political change. Writing in *The Guardian* in 2010, Eagleton called soccer "a dear friend to capitalism," insisting in a slavishly Marxist tone that soccer today "is the opium of the people, not to speak of their crack cocaine."[48] He had especially harsh words for the recently retired English soccer star David Beckham, whom he called "impeccably Tory" (referring to the ruling right-wing Conservative Party of Prime Minister David Cameron) and "slavishly conformist." Eagleton's positions on "the beautiful game" are rather pessimistic and lead him to call for the game's abolition: "Nobody serious about political change can shirk the fact that the game has to be abolished. And any political outfit that tried it on would have about as much chance of power as the chief executive of BP has in taking over from Oprah Winfrey."

Eagleton is unambiguous that soccer is a tool of crass "class warfare," thus preventing workers from seeing their authentic (that is, miserable) conditions:

> If every rightwing thinktank came up with a scheme to distract the populace from political injustice and compensate them for lives of hard labour, the solution in each case would be the same: football. No finer way of resolving the problems of capitalism has been dreamed up, bar socialism. And in the tussle between them, football is several light years ahead.[49]

Eagleton hints that there might be a trace of rebellion left in the working classes with respect to soccer, or what he calls a "supporters revolt against the corporate fat cats who muscle in on their clubs."[50] Yet he ends his piece with the same depressing tone that soccer is "the opium of the people."[51] Soccer clubs are increasingly transnational and their owners often have little intimate knowledge of the game and its supporters. Liverpool FC now belongs to the Fenway Sports Group from the United States and the American basketball superstar LeBron James. Examples of corporate takeovers abound in soccer today. Maccabi Tel-Aviv FC of Israel is owned by a Canadian businessman Mitchell Goldhar. Manchester City is owned by the Abu Dhabi United Group, thus making it one of the richest clubs in the world. Queens Park Rangers are owned by the Mittal-Fernandes group, an Indian-Malaysian joint venture. The trend in foreign ownership of soccer clubs around the world led FIFA president Sepp Blatter to critically opine on the subject: "You get people turning up with banker's guarantees who are not interested in football and then they lose interest in the clubs and leave. What happens to the clubs then?"[52] "There is always a danger that these people will just one day leave," he added, referring to Manchester City's former Thai owner Thaksin Shinawatra, who sold the English club to the Abu Dhabi United Group while facing corruption charges in his homeland.[53]

While AC Milan was spared the problems associated with foreign ownership, Paolo Maldini and Silvio Berlusconi were ultimately representatives of big business and corporate gigantism. Maldini was the best of company men for AC Milan for more than two decades. This is a trend that will likely be imitated by his two sons. While the working-class fans could idolize Maldini and other AC Milan stars, the team was a representative of global capitalism rather than working-class solidarity. AC Milan was ranked as the sixth wealthiest soccer club in the world by *Forbes*, thus making it the wealthiest club in Italian soccer.[54]

Yet AC Milan, and Berlusconi especially, was interested in winning hearts and minds beyond the soccer field, or in the symbolic and cultural capital of the game. While I will highlight the possibilities of social change through soccer in the next chapter, one is tempted to see how Eagleton's assessment of Beckham as "slavishly conformist" could be applied to Maldini, or any other AC Milan player. A precondition for remaining with AC Milan is understanding its scripted and controlled corporate culture, which is again officially led by Silvio Berlusconi after his political exit. There are strong rumors that Berlusconi will make a political comeback, no doubt aided by his big money ties to AC Milan and his controlling share in Mediaset, the largest commercial broadcaster in the country. As in the late nineteenth century or early twentieth century in England or South America, Eagleton and others argue that soccer today acts as the "drug" of the working class in an age when obscene state corporate support and tax loopholes rise, welfare benefits decline, and economic uncertainty and debt hang like a sword on all working people. From this perspective, Maldini might be a legendary player and a wonderful example to young people of service to his club, but he is merely the handsome face of a structurally inhumane capitalist system. This capitalist system has at its aim neither the welfare of soccer players, nor ordinary people in Milan or beyond. Or as French philosopher Jean Baudrillard argued in 1983 *In the Shadow of the Silent Majorities*, soccer remains an opiate of the masses: "Power is only too happy to make football bear a facile responsibility, even to take upon itself the diabolical responsibility for stupefying the masses."[55]

In conclusion, this chapter advanced the idea that soccer is a terrain for ideological struggle and "class warfare." I used the examples of soccer clubs during the rise of the industrialized working class, the Soccer War, Silvio Berlusconi's (and Paolo Maldini's) AC Milan and Italy, and Salvador Mariona's FC Alianza and El Salvador to demonstrate that, from Marxist or neo-Marxist perspectives, the "ideological state apparatus" engenders mass support in defense of capitalism and social control. In authoritarian regimes such as Honduras and El Salvador in the late 1960s, the "repressive state apparatus" is more likely to be used than in liberal democracies, as we saw with the Soccer War. In liberal and non-liberal societies alike, soccer is used to promote nationalism and subdue working-class consciousness. One of the greatest left backs of all time, Paolo Maldini neatly highlighted lesson three through his associations with AC Milan, Silvio Berlusconi by extension, and the Italian national team. Although he was an obscure yet talented El Salvadoran national team defender during the Soccer War, and later an executive for FC Alianza, Salvador Mariona's example allowed us to see the interactions between the "ideological state apparatus" and "repressive state apparatus," as well as how the latter is far less refined in authoritarian societies. As part of the "ideological state apparatus," soccer clubs and national teams reinforce "hegemonic" values such as competition, individualism, the notion that the power of money wins titles, and defense of capitalism. They can also legitimize the violence inherent in the "repressive state apparatus." In the next chapter, I examine how some soccer clubs and their supporters have created counter-hegemonic discourses and practices in order to challenge the establishment or dominant conceptions of viewing the world.

Chapter Four

"One Ball Can Change the World"

Soccer and Social Change

In previous chapters, I examined the way soccer is related to competing discourses of nationalism, how it has been manipulated by authoritarian and totalitarian governments, and soccer as a terrain for ideological struggle and "class warfare." This chapter seeks to ask the question: Can soccer be a vehicle for social change? Or has professional soccer so cemented its ties with extreme nationalism, authoritarian militarism, and big business interests that it is incapable of playing the role of social transformation?

It is important to keep in mind that in speaking of social change, I am referring to social transformation in a broad sense. That is, social change connotes anti-racist, anti-homophobia, anti-sexist, and anti-violence campaigns of concerned clubs, organizations in civil society, and even FIFA. Yet social change also entails attempts by individual players and fans, soccer collectives, anarchists, and liberal and left-wing groups to undermine the game's crass commercialism, corruption, and anti-democratic tendencies. In lesson four, I highlight a number of examples of soccer as a mechanism for social change: the anti-racist orientation of Dutch club side Ajax of Amsterdam, anti-racism campaigns led by Kick It Out in Britain, the struggle for democracy within Brazilian club Corinthians during the military dictatorship in the early 1980s, and the Homeless World Cup.

It is interesting to note that anti-racist campaigns around the globe have become so embedded within professional soccer that not participating in such programs gets you branded racist and neo-fascist (recall the discussion of neo-fascist players and fans in chapter 1 in relation to differing conceptions of nationalism), or hurts your corporate bottom line (see chapter 7). In this respect, Italian professional club SS Lazio opened the 2013 season without a major sponsor on its shirt because the club's hardcore fans are virulently racist and neo-fascist and the management has been seen as too tolerant of such excesses, thus turning away any potential corporate sponsors. Remember from chapter 1 that Lazio was also the club supported by Italian Fascist leader Benito Mussolini.

JERSEY #4: A DEFENDER OR DEFENSIVE MIDFIELDER

Before delving into the details of lesson four, I need to choose a number 4. Remember that the number 4 typically plays in defense, or as a defensive midfielder. A number 4 might play as a central back, a right halfback, or a combative defensive midfielder. Number 4s are often determined, tiger-like ball winners. They do the dirty, grinding work in a match. They are the coalminers of soccer, going deep down into the mines each day and doing the hard back-breaking work in order to make their respective teams successful. Some number 4s can also score and turn a game on its head. A number 4 is a complete player sacrificing for the team defensively, while demonstrating their often overlooked technical skills offensively.

Four players have been chosen to represent lesson four: Cesc Fàbregas, Patrick Vieira, Tom Huddlestone, and José Leandro Andrade. The first three players all played key roles in recent years in bringing awareness to issues surrounding racism in soccer in various countries: England, Spain, France, and arguably throughout Europe. In addition, I have selected an obscure yet brilliant black Uruguayan soccer star of the 1920s and 1930s named José Leandro Andrade. If we are to defeat the scourge of racism in soccer and society, we will need the efforts of soccer players, managers, administrators, politicians, journalists, and fans from various nations.

The player selected should be a champion of a cause, a representative of social change, or a symbol of the democratizing possibilities of soccer. In fact, the rule is that most professional players are not politically active because this gets you branded as a radical and undermines your local or global marketing potential.

Unfortunately, the efforts of these four aforementioned players and trailblazing British players such as Andrew Watson (the first black player to play professional soccer in Britain, who played for Queens Park Rangers and Scotland in 1881) and Jack Leslie (along with Arthur Wharton and Walter Tull, he is one of the first non-white players to play professional soccer) are countered by neo-Nazi skinheads, recruitment at soccer stadiums by extremist, racist, and ultra-nationalist organizations such as the National Front in England, and pro-fascist players such as Gianluigi Buffon (one of the representatives of chapter 1).

Patrick Vieira

Patrick Vieira was born in Dakar, Senegal, on June 23, 1976. A former French international, Vieira retired from professional soccer in 2011. Today he is the football development executive at Manchester City in the English Premier League. His role at Manchester City is to oversee youth development, commercial partners, and the club's social responsibility program, "City in the Community." Manchester City was Vieira's last club and in the 2011–2012 season the club won the Premier League title on the last day of the season, thus ending a forty-one-year drought for the Manchester club. In 2010, Vieira was also nominated Goodwill Ambassador of the Food and Agriculture Organization of the United Nations. In short, Vieira is a player with a social conscience. He is also a brilliant French international and hence a role a model in his country for many soccer players of African descent, who complain of systematic discrimination in French soccer and society.

Vieira made a name for himself at London-based club Arsenal from 1996 to 2005, where he won three Premier League titles, including an undefeated season, and four FA Cups. He scored twenty-nine goals for Arsenal and made 279 appearances for the club, while also securing the captain's armband. After leaving Arsenal in 2005, Vieira spent one season at Turin-based Juventus before joining Inter Milan in 2006. At Inter Milan from 2006 to 2010, Vieira made sixty-seven appearances and scored six goals.

On the international stage, Vieira was a driving force behind France's soccer resurgence. He amassed an incredible 107 caps for France. He will be most remembered as an integral member of the French team that won the 1998 World Cup for the first time in the country's history. Vieira set up Emmanuel Petit's third goal in the 3–0 victory against Brazil in the finals. In 2000, he was a member of the French national team when it won the European Nations' tournament. He played a key role on the French team that finished runner-up to Italy in the 2006 World Cup, scoring goals against Togo and Spain.

When Zinedine Zidane retired from the French national team, Vieira was appointed France's captain. Vieira was also instrumental in convincing Zidane to end his retirement and help France qualify for the 2006 World Cup. When Zidane returned to the French national side, Vieira nobly handed the captain's armband to the legendary Zidane.

Cesc Fàbregas

Francesc "Cesc" Fàbregas Soler was born on May 4, 1987. He is a contemporary Spanish player who plays for FC Barcelona and the Spanish national team. While Fàbregas wears the number 4 jersey, he often orchestrates attacks and plays mainly as a central midfielder. His versatility is his strong suit and this has allowed Fàbregas to even play as a winger or second striker.

Although he trained with Barcelona in his youth, Fàbregas was signed by Arsenal in September 2003 at the tender age of sixteen. He eventually established himself as Arsenal's starting central midfielder, playmaker, and captain. His Arsenal career lasted from 2003 to 2011, amassing thirty-five goals in 212 appearances. Since 2011, Fàbregas has already scored twenty goals for FC Barcelona.

As Spanish soccer underwent a revolution in the first decade of the twenty-first century, Fàbregas was a key plank in the most talented sides in the history of Spanish soccer. Despite his relative youth, Fàbregas played in the 2006 World Cup, European Nations' Championship in 2008, 2010 World Cup, and the European Nations' Championship in 2012, helping Spain to victories in the latter three tournaments. Along with the likes of midfielder generals such as Iniesta, Xavi, Xabi Alonso, Sergio Busquets, the rocks of Puyol, Piqué, and Ramos at the back, as well as the spectacular Casillas in goal, Fàbregas was an integral member of these successful Spanish national teams. He has made more than eighty-five appearances for Spain since 2006, a remarkable achievement for a young player. Before the achievements of these Spanish wonder teams, the highest a Spanish team finished internationally was winning the European Nations' Cup in 1964.

For the purposes of lesson four related to soccer as a vehicle of social change, Fàbregas is an Honorary Patron of the campaign against racism in soccer and society, namely, Show Racism the Red Card.[1] Established as an educational charity in the United Kingdom in 1996, Show Racism the Red Card uses high-profile soccer stars from Cesc Fàbregas to Rio Ferdinand "to help tackle racism in society" and deliver "education to young people and adults in their schools, their workplaces and at events held in football stadiums."[2] Films featuring famous professional players such as Thierry Henry, Samuel Eto'o, and Ryan Giggs allow teachers and other professionals to address issues related to racism.

It could be argued that as Fàbregas has Catalan roots; these origins played a role in sensitizing him to issues related to racism. The history of Spanish repression against the Catalans under Franco's dictatorship and during the Spanish Civil War is indeed lengthy and sad. As Fàbregas spent time in multiracial London with an Arsenal club that has been committed to anti-racism, this also undoubtedly played a role in Fàbregas's support for Show Racism the Red Card.

Tom Huddlestone

Tom Huddlestone (b. 1986) is a contemporary English soccer player who is an ambassador for the Kick It Out anti-racism campaign in professional soccer. Huddlestone has played as a number 4 for England and is a former midfield star with the London-based club Tottenham Hotspur. In 2013, Huddlestone joined Premier League club Hull City. Kick It Out made headlines in 2012 when Manchester United star Rio Ferdinand and a number of other black English players refused to wear their anti-racist t-shirts. I return to this issue later in the chapter when I discuss the effectiveness of anti-racist campaigns.

A tall midfielder at six foot two inches, Huddlestone was born in Nottingham, England. He was given his professional debut at the age of sixteen in 2005. From 2005 to 2013, Huddlestone made 143 appearances for Tottenham and scored eight goals for the London club. His exceptional passing skills have led to comparisons with the Tottenham legend and former England international Glenn Hoddle. Huddlestone has a ferocious shot from long distance.

Huddlestone received his first England cap in 2009 in a friendly match against Brazil. In another 2010 World Cup warm up game against Japan, Huddlestone started for the first time in a 2–1 victory. Although Fabio Capello announced that Huddlestone was in his preliminary 2010 World Cup squad of thirty players, the Tottenham star was not selected for England's final twenty-three-man squad. In 2012, Huddlestone made his first appearance for England in two years for a friendly match against Sweden.

Let's Kick Racism Out of Football was a campaign established in 1993 and Kick It Out was established as an organization in 1997. As its website points out, "Kick It Out works throughout the football, educational and community sectors to challenge discrimination, encourage inclusive practices and work for positive change."[3] It also notes that Kick It Out is supported and funded by the game's governing bodies, including founding body the Professional Footballers Association (PFA), the Premier League, and the Football Association. Moreover, Kick It Out has not been content to limit its anti-racism campaigns to Britain. Kick It Out "plays a leading role in the Football Against Racism in Europe (FARE) network and has been cited as an example of good practice by the European governing body UEFA, the world governing body FIFA, the Council of Europe, the European Commission, European parliamentarians and the British Council."[4] Another dynamic anti-racist initiative in British soccer was founded by fans and is called Football Unites, Racism Divides (FURD).

Along with Huddlestone, numerous retired and active soccer players and managers are involved with Kick It Out: Sir Alex Ferguson, Hope Powell, Steven Gerrard, Chris Powell, Samuel Eto'o, Rio Ferdinand, Paul Elliott, John Barnes, Dickson Etuhu, Florent Malouda, Steven Pienaar, Ji-Sung Park, Neil Etheridge, Wes Brown, Martin Kelly, and Jason Roberts. While it took until 1978 before a black player, Viv Anderson, represented England internationally, since then one in every four players making an England debut is black and seventy black players have represented England in senior professional competitions.[5] A black English soccer star, Huddlestone has been a beneficiary of changing attitudes toward black players in England. He acknowledged that attitudes in Britain are changing compared to other places in Europe where racism is a serious problem in the stands, particularly in Russia, Poland, Ukraine, Hungary, Italy, Spain, France, and numerous other countries: "I believe it has had a positive effect and the Premier League is certainly one of the best leagues in the world when you consider how little racism there is amongst players and fans. You hear stories about other major leagues in Europe and it's disappointing, but I believe we have got it right in this country with campaigns such as Kick It Out."[6] Yet as Liverpool legend and former England international John Barnes correctly pointed out, racism in soccer is a wider societal concern: "Racism is not only a problem in football, it's a problem in society. Until we tackle it in society, we can't tackle it in football."[7] Moreover, when black English international Rio Ferdinand refused to wear the Kick It Out jersey, perhaps he was trying to make a point that fighting racism needs more systematic changes than merely wearing anti-racism t-shirts. His stance was more realistic than players and administrators who suggested that black players should just play good soccer, ignore the racial taunting, and hope that the problem goes away.

José Leandro Andrade

José Leandro Andrade (1901–1957) was a sensational Uruguayan international who played the right half position and wore the number 4. He was nicknamed the "Black Marvel" (*Maravilla Negra*) and was "the first international idol of soccer."[8] "In one match he crossed half the field with the ball sitting on his head," writes Eduardo Galeano.[9]

Andrade's greatest domestic accomplishments came when he played for Nacional in his native Uruguay, scoring twenty-nine goals in 105 appearances from 1924 to 1930. He won a domestic title with Nacional and two more with Peñarol in 1932 and 1935.

Andrade also played for Uruguay internationally from 1923 to 1930, scoring one goal in thirty-four matches. In addition, Andrade played on Uruguay's *Copa América* winning teams in 1923, 1924, and 1926. Andrade also won an Olympic gold medal at the 1924 Olympic soccer tournament in Paris, where he first came to international prominence. He is the first black international player to play Olympic soccer. As Eduardo Galeano points out, Uruguay was one of the few countries in the 1920s and 1930s to field black players.[10] Andrade's spectacular performances and complete dominance in midfield in Paris led to the label the "Black Marvel." In 1928, he won his second Olympic gold medal for Uruguay. He also led Uruguay to win the first World Cup in 1930 on home soil. He made the all-star team for the 1930

World Cup and was voted the third best player of the tournament behind two great soccer legends: teammate José Nasazzi and the Argentinean star Guillermo Stábile. Andrade's supreme qualities are recognized by the IFFHS, which rates him the twenty-ninth best soccer player worldwide and the twentieth greatest in South America in the twentieth century.

Andrade's value for a team was not scoring, but rather controlling the defensive end of midfield and contributing in attack. Andrade was also an intelligent and honest player, allegedly never celebrating his goals.[11] He dominated the pitch with his speed and technique, not through an imposing physical presence. Andrade was not a short man, standing at five feet eleven inches, but a technical artist who relied on intelligence above physicality.

Andrade is considered one of the first great black players, as well as one of the world's first international soccer stars. He thus paved the way for numerous other non-white players in his own country, South America, and arguably worldwide. Andrade was a living example of "Kick Out Racism" in soccer long before Kick it Out was created. Yet it was not always clear that Andrade would be a world soccer star. Before the rise of professional soccer in Uruguay, Andrade worked a number of odd jobs: carnival musician, shoe shiner, and newspaper salesman.[12]

After his soccer career ended, Andrade was feted as a guest at the 1950 World Cup when Uruguay won its second World Cup in Brazil. His nephew Víctor Rodríguez Andrade was a member of the 1950 Uruguayan World Cup team. But by the mid-1950s Andrade was living in squalor in the Uruguayan capital city, Montevideo.[13] He had descended into a life of alcoholism. In his time in Paris in 1924, Andrade already had a reputation for being a drinker, a bohemian, the "king of the cabarets," and a man that was always "dressed to kill."[14] In 1957, Andrade contracted tuberculosis and died at a nursing home in Montevideo. For Andrade soccer was, for a time, an escape from death. Yet Andrade's accomplishments are engraved in soccer history. He is also a tremendous role model for blacks throughout Uruguay and Latin America because he was an exceptional and honest black athlete in a predominantly white soccer era.

SOCIAL TRANSFORMATION THROUGH SOCCER?

Lesson four examines the possibilities of using soccer as a mechanism for social transformation. Does the inherently "us" versus "them" on the playing fields and in the stands reinforce a militaristic ethos and consequently stunt social progress? Do the billions of soccer fans worldwide and the immense popularity of the sport provide us with opportunities for social change? Or are soccer campaigns against racism or homophobia merely co-optation schemes that rarely challenge the wider systematic racism of society and structural realities connected to global capitalism? Can the Homeless World Cup change individuals and help us question existing economic and political structures? Do ethnically based soccer clubs such as Syrianska FC in Sweden (founded by Arameans in 1977 and currently playing in the Swedish first division) or Hakoah Vienna (winner of the Austrian championship in 1926) reinforce ethnic differences or promote greater tolerance?

Many of the billions of poor worldwide might feel relief from a soccer match. Yet can soccer assist us in changing our unequal economic and political structures? Despite a globalized world with, for example, 5,000 Brazilian professionals worldwide (more than the number of its diplomats),[15] can ugly bouts of soccer "tribalism," localism, or hyper-nationalism change? Can soccer really tackle systematic racial discrimination? Can soccer help in the struggle against sexism?

Soccer is a mirror of our world, with all its ugly warts. Despite noble and passionate campaigns to end racism, xenophobia, or homophobia by some players, clubs, leagues, and FIFA, these sentiments persist. Justin Fashanu, the great English soccer striker of the 1970s and 1980s, was struggling with being gay in a sport that privileges masculinity and tragically took his own life. Fashanu was an intelligent, soft-spoken, kind, and humble player. He received little support from institutionalized professional soccer merely because he was gay in a sport that pretends that there are no gay players.

In 2013, there was not one openly gay player in British professional soccer. An anti-homophobia campaign that encouraged British soccer players to wear rainbow-colored laces was promoted by Stonewall, a gay rights charity, as well as Irish bookmaker Paddy Power.[16] It sent laces to 5,000 soccer players throughout the country. The slogan of the campaign, "Right Behind Gay Footballers," was controversial and for some critics strengthened stereotypes against gays and lesbians. As a result, Manchester United was one club who chose not to wear the laces, while anti-homophobia organization Football v Homophobia (FvH) criticized the initiative.[17]

As Chris Greenberg of *The Huffington Post* pointed out in 2013, our views about gay athletes might be finally changing:

> In the 77th minute of a regular-season Major League Soccer match between the Los Angeles Galaxy and the Seattle Sounders on Sunday evening, Robbie Rogers made history.
>
> The 26-year-old midfielder entered the game as a substitute for the Galaxy, becoming the first active openly gay male athlete to compete in a U.S. professional team sport.
>
> Rogers came out in February in an emotional note on his personal website. In that same post, he also announced his decision to "step away" from the game. With a smile on his face and the No. 14 on his back, he stepped back on to the field on Sunday evening. The crowd at the Home Depot Center welcomed him with a loud cheer.

The reaction on social media among fellow players, fans and media was similarly positive. [18]

Franklin Foer, in his *How Soccer Explains the World: An Unlikely Theory of Globalization,* points out that modern soccer is a form of "commodified tribalism." [19] This tribalism is often local, regional, or national, while historically it has not been gay friendly. As clubs, major corporations, the EU (the Bosman ruling allowed soccer players with EU citizenship not to count as foreign players), and FIFA increasingly dictate the rules of the game, soccer sells and makes billions of dollars worldwide. At the same time, soccer has simultaneously witnessed ugly pitch fights between Serbian and Croat clubs, the Celtic-Rangers rivalry in Glasgow, Scotland with its Catholic versus Protestant overtones, and the refusal of most Arab and Muslim nations to play against and hence recognize Israel. As a result of this "commodified tribalism," where Nike, Adidas, and Puma are content to make millions from their logos on national or club jerseys, Foer argued that

> it becomes so much easier to slip in and out of a group identity. You're no longer just born into who you are, you get to choose it, and it can get sold to you by corporations. That to me is kind of scary. But then again, you can see the upside to it—when you can slip into an identity more easily, you can also slip out of an identity more easily and maybe that makes it ultimately more harmless. [20]

Asked about whether "tribalism" could disappear from soccer, Foer is realistic: "I don't see tribalism ever really disappearing entirely. I just think that people are almost hardwired to identify as groups. And that sort of group identity always runs the risk of being chauvinistic." [21] Foer is not afraid to hold the corporations and ultimately soccer authorities responsible for "commodified tribalism":

> And what ultimately makes it such a disturbing parable is that it highlights the ways in which multinational capitalism can make such peace with the tribalism. These corporations find ways to exploit tribalism to make a buck, rather than trying to snuff it out. So you have Nike selling orange jerseys to the fans at Rangers games. In any other context an orange jersey would be harmless, but in the context of this rivalry it alludes back to King William of Orange and the re-conquest of the monarchy from the Catholics. They know it's an extremely inflammatory symbol. Yet Nike puts a swoosh on it and sells it because they know a lot of people will buy it. [22]

Markovits and Rensmann are more positive about soccer in the twenty-first century as "an engine of cosmopolitan political and cultural change." [23] While they do not doubt that the sport still retains its ugly bouts of ultra-nationalism, anti-Semitism, and hooliganism, especially in Europe, soccer

clubs today help to promote cosmopolitanism through globalization processes in which there is increasingly "respect for strangers and the universal
recognition of individuals independent of their cultural background, citizenship, and heritage."[24] Major soccer clubs from AC Milan to Bayern Munich
"play a crucial role in shaping more inclusive collective identities and a
cosmopolitan outlook open to complex allegiances."[25] As a result of multi-
ethnic global soccer clubs, fans increasingly accept and admire foreign
players, or those players belonging to ethnic minorities. National teams are
also less homogeneous and more inclusive than in the past with players of
Turkish origins playing for Germany, black players playing for Germany or
Italy, or Israeli Arabs playing for Israel. Soccer is, to use Robert Putnam's
notion of "bridging capital," an "integrative force among different groups
and their cultural boundaries."[26] Yet these ethnically diverse players do not
completely undermine what Putnam calls "bonding capital," or "a hardening
of boundaries among different constituencies and their cultures."[27] Whether
it is the national team or the local club, fans want to see great players that
play because of their merit and skills, not their race, religion, or ethnic
background. For Markovits and Rensmann, soccer thus creates new forms of
belonging, enhances "global citizenship," and can even be "a powerful force
of political and cultural change around the globe."[28]

CAMPAIGNS FOR SOCIAL CHANGE: AJAX, SÓCRATES, AND THE HOMELESS WORLD CUP

It is undoubtedly very difficult to change entrenched and unequal political
and economic structures, with or without soccer. As chapter 2 pointed out,
dictators and military generals use soccer as a vehicle to maintain their iron
grip on power. Power cannot stem from the barrel of the gun alone. In the
twentieth century, totalitarian regimes such as Fascist Italy, Nazi Germany,
or the Communist Soviet Union relied on brute force and "politics as religion,"[29] but could last merely twenty-one, twelve, and seventy-four years
respectively. All governments know that in order to stay in power they must
be legitimate and accountable in the eyes of their populations. Soccer will not
spare illegitimate governments. Changing the inequalities associated with
capitalism is possible but complex, as socialists and anarchists discovered in
bloody battles from the nineteenth to twenty-first centuries. So what can
soccer do to promote substantive social change? I use the examples of the
Dutch club Ajax of Amsterdam, Sócrates and his campaign for democracy
through his club Corinthians, and the Homeless World Cup in order to highlight the possibilities of soccer as a vehicle for social change. As a fan of
these three endeavors for social change, I am under no illusions that soccer
can radically change the world. If we want to change the world, we need to

change ourselves (our hearts and minds), our hierarchical political and economic structures, and the dominant patterns of interactions between and within states and civil society.

Anti-racist campaigns by many professional European soccer leagues and FIFA have been positive initiatives for social change. At the 2010 World Cup in South Africa, players from opposing teams read out anti-racist statements. At the 2012 European Nations' Championship in Poland and Ukraine, there were various anti-racist initiatives at the tournament, as well as at the governmental and civil society levels. In England, the country that is at the forefront of anti-racist campaigns in soccer, there are important organizations such as Show Racism the Red Card (the organization that has Cesc Fàbregas as its honorary patron), Kick It Out (Tom Huddlestone is a member), and Football Against Racism in Europe.

Black English soccer players in the 1970s and 1980s faced terrible racial abuse. There were rumors that the English national soccer team made it difficult for talented black players to make the squad. Viv Anderson and John Barnes were the rare black English players who made it and performed admirably with the national team in the 1980s. There was some evidence of white and black cliques within clubs such as Crystal Palace. A former manager Ron Atkinson was working as an analyst and made this racist comment directed at former Chelsea and French international defender Marcel Desailly: "He's what is known in some schools as a fucking lazy thick nigger."[30] When West Bromwich Albion, a talented side in the late 1970s and early 1980s, stepped on to the pitch, "they got the bananas and the treatment," because it was the team of three talented black players: Cyrille Regis, Laurie Cunningham, and Brendon Batson.[31]

Anti-Semitism was also a major problem in English soccer. This anti-Semitism within major English clubs was a reflection of the anti-Semitism in British society. Although there are today very few Jewish professional players in English soccer (Dean Furman, the South African international and Doncaster Rovers midfielder, is an exception), the reasons have more to do today with the decline of the Jewish working classes than anti-Semitism.[32] In short, Jews historically played soccer in England and produced professionals such as the Queens Park Rangers striker Mark Lazarus in the 1960s and the midfielder Barry Silkman, the last British-born Jewish player to play in England's top division with Manchester City in the 1979–1980 season. Today there are lots of Jews involved in English soccer as fans, administrators, owners, and agents, but hardly any professional Jewish players. No Jewish soccer player has ever played for England. Antony Clavane argues that soccer is largely a working-class sport and Jews were once part of the immigrant working classes, but are today largely middle class.[33] Thus, English Jews do not produce soccer players because they are no longer working class in their origins.

In contemporary soccer, Marc Zoro, Samuel Eto'o, Kevin Constant, and countless other black players in England, Spain, Italy, Croatia, Israel, Ukraine, and Poland have been subject to hurled bananas and denigrating monkey noises. John Terry, the Chelsea captain, was banned for four games when he was found guilty of racially abusing Queens Park Rangers' defender Anton Ferdinand. Luis Suárez of Liverpool was banned for eight matches for racially insulting Patrice Evra, a French international defender playing with Manchester United. Sol Campbell, a brilliant and retired English international, said that he sometimes felt alone as soccer authorities wanted to keep the "carnival" going and did little to stamp out racism in the sport: "I had to go down this road by myself. No authorities wanted to take notice."[34] Clyde Best, a trailblazing black Bermudan international striker that played with West Ham in the 1960s and 1970s and endured regular racist abuses, was exceptional as a role model and mentor for future black players in England. After retiring from professional soccer in 1984, Best said the following: "You knew you had a job to do. You were playing for people of color, not just in England, but all over the world."[35] In 2012, the English national soccer team consisted of nine black players, a far cry from the days when Best was one of the few black players in English first division soccer.

In 2012, Stan Collymore, a retired "mixed" English player that played from 1990 to 2001 and was capped by the national team three times, reported to English authorities that Joshua Cryer, a law student at Newcastle University and the captain of the department's soccer team, sent Collymore offensive tweets. One sadly read: "@StanCollymore has anyone ever referred to you as semi pro as in a semi pro coon #neitherwhitenorblack."[36] In the same year, twenty-one-year-old student Liam Stacey was jailed for tweeting racist comments about Fabrice Muamba, after the Bolton Wanderers player from the Democratic Republic of Congo had a cardiac arrest on the pitch. In short, anti-racist campaigns are not completely stamping out racism in soccer, but perhaps making racism less acceptable in the eyes of soccer clubs, national associations, FIFA, professional players, and the fans.

Ajax of Amsterdam is the most famous club in the history of Dutch soccer. This Dutch club has unwittingly played a role in the anti-racist struggle. Ajax was the club of the legendary Johan Cruyff, who played at Ajax between 1959–1973 and 1981–1983, winning three European Cup titles. Cruyff's number 14 jersey is the only squad number Ajax has ever retired. Cruyff also managed the club from 1985 to 1988. In its history, Ajax won two Intercontinental Cups in 1972 and 1995, the European Champion Clubs' Cup/Champions League four times (1971, 1972, 1973, and 1995), the European Cup Winners' Cup in 1987, the UEFA Cup in 1992, and the UEFA Super Cup twice in 1973 and 1995.

Ajax became known in the 1980s and 1990s for its multi-ethnic outfits and its "Jewish connection." As far back as the 1930s Ajax was seen among ordinary soccer fans as having "Jewish roots."[37] The Ajax stadium was historically located next to the old Jewish neighborhood of Amsterdam. The Jewish middle classes were said to support Ajax. When I visited the newly built Amsterdam Arena early in the new millennium to see a European match between Ajax and AS Roma, I was surprised by the number of Israeli flags in the stadium and the displays of the Star of David on hats and caps. There were probably more Israeli flags at the stadium than at Israeli national soccer matches! One could even buy scarves with the Star of David, a specialty of the hardcore fans of Ajax's F-side. Stephen Wagg points out that Ajax fans, very few of who are actually Jewish, responded by embracing Ajax's "Jewish" identity after anti-Semitic abuse from traditional rivals Feyenoord of Rotterdam.[38] The Ajax fans called themselves "super Jews," chanting "Jews, Jews" during matches. The flag of the state of Israel is a badge of honor.

A brilliant number 4 was Frank Rijkaard (b. 1962), the retired Dutch international and former Barcelona and Saudi Arabian national team manager. Rijkaard played for Ajax, Real Zaragoza, and AC Milan from 1980 to 1995, while representing his country seventy-three times and scoring ten goals. He scored seventy-four goals in 414 domestic matches in Europe. Rijkaard's work rate was impressive, recovering balls frequently. Rijkaard was like a steady rock at the heart of the midfield. He led AC Milan to two Italian domestic titles and he won another five domestic trophies with Ajax in Holland. As an exceptional black Dutch player with the national team (his mother is Dutch and his father from Suriname), Rijkaard helped pave the way for countless other black professional players in Holland. Yet Rijkaard was not a strong proponent of official anti-racism campaigns in soccer, instead arguing that clubs should proceed with "caution" on the issue of racism and players need to merely "ignore" fans that engage in racist chanting.[39]

Tottenham Hotspur, a London-based club in the English Premier League, has also been identified as a "Jewish club" and their supporters call themselves "Yid army." In 2013, the English Football Association's general secretary, Alex Horne, wrote the association to tell them that the term "Yid" is considered "offensive by the reasonable observer and considers the term to be inappropriate in a football setting."[40] He also suggested that the "use of the term in a public setting could amount to a criminal offense, and leave those fans liable to prosecution and potentially a lengthy football banning order."[41] It will be interesting to see if the English Football Association enforces their tough policy, ironically against the "Yid army" and especially against its anti-Semitic opponents.

In any case, the symbolic displays of defiance by Ajax and Tottenham fans are intended to enhance tolerance and multi-ethnic inclusiveness through soccer. They give the simple messages that we are all Jews and all of us will thus combat anti-Semitism and racism.

Markovits and Rensmann argue that "European soccer arenas function as political battlefields over identities and cosmopolitan change in the age of postindustrial globalization, which is embodied in global players as highly visible minorities on the field."[42] Moreover, the authors demonstrate how "anti-Semitic images of a 'globalized Jew' have reappeared among fans in European soccer over the last twenty or thirty years, in which the vilest insults and hostilities against Israeli soccer players and professional soccer clubs like Tottenham Hotspurs, Ajax Amsterdam, MTK Hungaria Budapest, FK Austria Wien, and Bayern Munich—Europe's so-called 'Jew' clubs— have become commonplace."[43]

The anti-Semitism sometimes reaches great heights. Since the 1980s, fans of Ajax's rivals escalated their anti-Semitic slogans, even chanting "Hamas, Hamas, Jews to the gas," in reference to Hamas, the anti-Semitic Islamist terrorist group that specializes in suicide bombing and calls for the elimination of the Jewish people and the state of Israel. Nazi salutes were not uncommon by rival fans. As a result of the excesses and politically incorrect and anti-Semitic chants, many Jewish Ajax fans stopped attending the matches. Moreover, Ajax tried to persuade its fans to drop the "Jewish identity" in the new millennium, hoping to take the thunder away from Ajax's racist and anti-Semitic rivals.

Despite the fact that Ajax fans display the Star of David at their matches, there has not been greater tolerance in Dutch society. Or as Markovits and Rensmann correctly observe, "anti-Semitism has far from disappeared from Europe's public discourse."[44] Dutch society is perhaps growing more intolerant, whether anti-Semitic or anti-Islamic. Extreme anti-Zionism is on the rise in Holland and throughout Europe and masks a more sinister anti-Semitism.[45] Geert Wilders, an extreme right-wing and anti-immigrant populist, is the leader of Holland's fourth biggest parliamentary outfit, the Party for Freedom (*Partij voor de Vrijheid*—PVV). Wilders is the parliamentary group leader of his party in the Dutch House of Representatives and his party gained twenty seats out of 150 in the Dutch House of Representatives in the 2008 elections. Wilders is best known for his vehement criticism of Islam, saying, "I don't hate Muslims, I hate Islam." It is true that Wilders is pro-Israel, but he is virulently anti-immigrant and anti-Muslim, going so far as to grotesquely suggest that the Muslim holy book the *Qur'an* is equivalent to Hitler's *Mein Kampf.*[46]

Despite anti-racism initiatives in soccer, racism and anti-Semitism have not disappeared from Dutch or other European soccer stadiums. Anti-racist campaigns throughout Europe have not prevented the rise of anti-immigrant political parties throughout Europe, which increasingly structure political debates around immigration and multiculturalism and have joined national governments in nine European countries since the early 1990s: Holland, Italy, Austria, Denmark, Norway, Estonia, Poland, Romania, and Slovakia.[47]

The right's power only grew in European politics and culture after the fall of the Communist Soviet Union and the rapid demise of once-powerful leftist parties.

The left, on the other hand, has generally supported anti-racist soccer campaigns, although some sectors of the radical left insist that anti-racism campaigns in soccer are merely cosmetic if they fail to tackle systemic discrimination and the gross inequalities associated with capitalism. These critics insist that anti-racism must supersede a Benetton-style anti-racism approach where what matters is the multicultural photo opportunity and profits more than systemic inequalities. The former French international captain Lilian Thuram, who is at the forefront of anti-racist education struggles, has suggested that we are not born with racism but rather learn it, soccer is a useful terrain for anti-racist struggle because it reaches millions of people, and soccer authorities need to ban racists from soccer stadiums.[48]

It was back in 1990 that Paul Gilroy argued that anti-racist movements were designed to free whites and blacks from the shackles of racism, but were initially portrayed by the right as a challenge to the British way of life and patriotic nationalism.[49] He argued that anti-racism campaigns cannot be "divorced" from wider political processes and their aim should be to "lay bare the benefits of white people."[50] Finally, Gilroy was self-critical, insisting that anti-racist movements could lapse into a "dictatorial character," "moralistic excesses," and an exaggerated "orthodoxy."[51] If we are to follow Gilroy's insights from more than twenty years ago, racism must be simultaneously tackled both on and off the soccer field because it is in the interests of society at large.

A key Brazilian player of the wonderful, free-flowing national teams of the 1980s was Sócrates, a gifted attacking midfielder. He was a great proponent of democracy within his club Corinthians, but also a champion of democracy throughout Brazil during the dark years of the military dictatorship. Although Sócrates is not our official choice because he wore the number 6 jersey, I will extensively draw on the example of Sócrates.

He was born with a name as long as Pelé's, Brasileiro Sampaio de Souza Vieira de Oliveira, on February 19, 1954. He was tall, lean, and elegant, standing a smashing figure of six feet four inches with his beard and headband, orchestrating the Brazilian midfield like a genius general. He was the Napoleon of soccer, although not as short as the French general. He was, like many Brazilian superstars, given a nickname: Sócrates. Like the ancient Greek philosopher, he loved intellectual debates, or the exchange of ideas reminiscent of ancient Greek democracy. He was even a medical doctor, earning the title while he played soccer. He is undoubtedly one of the greatest attacking midfielders to ever play the game. Tall yet never clumsy, Sócrates was a joy to watch. He could read the game like a gifted chess grandmaster, ten steps ahead of his opponents. It is from Sócrates and his Brazilian teammate Falcao that I first learned to really love soccer. His physical strength, blind heel passes, mastery of the midfield, and ability to score with both feet made him an invaluable member of the Brazilian teams in the 1982 and 1986 World Cups. Those Brazilian teams made soccer attractive, fun, attacking, and spontaneous. Apart from the Hungarian national team at the 1954 World Cup, these Brazilian teams were the best national teams that never won the World Cup. They represented a ludic and beautiful soccer, which is pleasurable in itself.

In his scintillating career, Sócrates played for largely Brazilian sides from 1974 to 1989. He played for Botafogo-SP and later joined Corinthians in 1978, a team for which he became famous due to his campaign to extend democracy within the club and the wider Brazilian society. He then moved to Italy to play for Fiorentina, before returning to Brazil in 1985 to end his career with Flamengo, Santos, and Botafogo. On the international stage, he was the captain of the Brazilian team in the 1982 World Cup; scored twenty-two goals for his country in only sixty international matches; was named South American Soccer Player of the Year in 1983; and was selected to Pelé's list of the 125 best living players in 2004. In the 1986 World Cup, the Brazilian superstar scored twice, including a penalty kick against Poland in the round of sixteen without a run-up! In the quarterfinals against France, he tried to convert his penalty in the same way again, but had his penalty in the shootout saved by goalkeeper Joël Bats.

What was fascinating about Sócrates was that he was no mere soccer player. He understood clearly that soccer is a part of life, culture, and politics. He was a fan of Che Guevara and John Lennon, two leftist idols of the 1960s. Sócrates was a doctor of medicine: a graduate of the Faculty of Medicine at Ribeirão Preto. After retiring as a player, he practiced medicine at Ribeirão Preto and lived there with his wife and six children. A columnist for numerous newspapers and magazines, the Brazilian legend wrote about sports, politics, and an array of other themes. At the time of his death, Sócrates was writing a work of fiction about the 2014 World Cup in Brazil. Known for his *joie de vivre*, intellectual debating, drinking, and smoking, Sócrates was the Christopher Hitchens (1949–2011) of modern soccer. Or the soccer equivalent of a Left Bank Parisian intellectual in the 1960s or 1970s.

On December 1, 2011, Sócrates was hospitalized with food poisoning, went into shock, and was put on life support. He had been fighting a liver ailment. He died on December 4, 2011, at the age of fifty-seven. The tributes came pouring in from even Brazilian president Dilma Rousseff, who stated that the country has lost "one of its most cherished sons."[52] The Brazilian president paid homage to the achievements of the Brazilian soccer legend on and off the pitch: "On the field, with his talent and sophisticated touches, he was a genius. Off the field . . . he was active politically, concerned with his people and his country."[53]

What is of interest to us here is that like José Leandro Andrade, Cesc Fàbregas, Patrick Vieira, Tom Huddlestone, or English-based soccer stars of the 1960s and 1970s such as Clyde Best and Laurie Cunningham, Sócrates was more than just a soccer player. He helped to transform the world with his ideas. During his sojourn at Brazilian club Corinthians from 1978 to 1984, Sócrates scored an impressive 172 goals in 297 matches. He became known throughout Brazil because he co-founded the Corinthians Democracy movement, in opposition to the ruling military junta. Sócrates and his Corinthian teammates emblazoned their soccer jerseys with the simple yet effective *Democracia* (Democracy), a direct shot at the Brazilian military generals ruling the country at the time. A leftist with a distaste for social injustice and the authoritarianism in his country, Sócrates took the courage to openly protest against the military junta's treatment of soccer players. Recall that in chapter 2 I used the example of the gifted Chilean international Elias Figueroa and how he won favor with the Pinochet military regime. Sócrates was the anti-authoritarian, or the antithesis of Elias Figueroa. He undoubtedly began a risky and courageous campaign through Corinthian Democracy connected to a professional soccer club from São Paulo, which then spread to a Brazilian-wide movement for democratization.[54]

Sócrates was aware of his role in life, not merely as a soccer player, but also as an ambassador for political engagement and social change. He knew that human beings can create a better and more democratic world through collective, non-violent political action. Uniting his love for soccer, life, and politics, Sócrates stated his goal in the campaign for Corinthian Democracy:

> I'm struggling for freedom, for respect for human beings, for ample and unrestricted discussions, for a professional democratization of unforeseen limits, and all of this as a soccer player preserving the ludic, joyous, and pleasurable nature of this activity.[55]

These lines are indeed moving and a statement of the reality that soccer is ultimately a beautiful, joyous game and that it can also act as a voice for social conscience and democratization. Del Burgo points out that Sócrates used soccer as a vehicle to enter into dialogue with the wider society and military junta.[56] He did not merely accept the military dictatorship as a fact of life like Elias Figueroa and many other soccer players. Jorge Valdano, a member of the gifted Argentinean side that won the 1986 World Cup, went so far as to suggest that Sócrates represented the dialogical, humanistic, and creative soccer of the left versus the jackboot brutality and chicanery of the right.[57]

The Brazilian military regime did fall in 1985, thus ending a military junta that began in 1964. Perhaps Sócrates and the struggle for Corinthian Democracy had a hand in the raising of mass consciousness against the military regime and the Brazilian transition to democracy. What is clear is that such campaigns for democratization help push social change, but are less frequent than some of us would like and do not fully undermine unjust socio-economic structures or rampant corruption.

In recent years, dictators like Hosni Mubarak in Egypt or Mahmoud Ahmadinejad in Iran have felt the wrath of soccer supporters and players alike. Some soccer players on Iran's national team wore green arm bands in honor of the opposition movement after state-led killings of peaceful demonstrators and rigged elections in 2009. The Al-Ahly supporters in Cairo have been at the forefront of the Egyptian variant of the "Arab Spring" and they blame the regime of deposed dictator Mubarak for a tragic stampede that killed seventy-four people in 2012.

We have thus far highlighted the case of Ajax Amsterdam, anti-racist campaigns in soccer, and Corinthian Democracy as vehicles for social change. Our last example of soccer as an agent for social change is the Homeless World Cup.[58] The 2012 edition of the Homeless World Cup took place in the heart of bustling Mexico City. The 2012 Homeless World Cup was held at *Plaza de la Constitución* or the *Zócalo*. The *Zócalo* has numerous Aztec ruins and was part of the Aztec capital Tenochtitlan. It has been the major gathering place for Mexicans since the Aztecs. Later it became the site for swearing in viceroys, royal proclamations, military parades, national independence ceremonies, and even modern religious events such as the festival of Holy Week. Foreign heads of state often visit the *Zócalo*. Key national celebrations and national protests are held there.

The slogan of the organizers of the 2012 Homeless World Cup is "Beating Homelessness Through Football." Seventy-three partner countries were involved with the Homeless World Cup. For the Mexico City 2012 Homeless World Cup, a total of forty-three nations were involved: Argentina, Austria, Bosnia and Herzegovina, Brazil, Bulgaria, Cambodia, Canada, Chile, Costa Rica, Czech Republic, Denmark, England, Finland, France, Germany, Greece, Guatemala, Haiti, Hong Kong, Hungary, Indonesia, Ireland, Italy, Lithuania, Mexico, Morocco, Namibia, Netherlands, Norway, Peru, Philippines, Poland, Portugal, Romania, Russia, Scotland, South Africa, South Korea, Sweden, Switzerland, Ukraine, the United States, and Wales. Note that the regular World Cup competitions only have thirty-two qualifying nations, with the vast majority of the world's approximately 200 countries unable to qualify. There was also a Women's Homeless World Cup held in Mexico City in 2012 with fourteen participating nations: Argentina, Brazil, Canada, Colombia, England, Hungary, India, Kyrgyz Republic, Mexico, Netherlands, Nigeria, Paraguay, Chile, and the United States.

Since 2003 the annual Homeless World Cup has been hosted by cities across the world as "homeless players unite to celebrate changing their lives and raise awareness of homelessness."[59] In 2012, Brazil, Mexico, Scotland, Ukraine, and Chile were the top-ranked men's teams, while Mexico, Brazil, Kenya, Colombia, and Argentina were the top-ranked women's nations.

At the 2012 edition of the tournament in Mexico City, Mexico defeated Brazil 6–2 in the Women's Cup final, while in the men's Homeless World Cup finals, Chile defeated the host nation 8–5. In a tournament based on a small four versus four pitch concept, I was impressed by the players' technical skills, endurance, and tactical awareness. The atmosphere at the matches was electric and the matches were televised live on YouTube. Young boys and girls made friends with homeless players and were taught important lessons about life. Who could imagine that homeless soccer players would ever get a chance to leave their cities, play soccer, be safe in proper lodgings, get some regular sleep and food, and even be recognized for their talents?

The Homeless World Cup has professional soccer players who act as Global Ambassadors supporting the aims of the tournament. These ambassadors include Emmanuel Petit, who won the 1998 World Cup with France. Another is the mercurial former Manchester United and French international Eric Cantona. Rio Ferdinand, an English international and Manchester United star, is also a Global Ambassador.

While soccer alone cannot undermine homelessness, individual players have changed their lives. People who watch the games are impressed by the personal and excessively sad and difficult journeys of the players. People can increase their social consciousness and engage in social solidarity by watching the Homeless World Cup. As the website of the Homeless World Cup points out, the journey of Homeless World Cup star Michelle Da Silva from Brazil is instructive:

> Michelle was born in 1990 in the famous favela portrayed in the film "The City of God." All her life, Michelle has lived for football—on a courageous journey out of poverty and exclusion through sport.
>
> Michelle was selected to represent Brazil at the Homeless World Cup in Copenhagen in 2007, when she won the Best Female Player award and was noticed by Eric Cantona as an outstanding player, during one of his training sessions—a speedy and powerful striker determined to do her best on the pitch and off.
>
> So it was no surprise that after she returned to Brazil she was swiftly selected for the Brazil women's under 20s national team and later went on to play in the 2010 South America Cup.
>
> Michelle says: "The Homeless World Cup is a major life experience. You create friendships and set the right attitude to succeed in your life and in football."[60]

Or there was the case of Homeless World Cup star Ginan Koesmayadi. He played for Indonesia at the 2011 Homeless World Cup in Paris. He was awarded the Best Male Player and has since been a very inspiring leader for his community. The website of the 2012 Homeless World Cup tells his inspiring story:

> At 20 years old, Ginan was diagnosed with HIV. Ironically, that is when his whole life turned around.
>
> The young man started using drugs when he was 14. At this point, it seemed that the whole world had turned against him, as he says. But after a few years, he decided to take control of his life: "I had grown tired of living on the streets, doing petty crimes to support my dependence on drugs. In 2000, I asked my family to get me into rehab. But I encountered yet another bump on the road when I was told that I had contracted HIV, possibly through used needles I used to inject drugs."
>
> "The biggest barrier a person with HIV has is self-doubt. When you limit your own ability because you are HIV positive, then you are doomed to failure," he said.
>
> After three years in rehab, Ginan, together with four friends, founded Rumah Cemara, a community-based organisation whose aim is to improve the quality of life of society's outcasts—HIV positive people, drug addicts and the homeless.
>
> The organisation also uses football as a universal language to overcome local stigma and discrimination towards people living with HIV/AIDS, and engage both HIV-positive and HIV-negative players.
>
> "In the long run, we would like society to treat us as normal human beings—neither discrimination nor privilege is needed. We would like to change the prevailing mindset that we are a useless, sinful bunch. That's all," insisted Ginan Koesmayadi.
>
> In the lead-up to the Rio 2010 Homeless World Cup, Rumah Cemara was chosen as the Homeless World Cup's national partner in Indonesia. Unfortunately, due to lack of funding, the team could not make it to the tournament that year.
>
> So Rumah Cemara and Ginan waited and made their amazing debut at the Paris 2011 Homeless World Cup.
>
> The trip was made possible thanks to a few donations and sponsorships and to show his gratitude, Ginan decided to walk from Bandung to Jakarta (215 km).
>
> This garnered him nationwide sympathy and recognition.
>
> Indonesia did not win in Paris but finished 6th overall and were one of the crowd's favourite teams.
>
> When asked about the power of football, Ginan always quotes French author, Albert Camus: "Everything I've learned about human morality and duty, I've learnt from football."[61]

The stories of Ginan Koesmayadi and Michelle Da Silva are inspiring and even heroic. The Homeless World Cup does change lives. On the left, critics insist that the Homeless World Cup makes it merely appear that homelessness is a concern of governments and corporate sponsors. Real unjust economic and political structures remain the same. Carlos Slim, one of the richest men in the world and a major sponsor of the Homeless World Cup through Telmex, might disagree with this perspective. The right, on the other hand, is sure that the personal self-empowerment narratives of the players associated with the Homeless World Cup makes a difference and that the world changes by transforming the lives of individuals. Similarly, anti-racist campaigns in soccer and the struggle for Corinthian Democracy have their supporters and critics. The debate rages on about whether soccer can change the world.

In conclusion, this chapter attempted to assess whether soccer can act as a vehicle for social change. We should remember Paul Gilroy's insight that anti-racist campaigns in soccer must not lapse into a cheap moralism and be divorced from racism in society and politics outside the field. Is it realistic for soccer to change racist attitudes? Does the intense atmosphere of soccer matches generate a space for the perpetuation of racism? Recall that in chapter 1 I pointed out how soccer arenas become spaces to voice politically incorrect ideas, including neo-fascism and racism.

* * *

The representatives of lesson four are Patrick Vieira, Cesc Fàbregas, Tom Huddlestone, and José Luis Andrade. Andrade is the flag bearer of lesson four. Andrade was the first major black star in Uruguay and an international soccer legend long before anti-racism campaigns began in professional soccer. By helping his national team to win international trophies, including the 1930 World Cup, Andrade helps us underscore four key points: 1) Uruguay was a country well ahead of its time in terms of anti-racism; 2) as an international soccer star in the 1920s and 1930s, Andrade became a hero and role model for blacks in Uruguay, Latin America, and perhaps around the world; 3) Andrade demonstrated that blacks could play daring, skilled, and honest soccer; and 4) if blacks excelled on the soccer field, it might be appropriate to afford them opportunities in important professional jobs outside of the soccer field (that is, in government, businesses, media, or universities).

Successful players from minority groups such as Andrade help to break down societal barriers and ultimately combat racist attitudes in society. The former Mexican international and Barcelona defender Rafael "Rafa" Márquez Álvarez (b. 1979) was the first Mexican to play for Barcelona. Márquez increased the standing of all Mexicans in Spain and abroad through his accomplished performances with Barcelona. Paulino Alcántara Riestrá (1896–1964), a Filipino-Spanish player, was the first Asian superstar in Spanish soccer. He was the first Asian player to play on a European club. He also played internationally for Catalonia, the Philippines, and Spain. Making his debut for Barcelona at the age of fifteen, the Filipino-born player remains the youngest player to play or score for the club. He scored a whopping 369 goals in 357 matches (friendly and non-friendly) for Barcelona, thus making him the club's highest goalscorer.[62]

Andrade, Márquez, and Alcántara paved the way for future black, Mexican, and Asian soccer players in major professional clubs. Vieira, Huddlestone, and Fàbregas carry the noble, anti-racist torch of these older soccer giants. Markovits and Rensmann are adamant that the former black Brazilian soccer star Júlio César, a member of the most successful squad in the history of German club Borussia Dortmund and an all-time fan favorite, has "arguably done more to undermine—and delegitimize—widely spread racial stereotypes and racist hatreds in the stands and in town than most educational campaigns."[63]

Institutional interventions of major politicians, civil society organizations, mainstream media, soccer clubs, and soccer bodies can also help to dramatically fight racism or contribute to social transformation. Beitar Jerusalem's and Israeli society's wide support for two Muslim Chechen signings in 2013 contributed to marginalizing its minority of hardcore, violent, ultra-nationalist, anti-Arab, and anti-Muslim fans. At the turn of the twentieth century, some Argentinean club sides could wear their ideology on their sleeves. Argentinos Juniors was initially called the Chicago Martyrs in homage to the anarchist workers imprisoned or hanged in Chicago after the riots in 1886 and Chacarita was founded by a group of socialists on May 1, 1906.[64] May 1 is celebrated by anarchists and socialists worldwide as International Workers' Day. Remember from chapter 3 that Gramsci could see soccer as a tool to promote the dominant ideology, but also a mechanism to challenge hegemonic thought through counter-hegemonic initiatives in civil society.

While some critics argue that soccer or sports in general can be a ghetto for minority athletes and they will not have opportunities outside of the world of soccer, others insist that positive change in the sporting realm will lead to changes in the larger society. While extreme forms of nationalism, racism, anti-Semitism, and narrow and exclusive identities based on ethnically driven concepts of citizenship will not necessarily disappear, soccer clubs, national teams, and fans today increasingly create "new inclusive attachments, multiple allegiances," and transformed cosmopolitan collective identities that focus on players' performances and merit rather than their ethnicities, faiths, or countries of origin.[65] According to this view, soccer "might provide an important bulwark against racism and cultural exclusion, and offer a major challenge to inward-looking identity politics."[66] From this perspective, the anti-racist campaigns in European soccer, the struggle for Corinthian Democracy, or the Homeless World Cup influence the wider world beyond the pitch. As the slogan of the 2012 Homeless World Cup stated, "One ball can change the world."[67]

Chapter Five

Gods and Their Shrines

Soccer as a Pagan Religion

Chapters 1 through 4 highlighted the political lessons of soccer. This chapter is about soccer as a pagan religion in an age when increasingly "God is dead," to paraphrase the German philosopher Friedrich Nietzsche (1844–1900).[1] In his *The Gay Science* published in 1882, Nietzsche further declared the following as a consequence of the death of God: "Must we ourselves not become gods simply to appear worthy of it?"[2] This lesson might be surprising for some people and this chapter is not intended to be an attack on established religions. Rather, our aim in lesson five is to demonstrate that soccer takes on all the trappings of a pagan religion and that our gods are increasingly soccer stars.

Soccer is a "secular religion," to use the expression of Mexican writer Juan Villoro from his classic *Dios es redondo* (*God is round*).[3] The Italian filmmaker Pier Paolo Pasolini opined that soccer is "the last sacred ritual of our time."[4] Jock Wallace, the former Scottish soccer player and manager of the Glasgow-based Rangers, affirmed that "Soccer is my religion."[5] The Uruguayan writer Eduardo Galeano prayed for attractive soccer, irrespective of the club or nation: "A pretty move for the love of God. And when good football happens, I give thanks for the miracle and I don't give a damn which team or country performs it."[6]

In Africa, soccer is so "sacred" that witch doctors are used by clubs and nations in order to put spells on rival teams and thus assist their own team. As one journalist explains, "Just as every German team has a physiotherapist, every African team has a resident witch doctor. And the spells work, say some."[7] At the 2002 African Cup of Nations, Cameroon trainer Winnie Schäfer was left without his co-trainer Thomas N'Kono because, just prior to the semi-final, "he had been seen burying bones under the turf and spraying a strange elixir, in order to cast a spell on the playing field."[8] N'Kono, a legendary African goalkeeper, was arrested and led away in handcuffs and ended up spending the night in police custody.

Soccer fans can be Christians, Muslims, Jews, Hindus, Buddhists, atheists, agnostics, secular humanists, or Wiccans. The retired English player Linvoy Primus (b. 1973), who spent most of his career with Portsmouth, was openly Christian and was part of a prayer group of soccer players that included former Nigerian international Kanu, the retired English player Sean Davis, and the Zimbabwean striker Benjani.[9] A soccer stadium in Santiago, Chile is named *Juan Pablo Segundo* (Pope John Paul II). Numerous Latin American soccer players cross themselves, or fall to the ground in prayer before the start of matches, including the Manchester United star and Mexican international Javier "*Chicharito*" (Little Pea) Hernández.

In this chapter, I advance the argument that, irrespective of a person's faith or lack of faith, modern soccer is akin to a secular or pagan religion. Professional soccer matches in Israel usually take place on Saturday, the Jewish rest day. Sunday is a church day for many Christians around the world, but also the day when there are lots of soccer fixtures in England, Italy, and Mexico. When soccer fans enter soccer stadiums, which one might view as modern "cathedrals" or shrines, they are transformed by experiences that are mystical, mythical, or even religious. Soccer stadiums and their rituals (including songs, scarves, hats, and banners) are like "sacred sites" in the eyes of many fans, players, and coaches. These "sacred sites," as Desmond Morris points out in his *The Soccer Tribe*, are really "temples" that fulfill key human functions such as the need for belonging and the power of the group.[10] When he introduced Gareth Bale at Real Madrid's world record signing in September 2013 to 20,000 screaming fans at the Santiago Bernabeu, the club president Florentino Perez stated "we are in the temple of Real Madrid."[11] In short, clubs, national teams, soccer stadiums, and players are venerated in a quasi-religious fashion. Famous Mexican side Club Deportivo Guadalajara, more popularly known as "Chivas," is nicknamed *Rebaño Sagrado* (Sacred Flock).

Modern soccer stars such as Lionel Messi, Cristiano Ronaldo, Iniesta, Xavi, Edinson Cavani, or Radamel Falcao are the gods of our times. These soccer stars have followed Nietzsche's aphorism to "become gods" and thus appear "worthy of it." Legendary retired soccer stars such as Pelé, Maradona, Beckenbauer, Zidane, Puskás, Cruyff, Yashin, Best, Moore, Di Stéfano, Gento, Rahn, Fontaine, Hugo Sánchez, Platini, Sócrates, Boniek, Lato, Weah, Milla, and Cha Bum-Kun were seen by many soccer fans as blessed by godlike powers. Soccer fans saw these star players as miracle workers on the pitch. In Brazil, Pelé was seen as a *safo*, a player with divine inspiration who was quick and clever and could do "forbidden things" on the pitch. The

Brazilian striker Romario, the winner of the Golden Ball award and World Cup title in 1994, did not always have kind words for Pelé but recognized his transcendental significance: "I was never one for idols. That said, I'm a good Brazilian and so it's only inevitable I look up to Pelé. He's like a God to us— well, he is to me anyway."[12]

Or, as Vladimir Dimitrijević opines, a great soccer star is akin to the Spanish literary hero Don Quixote, or a brilliant novelist or poet, in that he has one dominant idea in his head.[13] This dominant idea, he points out, is "grandiose" and "divine." The idea is based on winning, but also winning with a breathtaking style that pleases the fans and soccer gods. It is the opposite of a "politically correct" soccer linked solely to results and the "fear of not winning."[14] In chapter 11, I further explore the relationships between soccer, art, and literature. For now, I point out that the greatest contemporary and retired soccer stars provide fans with divine experiences in soccer "temples" or "cathedrals" (stadiums).

For those of you that are soccer fans, you must have been moved by divine soccer experiences. Watching players like the retired Moroccan international Mohammed Timoumi (1986 World Cup and 1985 African Player of the Year), the Nigerian midfield general Jay-Jay Okocha (1994 World Cup), the elegance of Brazilian midfield masters like Sócrates or Falcao, the scintillating dribbling skills of Johan Cruyff or George Best, or the lethal, curling free kicks of Michel Platini, it was as if these soccer stars were touched by a divine spark! The delicate technical skills that these players possessed were not merely due to hard work, discipline, or training. It did not matter whether these players were religious or radical atheists. Soccer was for them and their legions of fans akin to a religious experience.

JERSEY #5: SOCCER "GODS"

We must now select our number 5 player. Typically, the number 5 is a sweeper. The sweeper is the final line of defense before the goalkeeper. He is an organizer, sure in defense, and a steady influence on the team. Moreover, the sweeper is the player who can orchestrate the rhythm of a game, stop star forwards with key tackles, and even make decisive passes through his distribution abilities. There has been an array of talented sweepers in soccer history.

Some recently retired sweepers that were seen as gods by their fans include the Egyptian international sweeper Hany Ramzy, the South Korean sweeper Hong Myung-Bo (the first Asian player to play in four consecutive World Cup final tournaments from 1990 until 2002), the rock at the heart of the World Cup-winning French side in the 1998 World Cup Laurent Blanc (1989–2000), or the Argentinean international Roberto Ayala (1994–2007).

Recall that Elias Figueroa, the representative of chapter 2, was also an accomplished sweeper with the Chilean national team. Sweepers' command of the game turns them into leaders and heroic figures, which pleases the gods and their legions of awe-inspired fans.

Current sweepers of note include Brazil's powerful Lúcio, the elegant English international Rio Ferdinand, the Portuguese internationals Pepe and Ricardo Carvalho, Belgium's Vincent Kompany, and Brazil's Thiago Silva. The newer generation is generally tougher and more hardened in its style of play compared to the older generation. In the age of win-at-all-costs and commercial soccer, it is results that really matter. Thus, the newer generation of sweepers is more jackboot than technical artistry. Of course the game of soccer has changed and those modern soccer players are excellent athletes.

Soccer is akin to a secular faith, and Franz Beckenbauer and Zinedine Zidane have been selected as soccer gods that both wore the number 5. Beckenbauer and Zidane could defend and attack with equal ability. Beckenbauer and Zidane were the conductors of the West German and French national teams and their respective club sides for many years. Zidane could score unexpectedly with his head, like in the 1998 World Cup, or with a howling rocket from distance that left the goalkeeper dazed. Or, like Beckenbauer, Zidane could make an incisive pass that could cut even the most expert of defenses and make them look wanting and amateurish. Both Beckenbauer and Zidane were like great poets; their movements were as elegant as a dancer, they loved their craft like a gifted artisan, and both understood that soccer is a game in which the struggle is with oneself more than against your opponents.[15] In chapter 11, I further discuss the relationship between soccer and the arts.

Among all sweepers in soccer history, one sweeper stands out. If one thinks of soccer as a religion, or soccer as a divine experience, I must pick Franz Beckenbauer over any living sweeper as one of the representatives for lesson five. Beckenbauer was a soccer god: one of the greatest soccer players of all time. Or, as Christoph Biermann of *The Observer* put it: "In a secular Germany, Beckenbauer embodies not only the royal idea (his nickname is 'The Kaiser') but also that of an overlord. He is the god of German football."[16]

Our second choice for the number 5 jersey is the recently retired French international Zinedine Zidane. He wore the number 5 jersey while playing for Real Madrid. Although he was a midfielder, Zinedine Zidane could have played any position on the pitch and would have also been an accomplished sweeper. Zidane was also a soccer god. BBC called the French superstar "Le football God."[17] The BBC could back up its claim: "What Zinedine Zidane lacks in hair, he makes up for in skill and vision. Bags of it. A silky turn, a cunning feint, a dazzling dribble or a stunning volley. And he never lets anybody down on the biggest of stages. In the 1998 World Cup final, his two headed goals saw off the might of Brazil."

What Beckenbauer and Zidane had in common was complete dominance on the pitch, technical artistry, and vision. In 2013, *World Soccer* picked its eleven best players of all time in a worldwide poll.[18] Both Beckenbauer and Zidane made the team, as did Paolo Maldini, one of the representatives of chapter 3.

Franz Beckenbauer

Franz Beckenbauer is a retired West German international and a world soccer legend. Franz Anton Beckenbauer was born on September 11, 1945, in Munich, Germany. From 1964 until 1977, he appeared 427 times and scored sixty goals for Bayern Munich. Beckenbauer was such a gifted player that he earned the nickname *Der Kaiser* (The Emperor) because of his elegant style, complete dominance on the pitch, exceptional leadership skills, and his first name "Franz" (akin to the Austrian emperors). He is perhaps the greatest German soccer star of all time, as well as one of the legends of world soccer. It was at the 1966 World Cup when Beckenbauer arguably revolutionized the game with his trademark galloping runs from the back, as well as his free-flowing *libero* role that allowed him to roam the entire field.

Beckenbauer's honors were vast and he requires an entire museum to house his trophies! He was twice selected the European Footballer of the Year (1972 and 1976), appeared 103 times for West Germany, and played in three World Cups: 1966, 1970, and 1974. Marking and stopping the legendary Johan Cruyff in the 1974 World Cup final was a major highlight of his career. Cruyff was also selected by *World Soccer* as one of the top eleven players of all time. Beckenbauer's defensive exploits and his command of the game stopped Dutch "total soccer" and handed Germany a 2–1 win in the finals of the 1974 World Cup. Beckenbauer was the captain of West Germany's World Cup-winning squad in 1974.

At the club level with Bayern Munich, more success came for Beckenbauer. He won the European Cup Winners' Cup in 1967 and three consecutive European Cup titles from 1974 to 1976. The latter accomplishment made Beckenbauer the only player to win three European Cup titles as the captain of his club.

In 1977, Beckenbauer accepted a rather lucrative contract to play in the North American Soccer League with the New York Cosmos. He played with the Cosmos for four seasons until 1980. The team won the North American championship known as the "Soccer Bowl" three times in 1977, 1978, and 1980.

It is interesting that Beckenbauer was not only a deity as a player, but as a coach. Along with Brazil's Mário Zagallo, Beckenbauer is the only man to have won the World Cup both as a player and coach. In 1990, West Germany won the World Cup, beating Argentina 1–0 in the final in what was one of the dullest World Cup finals in recent memory. Beckenbauer was the coach of the German-winning team. From 1984 to 1990, Beckenbauer managed West Germany. In 1993, 1994, and again in 1996, Beckenbauer managed Bayern Munich. As both a player and coach Beckenbauer was dubbed a god: "Franz is a god, and Jürgen a mere mortal,"[19] opined the BBC in pitting the combined playing and managerial skills of Beckenbauer and Jürgen Klinsmann, a former West German World Cup winner in 1990 and the coach of the USA national soccer team.

In terms of world soccer history, *Der Kaiser* is in the category of world legends. In 1999, he was voted second, behind Johan Cruyff, as the European Player of the Century. The IFFHS voted him third behind Pelé and Cruyff in the World Player of the Century category. To add to his accomplishments, the IFFHS voted Beckenbauer the Universal Genius of World Soccer in 2007 because he was the world's top player, its top coach, and its top administrative official. The IFFHS website highlights the prerequisites for this prestigious award:

> During his active career, a footballer must have demonstrated total world class both at club level and in the national team, shown creativity on the pitch and been successful by any standard.
>
> He must also have been successful at the highest international level as the coach of a club and/or national team and shown similar creativity and brilliance there.
>
> Finally, he must also have been successful at the highest international level as an official and contributed ground-breaking ideas to world football.[20]

Zinedine Zidane

Zidane gave soccer fans a mesmerizing and pleasurable experience because of his extraordinary technical skills. Zidane was the greatest player of his generation in the 1990s and early part of the new millennium, until his retirement from international soccer after a heartbreaking loss to Italy in the finals of the 2006 World Cup. Zidane was also, for millions of French men and women, Berbers, and Algerians (his ethnic origins), Africans, and others around the world, like a god on the pitch. He not only won trophies, but also played beautiful soccer. Zidane's talented teammate Thierry Henry told French newspaper *Le Parisien* that Zidane was a god after he announced his return to international soccer in 2005 following his retirement: "What I am about to say is strong, but it's the truth. In France, everybody realized that God exists, and that he is back in the French international team. God is back, there is little left to say."[21]

He will always be known as "Zizou," the affectionate nickname for Zinedine Yazid Zidane. He was born on June 23, 1972, in the southern French city of Marseille. Zidane's parents immigrated to Paris from the Berberspeaking region of Kabylie in northern Algeria in 1953. The family found little work in Paris and by the mid-1960s they moved to Marseille. Zidane grew up as the youngest of five children. His family, like other soccer legends, came from a humble background. His father worked at a department store, while his mother was a housewife. The neighborhood Zidane grew up in was noted throughout Marseille for its high crime and unemployment rates. It was in the tough La Castellane section of Marseille in a housing complex that Zidane first learned his silky smooth soccer skills.

It is out of such suburbs as those in which Zidane lived, with high concentrations of immigrant communities, that discontent at French authorities and the police led to one month of riots in 2005. Many of those rioting were, like Zidane, French youths of North African origins. The riots began in Clichysous-Bois and included Paris and other major cities in France. Poor housing projects throughout France saw lots of rioting. Public buildings, sports facilities, schools, and cars were burned. The situation was so grave that a state of emergency was declared on November 8, 2005, and the French Parliament later extended the emergency measures for three additional months.

Zidane began his career with modest French side Cannes in 1988 and ended it with Real Madrid in 2006, scoring thirty-seven times in 155 matches for the Spanish club. It was his performances at Bordeaux from 1992 to 1996, where he scored twenty-eight goals in 139 matches, which earned Zidane interest from the major European clubs. Zidane led Bordeaux to a runner-up finish at the 1995–1996 UEFA Cup finals. If Zidane's performances were almost always exceptional and divinely inspired for France, at the club level Zidane won La Liga and the UEFA Champions League titles for Real Madrid, two *Serie A* league championships for Juventus, and an Intercontinental Cup and a UEFA Super Cup for both Real Madrid and Juventus. In recognition of his superstar status, Zidane was voted FIFA World Player of the Year three times in 1998, 2000, and 2003.

Zidane played as an attacking midfielder, and was the key figure for a generation of talented French players, including Henry, Pires, Trezeguet, Deschamps, Blanc, Lizarazu, Desailly, Petit, and others that won the 1998 World Cup and 2000 European Nations' Championship. Zidane singlehandedly helped France win its first ever World Cup in 1998 after a decisive 3–0 triumph in the finals against Brazil, the favorite. He scored two goals in the finals.

Watching the French international play at the height of his majesty when France won its first ever World Cup in 1998 was like being transported into the realm of the soccer gods. He is undoubtedly one of the greatest soccer players of all time. Zidane was so technically complete that watching him was like a quasi-religious experience. An Algerian I used to run into habitually in downtown Toronto, also a "Zizou" fan, would often say to me in reference to Zidane's divine skills: "There is only one 'Zizou.' There is no other like him. There is only one 'Zizou'—like there is only one god."

When he played for Real Madrid from 2001 until 2006, the retired French international Zinedine Zidane also wore the number 5 jersey. Zidane chose the number 5 shirt because Raúl, a club idol, was wearing the number 10 jersey. While Zidane was typically a playmaking midfielder who traditionally wears the number 10 shirt, he was sometimes capable of coming back into very deep positions akin to a sweeper (the traditional number 5) and beginning a dangerous move that might end in a goal. Zidane transformed the French team from a very good squad into a great team, but with France he wore the number 10 jersey.

At the 2002 World Cup, Zidane was injured and far from his best. Yet when he returned for his curtain call at the 2006 World Cup he was awesome, a divine force, and a magical performer. For his performances at the 2006 World Cup, Zidane won the Golden Ball as the tournament's most outstanding player. He will unfortunately always be remembered for the infamous head-butting of Italian defender Marco Materazzi. The head-butt led to Zidane's red card dismissal, but he almost won the World Cup for France shortly before his sending off a thumping header, which was miraculously saved by the Italian goalkeeper Gianluigi Buffon. Italy won the World Cup in a penalty shootout, denying the French legend and France a second World Cup win. Zidane ended his international career with thirty-one goals in 108 matches for France. Laurent Dubois points out that while Zidane's gesture elicited many different responses, regret about the incident prevailed among many French observers, including President Chirac.[22] They refused to pronounce judgment on Zidane, insisting on the nation's admiration for the superstar and respect for Zidane as a brilliant French player.

When Zinedine Zidane retired in 2006, he left us all with a soccer hole. A "Zizou" is like a gift from God. He comes around once every twenty, thirty, fifty, or one hundred years. There are good soccer players or excellent soccer stars, but the divine players are the very few that we can count on the fingers of our two hands.

Today Zidane's situation is a far cry from his childhood in the tough and poor La Castellane section of Marseille. He is Real Madrid's director of football. He also has aspirations to be a coach. Yet he will always be remembered for his exceptional gifts on the pitch. When Zidane retired in 2006, the tributes paid to the French superstar were stunning and extended well beyond the soccer world. He visited the Algerian birthplace of his parents, and had an official meeting with Algerian president Abdelaziz Bouteflika.

Other soccer legends have also sung Zidane's praises. Franz Beckenbauer, the other representative of lesson five, called Zidane "one of the greatest players in history" and David Beckham went further when he dubbed him "the greatest of all time."[23] Pelé called Zidane "a magician."[24] Italy's former manager Marcello Lippi, who coached Zidane when he played for Juventus, said: "I think Zidane is the greatest talent we've known in football these last 20 years, yet he never played the prima donna. I am honored to have been his manager."[25] Cesare Maldini, the former manager of the Italian national team, wished Zidane was on his side: "I would give up five players to have Zizou in my squad."[26]

Off the pitch, Zidane was also a great soccer ambassador: he was a FIFA representative in a Match Against Poverty in Spain in 2008; he played soccer for children with AIDS in Malaysia in 2007; acted as a UN goodwill ambassador since 2001; and is the official representative of Qatar's successful bid for the 2022 World Cup. Thus, Zidane has a social conscience like a number of players I discussed in chapter 4.

It is true that Zidane is also a rich man, with official endorsements from many big companies such as Adidas, Lego, France Telecom, Audi, and Christian Dior, to name a few. These sponsorship deals earned Zidane a hefty 8.6€ million ($11.6 million USD) in addition to his 61.4€ million ($83.2 million USD) salary with Real Madrid in his final season, making him the sixth-highest paid soccer player.[27] Yet the man that came from a humble background from the tough streets of Marseille will always be remembered neither for his fortune, nor his fame. Not even for his head-butting of Marco Materazzi. Zidane will be remembered for his divine soccer talents on the pitch.

Zinedine Zidane was the closest we have witnessed to a soccer deity since the days of Beckenbauer, Cruyff, and Pelé. At the end of his career, the legendary Pelé called him a master without equal in his generation.[28] After his stunning performance against Brazil in the 2006 World Cup, a writer for *The Independent* made this comment about Zidane: "There was something almost beatific in his performance. From the moment he walked slowly on to the pitch, with his eyes raised heavenwards, to when he finally departed, the first French player to leave following the final whistle, he was serene."[29]

Zidane's North African roots (that is, Berber and Algerian) were conspicuous in soccer circles and beyond after France won the 1998 World Cup. As pointed out in chapter 1, anti-immigrant and ultra-nationalist politicians within the Front National and the French public now had an image of a successful French national soccer team captain of North African origins. In addition, Zidane was a secular Muslim. He was neither a criminal, nor a jihadist sympathizer. He did not abuse the welfare system, a charge from the extreme right aimed at many North African immigrants in France and throughout Europe. Zidane was the model of a well-integrated Frenchman of North African origin.

Other soccer stars recognized Zidane's unique soccer skills and could even compare him to a god. Kevin Keegan, the retired English international, insisted that Zidane was better than two other soccer gods and compared him to the leader of an orchestra: "You look at Zidane and think 'I've never seen a player quite like that.' Diego Maradona was a great player. Johan Cruyff was a great player. They were different—but with similarities. What sets Zidane apart is the way he manipulates a football, buying himself space that isn't there. Add his vision and it makes him very special."[30] I pointed out that Thierry Henry, a former teammate of Zidane's with the French national team, paid Zidane the best tribute when he called him a soccer "god."[31]

SOCCER AS AN EXTENSION OF THE SENSES

Soccer is, like politics, a new religion of our age. Emilio Gentile, the Italian political historian, sees the twentieth century as the age of "politics as religion."[32] As traditional religions waned in a more secular age, the chosen race or class (the proletariat), the political party, the omniscient leader, the nation, state, or secular ideologies became our objects of worship. Fascism, Nazism, Maoism, and even liberalism are akin to forms of secular religious worship, complete with sacred commandments and scriptures, revered holidays, and anointed texts and leaders. Gentile insists that both co-optation and mimicry of traditional religion exists in the age of modern secular politics. Try as we may to banish the gods from the political sphere, they reappear as secular gods with new names, sacred commandments, and divine-like rituals.

In the case of both modern politics and soccer, we are not aware of the religious-like dimensions of the activities involved. In the modern epoch, it is not merely a question of what belongs to God belongs to the Church and what belongs to Caesar belongs to the state. With modern soccer, Caesar and God are united in the experiences of millions in soccer stadiums. Stadiums are our pagan temples and soccer heroes are our gods. Soccer players and fans obey sacred commandments by always following their respective teams, irrespective of the results. Both players and fans engage in superstitious rituals such as songs in order to invoke the gods to side with their team. Alan G. Ingham makes this point in a manner that does not negate the expanding commercial imperatives of soccer (chapter 7):

> Yes, winning and losing are important in the emotional experiences, but what is far more important is that, regardless of whether our team is winning or losing, the faithful seem compelled by an abstract force, larger than themselves, to go and worship at the shrine. We buy symbols of our devotion even though we know symbols such as "away" shirts are changed frequently as a money-making ploy (the English Premier League). We listen to the "liturgies"

and sing the "hymns." We buy souvenirs to keep the sacred alive after our pilgrimages. [33]

Soccer temples or shrines are not new in the history of humanity. Soccer and games more broadly have long been for humanity akin to religions, substitute religions, or a reflection of the struggle of the gods. Soccer, like all sports, is a medium of communication, or extension and amplification of our psychic and social selves, as Canadian communications giant Marshall McLuhan argued. [34] McLuhan rightly pointed out that in the ancient world sporting contests and games were models of our inner psychological lives, forms of collective popular art, and live and dramatic microcosms of both the universe and the cosmic realm. [35] In antiquity, opined McLuhan, sporting contests were seen as a preparation for war and required stoic discipline in order to combat external foes and the "enemies" within. [36] In line with the notion of soccer as a pagan religion, in pre-modern and non-literate societies, the spectators' role was unambiguously religious or spiritual. The sporting contest was viewed as a direct replica of the struggle of the gods and the wider cosmic drama. [37]

Modern soccer stadiums are the temples of our times, heightening what the Indians call *darshan* awareness, the mystical experience created by the physical congregation of vast numbers of people. [38] The Mexican writer Juan Villoro colorfully pointed out that a soccer match "without people is like a baptism without a child." [39]

If modern soccer stadiums are our contemporary temples or shrines, the largest soccer stadiums in the world heighten the mystical experience created by the physical congregation of vast numbers of people. Both Zidane and Beckenbauer played in soccer temples such as Santiago Bernabéu and Munich's Olympic Stadium, Bayern Munich's stadium for thirty-three years. It will surprise many to know that Rungrado May Day Stadium in Pyongyang, North Korea, is the largest soccer stadium in the world with a capacity for 150,000 spectators. Opened in 1989, "the primary purpose of the stadium is to host vast parades and other public spectacles in North Korea." [40] However, the stadium has also been used to host some of the North Korean national soccer team's matches. As the stadium is located in Communist, totalitarian, and isolated North Korea, "it is extremely unlikely that this magnificent arena will ever play host to a major tournament or have its turf graced by some of the world's best players." [41]

Estadio Azteca in Mexico City is the world's third largest stadium with a capacity for 105,000 fans. In terms of a stadium rich in soccer history, there is nothing to compare with the Azteca, except perhaps Brazil's Maracanã. Azteca is the home of the Mexican national team and hosted two World Cups, in 1970 and 1986. Those two World Cup finals included the two greatest soccer gods the game has ever seen: Pelé and Maradona. The 1970

World Cup-winning Brazilian team, which defeated Italy 4–1 in the finals, is arguably the greatest team of all time. This Brazilian side included the soccer legends Pelé, Clodoaldo, Carlos Alberto, and Jairzinho. The open, attractive, attacking, fluid, and flowing soccer that this Brazilian side played has never been matched by any team in the world.

The Azteca was also the setting for Argentina's entertaining 3–2 triumph against West Germany in the 1986 World Cup finals. During the quarterfinal match between England and Argentina, the Azteca was the site of two of the most memorable goals in soccer history: Maradona's "hand of God" goal and a solo effort that saw Maradona weave through seven English players, and seal his place in soccer greatness by sliding the ball past the English goalkeeper. Although the gifted Jorge Burruchaga scored the winning goal, it is Maradona that will be immortalized for what is perhaps the greatest goal in soccer history.

Located in Rio de Janeiro, the Maracanã (officially Estádio Jornalista Mário Filho) is a soccer pantheon. In his book entitled *Passion of the People?: Football in South America*, Tony Mason writes that the Maracanã is "a place of pilgrimage."[42] Frommer's called it "the temple of Brazilian soccer."[43] Writing for the Canadian Broadcasting Corporation, Connie Watson called the Maracanã "soccer's shrine" and "the temple of soccer."[44] The recently refurbished Maracanã was described by *The Guardian* as the "new temple to [the] national religion."[45] Built for the 1950 World Cup, the Maracanã became a place of tears after Brazil lost the World Cup final to Uruguay 2–1. Moacyr Barbosa, the Brazilian goalkeeper who was the scapegoat in the 1950 World Cup, tragically died, penniless, of a heart attack in 2000. Although he was one of the world's best goalkeepers in a career that spanned twenty-two years, he was forever haunted by the ghosts of Maracanã and Alcides Ghiggia's "soft" game-winning goal. More than 199,000 spectators watched the final. Scores of Brazilians committed suicide after the loss. According to one Argentinean writer, crucial national soccer team losses might drive some fans to "question god," toward agnosticism, or even toward the "death of the divine."[46]

Famous Brazilian club sides Flamengo, Fluminense, Botafogo, and Vasco da Gama have all used the Maracanã as their home at various points in their history. The Maracanã is today undergoing major refurbishing and it will host both the World Cup and the Olympic Games in 2014 and 2016, respectively. Brazil will seek to overcome the "curse" of the Maracanã in 2014 and 2016: the national tragedy of losing the 1950 World Cup final against tiny Uruguay.

Modern soccer shrines today compete with clubs run along a business model, as well as large corporations that sponsor and sell the game. I return to this theme in chapter 7 when I examine the relationships between soccer, business, and marketing. Corporations and even some clubs see very little in the stadiums except business opportunities. Club, country, or nation matter little for them, except the ability to sell themselves to the highest bidder. It is not unknown these days for players to play for five or six clubs. Yet despite the fact that soccer today is a transnational business opportunity, it still produces a soccer god like Zidane, worshipped by legions of fans. As one Zidane worshipper from Australia commented on a movie about the French star: "The guys who made this movie got it so wrong. They actually show Zidane as a tired static player and not the football god he is."[47]

SOCCER CROWDS AND THE STADIUM AS A SACRED EXPERIENCE

Gustave Le Bon, in his classic *The Crowd: A Study of the Popular Mind*, could see in soccer matches and all crowds the "intensification of the emotions" and "the inhibition of the intellect."[48] In soccer crowds, we substitute the unconscious actions of the crowd for the conscious activity of individuals. We are led by the "higher calling" of the team. As the crowd is ephemeral and "the intensification of the emotions" is tied to the team, once the match ends it might be difficult to engage in forms of solidarity outside the soccer temples with the same people that you see at the game. This might help to explain why various groups in civil society have sought to use the intense emotions and "thirst for obedience" inherent in soccer crowds to win supporters for their cause (as highlighted in chapter 1 with respect to nationalism, in chapter 3 in relation to the struggle for ideological hegemony, and in chapter 4 when I examined initiatives for social change).

According to Marshall McLuhan, like traditional religions, sporting contests such as soccer provide a frame of meaning: a mimetic re-creation of life's uncertainty and the mechanistic rigor of life in the early twenty-first century (that is, the mystery of the game's outcome determined by the soccer gods versus the rational, mechanistic rules of the game); the magical and mystical entrance into new realities; the breaking of the boundaries between the serious (for example, winning for one's country) and the frivolous (that is, it is after all just a game); the temporary release from the grinding realities of work and the material pressures of life; an implicit questioning of the concept of work (are professional soccer players working or playing?) and the boundaries between leisure time and work; and the derisive laughter and play element directed at the serious person, intellectual, or society.[49] For the Mexican writer Eloy Caloca Lafont, leisure activities such as sports are an integral part of the history of humanity: we play, distract ourselves, create magic rituals, and seek a space for social catharsis.[50]

The French sociologist Emile Durkheim argued that sacred spaces can be found outside the traditional religious realm. Thus, it was no accident that

John Bale, in his *Sport, Space and the City*, insisted that stadiums generate "love of place" and "some stadia have become what amounts to sacred spaces, worthy, perhaps, of future protection and preservation like other revered monuments."[51]

The congregation of large numbers of people at soccer stadiums, as well as the ritualistic choreography of opposing fans (including songs, banners, and colorful hats and scarves) is for some fans, players, and managers like a religious or mystical experience. As Christian Derbaix (Catholic University of Mons), Alain Decrop (University of Namur), and Olivier Cabossart (Catholic University of Mons) wrote in 2002, "Football fans express their identification with their team as a unified community during sacred sport moments."[52] They interviewed Belgian soccer fans from various clubs and insist that scarves and hats fulfill four symbolic functions: identification, integration, expression, and *sacralization*.[53] They conclude with the "ideas of players as heroes, stadiums as temples and artifacts [shirts or gloves given by the players to fans] as sacred relics."[54]

Christopher Gaffney (University of Texas) and Gilmar Mascarenhasa (University of the State of Rio de Janeiro) describe the stadium as an otherworldly realm: "Mecca of profane chants, upon entering into this space the individual lives in a time-world different than that on the outside."[55] Before a Champions League soccer match in Napoli in 2013, Borussia Dortmund manager Jürgen Klopp said the following: "Playing at the San Paolo will be a mystical experience for me, because it was the stadium that was home to Diego Armando Maradona. 'We will try to make ourselves be influenced positively by this 'presence.'"[56] One soccer fan could highlight his experiences at Barcelona's Camp Nou in ecstatic or religious terms: "I've died and gone to heaven."[57] The former West German national team goalkeeper and Turkish club Fenerbahçe captain Toni Schumacher, in his first season with the team in 1988, paid the ultimate tribute to the fans in Turkish soccer stadiums: "To experience a match in a Turkish stadium with these supporters is the ultimate for any football fan. Football is like a religion there."[58]

Soccer chants also add to the aura of the stadium as a sacred experience. Win, lose, or draw, die-hard soccer fans stick with their teams and sing their songs throughout the match. Some of those songs, such as "We'll Never Die," sung by Manchester United fans, see the team as an eternal faith linking past, present, and future generations:

> United's flag is deepest red
> It shrouded all our Munich dead
> Before their limbs grew stiff and cold
> Their heart's blood dyed its ev'ry fold
> Then raise United's banner high
> Beneath its shade we'll live and die
> So keep the faith and never fear

We'll keep the Red Flag flying here
We'll never die, we'll never die
We'll never die, we'll never die
We'll keep the Red flag flying high
'Cos Man United will never die.[59]

In conclusion, Beckenbauer and Zidane are divine soccer stars. The soccer temples and their fans now worship new heroes from Messi to Neymar. To millions of soccer fans around the world, it was obvious that Beckenbauer and Zidane loved to play soccer. For Zidane, there was still the little boy in him from the harsh streets of Marseille who loved to play all day, until his mother called him in for dinner. There was still the trickster in him; tricks that one can only learn through the madness and spontaneity of street soccer. Moreover, there was a soccer gift within him, as if providence had sent him to give millions of soccer fans pure joy. Zidane was a soccer god, yet possessed a humble personality. He could say to *Marca* in an interview in 2003 that he was a mere mortal and not a god.[60] Yet the fact that he made the comment confirms that his fans, journalists, coaches, and peers could see in him a "divine spark." He was the greatest soccer player of his generation, but he was the immaculate team player. Aware that the soccer gods are watching, Zidane was never cocky on or off the field. He remembered his immigrant roots, which made sure that he cultivated his God-given talents with hard work.

Zidane's kids are currently all enrolled in the Real Madrid soccer academy. This is no assurance that Zidane's children will be soccer gods. It is true that there are soccer families in which the sons follow in the famous footsteps of the father: Maldini, Ayew, and Hernández. Yet soccer gods like Zidane or Beckenbauer cannot be easily produced. Soccer gods are molded through the help of providence. Countless soccer players may have practiced for more hours than Zidane or Beckenbauer yet never reach the technical mastery, control, shooting skills, passing vision, and tender touch of Zidane or Beckenbauer. Good genes, discipline, intelligence, and hard work can all pay off, but a Zidane or a Beckenbauer are like a single star in the galaxy—they are one (or two) of billions.

The soccer temples where we view our soccer gods are increasingly tainted by violence, hooliganism, crass commercialism, and an unethical win-at-all-costs philosophy. Despite these negative tendencies, soccer is for most of its fans, players, and even owners more than a mere business, as many professional clubs are in debt. Soccer fans are known for their "love" of the game and "the shirt" (club or nation), which verges on the sacred.[61] As Nietzsche pointed out in the late nineteenth century, we murdered god and thus we must become gods. Soccer stars are our gods. Amazingly, we still produce soccer gods: Iniesta, Xavi, Cristiano Ronaldo, Neymar, Ibrahimović, and Messi, to name a few. Spain won the 2010 World Cup and the European

Nations' Championship in 2008 and 2012 with a squad that brought back the beauty of soccer: short passes in triangles, quick give and gos, control and mastery in midfield, working the ball out from the back, and a lethality in front of the goal. As human beings, we crave the festival, the carnival, and the party that is soccer. A soccer that is based on skill and guile more than strength; attacking, free-flowing, spontaneous, and unpredictable soccer; a soccer that would make the soccer gods proud. Beckenbauer and Zidane were the supreme practitioners of this divine style of soccer.

Chapter Six

Playing Fair

Soccer and Ethics

This chapter is about the relationship between soccer and ethics. These days, ethics is a term that is on everyone's lips, from soccer's governing body FIFA to military, corporate, and religious officials. Akin to the term democracy in the twentieth century, when even the most authoritarian regimes such as Communist East Germany claimed that they were democratic, today organizations, businesses, states, and non-governmental organizations have found in ethics a new discourse for the age. In the contemporary world, the discourse of ethics pervades all realms of life, from robotics and business to medicine and the military.[1] Aware of changing world consciousness, soccer clubs, players, fans, and FIFA have brought issues related to ethics to the forefront of the sport in recent years.

In an age "when corporations rule the world," to use the colorful phrase from David Korten's 1995 book,[2] is professional soccer losing its ethic of fair play? Fans, managers, and soccer administrators complain of excessive diving as players fake fouls in order to win free kicks and penalties. FIFA administrators have been recently embroiled in corruption scandals, which tarnish the image of "the beautiful game." Some fans, journalists, and academics insist that bribery, match fixing, and favoring elite soccer clubs and nations is endemic to soccer.[3] In 2013, El Salvador banned fourteen internationals for life for match fixing, including some of the country's most recognized soccer players.[4] Fans are turning away from professional soccer because they insist that it is infected with crass commercialism and game fixing. Why has instant replay been resisted by FIFA for so many years when there are clear errors in judgment by referees?

Recall from chapter 3 that Gramsci pointed out that while soccer was a reflection of competitive and individualistic values associated with capitalism, it was simultaneously wedded to the ethics of fair play, official rules, and "human loyalty." George Orwell was suspicious about fusing soccer and ethics together: "Football has nothing to do with fair play. It is bound up with hatred, jealousy, boastfulness, disregard of all rules and sadistic pleasure in witnessing violence: in other words it is war minus the shooting."[5] This chapter will evaluate Orwell's powerful proposition. An understanding of basic ethics and what philosophers have said about ethics will allow us to better grasp the relationship between soccer and ethics. Before I do this, I need to pick the number 6 jersey.

JERSEY #6: A SOCCER GENTLEMAN

My official choice for the number 6 jersey is more unconventional because I need to be inclusive of countries around the world. With this in mind, my official choice for the number 6 jersey is Igor Netto, a legendary former captain and box-to-box midfielder with the Soviet Union in the 1950s and 1960s. Netto came from another less materialistic age in soccer history. Despite the stereotypical Cold War image of the Marxist-Leninist Soviet Union as a state that would do anything to attain sporting glory in order to demonstrate the superiority of socialism, Igor Netto was both a socialist and a soccer gentleman known for his leadership, technical skills, determination, and fair play.

Igor Netto

Born on January 9, 1930, in Moscow, Igor Netto was a child when Soviet dictator Joseph Stalin was accelerating his chilling Reign of Terror. Netto was the son of Estonian migrants living in Russia. Mass party purges and executions, the Ukrainian famine, population transfers, genocide, and the gulag system were all part of the Stalinist totalitarian network of state terror. Robert Conquest suggested that at least 15 to 20 million individuals, perhaps 30 million people, died under Stalin's "Great Terror" from the 1920s until the early 1950s.[6]

Netto's childhood concerns seemed far removed from Stalin's "Great Terror." The website World Football Legends describes his normal childhood and love of two sports:

> As a child, he wanted to do little else but play football and regularly spent many hours each day kicking a ball around in the yard. Much to his mother's displeasure, he wore out football boots at a remarkable rate. As a youngster he also played ice hockey, but eventually turned his back on that game after being

on the receiving end of some big hits and worrying that injury would leave him unable to play football.[7]

Netto's talents were first spotted by Spartak Moscow when he was only nineteen years old. He made his debut with the Moscow-based club in the 1949 season. Historically, Spartak was the first and largest All-Union Voluntary Sports Society of workers of state trade, producers' cooperatives, light industry, civil aviation, education, culture, and health services. It was officially established in 1935.

Netto began his career at halfback, but he was rather more attack-minded than most halfbacks. He was known for his supreme confidence on the ball, which made him well suited for the role of central midfielder. He was especially critical of the long-ball style of play and encouraged teammates to play a possession game. Netto once said the following to a teammate shortly after the match began, which demonstrated his keen desire to play a possession game: "Straight from the kick off, in front of 50,000 supporters, a player received the ball and hoofed it up field in typically British style. 'Pass to a man. Not the crowd.'"[8]

Although Netto started out as a defender, he became one of the greatest wide midfielders and box-to-box midfielders the game has ever known. He scored thirty-six goals in 368 league games for FC Spartak Moscow from 1949 to 1966, winning five Soviet championships and three domestic cups. Netto was dynamic, stylish, composed, and technically gifted. He was tireless in defense and in assisting the attack. He was the engine of the great Spartak Moscow teams that were Soviet league champions in 1952, 1953, 1956, 1958, and 1962, as well as Soviet Cup winners in 1956, 1958, and 1963. In line with an ethic of loyalty to the club, Netto played his entire seventeen-year professional career with Spartak Moscow.

Internationally, Netto was also a Soviet Union legend. He was the captain of the Soviet Union from 1954 until 1963. One website called Netto "the heart and soul of the multiracial Soviet team."[9] He was part of the great Soviet Union team that won the European Championship in 1960, beating Yugoslavia 2–1 in the finals: Lev Yashin (Dynamo Moscow), Givi Tchekeli (Dinamo Tbilisi), Anatoli Maslenkin (Spartak Moscow), Anatoli Kroutikov (Spartak Moscow), Yuri Voinov (Dynamo Kiev), Igor Netto (Spartak Moscow), Slava Metreveli (Torpedo Moscow), Valentin Ivanov (Torpedo Moscow), Viktor Ponedelnik (SKA Rostov), Valentin Bubukin (Lokomotiv Moscow), and Michail Meshki (Dinamo Tbilisi).

Netto also anchored the Soviet Union squad that won the Olympic gold medal at the 1956 summer games. Although he was injured for all but one match at the 1958 World Cup, Netto helped the Soviet Union to consecutive quarterfinal berths at the 1958 and 1962 World Cups, in Sweden and Chile respectively. Netto earned fifty-four caps and scored four goals for the Soviet Union's national team from 1952 until 1965.

Igor Netto's great gentlemanly soccer qualities came to the forefront in the 1962 World Cup in Chile. In its first two matches, the Soviet Union tied Colombia 4–4 and defeated Yugoslavia 1–0. They need a tie to advance to the next round. Although there was no Fair Play Award in his day, Netto's fair play moment in a key World Cup match would have surely earned him a Fair Play Award today:

> In the 1962 World Cup Finals played in Chile, Igor Chislenko scored late in the game for the Soviet Union against Uruguay. That made the score 2–1 for the Soviets. The USSR captain, Igor Netto, then reported to the referee that the ball had gone through a hole in the side netting of the goal. The referee then changed his decision and disallowed the goal and the score reverted to 1–1. Later on, the USSR scored again to win 2–1. [10]

Many Fair Play Awards are given to players for which the game has little consequence for the team in question. In contrast, Netto abided by the ethic of fair play, even if it meant that his team could conceivably be eliminated from the World Cup, the most important world soccer competition. Netto's gentlemanly and fair play moment might be the greatest fair play moment in the history of soccer. Not only was Netto a leader on the pitch, he was also one of the most honest players the game has ever known.

Netto was recognized by the political authorities in his native Soviet Union. He received the prestigious Order of Lenin in 1957. His club side did not forget Netto, too, and they named the Spartak Moscow stadium after the Soviet Union soccer legend. Interestingly, after his retirement in 1966, Netto became an ice hockey coach, thus fulfilling a childhood dream. While Netto was a world-recognized player, as a manager he did not have great results, whether with AC Omonia (Cyprus), FC Shinnik Yaroslavl (Russia), Panionios (Greece), Neftchi Baku (Azerbaijan), or the Iranian national team. Netto later returned to Spartak Moscow, working with their youth team. He also wrote a book about soccer in Russian.

In the late 1980s, Netto began suffering from Alzheimer's disease. He died in 1999 at the age of sixty-nine. When Netto died, Russian and former Soviet Union fans rated him as the best Russian or Soviet Union midfielder of all time and seventh best player of all time, behind the legendary goalkeepers Lev Yashin and Rinat Dasayev and the strikers Oleg Blokhin, Igor Belanov, Eduard Streltsov, and Andrei Arshavin. [11] After he died, I preferred to remember Netto in happier times: holding the Henri Delaunay trophy aloft in 1960 after defeating Yugoslavia in the finals of the European Championship. Or there is a famous 1962 photograph of Netto and the legendary goalkeeper Lev Yashin immaculately dressed in well-tailored suits laying a wreath in Arica, Chile, at the monument for Chile's national hero Bernard

O'Higgins. Netto and Yashin were both participating in the 1962 World Cup in Chile. We should also remember Netto's exceptional courage, honesty, and fair play in declining to take advantage of his opponents Uruguay in a crucial World Cup match.

John Terry: Anti-ethical?

In contrast to Netto's spirit of ethical fair play, a contemporary English soccer star, John Terry, is the epitome of an anti-ethical player on and off the field. A number 6 with England's national team from 2003 to 2012, Terry currently wears number 26 for London-based club Chelsea. Terry was the England captain from 2006 to 2010, as well as from 2011 to 2012. Terry is undoubtedly a brilliant talent: a combative and determined defender and a player that scores key goals. He was named UEFA Club Defender of the Year in 2005, 2008, and 2009, as well as the Professional Footballers' Association Players' Player of the Year in 2005. In addition, Terry was included in the FIFPro World XI for five consecutive seasons from 2005 to 2009.[12] (Based in the Netherlands, FIFPro is the worldwide representative organization for 65,000 professional soccer players.) To add to his accomplishments, Terry was the only English player named in the all-star squad for the 2006 World Cup. At the club level, Terry is Chelsea's most successful captain: three Premier League titles, four FA Cups, two League Cups, and a UEFA Champions League title. He is one of only five players to make more than 500 appearances for Chelsea and is also the club's all time highest scoring defender (thirty-three goals in about 400 appearances since 1998).

Terry's problems are not directly related to soccer or his skills, but to his unethical behavior on and off the field. Terry is the anti-Netto; the unethical equivalent to Netto's ethic of fair play. In 2001, Terry and three teammates were fined two weeks' wages by Chelsea for drunkenly taunting American tourists at a Heathrow airport bar in the aftermath of the September 11 terrorist attacks.[13] In 2002, Terry was caught on camera urinating in a beer glass and was charged with assault after a confrontation with a nightclub bouncer. During the case, Terry was banned from selection for the England team, but was later acquitted of the charges. In the same year, Terry was fined for parking his car in a disabled spot. In 2009, Terry was investigated by Chelsea and the FA for allegedly taking money from an undercover reporter for a private tour of Chelsea's training facility, but the club cleared him of wrongdoing.[14]

In 2010 and 2011, it went from bad to worse for Terry. In January, after a court injunction was lifted it was revealed that Terry allegedly had a four-month affair in 2009 with Vanessa Perroncel, the former girlfriend of Wayne Bridge, his former Chelsea and England teammate. Bridge is currently a defender with Reading. The swirling rumors about Terry's unethical behav-

ior toward a teammate and his wife led to former England manager Fabio
Capello removing Terry from the captaincy in February 2010. Rio Ferdinand
became the new England captain. On February 25, 2010, Bridge announced
his permanent withdrawal from international duty following the allegations
regarding Terry and Bridge's former girlfriend Vanessa Perroncel. Terry was
reinstated England captain about one year later. In November 2011, Terry
was placed under police investigation following an allegation of racist abuse
made at a black professional soccer player, Anton Ferdinand, during a match
versus Queens Park Rangers. He is the brother of Rio Ferdinand. In December 2011, he was charged with using racist language by the Crown Prosecution Service.

In February 2012, the Football Association stripped Terry of his England
captaincy for the second time. The court found Terry not guilty because it
could not be proven beyond a reasonable doubt the words that were uttered at
the time. Yet under questioning Terry admitted that he had uttered the words
"fucking black cunt" at Ferdinand, which was confirmed by two expert lip
readers.[15] In July 2012, the Football Association charged Terry with using
"abusive and/or insulting words and/or behavior," which "included a reference to the ethnic origin and/or colour and/or race of Ferdinand."[16] The
Football Association had delayed the charge until after the conclusion of
Terry's criminal trial. On the eve of the trial, Terry announced his retirement
from the English national soccer team. On September 27, 2012, Terry was
found guilty and punished with a four-match ban and a £220,000 fine. Terry's light four-match ban was contrasted with Luis Suárez's eight-match ban
for repeatedly racially abusing Patrice Evra. Terry's club, Chelsea, was accused of hypocrisy because of the team's "zero tolerance for racism" policy.
Terry was only fined by the club, but not stripped of his captaincy. In
contrast, a Chelsea fan who racially abused Ivory Coast international and
former Chelsea star Didier Drogba, was given a life ban.

WHAT IS ETHICS?

Recall that John Terry is my anti-ethical choice and Igor Netto is the official
and ethical number 6 choice. Soccer is less ethical today compared to the
epoch when Netto played, in the 1950s and 1960s. Rampant commercialism,
doping, on-field cheating and diving, and game fixing are serious problems
in contemporary professional soccer. All this begs the question: What is
ethics? In order to assist us with this task, we turn to the world-renowned
philosopher Peter Singer.

Peter Singer was born on July 6, 1946. He is an Australian moral philosopher and one of the most important philosophers alive today. Currently Singer is a professor of bioethics at Princeton University, as well as laureate

professor at the Centre for Applied Philosophy and Public Ethics at the University of Melbourne. Singer is known worldwide for his secular and utilitarian approach to applied ethics. He first received notoriety for his book, *Animal Liberation* (1975), a seminal text in animal rights theory. Other key books penned by Singer include *Practical Ethics* (1979), *How Are We to Live?: Ethics in an Age of Self-interest* (1993), *Rethinking Life and Death: The Collapse of Our Traditional Ethics* (1994), *One World: The Ethics of Globalisation* (2002), and *The Life You Can Save: Acting Now to End World Poverty* (2009).

What is interesting about Singer is that his views on ethics have attracted many critics. Advocates for disabled people and right-to-life groups claim that Singer's utilitarian ethics leads to a position in favor of eugenics. This claim was particularly touchy for Singer as both his paternal and maternal grandparents were killed by the Nazis in concentration camps. What is of interest to us here is that Singer opines on nearly everything under the sun, including the ethics of soccer. Moreover, Singer proposed a useful definition of ethics in the 1985 edition of the *Encyclopaedia Britannica*:

> The discipline concerned with what is morally good and bad, right and wrong. The term is also applied to any system or theory of moral values or principles.
>
> How should we live? Shall we aim at happiness or at knowledge, virtue, or the creation of beautiful objects? If we choose happiness, will it be our own or the happiness of all? And what of the more particular questions that face us: Is it right to be dishonest in a good cause? Can we justify living in opulence while elsewhere in the world people are starving? If conscripted to fight in a war we do not support, should we disobey the law? What are our obligations to the other creatures with whom we share this planet and to the generations of humans who will come after us?
>
> Ethics deals with such questions at all levels. Its subject consists of the fundamental issues of practical decision making, and its major concerns include the nature of ultimate value and the standards by which human actions can be judged right or wrong.
>
> The terms ethics and morality are closely related. We now often refer to ethical judgments or ethical principles where it once would have been more common to speak of moral judgments or moral principles. These applications are an extension of the meaning of ethics. Strictly speaking, however, the term refers not to morality itself but to the field of study, or branch of inquiry, that has morality as its subject matter. In this sense, ethics is equivalent to moral philosophy.
>
> Although ethics has always been viewed as a branch of philosophy, its all-embracing practical nature links it with many other areas of study, including anthropology, biology, economics, history, politics, sociology, and theology. Yet, ethics remains distinct from such disciplines because it is not a matter of factual knowledge in the way that the sciences and other branches of inquiry are. Rather, it has to do with determining the nature of normative theories and applying these sets of principles to practical moral problems. [17]

If we summarize Singer's aforementioned definition of ethics, we can high-light five main points:

1. Ethics is concerned with appraisals of what is right and wrong.
2. It connotes a theory of moral values.
3. It is a discipline that opines about how humans should live in relation to other human beings.
4. Ethics is linked to practical decision making in that it contains reflections about the "nature of ultimate value" and a set of standards to judge human actions.
5. The discipline of ethics includes many other disciplines under its ambit from politics and economics to theology. Yet ethics is a unique and autonomous discipline, attempting to apply ethical principles to "practical moral problems."

From the above, it follows that we may use ethical principles to resolve moral problems associated with professional soccer. So, for example, can coaches turn a blind eye when their players are doping? Can FIFA administrators speak about "cleaning up the game" when they are stealing from the organization's coffers? In this respect, I recommend that all soccer fans read Andrew Jennings's *Foul! The Secret World of FIFA: Bribes, Vote Rigging, and Ticket Scandals*, which details FIFA's corrupt practices from nepotism and shoddy accounting to kickbacks and theft of funds.[18]

In an age of greater democratization worldwide, FIFA may no longer be able to turn a blind eye to authoritarian regimes hosting World Cup contests. Instant replay technology for controversial goals or penalty calls is probably a good idea. There is a perception by many fans that big nations and clubs are favored by referees. Or that the punishments for game fixing are not harsh enough. Do soccer players make too much money? Do players have an obligation to point out their own rule violations when they are missed by referees? Have the ethics of soccer changed since the days of Igor Netto? What can modern soccer stars teach young people? Should soccer players promote social change? Recall that in chapter 2 I highlighted the relationship between soccer and dictatorships and in chapter 4 I examined initiatives for social change associated with professional soccer. From liberal and left-wing perspectives, professional soccer organizations should take a stance against dictatorships that host international soccer competitions. From this perspective, FIFA and soccer clubs should be involved in more social change initiatives related to undermining poverty, environmental protection, or gender equality.

CAMUS, NETTO, TERRY, MOORE, AND THE ETHICS OF SOCCER

Perhaps the greatest number 6 to ever play the game was the England inter-national Bobby Moore. As a result of his gentlemanly qualities, Moore helps us to better understand the relationship between soccer and ethics. Born on April 2, 1941, Moore was such a distinguished English defender that he received the Order of the British Empire (OBE) title. A West Ham United player for twelve years from 1958 to 1974 (544 appearances and twenty-four goals), Moore was also captain of the England team that won its only World Cup in 1966. Moore made a whopping 108 appearances for his country and scored two goals. In his 108 appearances, Moore amazingly played in every minute of every game! This was a record in appearances for England, until it was broken by the gifted goalkeeper Peter Shilton and later David Beckham. Moore is regarded by learned soccer fans as one of the greatest players of all time. Pelé gave him a fantastic honor when he dubbed Moore the "greatest defender" that he had ever played against.[19]

Moore battled testicular cancer in 1964, but in that year still led West Ham to a 3–2 FA Cup finals triumph against Preston North End. In 1965, he lifted the European Cup Winners' Cup trophy after West Ham defeated 1860 Munich 2–0 in the finals. In 1966, Moore scored his first goal for England and captained the national team as it won the World Cup on home soil.

Moore also captained England in the 1970 World Cup and played a lead-ing role in England's progress beyond the group phase. In the second game against favorites Brazil, there was a wonderful moment when Moore tackled Jairzinho with such precision that it became known as "the perfect tackle."[20] Brazil won the game 1–0, but England advanced to the next round. After the game, Moore swapped jerseys with Pelé. Moore was voted runner-up behind West Germany's Gerd Müller for the 1970 European Footballer of the Year award.

In 1993, Moore announced that he was suffering from bowel and liver cancer. On February 24, 1993, Moore died at the age of fifty-one. The first West Ham home game after his death was on March 6, 1993. The West Ham ground became a shrine to the legendary Moore, with flowers and memora-bilia from both West Ham fans and even other clubs. His number 6 shirt was officially retired in 2008, fifteen years after Moore's death.

The legendary Bobby Charlton, a member of England's World Cup-win-ning squad in 1966, took Moore's death to heart. In a 2012 BBC documen-tary entitled "Hero: The Bobby Moore Story," after a long pause and plenty of reflection Charlton said: "Well, I only ever cried over two people, Billy Bremner and Bob. . . . He was a lovely man."[21]

In 2007, Moore received another honor posthumously. The Bobby Moore Sculpture was unveiled by Sir Bobby Charlton outside the entrance of the newly refurbished Wembley Stadium. The words attached to Moore's bronze sculpture are a testament to the great love for Moore both on and off the field: "Immaculate footballer. Imperial defender. Immortal hero of 1966. First Englishman to raise the World Cup aloft. Favourite son of London's East End. Finest legend of West Ham United. National Treasure. Master of Wembley. Lord of the game. Captain extraordinary. Gentleman of all time."[22] The words "gentleman of all time" makes one wonder: How many modern soccer stars are gentlemen? Certainly John Terry was no gentleman, if we remember his unethical actions and racist comments on and off the field. In chapter 11, I further discuss how the Moore sculpture and other forms of art immortalize soccer stars.

Tributes for Moore came pouring in from around the world. Alf Ramsey, England's manager at the 1966 World Cup, paid the highest tribute to Moore: "My captain, my leader, my right-hand man. He was the spirit and the heartbeat of the team. A cool, calculating footballer I could trust with my life. He was the supreme professional, the best I ever worked with. Without him England would never have won the World Cup."[23] Sir Alex Ferguson called him "the greatest defender" he had ever seen, while Franz Beckenbauer went further when he said Moore was "the best defender in the history of the game."[24] Pelé alluded to Moore's moral compass and called him an "honorable gentleman" and "one of the greatest footballers" in the world.[25] Even the former British prime minister Tony Blair showered Moore with great praise by suggesting that children could look to him for moral inspiration: "He was a superb footballer. If you wanted a role model from public life, Bobby Moore is a pretty good one to take."[26]

Recall that in the introduction I pointed out that the French writer Albert Camus was deeply touched by his experiences with respect to soccer, particularly his time with the Racing Universitaire Algérios (RUA) junior team that Camus played for in goal. Camus was a real soccer fan and his friend, Charles Poncet, once asked him if he preferred soccer or the theater. Camus unambiguously replied, "Football, without hesitation."[27] As a goalkeeper playing a unique position in soccer, Camus also learned lessons: "I learned that the ball never comes when you expect it to. That helped me a lot in life, especially in large cities where people don't tend to be what they claim."[28] Finally, Camus made this profound statement with respect to soccer and ethics: "After many years during which I saw many things, what I know most surely about morality and the duty of man I owe to sport and learned it in the RUA."[29]

Camus is correct. The soccer ethic of fair play is something we should admire. Netto and Moore embodied the ethic of fair play. Terry was unethical due to his racist comments, cheating on his wife with a teammate's girlfriend, drunken fights, and wildly inappropriate behavior after the tragic events of September 11. If a player is down and injured, you kick the ball out of play. You should not purposefully dive in the penalty area in order to win a penalty kick. It is a nice gesture to shake hands with your opponents and the officials at the end of a match. Selling a soccer match is morally wrong. Children see the players as gods and they should conduct themselves respectfully on and off the field. At least, these are our hopes.

In Singer's aforementioned definition of ethics, the philosopher asks: "What are our obligations to the other creatures with whom we share this planet and to the generations of humans who will come after us?" Similarly, Camus insists that what he learned about "morality and the duty of man" he owes to sport and his soccer experiences. In addition, as a result of his soccer experiences, Camus was making judgments about morality, soccer, and more broadly sport. Similarly, Pope Benedict XVI could see the moral power of soccer: "The sport of football can be a vehicle of education for the values of honesty, solidarity and fraternity, especially for the younger generation."[30]

Yet the ethical framework proposed by Camus is certainly different from Singer's. Singer is concerned with those that cannot speak for themselves, or individuals without a voice in a more self-interested age: animals, nature, or the poor. Camus, on the other hand, is proposing a universalistic ethics born out of his soccer experiences, which is more simple and straightforward. In his early books such as *The Myth of Sisyphus* (1942), *The Outsider* (1942), and *The Notebooks* (1935–1942), Camus hinted at a simplistic morality. While Camus understood that modern man was faced with a crisis of meaning in an age where faith was increasingly a private matter, Camus was no nihilist. Rather Camus sought to find meaning in the simple actions of life, like Sisyphus pushing the heavy boulder up the mountain each day, even with the knowledge that it would fall and the task of pushing the boulder up the mountain must begin each day anew. Also, Camus saw in soccer a simple morality: the principle of siding with and defending your teammates (friends), valorizing bravery (especially in the goalkeeper), and subscribing to the ethos of fair play. Camus understood that political and religious authorities complicate moral questions, or issues related to the way human beings should live and how they should act. In contrast, in soccer Camus saw a simple and universal game with a basic moral code, which is applicable to all peoples from different cultures throughout the world.

For Igor Netto and Albert Camus, soccer teaches us lessons that are helpful both on and off the pitch. In 1960 Camus's life ended in tragedy when he died in a car accident at the age of forty-six. He had lived a difficult life in French-controlled Algeria. Born into poverty, he never knew his father, as he had died in the First World War when Camus was merely one. His mother raised him and his grandmother beat him often. This might explain his love for street soccer as an escape from his difficult life. One writer viewed the decision by Camus to become a goalkeeper using the author's philosophical framework:

> But there is something appropriate about a philosopher like Camus stationing himself between the sticks. It is a lonely calling, an individual isolated within a team ethic, one who plays to different constraints. If his team scores, the keeper knows it is nothing to do with him. If the opposition score, however, it is all his fault. Standing sentinel in goal, Camus had plenty of time to reflect on the absurdist nature of his position.[31]

The same writer also insisted that Zinedine Zidane's dramatic head-butt in the 2006 World Cup finals could be analyzed using a famous character from Camus's novel *The Outsider*:

> Take the last World Cup final. Zinedine Zidane was France's finest player, a brooding, enigmatic, yet hugely talented individual. Towards the end of the game, without apparent provocation, he headbutted an Italian opponent. In doing so, Zidane behaved uncannily like Meursault, the anti-hero of Camus's finest work, *L'Etranger*, who, for no obvious reason, one day shoots an Arab he encounters on the beach. And like Meursault, with whom the reader instinctively sides despite the indefensible nature of his actions, Zidane was lauded by the French public.[32]

I do not know that Camus would have "lauded" Zidane's head-butt after Marco Materazzi had insulted Zidane. Camus would have probably chastised both Materazzi and Zidane for abandoning the soccer ethic of fair play. What would Camus say about a five-meter-high statue of Zinedine Zidane's head-butt on Marco Materazzi unveiled outside the Pompidou Centre in Paris in 2012?[33] The bronze statue was sculpted by the Algerian artist Adel Abdesseme and has attracted praise and moral outrage. Alain Michaud, the exhibition organizer, insisted that the statue "is an ode to defeat" rather than victory.[34] Or, had Igor Netto or Bobby Moore been alive today, they might have lamented what soccer has become: racism in the stands, doping, game fixing, excessive diving to win free kicks and penalties, an abundance of yellow and red cards, a win-at-all-costs philosophy, massive salaries, drinking and partying off the pitch, and the demise of the ethic of fair play.

Recall that Singer argued that ethics deals with "fundamental issues of practical decision making" and its key concerns include "the nature of ultimate value and the standards by which human actions can be judged right or wrong." In the age of modern soccer, we can think of lots of practical cases that "can be judged right or wrong." In particular, we are reminded of Diego Maradona's infamous "hand of God" goal against England in the quarterfinals of the 1986 World Cup.

In 2009, Thierry Henry of France handled the ball, and shortly after William Gallas scored a winning goal against Ireland, thus allowing France to qualify for the 2010 World Cup. After the game, Henry was honest enough to admit his handball, yet he opted for a different ethical framework related to the referee's responsibilities: "I will be honest, it was a handball. But I'm not the ref. I played it, the ref allowed it. That's a question you should ask him."[35] Giovanni Trapattoni, Ireland's Italian manager at the time, advanced a different ethical perspective: Henry should be given the opportunity to admit his offense.[36] Trapattoni elaborated on his position: "All European people saw the situation. I am sure that, if the referee had asked Henry, he would have admitted to the handball. I would prefer to go out on penalties than this. I am sad because the referee had the time to ask the linesman and Henry."[37] Yet the Ireland manager saw ethical implications in the Henry handball beyond the soccer field: "I am upset for fair play because we are told many times about fair play. We didn't change the rules three months ago. I go into schools to talk about fair play and tell the young kids that it's important for their life."[38] The Irish captain Richard Dunne was less magnanimous than Trapattoni in defeat and blamed the match officials: "I think it was quite blatant that he cheated. The linesman was in line with the incident, it wasn't even a hard decision to make."[39]

William Gallas, the French scorer of the controversial goal, claimed innocence: "It all happened so quickly. I received the ball from Thierry, but I couldn't see. I saw Thierry's pass, the Irish were surprised and I put my head and my chest out."[40] The French coach Raymond Domenech reacted angrily to the Irish complaints of cheating: "I didn't see the hand. You people [media] are talking of this after seeing it from 80 yards. The referee gave the goal, but I couldn't see anything from where I was. I didn't see the replay."[41]

Geoff Hurst scored three goals in the finals of the 1966 World Cup for England against West Germany. He scored the perfect hat trick, one with his head, another with his right foot, and the third with his left foot. England won the match 4–2. Yet Hurst will always be remembered for the third goal that modern technology clearly shows was not a goal. Many years later in a second round match at the 2010 World Cup, England met Germany. England's Frank Lampard was denied a goal as England was trailing 2–1. Lampard hit a rocket from twenty yards near the end of the first half. The shot looped over German goalkeeper Manuel Neuer. Instant replay clearly showed the ball hitting the bar and crossing the line. In a reverse of historical fortunes for England, Germany won the match 4–1 and the referee denied a legitimate England goal.

As he has written about soccer, Peter Singer can enlighten us about the Maradona, Hurst, and Henry goals, as well as Lampard's no-goal. Singer was asked the following question after Lampard's no-goal: Does a soccer player have a duty to own up to his or her knowledge about the "right" outcome of a given play? Should the German goalkeeper, Manuel Neuer, have told the referee that Frank Lampard's shot had crossed the line? Singer's answer is unambiguously in the affirmative:

Yes, we can deal with the problem to some extent by using modern technology or video replays to review controversial refereeing decisions. But, while that will reduce the opportunity for cheating, it won't eliminate it, and it isn't really the point. We should not make excuses for intentional cheating in sports. In one important way, it is much worse than cheating in one's private life. When what you do will be seen by millions, revisited on endless video replays, and dissected on television sports programs, it is especially important to do what is right.

How would football fans have reacted if Neuer had stopped play and told the referee that the ball was a goal? Given the rarity of such behavior in football [soccer], the initial reaction would no doubt have been surprise. Some German fans might have been disappointed. But the world as a whole—and every fair-minded German fan too—would have had to admit that he had done the right thing.

Neuer missed a rare opportunity to do something noble in front of millions of people. He could have set a positive ethical example to people watching all over the world, including the many millions who are young and impressionable. Who knows what difference that example might have made to the lives of many of those watching? Neuer could have been a hero, standing up for what is right. Instead, he is just another footballer who is very skillful at cheating. [42]

From Singer's perspective, the players themselves should jettison cheating, speak out honestly when they see rules being broken (irrespective of the team in question), and do what is right because they are in a society consisting of billions of other soccer fans. Like Camus, Netto, and Moore, Singer calls for fair play, simplicity, and individual responsibility. Yet Singer admits that while modern technology and video replays of controversial plays or goals "will reduce the opportunity for cheating," it will not eliminate cheating completely. Singer also points to a rare incident in 1996 that the German goalkeeper Manuel Neuer could have used as his model:

Liverpool striker Robbie Fowler was awarded a penalty for being fouled by the Arsenal goalkeeper. He told the referee that he had not been fouled, but the referee insisted he take the penalty kick. Fowler did so, but in a manner that enabled the goalkeeper to save it. [43]

Similarly, in 2012 the German international and SS Lazio striker Miroslav Klose confessed that he used his hand when scoring a goal against Napoli. After scoring in the fourth minute of the match, Klose went to inform the referee that the goal should not stand because he handled the ball. The goal was disallowed. Klose's team Lazio lost the match 3–0. On his Twitter account, FIFA president Sepp Blatter praised Klose: "Bravo Miro Klose. With your gesture you have shown yourself to be a champion and a proper player." [44] Inter Milan's Argentinean midfielder Esteban Cambiasso also heaped praise on Klose as a role model for children and future professional soccer players: "We should praise the honesty of Klose. We must honor this gesture. It is an example for all children to follow."[45]

The French paper *Le Monde* claims that in the course of investigating Operation Puerto in 2006, a doping bust primarily related to professional cycling, extensive documentation was discovered of "seasonal preparation plans" for Real Madrid and FC Barcelona players that include notes suggesting doping practices.[46] Probably the highest-profile case of doping in world soccer is of Diego Maradona at the 1994 World Cup in the United States, who was suspended and sanctioned for eighteen months for taking ephedrine. In 2005, Middlesbrough's former Portuguese international defender Abel Xavier was banned from soccer for eighteen months by UEFA for taking anabolic steroids after a UEFA Cup match on September 29, 2005, thus becoming the first player in English Premier League history to be banned for using performance-enhancing substances.[47]

Singer has opined on doping in soccer. It is rather surprising and disappointing that while Singer seeks to uphold an ethic of honesty and individual responsibility with respect to soccer cheats, he simultaneously supports doping in sports. Julian Savulescu, who leads the Uehiro Centre for Practical Ethics at Oxford University, insists that "we should drop the ban on performance-enhancing drugs, and allow athletes to take whatever they want, as long as it is safe for them to do so."[48] Singer agrees with Savulescu's solution. Singer thus controversially argues that the use of drugs in combination with intense training levels the playing field for "those with the best genes have an unfair advantage."[49] While I subscribe to Singer's ethics with respect to technology and goals, I cannot accept it when it comes to doping. We might ask Singer: Are not billions of soccer fans watching when players are doping and do the players not have any obligation to those fans? Moreover, it is rather troubling that Singer, who lost family members in the Nazi Holocaust because of Hitler's twisted notion of Aryan superiority, chillingly argues that "those with the best genes have an unfair advantage." Netto, Moore, and Camus would have seen such mental gymnastics as a clear effort to skirt the ethic of fair play. It is true that in soccer doping does not mean you win the match, because soccer is more than merely training, fitness, or genes. It is about tactics, skill, accuracy, luck, spirit, character, teamwork, and even individual genius. Yet recall that the soccer ethic highlighted by Camus is universal and thus applies to all peoples worldwide, irrespective of the game's result.

Singer's inconsistencies with respect to soccer ethics should alert us to the idea that we should not merely rely on expert knowledge in the realm of ethics. Moreover, using Singer's definition of ethics highlighted earlier, the Australian philosopher asked two relevant questions: "Can we justify living in opulence while elsewhere in the world people are starving?" and "What are our obligations to the other creatures with whom we share this planet and to the generations of humans who will come after us?" If we apply these insights to soccer, we might ask how players with astronomical salaries for major clubs such as Real Madrid, Barcelona, Manchester United, or Bayern Munich can justify "living in opulence," while "people are starving" in Africa, Latin America, Asia, and sometimes even in the players' backyards in Europe? Do professional players, FIFA administrators, club officials, and coaches not have "obligations to the other creatures with which they share this planet"? Can professional clubs treat their players like "property," as former USA international and Club Tijuana star Hércules Gómez claimed with respect to Mexican soccer clubs?

Cognizant of the role of morality and soccer on and off the pitch, FIFA created the Fair Play Award in 1987. It is designed to recognize good sporting behavior, or "fair play" actions, by people or organizations involved in soccer around the world. Individuals, teams, fans, spectators, soccer associations, and soccer communities have all won the award. The award choices have been interesting and diverse. In 1987, the German professional Frank Ordenewitz won the award after admitting to a handball in a penalty situation. In 1989, the award went to the Trinidad and Tobago fans for their sporting behavior, despite a narrow 1–0 home loss to the United States in their final World Cup qualifying match. A tie would have sent the island nation through to the World Cup tournament in 1990. In 1990, the great English striker Gary Lineker won the Fair Play Award after fifteen years as a professional soccer player without receiving a yellow or red card. In 1997, the Slovak amateur player Jozef Zovinec won the award after playing sixty years of soccer without receiving a yellow card. The USA and Iranian Soccer Federations jointly shared the Fair Play Award in 1998 for good sportsmanship during a World Cup match, despite the fact that the two countries have hostile relations and broke off diplomatic ties in 1980 in the aftermath of the 1979 Islamic Revolution. In 2000, Paolo Di Canio, a pro-Fascist Italian soccer star we encountered in chapter 1, won the award after taking the ball out of play with his hands when goalkeeper Paul Gerrard was injured on the ground. A year earlier the former South African international and Leeds skipper Lucas Radebe won the award for his excellent anti-racism work.

In addition, FIFA created a Fair Play Trophy in 1970, awarded to the cleanest team that progresses past the second round of the World Cup. The first winner was Peru in 1970. England won the trophy in 1990 and 1998. Brazil won the trophy four times in 1982, 1986, 1994, and 2006. Spain won the trophy in 2010. Other winners have included Argentina, France, and Belgium.

While FIFA officially promotes fair play and fair play awards, its own record is far from fair for many soccer fans. In 2006, Andrew Jennings wrote *Foul! The Secret World of FIFA: Bribes, Vote-Rigging and Ticket Scandals.* It details an international cash-for-contracts scandal after the collapse of

FIFA's marketing partner ISL. Jennings insisted that some FIFA officials had been bribed and there was extensive vote rigging as FIFA president Sepp Blatter sought to maintain control over the organization.

In 2010 and 2011, a series of major corruption scandals rocked FIFA, which confirmed some of Jennings's allegations. One claim was about Russian kickbacks of cash and gifts given to FIFA executive members, who secured Russia's 2018 World Cup bid. When Qatar received the 2022 World Cup instead of Britain, there were serious allegations by the *Sunday Times*: FIFA officials Issa Hayatou of Cameroon and Jacques Anouma of Ivory Coast were paid by Qatar's government.[50] At the time of writing, Qatar's hosting of the World Cup is in doubt because more FIFA officials are being investigated for the corruption surrounding the Arab state's bid. In addition, there are reports of forced Qatari labor of foreign workers and even deaths, especially from Nepal.[51]

As a result of the corruption scandals, on May 25, 2011, FIFA announced that it had opened an investigation to examine the conduct of four key officials: Mohamed bin Hammam, Jack Warner, Debbie Minguell, and Jason Sylvester. FIFA executive committee member Chuck Blazer, who is also the general secretary of CONCACAF (North America including Mexico, Central America, and the Caribbean), alleged that violations were committed under the FIFA code of ethics during a meeting organized by bin Hammam and Warner. Warner, a former vice president of FIFA, president of CONCACAF, and the owner of Trinidad and Tobago club side Joe Public FC, was accused of wanting kickback money for a World Cup 2018 vote in relation to the 2011 FIFA presidential election. Bin Hammam, who played a key FIFA role in the Qatar 2022 World Cup bid, allegedly offered financial incentives for votes cast in his favor during his presidential bid to oust Blatter. Bin Hammam and Warner were suspended by FIFA.

Warner did not go gently. He claimed that FIFA secretary general Jerome Valcke told him in an e-mail that Qatar "bought" the 2022 World Cup. Bin Hammam, too, did not go without a fight. He wrote to FIFA, claiming "unfair treatment" by both the FIFA Ethics Committee and its administration. In May and June 2011, further evidence of FIFA corruption surfaced as Fred Lunn, vice president of the Bahamas Football Association, claimed that he was given $40,000 in cash in order to vote for FIFA presidential candidate Mohamed bin Hammam. Louis Giskus, president of the Surinamese Football Association, alleged that he was given $40,000 in cash for a "development project," with the understanding that he would vote for bin Hammam and against current president Sepp Blatter.

In June 2011, João Havelange, the seventh president of FIFA, from 1974 to 1998, as well as the longest-serving member of the International Olympic Committee (IOC), from 1963 to 2011, resigned after an ethics committee was formed to investigate whether Havelange received a bribe of $1 million.

Citing ill health, Havelange resigned as a member of the IOC and the investigation was strangely closed.

Scanning Havelange's record, one realizes that the Brazilian represented all that was unethical about FIFA. It was under Havelange's reign in 1982 that Carlos Lacoste, a president of Argentina during the military junta, became vice president of FIFA. Lacoste was a key member of the organizing committee for the 1978 FIFA World Cup in Argentina. He was also the cousin of President Jorge Rafael Videla, the man responsible for the brutal policy of "disappearances." Recall that this was a theme I dealt with in chapter 2. Havelange also once signed a character reference and was an associate of Brazilian criminal Castor de Andrade, who was sentenced to six years in prison in 1994 for racketeering. Finally, Havelange had a turbulent relationship with Pelé. It turns out that João Havelange's daughter, Lucia, was married to Ricardo Teixeira for thirty years until 1997. Teixeira was president of the Brazilian Soccer Confederation (CBF) between 1989 and 2012. Pelé was upset that his television company was rejected in a contest for domestic rights and he accused Teixeira of corruption in 1993.[52] Havelange took his revenge, yet was roundly criticized for banning Pelé from the 1994 World Cup draw in Las Vegas.

Despite charges that FIFA's current president Sepp Blatter is a "dictator" leading a corrupt organization that pockets billions of dollars, the Swiss administrator shrugged off allegations of corruption within FIFA and was re-elected as president for a fourth time in 2011. Blatter took the FIFA reigns from Havelange in 1998 and was re-elected without much of a struggle in 2002, 2007, and 2011. Blatter is not much better than Havelange in terms of transparency and corruption within FIFA. There are swirling allegations that Blatter intimidated or paid off potential opponents.

Sepp Blatter's lack of moral compass was clear during the FIFA corruption scandals in 2010 and 2011. Blatter is merely concerned with his hold on power and the effects that the corruption scandals are having on corporate sponsors such as Visa, Coca-Cola, and Adidas. These companies pay large sums of money to have their logos advertised at World Cup soccer matches. Commenting on FIFA corruption allegations, a Visa spokesman opined that "The current situation is clearly not good for the game."[53] Or, as Adidas chief communications officer Jan Runau insisted in relation to the FIFA corruption scandals, "The negative tenor of the public debate around FIFA at the moment is neither good for football nor for FIFA."[54]

Instead of taking this as an opportunity to "clean" FIFA's house, Blatter could merely state the following at a press conference: "We are not in a crisis, we are only in some difficulties and these can be solved inside our family."[55] "FIFA is strong enough to deal with our own problems," added Blatter, shortly before elections by the FIFA Congress.[56] Although Blatter was cleared of any wrongdoing, the scandals are hurting FIFA and the image of professional soccer. FIFA and Blatter are increasingly seen as outdated in their desire to cling to power. Australian senator Nick Xenophon accused FIFA of "scamming" his country of the A$46 million it spent on the Australia 2022 FIFA World Cup bid.[57] Dick Pound, a former vice president of the IOC, accused FIFA of lacking any real transparency.[58]

All these scandals within FIFA raise the following questions: How can FIFA stop match fixing, doping allegations, or the undue power of major sponsors and clubs in soccer when it does not have its own house in order? In 2006, a terrible match-fixing scandal rocked top Italian professional soccer league teams in Serie A and Serie B. The scandal was uncovered by the Italian police. The league champions Juventus were one of the key culprits. The club lost its 2005 and 2006 Serie A titles, was forced out of the 2006–2007 UEFA Champions League, and was relegated to Serie B after it appealed its original relegation to Serie C1. Other major teams involved in the scandal included AC Milan, Fiorentina, Lazio, and Reggina. Secret telephone interceptions revealed a shady network of relations between team managers and referee organizations. The various teams were accused of rigging matches by selecting favorable referees. The Canadian journalist Declan Hill suspects that the 2006 World Cup second round match between Ghana and Brazil was fixed.[59] In 2009, fifteen people were arrested and an investigation initiated in Bochum, Germany about alleged game fixing of about 200 European matches, including many lower league matches in which there is no official oversight.[60]

Sensing public disdain over soccer and match fixing, UEFA president Michel Platini opened an anti-corruption department in 2009. How can players, coaches, referees, and administrators be told to advance the ethic of fair play when the world's soccer governing does not play kosher? And given all these corruption scandals, more fans are asking: How can we be certain that players who put on the national colors are not ever bribed by nations with major funds at their disposal? The soccer show must go on, we are told, but at what price? How many soccer fans no longer watch the game because of its rampant commercialism and corruption? Or is it too few for the major clubs, corporations, and FIFA to really care?

Furthermore, FIFA is accused of inflicting light penalties on racism, like CSKA Moscow fans' racial taunting against Manchester City's Ivory Coast international Yaya Touré in 2013, which resulted in a one-match partial closure and a full stadium closure with a fine of €50,000 if there is a second offense. Terry paid a heavy price for racial abuse with his England career, but his club and the Football Association could have taken more severe measures. Former England international John Barnes suggests that England should target its racism fight at home with respect to talented blacks denied management positions in soccer or young blacks suffering from poverty and discrimination in inner-city Brixton (a district in South London with a high percentage of the population of African and Caribbean descent, made infamous by riots in 1981, 1985, 1995, and 2011), rather than focus on "rich guys" that have a lot in common such as Touré, Terry, Suárez, or Anton Ferdinand.[61] "A millionaire getting booed in Russia is nothing compared with generations of people never getting the chance to better their lives and those of their children,"[62] insists Barnes in reference to disenfranchised blacks in England. Writing in *The Guardian*, Barnes opted for a measured response against racism in soccer, which he views as a reflection of racism in British society and not merely a problem in Russia or Eastern Europe:

> Personally, I don't blame Suárez or Terry for what they did—they are simply products of a society and environment that allows them to think it is OK to speak about certain people in a certain way. It would be far better if instead of banning them and demonising them, the Football Association aimed to educate them and make them see that black people are undeserving of racial abuse.[63]

What about the perception that there is no longer any ethics or beauty in contemporary soccer's win-at-all-costs philosophy? Players should play to entertain as much as to get results. What would George Orwell have said about the demise of fair play in soccer, a trend he already witnessed in 1945? And if Albert Camus, Igor Netto, or Bobby Moore were alive, what would they say to help us out of professional soccer's moral darkness?

Chapter Seven

The Business of Business

Soccer, Business, and Marketing

U.S. president Calvin Coolidge (1923–1929) once remarked that "the chief business of the American people is business. They are profoundly concerned with buying, selling, investing and prospering in the world."[1] Coolidge could have easily been speaking about the business of professional soccer. This chapter is about the relationships between soccer, business, and marketing.

Any cursory examination of sports makes it obvious that soccer is used as a marketing tool to sell the world's most popular game, professional clubs, players, corporations, and advertisers. Major clubs such as Barcelona or Manchester United even sell their soccer matches as unique experiences. When you enter Old Trafford, Manchester United's fabled stadium opened in 1910, you are entering the "Theatre of Dreams"—a name coined by United and English international legend Bobby Charlton.

Moreover, the North American Soccer League (NASL), which existed from 1968 to 1985, was a veritable marketing invention, a creation of the marketing "spin merchants," to borrow Ingham's phrase from chapter 3. Markovits and Rensmann argue that the NASL's New York Cosmos, with legends such as Pelé and Beckenbauer at its core, "represented the first truly globalized sports club of the modern age."[2] How could it be that Toronto-based NASL teams could draw merely 5,000 to 15,000 fans on average and yet pay such talented and high-priced stars such as David Byrne (South Africa), Jomo Sono (South Africa), Clyde Best (Bermuda), Željko Bilecki (Yugoslavia), David Fairclough (England), Roberto Bettega (Italy), Jimmy Nicholl (Northern Ireland), Eusébio (Portugal), Jimmy Bone (Scotland), Jan Moller (Sweden), and Arno Steffenhagen (West Germany)? These were merely the Toronto players and there were other more famous stars throughout the NASL such as Carlos Alberto, Vladislav Bogicevic, Johan Cruyff, Johan Neskeens, George Best, and Roberto Cabañas. The NASL was so marketing conscious that it instituted a soccer rarity, a shootout in case of a draw, in order to make the game more exciting for a North American audience. Borrowing from baseball and American football, teams even had mascots in order to make the club brand more identifiable to fans.

The NASL lasted less than twenty years. One of the main problems with the league was the lack of local talent and excessive reliance on foreign talent, often beyond its prime. Another major problem with the NASL was overexpansion. New franchises were added quickly without consolidating the existing franchises. So, for example, in 1968 the NASL began with seventeen teams and by 1969 it had merely five teams. New growth occurred in the 1975 and 1976 seasons with a total of twenty teams and a high of twenty-four teams for the 1978–1980 seasons. In the NASL's final season in 1984, only nine teams remained. Another factor in the demise of the NASL was when FIFA awarded Mexico rather than the United States the 1986 World Cup after Colombia withdrew.

It would take another ten years from the NASL's last season until a new professional soccer league, Major League Soccer (MLS), was created in the United States. The 1994 World Cup in the United States, which saw the highest attendance of any World Cup in history, added to the allure and marketing appeal of the MLS. The MLS learned three marketing lessons from the failed NASL: 1) rely on mostly local talent; 2) create franchise stability; and 3) accept expansion teams based on the league's financial stability.

Soccer marketing had its growth period in the 1960s and 1970s with the emergence of soccer superstars such as Pelé and George Best. These soccer stars sold the game worldwide, as well as various products, services, and advertisers. The Manchester United legend George Best was the epitome of cool, an image promoted by marketing gurus who focused on his sexy image and fast lifestyle (pretty women, parties, and fast cars) as much as his exceptional soccer talents. With the New York Cosmos, Pelé became a global media celebrity—a worldwide icon—perhaps one of the most recognizable public faces of all time. It is no wonder that Brazilian politicians still invoke his name and companies such as the Spanish bank Santander still use the image of Pelé to promote their bottom line.

By the 1990s, soccer had become a marketing tool of extraordinary proportions. Players such as England's David Beckham and Brazil's Ronaldo Luís Nazário de Lima (winner of the 1994 and 2002 World Cups and three-time FIFA Player of the Year award) were transformed into global marketing icons. Manchester United has bought talented Korean, Japanese, Ecuadorian, Mexican, Brazilian, Portuguese, Dutch, and Serbian players in order to sell Manchester United to soccer fans around the globe. There are more players, clubs, coaches, administrators, corporations, and governments that understand the marketing thrust and appeal of soccer. In the age of YouTube, Facebook, and Twitter, even tiny and obscure soccer clubs and players recognize the importance of social media and marketing. While not all soccer players can be turned into the "Beckham brand," more soccer players are emulating his marketing chic both on and off the pitch.

Before highlighting the business and marketing lessons of soccer, we need to select our number 7, an outside right, right winger, or right midfielder.

JERSEY #7: A MIDFIELDER WORTHY OF BRANDING

Whereas with every number it was a real challenge to choose a player or players, it was not a difficult choice to select David Beckham as one of the number 7 choices. While I was writing *The World through Soccer*, Beckham retired in May 2013 after he won yet another trophy: the French first division league championship with Paris Saint-Germain FC. Beckham wore jersey number 23 with the Los Angeles Galaxy, but most of his career he wore the number 7 shirt. Cristiano Ronaldo, a Portuguese international currently playing with Real Madrid CF, is also a number 7 with great marketing appeal and has even more breathtaking individual skills than his English counterpart. He has also been selected as a representative of this chapter.

Yet there is nobody like David Beckham that can best highlight the links between soccer as a business and its marketing appeal. All of David Beckham's decisions—from joining Manchester United and later Real Madrid, AC Milan, the Los Angeles Galaxy, and Paris Saint-Germain—were made with the desire to push the ubiquitous "David Beckham brand." Beckham is perhaps the greatest marketing icon that soccer has ever seen. Even Beckham's decisions off the pitch such as his numerous tattoos or his marriage to a "Spice Girl" are cultivated to enhance his marketing appeal. When Beckham sells, he sells Beckham, his club, the English national team, shirts, match tickets, paraphernalia, sponsors, advertisers, products, and also the game itself. Beckham's marketing pull is so profound that Markovits and Rensmann invented the term "Beckham effect," which connotes "the arrival of a foreign, bona fide, crossover, global superstar to help a struggling sport in a country where it has languished at the cultural margins."[3] Once-obscure soccer leagues such as in the United States, Qatar, China, or India have seen the arrival of foreign superstars help the sport achieve more mainstream cultural appeal. Beckham was responsible for almost single-handedly changing the image and quality of the MLS, increasing fan attendance, bringing major sponsors, and pushing other European, South American, African, and Asian stars to play in North America.

"Becks"

David Beckham, or "Becks" as he is affectionately known, was not only an exceptional right-sided midfielder, but he neatly embodies lesson seven's insights about soccer as a global business and its marketing appeal. David Robert Joseph Beckham is only thirty-eight and has already received the distinction of the Order of the British Empire. He was born in Leytonstone, England on May 2, 1975. In 2013 he retired, playing his last professional match with French club Paris Saint-Germain.

Beckham first made his name and his marketing appeal with Manchester United from 1993 to 2003. He also had a short spell at Preston North End in England (1994–1995) and a few loan spells at AC Milan (2009–2010), as well as spending a good portion of his career at Real Madrid (2003–2007). From 1996 until 2009, Beckham scored seventeen goals and made 115 appearances for England's national team, a record for outfield players only surpassed by the legendary goalkeeper Peter Shilton. Beckham was England's captain from 2000 until the 2006 World Cup tournament. He also played in three World Cups for his country in 1998, 2002, and 2006. When he scored a sublime free kick goal against Ecuador in the second round of the 2006 World Cup to win the match 1–0, he became the only English player to score in three World Cup tournaments. He was only the fifth player in World Cup history to score twice from a direct free kick, sharing the honor with free kick masters Pelé, Roberto Rivelino (Brazil), Teófilo Cubillas (Peru), and Bernard Genghini (France). Beckham scored his other free kick goal against Colombia in the first round of the 1998 World Cup.

Beckham began his professional, first-team career at the tender age of seventeen with Manchester United. With the Manchester-based club, he won the Premier League title six times, the FA Cup twice, and the UEFA Champions League once. While Beckham became a marketing icon both at United and Real Madrid, he did not win a lot of silverware at the Madrid club. He only won La Liga championship in his final season with the club in 2007.

On July 1, 2007, David Beckham signed a five-year contract with the Los Angeles Galaxy. His two loan spells in Italy with Milan in 2009 and 2010 angered many Los Angeles Galaxy fans, some of who called him a "fake" and "traitor." Despite the angry accusations, in 2011 and 2012 Beckham helped the Los Angeles Galaxy win its third and fourth MLS Cup trophies. He thus became one of those rare players who won league titles with three different professional clubs in three countries. At the end of the 2012 season, Beckham declared his mission of making soccer more popular in the United States accomplished and said that he was leaving the Los Angeles Galaxy for a final soccer adventure. He spent the 2013 season making ten appearances for Paris Saint-Germain, which won the French first division championship for the first time since 1994. As a result of Beckham's time in the MLS, Los

Angeles Galaxy and MLS league attendance figures rose, more clubs joined the MLS, the league was on solid financial footing, and the league won new fans, sponsors, and advertisers. Yet some critics like Ben Rycroft argue that while Beckham attracted new media attention for soccer in the United States, the MLS has "driven its own growth."[4]

In honor of his soccer exploits, Beckham was twice runner-up for World Player of the Year. Noted for his exceptional and precise crossing of the ball, Beckham is third in the English Premier League's all-time assist chart, with 152 assists in 265 appearances.[5] He scored sixty-two goals for Manchester United, including a gem from past the halfway line, another thirteen for Real Madrid, and eighteen for the Los Angeles Galaxy.

Beckham was England's first captain to collect two red cards and be sent off in a World Cup match. At the 1998 World Cup, after Argentina's Diego Simeone fouled him, Beckham foolishly kicked the Argentine midfielder and was given a red card. Despite his troubles with the Spanish giants Real Madrid (including an excessive forty-one yellow cards), he was noted for his extreme professionalism, even when he sat on the bench. He missed out on the 2010 World Cup with a torn Achilles tendon.

His manager at Manchester United, the fiery Scotsman Alex Ferguson, complained that Beckham lost his way after he got into a relationship and later married "Spice Girl" Victoria Beckham in 2007: "He was never a problem until he got married. He used to go into work with the academy coaches at night time, he was a fantastic young lad. Getting married into that entertainment scene was a difficult thing—from that moment, his life was never going to be the same. He is such a big celebrity, football is only a small part."[6] Yet while Ferguson complained, Beckham and the Manchester club kept winning titles. Ferguson guided the club to thirteen Premier League titles, five FA Cups, four League Cups, and two Champions League trophies. Although Ferguson had to admit that Beckham's off-field celebrity status was a distraction, he could say that the English star "practiced with a discipline to achieve an accuracy that other players wouldn't care about."[7] How else could we explain his indefatigable work rate, extraordinary assist total, sensational set pieces, incredible passing skills, and sublime free kick goals?

In 2013, *Alex Ferguson: My Autobiography* was released shortly after the manager's retirement.[8] In the autobiography, he devotes one chapter to Beckham. He points out that marriage changed Beckham. In addition, the day after their heated exchange in which Beckham swore at Ferguson and the manager threw a shoe at the star, Ferguson "told the board David had to go." Alex Ferguson's autobiography is one of the most popular imported English books in China's online shopping network. Moreover, before the release of Ferguson's biography, Beckham considered asking Ferguson to be the coach of the Miami Fusion, a team that folded in 2001, and now Beckham is seeking to buy the team for a new MLS expansion team.[9] Yet aware of his image and marketing goals, Beckham refused to be negative about Ferguson: "I'm not going to sit here and be negative about a man who gave me the chance to play for my boyhood team," while promoting his own book *David Beckham* in a global book signing televised on Facebook.[10]

What is extraordinary about Beckham is that while he sold numerous brands, including his various clubs, he also became the biggest brand in soccer history. Pelé, George Best, and Cristiano Ronaldo also branded themselves and were more complete players, but Beckham was the brand that beat them all.

Beckham used his marketing appeal in a way that could compare to no other soccer player in the history of the game. He was young, sexy, super fit, edgy (tattooed), a superb soccer star with the world's major clubs, a legendary English international, a family man with four children, and with a value-added wife who was a worldwide pop star herself. David Beckham's website cultivates his cool, sexy, alluring, and tattooed image.[11] In 2007, David Beckham joined the Los Angeles Galaxy in order to fully market the "Beckham brand" and sell soccer in North America. Beckham was humble and realistic about his new soccer adventure in the United States and won more admirers by stressing his love of soccer above profits:

> I'm coming there not to be a superstar. I'm coming there to be part of the team, to work hard and to hopefully win things. With me, it's about football. I'm coming there to make a difference. I'm coming there to play football. . . . I'm not saying me coming over to the States is going to make soccer the biggest sport in America. That would be difficult to achieve. Baseball, basketball, American football, they've been around. But I wouldn't be doing this if I didn't think I could make a difference.[12]

Beckham was awarded generously by the Los Angeles Galaxy, becoming the highest-paid player in league history. If we combine Beckham's earnings with those of Victoria Beckham, his wife, the couple's joint wealth in 2009 was estimated at £125 million (US$201 million).[13] Yet, his yearly salary with the Galaxy was estimated to be US$6.5 million and his net worth in 2011 was an absurd US$219 million.[14] The lowest Galaxy salary for a player was a mere US$11,000, what Beckham might earn in a day.[15] In 2012, at the age of thirty-seven and beyond his prime, he was pursued by French club Paris Saint-Germain. He signed with the French club and helped them win the French first division title in 2013.

Cristiano Ronaldo — CR7

Born Cristiano Ronaldo dos Santos Aveiro on February 5, 1985, in Funchal (the capital city of the island of Madeira), Portugal, Ronaldo is a contemporary Portuguese international who is one of the most talented players in the game today. He began his youth career with Andorinha and later Nacional, both Funchal-based teams, in the early 1990s. He is a sensational dribbler, a free kick master, and a player that terrorizes defenses with his dashing runs. Ronaldo is also a near equal to Beckham in branding himself and selling soccer: clubs, jerseys, tickets, products, advertisement, and the game.[16]

Ronaldo's professional career began modestly with Lisbon-based Sporting CP, where he scored three goals in twenty-five games in the 2002–2003 season. At Manchester United from 2003 to 2009, Ronaldo was transformed into a superstar on the field and marketing icon off the pitch. For Manchester United, he scored eighty-four goals in 196 matches. His boss Alex Ferguson dubbed him the best player in the world. He won three league titles, one FA Cup, a Champions League trophy, and a World Club championship with the Manchester club.

Since joining Real Madrid in 2009, Ronaldo has been a scoring sensation. He holds records for most goals scored in a season for Real Madrid, for being the first top European league player to reach forty goals in a single season in two consecutive years, for the fastest Real Madrid player to reach 100 league goals, and the first player ever to score against every team in a single season in the Spanish first division (La Liga).[17] As of September 2013, Ronaldo had scored 148 goals in 139 matches for Real Madrid. This outlandish strike rate is better than any player in the game. With Real Madrid, he has won one La Liga title, a Spanish Cup, and a Spanish Super Cup title.

With Manchester United he won eight trophies, and with Real Madrid another three. Ronaldo is the only player to have won the European Golden Shoe in two different leagues (English Premier League and Spanish La Liga). With his current club, Real Madrid, Cristiano Ronaldo has scored the most goals in a single season in all competitions (sixty), the most in one La Liga season (forty-six), and has already surpassed 300 club goals. Cristiano Ronaldo is the only player among Real Madrid's top league goal scorers who averages more than a goal per match (1.09). Playing for Real Madrid, he also has the record for most Champions League goals in a single season (twelve) and most hat tricks in a season (seven).

Ronaldo won the European Golden Shoe for highest goalscorer in 2008 and 2011. In 2008, he won the World Soccer Player of the Year award. He also led Portugal to a fourth place finish in the 2006 World Cup, and runner-up and bronze finishes at the European Championship in 2004 and 2012, respectively. He has scored thirty-nine goals for Portugal and made over 100 appearances for his country since his debut in 2003.

It is interesting to note that Ronaldo makes countless others goals for country and club through his guile, tremendous pace, and delicate passing abilities. The Manchester United and later Real Madrid star was honored for his skills. He won the prestigious *Ballon d'Or* in 2008 and 2013 and finished second in voting for the same award in 2007, 2009, and 2011.

Like Beckham, Ronaldo is rich. Through soccer and promotional model-ing, Ronaldo had a net worth of US$150 million in 2012.[18] In 2012, Ronaldo had the second-highest soccer salary in any league with US$20 million annu-ally, including bonuses (behind Cameroonian striker Samuel Eto'o who played for the Russian team Anzhi Makhachkala).[19] In 2009, Ronaldo be-came the most expensive soccer player in history after moving from Man-chester United to Real Madrid, in a transfer worth US$131.6 million.[20] Like the retired English star, Ronaldo is a marketing dream. He is the second soccer player when it comes to endorsement earnings, trailing only David Beckham.[21] In 2013, Ronaldo officially launched his new underwear range, CR7, in spectacular fashion: a nineteen-meter-tall campaign image featuring the winger modeling his new underwear suspended above Madrid's *Palacio de Cibeles* in the building's renaissance courtyard.[22] After seeing the launch of Ronaldo's new underwear line, one writer suggested that Ronaldo is the new Beckham:

> He filled the vacant spot left by Madrid bound David Beckham when he signed for Manchester United in 2003—but it would seem the similarities between the two footballers don't stop there.
>
> Indeed, the Portuguese winger has enjoyed a career comparable to the former England skipper, having followed him to the Bernabeu—albeit two-years after Beckham swapped Spain for Southern California and Los Angeles Galaxy.
>
> Like Becks, the moisturized midfielder has also developed separate inter-ests away from the pitch—and he was on hand to launch his latest at Madrid's Palacio de Cibeles on Thursday.[23]

MARKETING SOCCER

In the following section, I examine the phenomena of "marketing national-ism," the World Cup as a marketing dream, brand soccer stars such as David Beckham and Cristiano Ronaldo, and other number 7s with marketing ap-peal. From these examples, I argue that soccer is more than a game. Profes-sional soccer today provides unprecedented business and marketing opportu-nities for FIFA, national teams, major clubs, corporations, advertisers, ana-lysts, writers, journalists, and soccer players.

FIFA, the world's governing soccer body, was created in 1904. What distinguishes FIFA's structure from the United Nations is that it recognizes federations or nations rather than sovereign states. Based in Zurich, Switzer-land, today FIFA has 209 national associations under its ambit. In short, FIFA has more members than the United Nations, which currently has 191 member states. As former UN secretary-general Kofi Annan argued, world soccer led by FIFA is "the only truly global game, played in every country by every race and religion, it is one of the few phenomena as universal as the United Nations."[24]

As a result of FIFA's democratizing criteria for entrance into the organization, Northern Mariana Islands, Chinese Taipei (Taiwan), Hong Kong, Guam, Macau, and Palestine are all members of the Asian Soccer Confederation under FIFA's control. Yet none of these aforementioned "nations" are sovereign states recognized by the international community. Similarly, although they are not sovereign states, Réunion and Zanzibar are members of FIFA's African Soccer Confederation. Guadeloupe, Martinique, the U.S. Virgin Islands, Turks and Caicos Islands, and Puerto Rico are not sovereign states, yet all are members of FIFA's CONCACAF federation representing North America, Central America, and the Caribbean. New Caledonia, Tahiti, and the Cook Islands are part of FIFA's Oceania Soccer Confederation, although they are not independent states. Northern Ireland, Scotland, Wales, England, Gibraltar, and Faroe Islands are all members of the UEFA federation, although the Faroe Islands belong to Denmark and the five remaining are part of Great Britain.

Moreover, recall that in chapter 5 I examined soccer as a secular religion. There is a Vatican City national soccer team (*Selezione di calcio della Città del Vaticano*) that represents Vatican City. In this case, a secular faith intersects with an established religion and theocratic state. Yet the Vatican is one of only eight fully recognized sovereign states whose national team is not a FIFA member. The others are Monaco and Pacific micro-states Tuvalu, Kiribati, the Federated States of Micronesia, Nauru, Marshall Islands, and Palau.

Why are there more FIFA members than sovereign states? I argue that FIFA's democratizing criteria for membership is a practical business and marketing strategy designed to expand the growth of the global game and enhance the profits of the Swiss-based organization. FIFA controls six regional soccer confederations (Europe, Africa, Asia, Oceania, and two in the Americas) that it allows a degree of autonomy in day-to-day operations. Yet it is clear that FIFA's structure means that all six regional federations must respond to the dictates of FIFA's head office and its president Sepp Blatter.

FIFA's aforementioned regional structure allows the organization "to operate like a transnational business."[25] Each of the 209 FIFA members must pay the organization an annual fee. In addition, each international match that is played by any of the 209 members (including friendlies, tournaments, World Cup qualifying games, World Cup matches, Olympic Games matches, etc.) means that the participating "nations" or members must pay FIFA. In order for us to appreciate the business and marketing savvy of FIFA, here is a startling statistic. If FIFA was a sovereign state in 2006, it would have been the nineteenth biggest economy in the world with a gross domestic product of more than US$500,000 billion.[26] This extraordinary economic output would allow FIFA to join the G-20, the organization consisting of the world's twenty most powerful countries. Switzerland, the home of FIFA and a country with no shabby economy, has GDP roughly equal to that of FIFA.

Dejan Stanković, an Inter Milan midfielder from 2004 until 2013 and a Red Star Belgrade hero in the 1990s, is a good example of FIFA's strategy of "marketing nationalism." The Belgrade-born midfielder played in the 1998 World Cup for the Federal Republic of Yugoslavia, while numerous republics from Slovenia and Croatia to Bosnia-Herzegovina had already become independent nations. At the 2006 World Cup, Stanković played for Serbia and Montenegro. Montenegro is now an independent country since its referendum in 2006. Finally, at the 2010 World Cup Stanković played for Serbia and one year later retired from international soccer. Stanković thus became the first ever soccer player to represent three national teams in three different World Cups. The point is that in recognizing nations, irrespective of the unique political circumstances of a country or region, FIFA is using nationalism as a tool for building national brands and selling soccer.

FIFA's official slogan is "For the Game, For the World." This slogan might be true, but it masks FIFA's business and marketing bottom lines. The 209 federations are there to generate an important source of revenue for FIFA each year and give the world the positive impression that soccer is more democratic than the realm of international politics and nation-states. English, French, German, and Spanish are FIFA's official languages, thus cementing FIFA's global appeal in many nations. In addition, FIFA owns various companies that generate revenues through marketing, sponsors, and the sales of products. These companies include the following: FIFA Marketing and TV SA based in Switzerland, which exploits soccer marketing opportunities worldwide; FIFA Marketing Germany GmbH; Hitzigweg SA (Switzerland) for real estate services; FIFA Travel GmbH Zurich for travel agency services; FIFA Ireland Ltd. for an array of services; FIFA Media SA Zurich; and Footfin SA (Soccer Finance) (Switzerland).[27]

FIFA's business model, which is based on more federations than sovereign states and global marketing campaigns through a network of allied companies, allows it to engage in what one writer calls "opportunistic nationalism."[28] In chapter 1, I demonstrated how soccer is a site of contestation with respect to differing discourses of national identity. Soccer stars such as Chilavert, Buffon, or Zidane gave of themselves for the national cause through international soccer matches, although some of their compatriots in civil society question their politics or origins and thus their "fitness" to represent the national team. Within the civil societies of different national teams, there are different views of who should play for the national team and what soccer means to the nation. The multi-ethnic nature of the U.S. national soccer team is not the rule in all countries around the world. Given FIFA's political and economic control of global soccer, some fans see FIFA's legitimization of 209 soccer federations and the sponsoring of World Cup contests as part of an "opportunistic nationalism." For these fans and critics, FIFA cares little about Palestine, Gibraltar, or Guadeloupe, but is interested in the marketing potential and revenue base associated with structuring soccer along nationalistic lines. In short, Scotland versus England, Serbia versus Croatia, Iran versus the United States, or perhaps one day Israel versus Palestine, sells for FIFA.

Moreover, with the rise of a global soccer market, commercial necessities, greater migration flows, and the influence of major global club sides, foreigners are quickly supplanting local talent and cost far more than locals. This is particularly true with the major European clubs after the Bosman ruling (named after Belgian player Jean-Marc Bosman) by the European court of Justice in 1995, which gave all European Union (EU) citizens the ability to work and play within any nation in the EU without being considered a foreigner. Major club sides in Europe such as Chelsea, Manchester United, or AC Milan often have more foreign players than local, national talent. Even once-obscure leagues like Cyprus are now flooded with EU nationals from outside Cyprus who do not count as foreigners, as well as foreigners from outside of the EU.

The upshot is that FIFA controls all world soccer contests at the club, national, and international levels. On the one hand, FIFA exploits this "opportunistic nationalism" through the presence of 209 "nations" or federations, which generates nationalist sentiments and adds historical drama to some of the matches. Yet FIFA understands the marketing and revenue potentials of global soccer in which players are sold to clubs at alarming rates, irrespective of their nationality and largely in the interest of profits for the clubs, players, and ultimately FIFA.

The World Cup is also a marketing dream for FIFA and a variety of corporations and organizations. The first soccer World Cup was held in Uruguay in 1930. The World Cup began with merely thirteen nations. In the World Cups between 1934 and 1978, sixteen teams competed in each tournament. There were no World Cups during World War II, and there were two exceptions to the sixteen-team rule inaugurated in 1934. In 1938, Germany had completed its *Anschluss* with Austria as a result of Nazi expansionist aggression, and after qualifying matches, Austria was absorbed into Germany, thus leaving the 1938 World Cup tournament with fifteen teams. In the 1950 edition of the tournament in Brazil, the first one after World War II, India, Scotland, and Turkey withdrew, thus leaving the tournament with thirteen teams.[29] At the World Cup in Spain in 1982, the tournament expanded to twenty-four nations. By the 1998 World Cup in France, the tournament had expanded to thirty-two teams. This move to thirty-two teams was designed to expand the number of African, Asian, and North and Central American nations, as well as to increase the business growth of soccer beyond its traditional frontiers in Europe and South America. As a result, billions of fans around the world, even if they are not major soccer fans, watch the World Cup tournaments at least every four years. This even applies to countries such as the United States where soccer still languishes in relative "cultural marginality," although this is changing with the rise of global soccer clubs and fans, the "Beckham effect," the growing influence of the Latino communities, the rise of a professional soccer league (MLS), and the success of the national women's team and its global superstars such as Mia Hamm and Christie Rampone.[30]

It is rather interesting that all the winners in the history of the World Cup have come from Europe or South America: Brazil (5), Italy (4), Germany (3), Argentina (2), Uruguay (2), England (1), France (1), and Spain (1). Countries outside of Europe or South America have rarely been able to progress to the quarterfinals of World Cup tournaments. Since the tournament expanded to thirty-two teams, countries outside of Europe and South America have attained more success. Mexico reached the quarterfinals on home soil in 1986; Cameroon gained a quarterfinal berth in 1990; Korea Republic finished fourth in 2002; both the USA and Senegal reached the quarterfinals in 2002; and Ghana was a quarterfinalist in 2010. In 1930, before the 1998 World Cup and the expansion to thirty-two teams, the United States finished the tournament in third place. At the 2002 World Cup in Japan and South Korea, Turkey and South Korea finished third and fourth, respectively.

Teams from former Communist Eastern and Central Europe have fared much better in World Cup contests. Czechoslovakia (1934 and 1962) and Hungary (1938 and 1954) finished as runners-up twice each, Poland (1974 and 1982) garnered third place twice, Croatia placed third in 1998, and the Soviet Union (1966), Yugoslavia (1930 and 1962), and Bulgaria (1994) each finished in fourth place.

If we think of nations that have won the World Cup or finished in the top four, we realize that soccer still has a lot of growth potential in countries such as China, India, and South Africa. Few nations outside of Europe, South America, or North America (Mexico twice and the United States once) hosted the World Cup. In 2010, the first World Cup was hosted in Africa by South Africa. Only five World Cups have been hosted outside of Europe or South America: South Africa (2010), South Korea and Japan (co-hosts) in 2002, the United States (1994), and Mexico (1986 and 1970). Qatar will host the 2022 World Cup. This will mean that Asia will only host its second World Cup in 2022. Thus, officials with FIFA see great business growth and marketing potential in Africa, Asia, and even North America, Central America, and the Caribbean.

World Cup attendance figures averaged about 24,000 fans per game at the 1930 World Cup in Uruguay and reached a high of more than 68,000 fans per match at the 1994 World Cup in the United States. About 50,000 fans per match attended the last two World Cups in Germany and South Africa. The last three World Cups before South Africa and Germany with more than 50,000 fans were in England in 1966 (51,000), Mexico in 1970 (50,000), and the United States in 1994 (68,000). The lowest average attendance was when Italy won the World Cup in 1934 with about 21,000 fans per match. These figures also suggest that attendance growth is possible at World Cups in Brazil (2014), Russia (2018), and Qatar (2022). The choice of tiny Qatar to host the 2022 World Cup surely raised eyebrows around the globe but has a lot to do with allowing FIFA to expand its market share in Asia.

The World Cup is today the world's most widely viewed sporting event on television, with an estimated 715.1 million people in 214 territories and countries watching the final match of the 2006 World Cup in Germany between France and Italy.[31] Despite the hosting of the 2002 World Cup in Asia with its major time differences, an accumulated audience of a whopping 30 billion watched the tournament.[32] These types of numbers are heartwarming for FIFA, corporate sponsors, and advertisers.

The World Cup is a business and marketing bonanza for FIFA and its corporate sponsors. It is estimated that hosting a World Cup today makes FIFA the equivalent revenue of twelve Super Bowls and can provide 5,000 to 8,000 jobs for host cities.[33] FIFA's financial record is indeed healthy and robust, even during an economic downturn precipitated by the 2008 global financial crisis. In 2010, FIFA's financial statements indicated that its profits soared to US$1.1 billion.[34]

Corporations that sell and market soccer also look forward to the World Cup. The sales of Adidas products doubled as a result of the 2010 World Cup. "After the first ten days it is already clear that this World Cup will be a great success for Adidas. We will not only achieve our ambitious goals in football, we will over-achieve them. Our football business is growing worldwide. This underlines the global power this tournament has," insisted Herbert Hainer, a CEO of Adidas.[35] For Adidas the 2010 World Cup represented record sales of at least €1.5 billion in the soccer category, a 15 percent jump from 2008 and a 25 percent increase from the 2006 World Cup.[36] Sales are healthiest in Germany, Mexico, Argentina, and South Africa, with sales of one million units or more for each of those countries.

If Mexico does not qualify for the 2014 World Cup in Brazil, it will have severe economic repercussions, argues one marketing expert: "Rogelio Roa, commercial director of the sports marketing firm DreaMatch Solutions, says his company estimates that consumer brands and TV stations won't make about $600 million in selling products and services if Mexico stays home."[37] Thus, it was not without irony that when the United States defeated Panama 3–2 in injury time in the fall of 2013, it revived Mexican hopes for qualification by allowing them to enter the playoffs against New Zealand. It also led to a flurry of rare pro-America sentiments in Mexican newspapers and the press in general, including phrases such as "God Bless America" and "We

Love You." Mexican TV Azteca announcer Christian Martinoli fully captured this spirit after the United States scored a late equalizer against Panama:

> It is because of the USA that we are being placed in the playoff . . . BECAUSE
> OF THEM, NOT DUE TO YOU . . . NOT ANY OF YOU in the green
> shirts . . . IT WAS THEM!! NOT YOU! . . . THEY DID IT!!!!! NOT YOU!
> Remember this forever . . . KEEP THIS CLEARLY IN MIND FOR THE
> REST OF YOUR LIVES! You do NOTHING for the shirt, you do NOT put
> the effort, you have NOT placed us in the playoffs, you HAVE NOT placed us
> in the WORLD CUP . . . YOU WOULD NOT HAVE KEPT US ALIVE . . . IT
> WAS THE USA, NOT YOU! NOT YOU AND YOUR ARROGANCE/CON-
> CEIT . . . NOT YOU AND YOUR INFAMY . . . NOT YOU AND YOUR
> MORONS/PUNKS . . .
>
> IT IS A FAILURE . . . and UNDESERVED—to go through to the
> playoff—WE HAD NO ARGUMENTS to earn the playoffs, THE USA,
> WITH SUBS, WITH MANY SUBS as the visiting team shows us once again
> what the USA is all about . . . how to play the game with dignity, how to
> approach the sport . . . Mexico is a horror, just terrible . . . A FAILURE . . .
>
> THE USA HAS SURPASSED US . . . They are better than Mexico in
> SOCCER . . . THEY EVEN HAVE THE LUXURY OF PLAYING THEIR
> SUBS and KEEPING US LIVE . . . I hope our coach resigns . . . He has failed
> as a coach . . . [38]

Advertisers also make far more money from soccer World Cups than Olympic Games.[39] Deloitte's projected marketing revenue for FIFA between 2010
and 2014 stands at more than US$1.2 billion.[40] McDonald's Corp., Canon
Inc., Sony Corp., Coca-Cola Co., Continental, and Adidas pay large sums for
sponsorship to "broadcast their logos to billions of viewers across the globe
as well as stadium fans."[41] This creates a company presence, which helps to
generate sales and profits.

In addition, one author estimates that the World Cup host can be expected
to increase its GDP by an average of 4 percent as a result of hosting the
world's most popular sporting event.[42] The 1986 World Cup was to be held
in Colombia, but it was switched to Mexico. There are rumors that Nike
pressured FIFA to change the venue away from Colombia due its excessive
poverty and the violence of the "war on drugs," as well as because of its
desire to increase profits.[43] The World Cup in Mexico was one of the most
exciting in recent memory, with Diego Maradona of Argentina the indisputable star, and FIFA a winner as a result of having the World Cup in Mexico
instead of Colombia.

FIFA, soccer clubs, corporate sponsors, and many players also make
astronomical profits. Some soccer players are akin to brand names: David
Beckham, Cristiano Ronaldo, and Lionel Messi today, or Zinedine Zidane,

Ronaldinho, or Ronaldo in the 1990s and the beginning of the new millennium.

We do not typically think of professional soccer players as exploited, but most players are not brand stars such as Beckham and Cristiano Ronaldo. Alan G. Ingham explained the rise of brand sports stars and those that sell them by using Marxist language:

> Potential buys new, higher quality means of production. Eventually, we may exchange the products of our labor for a wage. Those who supply the means of production (sponsors, owners, organizations, associations, etc.) buy our potentials as labor power. They expect a return on investment. They sell us higher quality means of production (better facilities, uniforms, travel, etc.) only if our talents warrant it and only if the wages (and their investments in the means of production) are lower than the overall exchange-value. The cheapest payments are honorific (cups, medals, and other trophies). The more expensive are professional player contracts. But, the entire feeder system, from bottom to top, is overdetermined by the exchange-value creating capacities of labour—anticipated and real. Our commitment to produce at the Prolympic (the confluence of Olympic and Professional elite athletic systems) level renders us complicitous in our own and our parents' exploitation.[44]

Clubs make profits from the sale of players and in our age players are sold with extreme regularity. Paolo Maldini, who I covered in chapter 3, spent his entire career at AC Milan. This is a rarity in today's commercial-driven soccer. Steve Claridge (b. 1966), currently a commentator with BBC Sport, played at all levels of English professional and semi-professional soccer for nineteen different clubs and scored over 300 goals from 1983 to 2012. Paul Warhurst, who began his career with Manchester City, played for a whopping sixteen clubs. Christian Vieri, a former Italian international, played for thirteen clubs, including eight different clubs in seven seasons. His best performances were with Inter Milan, where he scored 103 goals in 143 appearances.

The Uruguayan striker Sebastián Abreu Gallo (b. 1976), who has represented Uruguay at two World Cups and is known as *El Loco* (The Madman), began the 2013–2014 season with Nacional in Uruguay and was loaned to Argentinean outfit Rosario Central. In a career that began with Montevideo-based Defensor in 1996, Abreu has played for more than twenty teams in seven different countries: Brazil, Uruguay, Mexico, Argentina, Greece, Israel, and Spain. He had eleven loan spells with different clubs around the world. His most prolific spells include the 2002–2003 loan spell with Mexican side Cruz Azul where he netted an impressive forty-six goals in fifty-two matches, as well as his twenty-four goals in fifty matches for Brazilian side Botafogo since 2010. Abreu scored the decisive penalty for Uruguay in the quarterfinals of the 2010 World Cup against Ghana in audacious Panenkastyle, thus taking Uruguay to the semi-finals of the World Cup for the first time since 1970. It was arguably the single greatest artistic moment of the 2010 World Cup in South Africa.

Another current journeyman is the Panamanian international striker Luis Tejada (b. 1982), known as *El Matador* (The Killer) for his impressive strike rate with various clubs and countries. His club side in 2013 was Mexico's Veracruz, his twelfth professional team in a career that began with Panamanian outfit Tauro FC in 2001 and has since taken him to Colombia, the United Arab Emirates, Peru, and Mexico.

In short, the regularity of player transfers and loans today nets clubs healthy profits and leads them to view soccer as a business rather than merely a game. Clubs do not consider the human impact of the transfers and loan spells on the players. Players might gain experience through loans, but they feel caught between their parent and new clubs. Writing in *The Guardian*, Richard Williams suggested an overhaul to the loan system in Britain:

> The whole business needs reforming, starting with a reconsideration of the rule allowing Football League clubs to borrow up to 10 players at any time and to play five of them in a single match. These numbers are too great. Supporters do not care who gets the promotion but, when times are bad, how can they be expected to maintain a deep and consoling affinity for a side stuffed with players who are, after all, only waiting for the call to return to their five-star lives in the Premier League?[45]

Forbes list of the twenty richest soccer clubs demonstrates the tremendous economic pull of the major European teams. The clubs on the list are all European. Italy's Napoli is listed at number twenty with $167 million in revenue. Manchester United is the richest club, with $532 million in revenue and the club is valued at $2.23 billion.[46] The other richest clubs in terms of their value include: Real Madrid ($1.88 billion), Barcelona ($1.33 billion), Arsenal ($1.29 billion), Bayern Munich ($1.23 billion), AC Milan ($989 million), Chelsea ($761 million), Liverpool ($619 million), Juventus ($591 million), and Schalke 04 ($587 million). Manchester City, the winners of the English Premier League title in 2011–2012, is valued at $443 million. Olympique Lyonnais and Olympique Marseille are the only two French clubs on the list, valued at $385 million and $359 million, respectively. The top twenty richest clubs are from only five countries: England (6), Italy (5), Germany (4) Spain (3), and France (2).

Very few players belong to wealthy clubs and thus benefit from belonging to the richest clubs in the world. The millennium opened with the highest transaction in the history of soccer when Real Madrid paid Juventus of Turin a whopping US$73 million for the services of French midfield genius Zinedine Zidane.[47] In 2013, the Uruguayan international striker Edinson Cavani was transferred from Italian club Napoli to Paris Saint-Germain for a whopping €64 million (US$85 million).[48] The Cavani signing surpassed another record transfer in the same year: Colombian international Radamel Falcao's €60 million (US$80 million) move from Atlético de Madrid to Monaco. Topping all player transfers in soccer history is the Welsh international Gareth Bale. When he moved from Tottenham Hotspur to Real Madrid in 2013, the Spanish media reported a transfer fee of €91 million (US$121 million), while the English press insisted that there was a world record transfer fee of €101 million (US$135 million).[49] If the latter figure is correct, Bale's transfer shatters Cristiano Ronaldo's old transfer record fee of €94 million (US$125 million) from Manchester United to Real Madrid.

Portugal's Cristiano Ronaldo, discussed earlier in this chapter, topped Zidane when he became the most expensive soccer player in history after moving from Manchester United to Real Madrid.[50] In addition, his contract with Real Madrid pays him €12 million (US$16 million) per year, making him one of the highest-paid players in the world.[51] In 2010, *France Football* put Ronaldo at third in a list of the world's best-paid soccer players.[52] Only David Beckham and Lionel Messi topped Ronaldo. In 2011, Messi earned a combined salary both on and off the field of €33 million (US$44 million), Beckham €31.5 million (US$42.1 million), and Ronaldo €29.2 million (US$39 million).[53]

The Portuguese international and the FIFA World Player of the Year in 1998 has so far rewarded Real Madrid handsomely, netting, at the time of writing in 2013, more than one goal per game for the Spanish club. His eighty-four goals with Manchester United from 2003 to 2009 and his breathtaking performances on the pitch earned twenty-two-year-old Ronaldo plaudits from a retired Dutch master, Johan Cruyff, who insisted the Portuguese winger was the best player in the history of Manchester United: "Ronaldo is better than George Best and Denis Law, who were two brilliant and great players in the history of United."[54] Ronaldo's former Manchester United manager Alex Ferguson, whom Ronaldo called "my father in sport," went further than Cruyff in 2009: "I have nothing but praise for the boy. He is easily the best player in the world. He is better than Kaká and better than Messi. He is streets ahead of them all. His contribution as a goal threat is unbelievable. His stats are incredible. Strikes at goal, attempts on goal, raids into the penalty box, headers. It is all there. Absolutely astounding."[55] In his autobiography, Ferguson insisted that Ronaldo was the most gifted player he ever managed, with only Paul Scholes and Ryan Giggs coming close in skill and determination.[56] In short, club sides have paid handsomely for Ronaldo, but he scores at an alarming rate that far surpasses Beckham, Messi (as of 2013, Messi scored 214 goals in 246 matches for Barcelona), Neymar, or any other contemporary soccer player.

Ronaldo already has an autobiography entitled *Moments* (2007). David Beckham penned *David Beckham: My Side* (2002) and two co-authored works with Dean Freeman and Tom Watt, respectively, entitled *Beckham: My World* (2001) and *Beckham: Both Feet on the Ground* (2003). These autobiographies help to promote the marketing cults of Ronaldo and Beckham.

The business ventures of Ronaldo are indeed extensive. Ronaldo opened two boutique shops in Portugal called CR7, named after his initials and shirt number. A YouTube video entitled "The CR7 Shop" shows Ronaldo modeling some of the high-priced fashion accessories of his boutique.[57] His official website, www.cristianoronaldoofficial.com, features the Portuguese international in the national kit sponsored by Nike. Ronaldo is posing as if he is ready for a match: proud, trim, and fit, and a menacing figure for defenses around the world. Ronaldo features prominently in Nike television advertisements. In December 2011, Cristiano Ronaldo, in conjunction with developer RockLive, launched an iPhone game called Heads Up with Cristiano. In 2012, Ronaldo worked with Castrol Edge in a live-streamed soccer challenge with fans. In 2013, Ronaldo became the public face of Pro Evolution Soccer 2013. At 10 million Facebook fans, Ronaldo is a worldwide icon on social media. According to *Forbes* (2012), Ronaldo had the fifth-highest social rank in social media in the world in 2012, with only Lady Gaga, Rihanna, Justin Bieber, and Katy Perry topping the Portuguese soccer star.[58]

If it was not for Lionel Messi (arguably the world's best player today), Cristiano Ronaldo would have won more personal trophies than (and his marketing thrust might have surpassed) Beckham. Furthermore, Renaldo's personality is at times a marketing hindrance, and he is perceived as more serious, a complainer, and more of a lady's man than David Beckham. Ronaldo is undoubtedly one of the most scintillating, exciting, and lethal players the world has ever seen. The Portuguese coach of Chelsea, José Mourinho, laments Cristiano Ronaldo's unfair treatment compared to Messi:

> If Messi is the best on the planet, Ronaldo is the best in the universe. If you are going to give out the *Ballon d'Or* because a player is the best, give it to Cristiano or Messi. But I ask: if the two are on the same level, is it normal that one wins four and the other one? It is not.[59]

While Cristiano Ronaldo did not do a shabby job of marketing himself and was clearly a more productive soccer player in terms of goal totals than Beckham or even Messi, Beckham could out brand them all. In 2012, one year before his retirement, David Beckham was the top-ranked soccer player, at thirty-two in the *Forbes* list of the World's Most Popular Celebrities.[60] He was in thirty-fifth place in earnings, forty-fourth spot in television and radio popularity, seventeenth highest in the press, sixth in the social ranking category, and twenty-sixth in terms of web presence.

In a piece entitled "Beckham the worldwide brand," Simon Moon writes that the English superstar is "as instantly recognisable as that of multinational companies like Coca-Cola and IBM."[61] His £116,000-a-week (US$186,500) salary at Real Madrid was "small change compared to the £17m-plus [US$27 million] he earns every year from the likes of mobile phone giant Vodafone and Gillette whose products he promotes."[62] "David Beckham is a sports marketer's dream—talented, photogenic and with a pop-star wife. He is the England captain, arguably England's most gifted player and almost certainly the world's most famous footballer," insisted Alex Chapman, a partner at London firm Briffa.[63]

Beckham and "Spice Girl" Victoria Beckham became fashion icons and his wife clearly helped his off-field marketing and business ventures. The two became spokespeople for major clothing designers, health and fitness specialists, fashion magazines, perfume and cosmetics manufacturers, hair stylists, exercise promoters, and spa and recreation companies. Beckham appeared on the cover of *Details* and his wife in *W*. David Beckham Instinct is a fragrance line that the English star promoted. He has a marketing collaboration agreement with Pepsi. His clean, sexy, extremely well-groomed image and appeal to gay and straight people alike earned Beckham the title of world's most famous "metrosexual" by the man who invented the term.[64] Mark Simpson joked about Beckham as a metrosexual: "He's well dressed, narcissistic and obsessed with butts. But don't call him gay."[65]

Beckham increased the appeal of the "Beckham brand" when he visited British soldiers in Afghanistan in 2010. His charity work has also earned him marketing appeal, including being a UNICEF Goodwill Ambassador, a patron of the Elton John AIDS Foundation, a spokesman for Malaria No More, and in conjunction with other MLS stars, teaching life skills to disadvantaged youth in Harlem. Films such as *Bend It Like Beckham* (2002) and the trilogy *Goal!: The Dream Begins* further promoted the marketing success of Beckham. Even his tattoos can be viewed as an art collage, which helps to add to the Beckham mystique and market the "Beckham brand." One of his tattoos is a giant winged cross on his neck and another is a Bible verse written in Hebrew.[66]

As "The David Beckham Brand," a marketing case study, made clear, the English star was a global marketing icon:

> David Beckham was one of the most popular soccer stars in the late 1990s and the early 21st century. His amazing ability to score from free kicks coupled with his good looks earned him a lot of admirers in Europe and Asia. He was also one of the most sought after celebrities to endorse products and a number of important companies vied to sign him on for endorsements.
>
> Born of middle class parents, David Beckham was obsessed with football from his childhood and always dreamed of playing professionally. He was

signed up by Manchester United, one of the most popular football clubs in
Europe, first as a trainee and later, as a full-fledged member of the club. [67]

Beckham quickly made a name for himself, with his signature free kicks
where he had the ability to curve the ball in the air toward the goal, mislead-
ing defenders and goalkeepers. Beckham and his wife, "Spice Girl" Victoria
Adams, were fashion icons in the United Kingdom and merited a lot of
tabloid coverage. They were also sought-after endorsers of a number of
products.

Beckham was roundly praised for his marketing acumen both inside and
outside the soccer world. Emilio Butragueño, a Real Madrid official, former
Spanish international, and legendary Real Madrid star, said this about Beckham's marketing impact in 2003: "Right now he is one of the most important
players in the world in terms of marketing. . . . Beckham is an icon."[68] "The
brand is exceptional and the potential is enormous. No other sports star has
the brand placing or personality of Beckham," wrote John Williamson of
Wolff Olins.[69] The sports analyst at Field Fisher Waterhouse, Michael Ster-
ling, said this about the former English international: "He's a sponsor's
dream: a fashion icon, associated with success, a family man. Because of
Beckham, football is no longer just about football, but about character and
personality."[70]

When he played, the "Beckham brand" transcended national borders.
Cristiano Ronaldo and Lionel Messi are global stars that sell the Real Madrid
and Barcelona brands to a global audience of billions of soccer fans. The
soccer superstars also sell brand names such as Nike or Adidas and they are
themselves branded by marketing companies with a truly global reach. Wied-
en and Kennedy, the marketing company that created Nike's global soccer
campaigns, can be credited for turning superstar soccer players into brands. It
was back in 1985 with a television advertisement that Nike turned a basketball star, Michael Jordan of the Chicago Bulls, into a player brand. As a
result of the branding of major soccer players and big clubs, you can travel
from Hong Kong to Accra and Milan to Toronto and you will see the same
jerseys of marquee players and major clubs. It was thus no accident that as
the 2006 World Cup began in Germany, Nike's advertisement slogan was
distinctly designed to sell soccer products by capitalizing on populist, anti-
government sentiments: "Leave the discussions to the politicians, it's the
year of the World Cup."

Aside from Beckham and Cristiano Ronaldo, my other possible number 7
choice was George Best (1946–2005). He was a real showman on the pitch,
repeatedly terrorizing defenders, nutmegging (putting a ball through a
player's legs) players with regularity, and scoring audacious goals through
sheer dribbling genius. There was perhaps no more entertaining player to
watch in his day than Best. Yet Best was afflicted by the vices of drinking

and womanizing. He admitted to have wasted 90 percent of his earnings on alcohol and women.[71] Best insisted that in 1969 he "gave up women and alcohol, and it was the worst twenty minutes of my life."[72]

Best was one of the earliest soccer pop icons with Manchester United in the 1960s. David Beckham and later Cristiano Ronaldo would take that pop icon status to another level in the 1990s and new millennium. Best was the Beckham or Ronaldo of his day, with no less than six autobiographies about him. He advertised sausages on television, made television and film appearances, and was featured in fashion magazine *GQ* as one of the fifty sexiest men.[73] George Best was such a legend that Belfast's international airport is named after the Northern Ireland international—George Best Belfast City airport. When he won the European Cup with Manchester United in 1968, he also won the prestigious European Player of the Year award. He is undoubtedly the greatest Northern Irish international of all time. In a career that spanned from 1963 to 1984, with stops at Manchester United, the Jewish Guild (South Africa), several NASL clubs, Fulham, Cork Celtic, and Brisbane Lions, among other clubs, Best scored 208 goals in nearly 600 matches. He added nine goals in thirty-seven matches for Northern Ireland, but never appeared in a World Cup. Yet Best was a brilliant player with Manchester United, where he was the club's leading scorer for six consecutive seasons, and was the First Division's highest scorer in the 1967–1968 season.

Like Best, Wynton Rufer (b. 1962) was right-winger or striker, wearing the number 7 for New Zealand's national team and the number 11 shirt for Werder Bremen. Born to a Swiss father and a mother of Maori descent in Wellington, Rufer is the greatest player in the history of New Zealand and the Oceania Soccer Confederation. Rufer was the Oceania Player of the Century and a three-time winner of the Oceania Footballer of the Year. He opened the door for many players in his region by performing admirably for European club sides Grasshoper Club-Zurich (Switzerland) and Werder Bremen (Germany). He helped Bremen win six domestic titles from 1989 until 1995 and scored fifty-nine goals in 174 matches for the German club. The 1992–1993 season was especially propitious for Rufer, when he scored seventeen goals for Werder Bremen as the club won its third championship in its history. He scored in the 1993 finals of the Cup Winners' Cup when Bremen defeated Monaco 2–0. In the UEFA Champions League season of 1993, he finished joint top scorer in the competition. Rufer also played in the 1982 World Cup for New Zealand. By the time he retired in his native New Zealand with club side Kingz in 2002, Rufer had amassed 224 goals in 539 club appearances in New Zealand, Switzerland, Germany, and Japan. His career began with New Zealand side Stop Out in 1980, meaning that he played professional soccer for an incredible twenty-two years! He was almost forty when he retired.

For New Zealand's national team, known as the "All Whites," Rufer scored twelve goals in twenty-three appearances from 1980 until 1997. He did not appear more times for his country because clubs like Zurich refused to release him for international duty, highlighting the importance of players' health for the business of professional clubs. At the age of seventeen, Rufer had already scored for New Zealand in World Cup qualifying. He scored the winner against China one year later, which allowed New Zealand to qualify for the 1982 World Cup in Spain for the first time in its history. He was only nineteen at the 1982 World Cup and played in all three first-round matches, the losses against Brazil, the Soviet Union, and Scotland. For all his soccer accomplishments, Rufer was awarded the prestigious New Zealand Order of Merit.

Rufer was fast, fit, technically gifted, and a lethal finisher. He stayed healthy long enough to have a very long and illustrious career. He would take his penalty kicks with the ease of a Sunday afternoon stroll in the park. Give him a few inches and Rufer could go around you in a flash. He was a true professional, a gifted winger, and a New Zealand legend. It is fitting that today Rufer is attempting to create the soccer stars of tomorrow. He now runs the Wynton Rufer Soccer School of Excellence in various cities in New Zealand, Germany, and Japan.[74] In short, the marketing of soccer stars continues long after they have ended their careers.

* * *

In conclusion, David Beckham and Cristiano Ronaldo are truly representative of the growth of modern soccer as a business and its global marketing appeal. The game brands star players such as David Beckham, Cristiano Ronaldo, and Lionel Messi. Beckham's marketing impact in North America was so great that the "Beckham effect" is named after him, namely, the ability to lure major soccer stars to once obscure domestic leagues around the world. I coined the term the "Raúl effect" with respect to brand soccer stars marketing obscure soccer leagues in Asia, playing on the term the "Beckham effect." A former Real Madrid legend, Raúl plays for Qatar Stars League club Al Sadd since 2012. Christian Benítez, the talented Ecuadorian international, played for El Jaish SC in the Qatar Stars League shortly before he died of peritonitis in 2013. As the commercialization of the game grows, brands connote "an integrated approach to marketing and business strategy and applied to a specific logo or brand" and they can even be found among left-wing and anarchist supporters' groups (for example, Beşiktaş Çarşı from Istanbul) selling their t-shirts, lighters, and mugs emblazoned with the popular, anti-capitalist logo of the movement.[75]

In addition, it is statistically proven that buying such high-priced stars with talent allows major clubs to win domestic and international championships as "the ball does not go in by chance."[76] Or, to quote one rabid Mexican soccer fan, "Soccer is a science"[77] and the richest clubs are the "scientists" of success through their profits and titles. World Cup contests are tools designed to expand business and marketing opportunities for FIFA, companies, and national teams beyond the traditional soccer markets in Europe and South America.

Moreover, although most hard-core nationalists would like us to believe that we should die on and off the pitch for the nation, FIFA views nationalism in pragmatic terms as a strategy designed to improve its image, market professional soccer, and generate profits. Finally, recall the discussion in chapter 3 about the role of "spin merchants" in promoting ideological hegemony. The "spin masters" include soccer's public relations, media relations, advertising, and marketing specialists. Ingham argued that the role of "spin merchants" is to "dream up euphoric rites/rituals to reaffirm the moral authority of liberal democratic societies as the capitalist classes and the functionaries of the State have envisioned it on their terms."[78]

Chapter Eight

Leading by Example

Soccer as a Leadership Opportunity

Lesson eight is about soccer as a leadership opportunity. This chapter highlights new leadership insights, which break down the static conception between leaders and followers, to argue that soccer is a leadership opportunity for all of us. In soccer, it's irrelevant whether we are young or old, men or women, or players, coaches, administrators, or fans. Soccer is a terrain to exercise our leadership skills, whether we are amateurs or professionals; whether we are in official positions of leadership, or far from official leadership roles. Winning and losing mirrors the high and lows associated with life and also provides us with excellent leadership opportunities.

Soccer's leadership opportunities apply to people of all ages, nations, cultures, faiths, genders, or sexual orientations. These leadership opportunities are available to players at the amateur and professional levels, FIFA administrators, officials leading national federations, coaches, referees, managers, journalists, and even companies and advertisers connected to soccer. From soccer's ups and downs, from winning and losing to injuries and personal adversities, we can learn leadership qualities that will allow us to grow as individuals. Jorge Valdano, a winner of the 1986 World Cup with Argentina and the former General Manager of Real Madrid, argues that soccer is akin to a "school of life," offering us countless leadership opportunities and lessons for self-improvement.[1] Individual leadership and growth also allows organizations associated with the game to change for the good of the game and for the benefit of all those associated with soccer.

All this begs the question: What is leadership? From the leadership courses I taught in Toronto, here are eleven key lessons with respect to leadership:

1. Leadership is about attitude, your attitude in any given moment of life, in a life that is transitory.
2. Leadership is about rolling up your sleeves, working hard, and maintaining discipline in pursuit of your goals.
3. Leadership applies to both so-called leaders and non-leaders. It does not matter what you do in life, whether you are Clint Dempsey, Xavi, Steven Gerrard, President Barack Obama, a pastry chef, a student, a community leader, or a recently unemployed worker due to the financial crisis or economic downturn. Take your life as a leadership opportunity to improve yourself, your skills, your interpersonal relationships, and your attitude.
4. Leaders can come from anywhere: the top, the middle, or the bottom of the social pyramid.
5. Leaders speak truthfully and honestly to people with or without power.
6. Leaders are made, not born, through their hard work, willpower, and through active participation in the communities around them.
7. Leaders are ethical. It is not true that you need to lie, cheat, be corrupt, and stab others in the back in order to achieve important positions of power.
8. Leaders have a grand vision for how to improve themselves and their communities.
9. Leaders do not merely talk. They listen.
10. Leaders make decisions based on input from the bottom, middle, and top.
11. Leaders admit when they are wrong and take steps to improve themselves and their communities.

We also can enhance our leadership insights by determining what leadership experts say about leadership. Today leadership is a burgeoning industry. There are leadership associations, research centers, and training courses around the world. There are leadership B.A., M.A., and Ph.D. programs, particularly in the United States and Britain. Leadership insights are said to be applicable for businesses, human resources departments, management studies, politics, sports, philosophy, ethics, education, and numerous other realms of existence. There are leadership journals and leadership experts. In short, there is growing knowledge about leadership and a plethora of leadership courses. Yet leadership is often a contested concept. Moreover, are we producing better leaders?

Veronica Bishop,[2] author of *Leadership for Nursing and Allied Health Care Professions* (2009) and a visiting professor of nursing at City University (London, UK), does not define leadership itself, yet provides useful characteristics and insights associated with leadership:

1. Allows for success in an organization.
2. Connotes clarity of vision.
3. Provides hope or direction, or can conversely turn the world upside down.
4. Is able to share information.
5. Using Max Weber's classification of leaders, receives his or her authority through charismatic, traditional, or rational sources of legitimation. Charismatic authority inspires great ideological commitment.
6. Has good communication skills.
7. Is able to gain support or followers.
8. Leaders have a number of key traits such as passion, risk taking, optimism, creativity, openness, magnanimity, dedication, people skills, and stamina.
9. Involves wisdom, personal knowledge, or expertise.
10. Leaders meet challenges, move forward, and extend their private world to embrace those around them.
11. Involves power, whether it is based on information, authoritarian command, or charisma (that is, personal, magnetic appeal, sometimes of a divine-like quality).
12. Is genetic, circumstantial, or learned.

In his book *Los 11 Poderes Del Líder* (*The 11 Powers of the Leader*), Jorge Valdano argues that a leader has the following characteristics and that soccer is a natural place to exercise one's leadership skills:[3]

1. Credibility
2. Hope
3. Passion
4. Style
5. Keeping one's word
6. Curiosity
7. Humility
8. Talent
9. Promotion of group (team) unity
10. Simplicity
11. Attaining success

Leadership studies are also full of examples of either competent and visionary leaders, or "toxic leaders." British prime minister Winston Churchill was considered a visionary leader for his role in rallying Britain and the Allied powers in defeating Nazism. Adolf Hitler, on the other hand, was viewed as a "toxic leader" who was excessively authoritarian, refused to create dialogue about alternative courses of action, engaged in childish behavior, and was obsessed with an unethical and scientifically indefensible racialist world-view.

A definition of leadership provided by Peter Northouse, professor emeritus of communication in the School of Communication at Western Michigan University, is simple and elegant: "A process whereby an individual influences a group of individuals to achieve a common goal."[4] From this aforementioned definition, it follows that: 1) leadership is a process of interaction; 2) it involves influencing others; 3) it takes place in groups; 4) it connotes goal attainment; and 5) the goals are shared by leaders and their followers. Northouse's definition can be praised for its simplicity. Yet the definition has no ethical component and could thus mean that a Churchill or Hitler could be pooled together in the same category as great leaders. We might combine the definition offered by Northhouse with the definition of ethical leadership provided by the Center for Ethical Leadership based in Seattle, Washington: "Ethical leadership is knowing your core values and having the courage to live them in all parts of your life in service of the common good."[5]

Before delving into the leadership lessons of soccer, I need to examine my choices for the number 8 jersey. The choices are getting tougher as players wearing higher numbers typically gain more recognition than other players because of their playmaking or scoring exploits.

JERSEY #8: LEADERS IN THE MIDFIELD

The number 8 is an inside right (forward), a second forward, or midfield playmaker. He sets up goals and also scores his fair share of goals. The second striker usually plays behind the center-forward or main striker. A number 8 typically plays in a very advanced forward position and is there to score goals. The number 8 often has less defensive responsibilities than a midfielder, but the best number 8s, such as Liverpool's and England's Steven Gerrard, do their fair share of quality defending.

In this chapter, I opted to choose a few number 8s from various continents in order to advance the notion that leadership takes place around the globe in different epochs and it transcends cultural barriers. The contemporary players selected are the following: Xavi Hernández (Spain), Steven Gerrard (England), and Clint Dempsey (United States).

Xavi represents leadership on the field through his mastery in midfield, but also for his off-the-field mediation skills. Jorge Valdano points out that FC Barcelona's Xavi and his Real Madrid counterpart Iker Casillas exercised concrete leadership skills:[6] they would speak on the phone regularly in order to minimize the "toxic" atmosphere of the derby matches and to prevent the breaking of the "magic" associated with the triumphs of the Spanish national team after it won the World Cup in 2010 (many Spanish internationals either

play for FC Barcelona or Real Madrid). Dempsey embodies leadership con-
tributions on and off the field. The United States international grew up in a
Texas trailer park, lost his sister Jennifer Dempsey to a brain aneurysm, and
became a superstar striker in England (Fulham and Tottenham Hotspur) and
the captain of the USA national team.[7] Since becoming captain of the USA
national soccer team in 2013, Dempsey led the United States to World Cup
qualification and won high praise from his German coach Jürgen Klinsmann:
"Having Clint Dempsey on your team is a privilege and he is one of the best
players in U.S. history."[8] Yet in an interview with *The Wall Street Journal* in
2013, Klinsmann challenged Dempsey's talent level: "[Dempsey] hasn't
made s—. You play for Fulham? Yeah, so? Show me you can play for a
Champions League team, and then you start on a Champions League team.
There is always another level. If one day you reach the highest level then
you've got to confirm it, every year."[9] One writer suggests that Dempsey
"appeared to take Klinsmann's remarks as a challenge responding with good
form for both his club and the national team, leaving very little room for
criticism from the U.S. coach."[10] Gerrard embodies leadership on the field,
but also off the field in overcoming life's obstacles. Zinedine Zidane, a
representative of chapter 5, said the following about Gerrard, thus highlighting his leadership qualities, including passion, talent, ability to engender
team unity and success (Jorge Valdano), and genetic, circumstantial, or
learned talent (Veronica Bishop):

> Is he the best in the world? He might not get the attention of [Lionel] Messi
> and Ronaldo but yes, I think he just might be. If you don't have a player like
> Steven Gerrard, who is the engine room, it can affect the whole team. When
> we were winning league titles and European Cups at Real, I always said
> Claude Makelele was our most important player. There is no way myself,
> [Luis] Figo or Raul would have been able to do what we did without Claude
> and the same goes for Liverpool and Gerrard. He has great passing ability, can
> tackle and scores goals, but most importantly he gives the players around him
> *confidence and belief.* You can't learn that—players like him are just *born*
> with that presence.[11]

Xavi

Barcelona and Spain midfield general Xavi is a brilliant player, true professional, and embodies leadership on and off the soccer field. Born in Terrassa,
Catalonia (Spain) in 1980, Xavi is a product of Barcelona's demanding La
Masia youth system since the age of eleven. Xavi progressed through the
youth and reserve teams and was a key member of the FC Barcelona B team
that won promotion to the Second Division. Since 1998, he has made over
450 appearances for Barcelona and scored fifty-five goals. For Spain, Xavi
has played 130 matches and scored thirteen goals.

Xavi wears the number 8 for Spain and number 6 for Barcelona, while his partner-in-crime Iniesta wears number 8 for Barcelona and number 6 for Spain. While Argentinean striker Lionel Messi, Xavi's Barcelona teammate, receives more accolades than the Spanish midfield star, Xavi has won more trophies than the Argentinean superstar. Messi won the prestigious Ballon d'Or in 2009 and the FIFA *Ballon d'Or* in 2010, 2011, and 2012, thus joining an elite group consisting of Dutchmen Johan Cruyff and Marco van Basten and Frenchman Michel Platini. Yet Messi has not been able to win a major tournament with Argentina, except for the gold medal at the 2008 Olympic Games in Beijing. While Xavi finished third in the *Ballon d'Or* nominations in 2009, 2010, and 2011, the Spaniard has won far more collective trophies for both club and country. Playing for Spain, Xavi won the 2010 World Cup and two European Nations' Championships in 2008 and 2010. In addition, Xavi won a silver medal for Spain at the 2000 Olympic Games in Sydney.

Interestingly, Xavi did finish ahead of Messi in one major competition: The IFFHS voting for World's Best Playmaker in 2012 saw Iniesta finish first (146 votes), Xavi second (128 votes), and Messi third (98 votes). Yet Xavi won the title in the same competition for four consecutive years in 2008, 2009, 2010, and 2011.

Xavi is in a play-making and success league of his own. He has won a whopping twenty-five trophies, more than any Spanish player in history. He has also won more domestic trophies (twenty-two) than any other Spanish player in history, all with FC Barcelona:

1. *La Liga*: 1998–1999, 2004–2005, 2005–2006, 2008–2009, 2009–2010, 2010–2011, and 2011–2012.
2. *Copa del Rey*: 2008–2009 and 2011–2012.
3. *Supercopa de España*: 2005, 2006, 2009, 2010, 2011, and 2013.
4. UEFA Champions League: 2005–2006, 2008–2009, and 2010–2011.
5. UEFA Super Cup: 2009 and 2011.
6. FIFA Club World Cup: 2009 and 2011.

Thus, there is no doubt about Xavi's play-making talent, a key attribute of leadership. If we recall Valdano's eleven leadership traits, Xavi demonstrates many of those characteristics: credibility, passion, talent, style, simplicity, promotion of team unity, and attaining success. His credibility was enhanced by regularly chatting with his Real Madrid counterpart Casillas and thus promoting the continued unity and success of the Spanish national team. His trophies are a testament to his success for club and country. He is extremely talented, as highlighted by his four consecutive World's Best Playmaker awards. Xavi is relatively short (five feet seven inches) but talented. Yet Valdano uses Xavi to point out how management has a tendency to mistakenly push for players who are taller and more physically imposing rather than merely assessing raw talent.[12] While his style of play is extremely technical, he plays simple soccer. Valdano is adamant that Xavi's leadership is based on the power of his talent and performance on the field: he hardly loses a single ball in midfield; dominates possession and hence tires his opponents; makes pinpoint passes into the opponent's dangerous penalty area; his passing, pin-point control, and constant movement are his specialties; and he is always calm, meticulous, and a huge performer on the field.[13] As Xavi stated with respect to his on-field vision and accurate passing: "That's what I do: look for spaces. All day. I'm always looking."[14] Xavi possesses what Valdano calls a capacity for "synthesis" that is "genius" because he outwits his opponents, often finds teammates in dangerous scoring positions, or can also score himself.[15]

Xavi is undoubtedly one of the greatest midfielders of all time, as well as the most gifted playmaker of his generation. Named the 2008 European Championship player of the tournament, Xavi was masterful when Spain defeated Germany 1–0 in the final. He was truly dominant in midfield, made an assist, tackled, ran tirelessly, and led Spain to their first major trophy since the 1964 European Championship. In the 2010 World Cup in South Africa, Xavi led Spain to its first World Cup title and provided the most passes and balls crossed inside the dangerous eighteen-yard box. It is estimated that he ran more than 15 km (9.3 miles) in the finals. In the 2012 European Championship finals, he set up two goals and became the first player to assist in two European Championship finals. In short, Xavi is a talented leader on the field, thus earning the moniker "Puppet Master."

Steven Gerrard

Steven Gerrard is the captain and central midfielder for Liverpool FC and England. Born the same year as Xavi in Whiston (Merseyside), England, in 1980, he has played for only one club, Liverpool, for his entire career. This is a rarity in today's professional soccer where club transfers are frequent. Gerrard loves the legendary Liverpool club, even refusing more lucrative offers from other European clubs. He has been recognized as a soccer leader through his Most Excellent Order of the British Empire (MBE) title, which he gained in 2007. Gerrard was picked as the England Player of the Year in 2007, Football Writers' Association Player of the Year in 2006, and won the UEFA Club Footballer of the Year and the bronze medal in the *Ballon d'Or* voting in 2005. Thus, if we follow Valdano's ideas about the importance of a leader's talent and his ability to attain success, Gerrard is a leader.

In 2013, Gerrard reached a milestone with his one hundredth Liverpool goal. He has made more than 450 appearances for Liverpool since 1998. Gerrard began his England career in 2000, amassing over 105 caps and twenty-one goals. He has represented his country at the 2000 and 2004

European Championships, as well as the 2006 and 2010 World Cups. At the 2010 World Cup, he was England's top goal scorer with two goals, in the absence of an attacking thrust from the strikers. At the 2010 World Cup he first captained England, as regular captain Rio Ferdinand missed the tournament due to an injury. Gerrard became England's permanent captain before the 2012 European Championship. As a result of his outstanding performance at the 2012 European Championship, including three assists in the first round, Gerrard was named to the tournament all-star squad.

There is no doubt that Gerrard is one of the greatest English soccer players ever. Perhaps only Kenny Dalglish for Liverpool was at Gerrard's level in terms of skill, performance, and commitment. Zinedine Zidane, one of the representatives of chapter 5, called Gerrard one of the best soccer players in the world in 2009.[16] In 2010, *The Guardian* honored Gerrard by placing him on their World XI team, which is a list of the eleven greatest soccer players of all time.[17]

A leader also makes the entire team (club and country) better, insisted Valdano. Recall that Northouse argued that leadership is interactive; it involves influencing others, it takes place in groups, it connotes goal attainment, and the goals are shared by leaders and their followers. Gerrard makes his entire team play better. A leader, insisted Bayern Munich's Spanish manager Pep Guardiola at a conference in Buenos Aires, is "one who makes the other better."[18] Gerrard is that leader and he rises to the occasion for major matches: he is the only soccer player to have scored a goal in an FA Cup Final, a League Cup Final, a UEFA Cup final, and a Champions League final. He has won the European Champions League Cup (2004–2005), a UEFA Cup (2000–2001) title, two FA Cups (2000–2001 and 2005–2006), and three League Cups (2000–2001, 2002–2003, and 2011–2012). When Liverpool was down 3–0 at the half against AC Milan in the Champions League finals in the 2004–2005 season, he rallied Liverpool to a historic 4–3 win in penalties. Gerrard scored one goal and helped make another when he was fouled by AC Milan's Gattuso in the box. It was one of the most dramatic comebacks ever witnessed in the history of soccer. It evoked comparisons with Portugal's dramatic comeback led by the great Eusébio against North Korea in the 1966 World Cup, reversing a 3–0 score to win 5–3.

Gerrard is also a leader because of his versatility, playing as a defensive midfielder, offensive midfielder, right defender, or even second striker. Like a true captain, his attitude is positive: he does what is necessary for club and country. His endless running in defense, crunching and diving tackles, and howling goals with his blistering right foot (sometimes from outlandish distances), are inspirational for the entire team. Recall that leadership is about attitude, your hopeful attitude in any given moment of life, in a life that is transitory. It is also about getting dirty, working hard, and maintaining discipline in search of your team's goals. Gerrard possesses all these aforementioned qualities.

Gerrard is all heart and inspirational leadership by example. In his autobiography, he ends with a very touching line: "I play for Jon-Paul."[19] Gerrard's cousin, Jon-Paul Gilhooley, was killed in the 1989 Hillsborough tragedy. Gerrard was only eight at the time and already an avid soccer fan. Sadly Jon-Paul was only ten when he died, the youngest of the ninety-six victims of the Hillsborough disaster. Gerrard insists that Jon-Paul's death spurred him to be a great, inspirational player.

The Hillsborough tragedy was caused by a human crush and a panic, and it occurred during the FA Cup semi-final match between Liverpool and Nottingham Forest on April 15, 1989, at the Hillsborough Stadium in Sheffield, England. To add to the ninety-six dead, there were 766 injuries in the tragedy. The disaster is the worst stadium disaster in British history and one of the worst in world soccer history. The official report of the Hillsborough tragedy, the 1990 *Taylor Report*, insisted that lack of police control was the main cause of the panic. As professor of criminology at Queen's University (Belfast), Phil Scraton, noted, Hillsborough was "an avoidable disaster."[20] A 2012 report cited the failures of emergency services and other public officials, as well as attempts to conceal the truth. As a result of the Hillsborough tragedy, standing terraces at all soccer stadiums in England, Scotland, and Wales were eliminated.

Leadership is also about inspiring hope, argued Valdano. Gerrard has used his cousin Jon-Paul's tragic death to inspire hope in himself, teammates, and Liverpool fans. He understands that Jon-Paul could have been him, or any other youngster in England or around the world who is taken to a soccer match by a father, mother, cousin, or friend. He understands that in the face of the pain and hardship of Jon-Paul's loss, soccer is merely a game. In being true to Jon-Paul, his family, and the memory of the Hillsborough dead, Gerrard is also invoking the spirit of Liverpool's chillingly beautiful anthem "You'll Never Walk Alone":

> When you walk through a storm
> Hold your head up high
> And don't be afraid of the dark
> At the end of the storm
> Is a golden sky
> And the sweet silver song of the lark
> Walk on through the wind
> Walk on through the rain
> Though your dreams be tossed and blown
> Walk on walk on with hope in your heart
> And you'll never walk alone.

Gerrard is that leader who converted a family loss into heroic moments for both Liverpool FC and England. Gerrard also faced more adversity when in 2007 he mistakenly hit a ten-year-old cyclist in Southport, who shot unexpectedly into Gerrard's path. The boy is a Wayne Rooney fan, and Gerrard visited him in the hospital to present him with a pair of boots signed by the Manchester United and England star.[21] He is a talented leader, has overcome life's obstacles, and gives more than 100 percent on the pitch both offensively and defensively. Gerrard is not perfect, but he always sullies his kit and this is also the sign of a leader. He gives everything on the pitch for his club and country.

While Steven Gerrard is a brilliant number 8, remember that in the introduction I pointed out that our choices for different lessons need to reflect the notion that soccer is a sport played by cultures and countries around the globe.

Clint Dempsey

The United States of America is not traditionally known as a soccer nation, but that is changing with the solid performances of the men's team at numerous World Cup tournaments, as well as the successes of the women's national team. The "Stars and Stripes" reached the semi-final at the inaugural World Cup in 1930, finishing third. This is the highest finish of any CONCACAF country at a World Cup tournament. The United States qualified for the 1934 World Cup, and then caused a stir at the 1950 World Cup in Brazil, defeating England 1–0 in their second group match. Yet the United States had to wait until 1990 before they qualified for the World Cup again.

The United States qualified automatically as hosts of the 1994 World Cup, losing to Brazil in the second round. Since 1994, the United States has been on a remarkable run and is no longer seen as a soccer pushover. The national team has qualified for every World Cup from 1994 to 2014. In the 2014 World Cup qualifying, it managed a respectable 0–0 tie against Mexico at the fabled Azteca stadium and a 2–0 triumph in Columbus, Ohio. Moreover, the United States reached the quarterfinals of the 2002 World Cup, where they narrowly lost to Germany 1–0.

In both 2005 and 2007, Dempsey helped the United States win the CONCACAF Gold Cup. In 2009, the United States reached the final of the FIFA Confederations Cup, defeating top-ranked Spain 2–0 in the semi-finals, but lost to Brazil 3–2 in an entertaining final.

While a number of players have been instrumental in the resurgence of the "Stars and Stripes" since the 1990s, including Eric Wynalda, Claudio Reyna, Kasey Keller, Marcelo Balboa, DaMarcus Beasley, and Landon Donovan, Clinton Drew "Clint" Dempsey has been a star and leader of the USA national team since his international debut in 2004. He wears the number 8 jersey for the USA national team and was handed the captain's armband for crucial qualifiers for the 2014 World Cup against Costa Rica and Mexico. Playing as a striker or attacking midfielder, the USA international has made 101 appearances for his country and is second in all-time national team goals (thirty-six). Dempsey had a long, illustrious career in England with Fulham and Tottenham Hotspur from 2007 to 2013 (fifty-seven combined goals and over 200 Premier League appearances), and in 2013 signed with the Seattle Sounders FC for a transfer fee of US$9 million.[22] Dempsey holds the record for most goals (fifty-seven) by an American in the English Premier League. He was the Fulham Player of the season twice in 2010–2011 and 2011–2012, while in the 2009–2010 season he helped the London-based club to reach the finals of the UEFA Europa League. Dempsey also finished fourth for the Premiership Player of the Year voting in 2011–2012.

Dempsey was born on March 9, 1983, near the Mexican border in Nacogdoches, Texas. He embraced the town's Latino influences. He played for one of the best youth soccer clubs in Texas, the Dallas Texans, and later Furman University. The Dempsey family lived with little means in a trailer in the backyard of Dempsey's grandparents' house. "Nothing was ever given to Clint. He had to work, I always felt like, twice as hard to get what maybe some other people already had," said his mother Debbie.[23] The experience shaped his character and creative style.[24]

In 2004, Dempsey joined the Major League Soccer club New England Revolution. He had a major jaw injury, but still scored twenty-five goals in seventy-one appearances for the New England outfit from 2004 to 2006. He helped the Revolution win the MLS Cup for two consecutive seasons in 2005 and 2006. He then caught the eyes of English scouts who were impressed by his no-nonsense style, commitment, and goal-scoring skills. From 2007 to 2012, Dempsey played for Premier League club Fulham. He is the club's highest Premier League goal scorer of all time (fifty goals).

Internationally, Dempsey has played for the United States in two World Cups (2006 and 2010), while he helped the "Stars and Stripes" qualify for the 2014 World Cup in Brazil. In the 2006 World Cup in Germany, Dempsey scored the team's only goal of the tournament. In the 2010 World Cup in South Africa, Dempsey scored against England, becoming only the second American, after Brian McBride, to score goals in multiple World Cup tournaments. Dempsey has also scored big goals for the United States against Spain and Brazil in the Confederations Cup, England in the World Cup, and the game winner against Italy in a friendly in 2012.

Dempsey's leadership is on the field: he was captain of the USA national team with a fiercely competitive nature. He has performed admirably in England and Europe with two top Premier League clubs, Fulham and Tottenham Hotspur. Moreover, Dempsey has battled several key injuries, including jaw and knee injuries, to come back stronger and more determined to win.

Dempsey has been accused of playing rough, including injuring several players throughout his career, but this is a product of his sheer tenacity and determination to win, rather than malice.

Dempsey's leadership is also off the field. That is why his national team coach Jürgen Klinsmann handed him the captain's armband for key qualifying matches for the 2014 World Cup. As a youth, Dempsey sometimes had trouble meeting commitments to soccer because of family financial problems and time constraints. His sister was a major tennis prospect, but as pointed out earlier, Dempsey lost his sixteen-year-old sister Jennifer to a brain aneurysm in 1995. This made Dempsey even more determined to be a soccer star and to honor the memory of his deceased sister. In conjunction with Texas rappers XO and Big Hawk, the soccer star recorded a hip-hop video for Nike for the 2006 World Cup, which is dedicated to the memory of his sister. The song is called "Don't Tread" and the refrain is the catchy "Don't tread on Clint."[25] The song seeks to capitalize on Dempsey's working-class roots to sell the game in the United States. Recall that in chapter 7 I explored the marketing appeal of soccer. In chapter 11, I will highlight the relationship between soccer and fine arts, including videos and songs.

In 2013, Dempsey made a bold decision to sign for the Seattle Sounders and leave Tottenham Hotspur, a club that plays in arguably the best league in the world. Dempsey was allegedly not satisfied with his playing time at the London-based club and the World Cup was around the corner in 2014. A great leader wants to always play and perform well on and off the pitch. His former coach at Nacogdoches High School, Farshid Niroumand, insists that Dempsey is a leader because of his talent and that his European sojourn downplayed his talents:

> When he was playing in Europe, knowing Clint, I always thought he was a tiger in a cage. He was afraid of losing the ball. Knowing him, he did not feel comfortable holding the ball as long as he'd like to. He was forced to play one-touch, two-touch or release the ball quickly. Clint has a very, very beautiful game of soccer if they let him hold the ball a little longer. Being in America, I think opportunity will arise. You'll see a better side of Clint—better soccer from Clint, more attractive, more productive.[26]

His former teammate at Furman University, Anthony Esquivel, saw in Dempsey leadership traits highlighted by Veronica Bishop, in which leaders meet challenges and move forward rather than remaining complacent:

> Knowing Clint, I think he's always looked to take on challenges. That's what is great about him. He's never quite satisfied and he's always been able to keep that hunger. I definitely think he'll see this as another challenge for him to up his game even more and help Seattle and help the league out as a different role—more than just a player. I think he'll be up for it.[27]

According to one astute commentator, Dempsey gained the captain's arm-band above other players (for example, Michael Bradley or Tim Howard) because of his talent, passion, and ability to bring team unity, three key leadership traits cited by Valdano:

> For a captain to be truly effective, they must have the respect and confidence of the other players on the field. Over the last five years, Dempsey's total commitment to the USMNT and his desire to help the team play to the best of its ability has been unquestionable. And with the absence of Landon Donovan for much of the last two years, Dempsey's presence has been the glue that has held the team together.[28]

Dempsey's style of leadership is not always the most vocal on the field. Yet even this is changing since he received the captain's armband: during the U.S.'s 4–3 win against Germany in 2013, "Dempsey was more than vocal with late-game substitute Terrence Boyd when Boyd lost possession several times when the U.S. was holding onto a late lead."[29] Remember Guardiola's notion that a leader makes the whole team improve. It was echoed by Seattle Sounders FC Nigerian star Obafemi Martins after Dempsey was signed in 2013: "Dempsey's a good player so he's going to be good for me and Eddie [Johnson] and Lamar [Neagle] as well and the other players because we need good players on the team."[30] A good leader also has the support of his teammates and leads through his example: "He definitely has the respect of players in this camp. He's one of those players who you like to see leading by example,"[31] the U.S. goalkeeper Brad Guzan insisted after Dempsey was handed the captain's armband.

LEADERSHIP CASE STUDIES

At this juncture, I take these aforementioned definitions and the insights about leadership and apply them to a number of case studies of soccer players (male and female), coaches, administrators, journalists (announcers), and fans. For players, I use the examples of anti-apartheid soccer players and prisoners at Robben Island in South Africa and the retired USA international Julie Foudy. For coaches, I contrast the successful leadership skills of José Mourinho and Alex Ferguson and the "toxic leadership" of former French national team coach Raymond Domenech at the 2010 World Cup. For administrators, I examine ways in which FIFA officials can demonstrate better, more ethical, and more inclusive leadership. For soccer journalists, I use the examples of play-by-play announcer Andrés Cantor. Finally, I use a few examples of how soccer fans have taken leadership responsibilities by controlling, or partially controlling, their beloved clubs.

Numerous soccer stars have demonstrated leadership on and off the pitch. Donald Simpson Bell VC (1890–1916) was an English schoolteacher and professional soccer player who died in World War I. During World War I, Simpson Bell was awarded the Victoria Cross for his heroic acts of bravery in the Somme.[32] Justin Fashanu was an English striker who played for a variety of clubs between 1978 and 1997 and was best remembered for his stellar performances with Norwich and Notts County. He had the leadership to be the first and only English professional player to openly declare his homosexuality.[33] In chapter 4, I pointed out that Fashanu tragically took his life in 1998. I also highlighted a new openness toward gay players in Britain and North America, including anti-homophobia initiatives in professional soccer.

Julie Foudy was a midfielder for the U.S. women's national soccer team from 1987 until 2004. She was capped 271 times by her country and scored forty-one goals. She also played professionally for the San Diego Spirit of the Women's United Soccer Association, which was founded in 2000 and began its first season in 2001. She served as the USA team's co-captain from 1991 to 2000 and the captain from 2000 until her retirement in 2004. Foudy won two World Cups in 1991 and 1999 and two Olympic gold medals in 1996 and 2004, as well as an Olympic silver medal in 2000.

The leadership of professional women players such as retired USA international Julie Foudy is indeed heartwarming. July Foudy has her own school, The Julie Foudy Sports Leadership Academy, which teaches twelve- to eighteen-year-old girls and women the power of leadership skills both on and off the field.[34] Foudy insists that "sports gave mc my voice" and she wants to now use soccer to give "voice" to a new generation of female soccer players.

Due to a history of rampant sexism, women's soccer was not taken seriously before the 1990s. Women players were taken more seriously when female stars, such as Julie Foudy, Mia Hamm (a double winner of the FIFA World Player of the Year award), and Brandi Chastain, emerged in the United States. World soccer stars, such as Japan's Homore Sawa, China's Sun Wen, Germany's Birgit Prinz, and Brazil's Marta, increased the seriousness of the women's game. Administrators and coaches of the women's game also played a key role in making women's soccer professional, exciting, and entertaining. At the 2011 World Cup, the average attendance per match was approximately 26,000 fans. At the 2012 Olympics in London, 80,000 fans saw the United States defeat Japan 2–1 in the finals at Wembley Stadium. The record for a women's World Cup final was set in Los Angeles in July 1999 when about 90,000 fans saw the United States beat China.

In a far different context, anti-apartheid activists who were imprisoned on Robben Island used soccer in order to keep their dreams alive of a better world based on freedom and the abolition of apartheid. The prisoners included famous anti-apartheid heroes: 1993 Nobel Prize winner and president of South Africa Nelson Mandela (1994–1999), Kgalema Petrus Motlanthe (South Africa's president from 2008 to 2009), and Jacob Zuma, president of South Africa since 2009.

Robben Island housed a who's-who of resistance to white-led apartheid South Africa, including the key leaders of the African National Congress, the militant anti-apartheid organization. Robben Island prisoners included the poet Dennis Brutus, the current mayor of Johannesburg Amos Masondo, the leader of the Soweto Uprising Murphy Morobe, and future Namibian politicians.

Robben Island is an island about 7 km (4.3 miles) west of the coast of Bloubergstrand, Cape Town, South Africa. Anti-apartheid hero and current South African president Jacob Zuma spent 27 and 10 years, respectively, on Robben Island. Today Robben Island is a reminder of the horrors of the apartheid era and a United Nations World Heritage site. Sepp Blatter, the current FIFA president, visited Robben Island in the run-up to the 2010 World Cup in South Africa and insisted that it tells "a story of humanity and a very important one."[35]

In 2005, a film directed by Junaid Ahmed called "More Than Just a Game" told the inspirational story of how prisoners at Robben Island created an organized soccer league.[36] The Robben Island soccer league, known as the Makana Football Association, was founded in 1966 and lasted until 1973. It was named after a nineteenth-century Xhosa warrior and prophet. It was no ordinary league. Since the seventeenth century, Robben Island was used to house political prisoners, but the organized league did not begin until the 1960s. The players used soccer as an order of passion and discipline. Yet soccer also generated a leadership opportunity for the prisoners as they struggled with their incarceration and hoped for a better world. It took vision and clarity, traits we associate with positive leadership, to create the Robben Island soccer league. It allowed the players to dream, a key ingredient of both leadership and the human condition. The league also became a vehicle for dialogue, democracy, the anti-apartheid struggle, and grooming the leadership skills of future leaders and presidents of South Africa.

A few interesting facts about the Robben Island soccer league are instructive because they highlight the leadership of all the prisoners collectively and their love for soccer:

1. Prisoners on the island demanded the right to play soccer and the prison authorities relented under pressure from the International Red Cross.
2. The league had three divisions based on abilities and each league had players, coaches, trainers, managers, and referees. A prison population of 1,400 provided the personnel for the league.

3. The league had standing committees to deal with various issues from rules to discipline, while a meticulous log of the meetings was kept.
4. Matches were played for two hours on Saturdays for nine months of the year.
5. Strict FIFA rules were adhered to because the prisoners wanted to show that if they could run a soccer league, they might also one day run a government.
6. The league allowed different anti-apartheid factions from the African National Congress to the Pan African Congress to cooperate through soccer, despite their sometimes profound ideological and tactical differences with respect to the apartheid-led regime and the future.
7. Nelson Mandela and other key political prisoners were banned from playing or watching the league games.
8. President Zuma was a referee in the league and Dikgang Moseneke, the deputy chief justice of South Africa, also participated in the league.
9. The players had such pride in the league that they even used colored uniforms instead of the drab prison outfits.
10. Training sessions were often held in communal bathrooms and the maintenance committee and players tended to the field and built the posts.
11. Trophies and certificates created by the prisoners were given to the winning teams, but they were often confiscated by the prison authorities. [37]

What experts say about leadership could be applied to the Makana Football Association. Recall when Northouse argued that leadership is "a process whereby an individual influences a group of individuals to achieve a common goal." In the case under consideration, it was not merely one individual, but numerous prisoners, who used soccer as a tool to influence each other positively and advance their individual and collective leadership skills. In addition, my definition of ethical leadership posited that it connotes "knowing your core values and having the courage to live them in all parts of your life in service of the common good." The players, coaches, and administrators associated with the Makana Football Association understood that apartheid was an evil that would one day be defeated, and used soccer to give their lives some joy while enhancing their leadership skills. In 1989, the Makana Football Association was recognized for its great accomplishments and was given honorary FIFA membership. [38]

In soccer, we can also learn leadership lessons from coaches and managers. Coaches and managers must know how to deal with players and management alike, the leadership style required for their teams, the style of play required for their teams, how to manage the different personalities in the dressing room, the changes needed in the club, who should be the leader or leaders on the pitch, and whether those leaders (captains or co-captains) are able to adapt themselves to the different circumstances that the team faces.[39] The coaches with the most leadership skills translate their passion and talent into success (titles).

Alex Ferguson, a former soccer player who scored 170 goals as a forward in Scottish professional soccer from 1957 to 1974, is one of the best managers in the history of the game. He retired on the summit of soccer professional coaches in 2013. From 1986 to 2013, Ferguson led Manchester United to numerous soccer trophies, as the team became one of the most successful soccer clubs in the world. Under the guidance of the fiery Scotsman, Manchester United won nearly forty trophies, including thirteen Premier League titles, ten FA Charity/Community Shield trophies, five FA Cups, four League Cups, two Champions League titles (1998–1999 and 2007–2008), the Intercontinental Cup in 1999, and the Club World Cup in 2008.

Ferguson became a Manchester United icon and a manager brand. His leadership style clearly got results, but former players under his helm such as David Beckham and even his compatriot, the talented and diminutive Gordon Strachan, criticized Ferguson for his authoritarian approach to managing. Numerous players had public dust-ups with Ferguson, including a shoe thrown at Beckham after an argument in 2003. While we cannot argue with Ferguson's titles (thirty-eight trophies in twenty-six years), we might wonder how ethical his leadership skills are if so many high-profile players leave the club? Supporters of Ferguson argue that Ferguson did everything in terms of a grand Manchester United vision. If this larger Manchester United vision means putting high-priced stars in line for lack of discipline and performance, this is what a great leader must do, argue his most ardent supporters. Gordon Strachan, a soccer manager with Celtic from 2005 to 2009 and a star player for Scotland at the 1982 and 1986 World Cups, had harsh words for Ferguson in his autobiography: "I decided this man could not be trusted an inch—I would not want to expose my back to him in a hurry."[40]

José Mourinho (b. 1963) is a Portuguese soccer manager and currently the head coach of Chelsea FC. Bayern Munich manager Pep Guardiola insisted Mourinho is perhaps the best coach in the world, while Chelsea idol Frank Lampard said he is the best coach he has ever played for.[41] Recall that Guardiola pointed out that a leader makes others better. Valdano argued that leaders instill passion and hope (confidence and belief), as well as engender team unity. Frank Lampard, the Chelsea midfield legend, is unequivocal about Mourinho's leadership skills:

> He made me believe I was better than I was at the time. I thought I was a decent player, but he said to me "listen, you can really get to the top" and he made me believe it. I tried to take it on and do it. Mourinho was the best. For

me he was. He brought my confidence to a level it had never been. . . . It's a presence and an aura and a way with people. He galvanises people. His own self-confidence reflects back on his teams. He did that to me personally. Tactically he's fantastic. He's very astute. As a team he sets you up brilliantly. But what he does is he gets the best out of players and gets this togetherness that I'd never known until he came to the club and I haven't seen it again since then.[42]

Mourinho has coached Benfica, União de Leiria, and Porto in his native Portugal, as well as Chelsea (twice), Inter Milan, and Real Madrid. Along with coaching legends Tomislav Ivić, Ernst Happel, and Giovanni Trapattoni, he is only the fourth coach to win league titles in at least four different countries: Portugal, England, Italy, and Spain. He also won the Champions League titles with Porto and Inter Milan in 2003–2004 and 2009–2010, respectively. In 2010, he won the first FIFA *Ballon d'Or* Best Coach award. Between 2002 and 2011, Mourinho went 150 home league matches unbeaten with four different clubs: thirty-eight (W36–D2) with Porto, sixty (W46–D14) with Chelsea, thirty-eight (W29–D9) with Inter Milan, and fourteen (W14–D0) with Real Madrid. Wherever Mourinho goes, it seems success follows him.

Yet Mourinho had rather humble soccer beginnings and chance led him to exert his incredible leadership talents. A central midfielder as a player, Mourinho played for rather modest sides in Portugal from 1980 to 1985, including Rio Ave, Belenenses, and Sesimbra. He scored very few goals and his career, by all accounts, was rather unspectacular. He then worked as a physical education teacher and a youth team scout until a fortuitous encounter with legendary English coach Sir Bobby Robson. Mourinho became an interpreter for Sir Bobby Robson at Sporting Lisbon and Porto in Portugal, as well as Barcelona. Mourinho speaks six languages. After Robson left Barcelona, Mourinho worked with his successor, the Dutchman Louis van Gaal. Thus, Mourinho learned invaluable leadership lessons from two famous and effective soccer coaches.

When Mourinho's start in professional coaching came with Benfica in 2000, he never looked back and made himself a legend in the game. His controversial comments sometimes landed him in hot water with soccer officials, but nobody denies that he is a leader and one of the greatest coaches in soccer history. His inability to win sufficient titles at Real Madrid in 2012 and 2013 led him back to the Chelsea coaching position. How he performs at Chelsea to rebound from the disappointments at Real Madrid will test his leadership skills.

Whereas Mourinho had the ability to set grand visions, concrete goals, and meet many of those goals as a coach in four different countries, a French coach named Raymond Domenech will forever be etched in the category of "toxic leaders." He was certainly a more spectacular player than Mourinho, as Domenech earned eight caps for France as a defender from 1973 to 1979, won two French cups with Lyon and Bordeaux, and a league championship with Strasbourg in 1979. Domenech's tenure as the manager of the French national team from 2004 until 2010 was controversial and unceremonious, though he did manage to lead France to the finals at the 2006 World Cup as a result of the heroic performances of Zinedine Zidane.

Domenech was criticized for creating a toxic atmosphere in the dressing room when France was disgraced in the first round of the 2010 World Cup in South Africa. There was a players' revolt against Domenech and the players refused to train before their third World Cup match. The French public, press, and parliamentarians were outraged with the players and the inability of Domenech to reign in his divided team.

During a 2–0 loss to Mexico, Nicolas Anelka, a mercurial French striker, reportedly insulted Domenech. Anelka was dismissed from the team the next day. Patrice Evra and team trainer Robert Duverne also had a confrontation, which supposedly caused Domenech to physically restrain Duverne. The French players responded by returning to the team bus and refusing to practice. The team returned to practice after protests by the French Soccer Federation. When France ended its miserable World Cup campaign with a 2–1 loss to South Africa, Domenech sadly refused to shake the hand of South Africa's coach Carlos Alberto Parreira. He had lost all legitimacy as both a leader and an ethical human being.

Liane Davey, a principal for Knightsbridge Leadership Solutions in Toronto, made an astute comment about Domenech's lack of leadership and responsibility after the players' revolt:

> After France's players refused to practice to protest star player Nicolas Anelka's expulsion, Raymond Domenech berated the team in the locker room, rather than open a dialogue. That's a mistake: If you make decisions that don't sit well with others, you need to acknowledge your part in creating the issue. [43]

Following the model of leadership from the leadership course I taught, leaders come from all parts of the soccer hierarchy: the bottom, middle, or top. Valdano argues that the entire team, its players, and the management can exercise their leadership skills by striving to win with style (that is, fairly and through both technical and moral superiority). [44] Seen from this perspective, the players themselves are all leaders and individually responsible for making the collective better. While it is true that, as Zinedine Zidane pointed out, Domenech "lost control" of the French national team at the 2010 World Cup, [45] players like Anelka and especially team captain Evra could have behaved differently and demonstrated greater leadership. The strike idea by the players was excessive in the middle of a World Cup. The players needed to realize that young children in France and around the world look up to them as role models. Leadership needs to be demonstrated when you win, draw, or lose. It should come from both players and coaches. It should be conscious that soccer is part of a larger society and that it has ethical responsibilities to society at large.

In chapter 6, we highlighted the ethical shortcomings associated with soccer and FIFA administrators. Following our leadership insights, we argue that FIFA needs to clean its own house, create more accountability in its practices, and get rid of corrupt administrators. While changes can come at all levels within the organization, including the officials that select World Cup bids, a strong message needs to be sent from the top beginning with FIFA president Sepp Blatter.

Blatter is perceived as autocratic, unaccountable, and unwilling to tackle the corruption within the organization. Recall that in chapter 2 the former Chilean international Elias Figueroa was going to be the ChangeFIFA candidate, but suddenly withdrew his name and thus did not challenge Blatter's reign. Blatter has gone essentially unchallenged in an organization that has a GDP that is higher than the majority of the countries across the globe. In a world where totalitarian evils were defeated in the twentieth century and where in the twenty-first century the "Arab Spring" has deposed authoritarian dictators in a region long resistant to democracy, is it right that FIFA and Blatter run worldwide soccer like a "benign dictatorship"?

Recall that I pointed out that leadership entails the ability to share information. Yet Blatter has refused to open up the voting process to challenge his presidency, thus acting like a modern soccer monarch. He has been slow to seriously investigate widespread corruption in the organization. Blatter is even losing his legitimacy in the eyes of corporations concerned with bribery and corruption allegations, as well as the world's fans. In addition, Blatter does not have very good communication skills when it comes to dealing with issues related to his accountability and that of the organization. Finally, Blatter has not demonstrated ethical leadership around accountability issues related to World Cup bids, corporate sponsors, the corruption of key officials, and his own authoritarian form of governance. He dismissed the anti-government protests taking place during the Confederations Cup in Brazil in 2013, saying FIFA was "stronger" and showed little empathy for the largely non-violent protestors demanding a re-jigging of government financial priorities, as well as less government corruption and lower transportation prices.[46] Blatter has become a big part of FIFA's troubles. If he begins to clean up the game's administrative structures within FIFA, he will be a real leader and a hero to billions of soccer fans. If he does nothing, or makes cosmetic changes within FIFA, he might stay in power and harm the good of the game as a whole. A veritable FIFA revolution will be needed to clean up professional soccer. FIFA needs to clean up its act, come up with fresh ideas, and foster popular participation and real change.

Some fans around the world have demonstrated better ethical leadership than Blatter. Remember that in chapter 6 I highlighted the Brazilian struggle for democracy, which was led by Sócrates and his club Corinthians. The club and its fans fought for human rights, individual rights, democracy, fan participation in the club, and the joys of soccer against its excessive commercialism. Around the world fans have organized collectively in order to gain greater control of their clubs and to prohibit majority ownership in the club's constitutional documents. Increasingly one finds fan-owned clubs around the world. We might view these fan-owned clubs as examples of collective leadership, which is inclusive and often more ethical than majority ownership. This is not, of course, to fully romanticize fan-owned clubs.

Fan-owned clubs can be found around the world. These clubs include: Zacatepec (Mexico), Liga Deportiva Alajuelense (Costa Rica), Jeanne D'Arc FC (from Mali's capital city Bamako), Might Jets FC (Jos, Nigeria), Yokohama FC (Japan), Seoul United (South Korea), Rapid Vienna (Austria), NK Varteks (Varaždin, Croatia), Prague-based Bohemians 1905 (Czech Republic), PFC Botev Plovdiv (Bulgaria), Aris FC (Thessaloniki, Greece), Rosenborg BK (Norway), Linfield FC (Northern Ireland), Shamrock Rovers FC (Republic of Ireland), Swansea City FC (Wales), the Seattle Sounders FC (United States), and Athletic Bilbao and Barcelona (Spain). England has numerous fan-owned, or partially fan-owned clubs from Wycombe Wanderers FC and Chester FC to Exeter City FC and AFC Rushden and Diamonds. Moreover, all soccer clubs in Sweden and Turkey are fully owned by the fans, thus giving the fans a high degree of democratic decision making.

While some of the aforementioned clubs have achieved great successes, others are languishing in obscurity and the lower divisions of professional soccer. Clint Dempsey's Seattle Sounders FC is a real MLS success story. Seattle has sold out every league match, set MLS records for average attendance, led the league in season ticket sales, and qualified for the MLS Cup playoffs in each of its first three seasons.[47] Those figures are set to remain stable or even increase after the Seattle Sounders signed the USA international and former Premier League star Clint Dempsey in 2013. Many fans prefer the fan-owned clubs because they are involved with the club and are ultimately responsible for its ups and downs. They see the game as less dominated by the principle of profits for a few individuals. With less control over the club, there is a tendency to blame a scapegoat like the investors, a management group, or a coach. With fan-owned clubs, leadership is an affair for all involved with the club from players and fans to administrators and the cleaning staff.

Soccer journalists can also display leadership by becoming icons in their profession. They help to transmit a love for "the beautiful game." One of my favorite journalists is Andrés Cantor (b. 1962), a native of Buenos Aires, Argentina. He is a Spanish-language sportscaster in the United States. He provides Spanish-language commentary of soccer matches and he has also provided soccer commentaries in the English-speaking world. Cantor is famous   for   imitating   the "GOOOOOOOOOOOOOOOOOOOOOOOOOOOLLLLLLLLL!" call of Latin American announcers. Working with Univision, Telemundo, and NBC Sports, he has a wonderful voice, passion, and love for the game. He adds real spice to soccer games with his dramatic announcing style. He is the exact opposite of the often dry and ironic English announcers. He is a real leader in his field. In 1994, Cantor was recognized for his leadership when he was honored as Sports Personality of the Year by the American Sportscaster Association.

* * *

In conclusion, this chapter has sought to draw leadership lessons from soccer. "It is easy to recruit one thousand soldiers, but hard to find a good general," argues an ancient Chinese proverb. This saying could apply to soccer players, captains, coaches, journalists, referees, and administrators. Xavi, Clint Dempsey, and Steven Gerrard are my leaders of choice because of their leadership skills on and sometimes off the field. Dempsey is a real leader because he came from an underrated soccer region (CONCACAF) and country (United States) and rose to international prominence. Moreover, Dempsey overcame great personal adversity to become a recognized USA national team captain. His new nickname is "Captain America." Gerrard's leadership skills are related to his talent, tenacity on the field, personality that helped to unify club and country, and ability to overcome adversity such as the death of his young cousin. Xavi is the midfield general-leader of Spain's soccer renaissance at the end of the first decade of the twenty-first century, while he also used his mediation skills at club level in conjunction with Casillas to maintain the "magic" of the Spanish national team.

Good leaders come from anywhere. They can be players, managers, coaches, fans, or administrators. The players can be amateurs or professionals and can come from all cultural backgrounds and sexes, as demonstrated by the heroic Robben Island prisoners and retired USA international Julie Foudy. Dempsey, Gerrard, and Xavi are brilliant contemporary soccer leaders. If he could have played with the Liverpool greats of the early 1980s such as Kenny Dalglish, Ian Rush, John Barnes, Jan Mølby, Alan Hansen, Craig Johnston, and Avi Cohen, Gerrard might have won far more trophies. A leader can help a team with his supreme efforts, but a talented team wins multiple trophies because each one of its players includes numerous responsible leaders striving toward a common cause.

When Canada won the bronze medal in women's soccer at the 2012 Olympic Games and nearly beat the United States in the semi-finals in a thrilling match, the Canadian press lauded the unexpected result and generally acknowledged the leadership commitment and "ownership" of all the players on the team.[48] Also, great leaders know how to overcome adversity through their talent, passion, and success, as highlighted by Dempsey and Gerrard. Moreover, leaders need to be ethical and have an attitude filled with hope and vision because they have a moral responsibility to their team, the fans, the world around them, and future generations of soccer players. Recall that the Center for Ethical Leadership pointed out that ethical leadership is "knowing your core values and having the courage to live them in all parts of your life in service of the common good." As *El Libro azul* (*The Blue Book*), given to all Real Madrid's players, states, players must behave ethically on and off the field because of the millions of fans worldwide watching them.[49] *The Blue Book* adds: "One must be respectful with one's teammates, referees, and opponents. Victory is also a consequence of moral superiority."[50]

Chapter Nine

Dreaming of Wembley or Anfield

Soccer, Dreams, and Childhood

In *The Interpretation of Dreams*, first published in Vienna in 1899, Sigmund Freud interpreted dreams as a wish fulfillment, or attempts by the unconscious to resolve conflict.[1] Carl Jung, in his 1912 work *Psychology of the Unconscious*, wrote: "Between the dreams of night and day there is not so great a difference."[2] Lesson nine is about the notion of soccer as a dream; a dream that begins in childhood and is lived day and night. Soccer is for many of its fans a dream—the dream of playing professional soccer. It is about dreams of representing our respective national teams. Those dreams are first aroused in childhood and continue for soccer fans, players, coaches, and administrators when they are adults. Soccer's earliest memories are formed in childhood, while in childhood we also form our earliest friendships and a profound love for the game.

Cesar Luis Menotti, the coach of Argentina's World Cup-winning team in 1978, said the following about soccer and dreams: "To be a footballer means being a privileged interpreter of the feelings and dreams of thousands of people."[3] Or perhaps millions and billions of fans, if we follow FIFA's staggering attendance figures for World Cup competitions. Menotti also saw in soccer a mechanism to defend the "dignity" of soccer in Argentina, an "artistic expression of the lower classes," and an expression of "respect" for "our own dreams and the hopes of the people that love and admire us."[4]

"We played until it was dark. I dreamt of becoming a professional footballer," wrote the world famous Algerian-born French philosopher Jacques Derrida (1930–2004).[5] Stephen Gill, one of the most esteemed international relations theorists today and a distinguished research professor of political science, communications, and culture at York University in Toronto, Canada, pointed out that his British father was a successful soccer player before sustaining injuries during World War II, while his own "ambition was to become a professional soccer player."[6]

Eduardo Galeano, the great Uruguayan writer and the author of *Open Veins of Latin America* and *Soccer in Sun and Shadow* (*El fútbol a sol y sombra*), like many of his compatriots, dreamed of becoming a professional soccer player. Uruguay is a small South American nation with a population of 3.25 million people that amazingly won two World Cups in 1930 and 1950. It also finished in fourth place at the 2010 World Cup in South Africa. Uruguay has also won a record fifteen Copa América titles, or South American championships. The South American nation won soccer gold at two Olympic Games in 1924 and 1928. In addition, Uruguay has produced a history of world-class players from José Leandro Andrade, one of the representatives of chapter 4, to Alcides Ghiggia, the hero of the 1950 World Cup finals triumph against Brazil. In more recent memory, Enzo Francescolli, Alvaro Recoba, Luis Suárez, Diego Forlan, and Edinson Cavani have continued the Uruguayan tradition of producing world-class players. Galeano points out that Uruguay's early soccer successes were built on a government policy that built soccer fields throughout the country in order to promote physical education.[7] As a result, Galeano insisted that "soccer pulled this tiny country out of the shadows of universal anonymity."[8] Recall that in chapter 1 I highlighted the relationship between soccer and nationalism. We might view Uruguay's soccer exploits as enhancing the nation's "soft power" in the international community.[9]

Uruguay's soccer accomplishments are profound and were surely founded on the childhood dreams of all Uruguayans to wear *La Celeste* (The Sky Blue) jersey of the national team. To put Uruguay's soccer prowess in comparative perspective, only five nations with a smaller population than Uruguay have ever participated in any World Cup: Northern Ireland (three), Slovenia (two), Wales, Jamaica, and Trinidad and Tobago. Yet none of those countries—and most of the countries of the world—cannot claim to have won two World Cup trophies, two Olympic gold medals, and fifteen regional trophies.

The most passionate soccer fans and players remain like children. They dream of playing at Wembley or Anfield, two "cathedrals" of English soccer. They are endlessly romantic and nostalgic. They recall the old days of attractive soccer. In this chapter, we advance the argument that soccer is a simple child's game that at its best turns adults into children filled with joy, creates friendships, and ultimately fills our hearts with love for this amazing game. Before we meditate upon this lesson, we need to pick the representatives of the number 9 jersey.

JERSEY #9: CENTER FORWARDS—LIVING THEIR DREAMS, INSPIRING OTHERS

There are many great number 9s in soccer history. The number 9 is a center forward, a target man, and a marksman. A soccer website, Football's Greatest, describes the role of the number 9:

> The traditional centre-forward was a big part of the game from its evolution until modern times, especially in England and northern Europe. The centre-forward was tall, strong and brave and an excellent header of the ball. His job was to act as a focal point for the attack, often playing with his back to goal he would hold the ball up and the lay it off to play his team-mates in. These players were also the main source of goals for the team and great finishing is a pre-requisite for the greats in this position. If not scoring himself, the centre-forward played an important role by dominating defenders physically and keeping them occupied and on the back foot. Much of his play would be about winning the ball in the air. Principally, a major source of goals was provided by him, getting on the end of crosses and heading the ball into the back of the net. The heyday of the traditional centre-forward was from the dawn of the game to the 1960s.
>
> In the modern game (and often in Latin and Mediterranean countries in earlier eras) teams do not always play this way. Playing with the ball on the ground does not require this type of centre-forward and many teams played without them, although they still remained important across the world, and especially in England. The new style centre-forward (exemplified by players such as Drogba) have to perform the role described above but, frequently operating alone, they must now also be able to turn with the ball and go for goal themselves, requiring them to be quick and good with their feet as well as in the air. This is a challenging role and it is becoming more important now that teams are typically playing with only one central striker (i.e., in a 4-2-3-1 or 4-3-3 formation). In this system it is vital that the ball can "stick" long enough when played to the centre-forward to give other players time to join the attack.[10]

The number 9 position demands holding up the ball for the attack and also scoring goals. Typically, nations with a history of winning World Cups, including Brazil, Italy, Germany, Argentina, Uruguay, England, and France, have produced excellent number 9s. Yet I will only comment on the number 9s that embody the notion of soccer as a childhood dream.

For the number 9 jersey, I have picked a North American (Mexico's Hugo Sánchez), an Asian (South Korea's Cha Bum-Kun), and an African (Cameroon's Roger Milla).

The 1982 and 1986 World Cups saw the emergence of Sánchez, Cha, and Milla. The selection of players from outside of Europe or South America, the traditional powers of world soccer, is purposeful. As the World Cup changed from sixteen to twenty-four countries in 1982, more non-European and non-

South American national teams entered the consciousness of fans worldwide. African teams performed heroically at the 1982 and 1986 World Cups. Cameroon, which never lost at the 1982 World Cup, was nonetheless eliminated in the first round after three draws. Algeria shockingly defeated West Germany 2–1 at the 1982 World Cup. Morocco impressively defeated Portugal and reached the second round of the 1986 World Cup. These African teams showed us that soccer's European and South American dominance might one day come to an end. Canada even qualified for the World Cup for the first time in its history in 1986.

Especially impressive were Cha, Milla, and Sánchez because not only were they non-Europeans who excelled playing for their countries, they made the journey to Europe to star in professional leagues in Germany, France, and Spain, respectively.

Hugo Sánchez

Sánchez was a man possessed in front of goal and one of the greatest players in the history of Real Madrid. Jorge Valdano, a former Argentinean teammate of Sánchez with Real Madrid, explains how the Mexican number 9 scored thirty-eight goals in one season and could score with one simple touch, whether with his feet, head, chest, or thigh.[11] From 1985 to 1992, the Mexican international scored a whopping 164 goals in 207 matches for the Spanish giants. He was the Spanish league's top goal scorer for five seasons and in the 1989–1990 season was the top scorer in all of Europe, "firmly cementing his place as one of soccer's all-time great strikers."[12] He also scored twenty-nine goals for Mexico in fifty-eight appearances from 1977 to 1994. His sensational bicycle kick goals and goal-scoring celebrations were also noteworthy, especially his backward somersaults. These kinds of spectacular goals and theatrical celebrations impress young people and add to the aura and mystique of the player in question. They made young Mexicans dream of emulating the exploits of Sánchez. Raúl Jiménez, a young striker with Mexico's national team and Club América insists that his vision is of "some day playing for Real Madrid," the team of his boyhood dreams.[13] Ivan Orozco argues that Jiménez "will continue to envision playing in Europe like his idols Hugo Sanchez and Raul Gonzalez, both former Real Madrid stars."[14] In a key World Cup qualifying match against Panama in 2013, Jimenez emulated his boyhood idol Sánchez by scoring a dramatic and spectacular late bicycle kick winner from 18 yards away.

Javier Hernández, whose father and grandfather both played for the Mexican national team, also dreamed of playing professional soccer. "The dream, the goal, always was to play in [Mexico's] first division and then, if I did really well there, with the national team. And then after that, Europe," insisted Mexico's Manchester United star.[15]

Mexico hosted the World Cup for a second time in 1986 and its indisputable hero was Hugo Sánchez (b. 1958). He led Mexico to the quarterfinals in the tournament. After his playing days ended, he coached Pumas UNAM, Necaxa, and Pachuca. As a player, Sánchez played in three World Cups for Mexico in 1978, 1986, and 1994. He was voted CONCACAF Player of the Twentieth Century by the IFFHS, ahead of four other Mexicans: Luis Fuente, Carlos Hermosillo, Horacio Casarin, and Raúl Cárdenas. The IFFHS also voted him the twenty-sixth greatest player of the twentieth century. Yet in the 1980s, Sánchez was the great hero of Mexican soccer because of his scoring exploits with Real Madrid. Previously with Pumas UNAM in Mexico from 1976 until 1981, Sánchez scored ninety-nine goals in 183 matches.

What fans loved about Sánchez was his impressive ability to score from tight angles and from nearly everywhere. His flashy and daring styles, including his trademark windmill goals and his celebratory somersault after scoring, were audacious and outlandish. In those celebrations, he was honoring his sister, who was a gymnast and participated in the Montreal Olympics in 1976. As a sign of adoration for him in his native Mexico, in 2007 Hugo Sánchez inaugurated a street with his name in Puebla.[16] In an official charity campaign for the 2006 World Cup, Sánchez continued to inspire the dreams of the children of Mexico through SOS Children's Villages: he met children and mothers and pledged his support for six villages that will provide 800 orphaned and abandoned children with a home in a family environment.[17]

Cha Bum-Kun

Cha had a blistering and thundering shot from a distance and was a terror in the air. His nickname was "Cha Boom" because of his deadly shots from long distance. Cha was a real hero of mine: a soccer star from far-away Asia. The South Korean international striker Cha Bum-Kun (b. 1953) was a hero with Eintracht Frankfurt (forty-six goals) and Bayer 04 Leverkusen (fifty-two goals) from 1979 until 1989. At Leverkusen, Cha won the UEFA Cup in 1988 and set a record at the time for most goals by a non-German player with ninety-eight career goals. With fifty-five goals, he is the all-time leading goal scorer of the South Korean national team, on which he played from 1972 until 1986. He played in the 1986 World Cup in Mexico and although he did not score and South Korea was eliminated in the first round, his dangerous runs, impressive physique, tireless work rate, and howling shots from long distance were memorable. He was voted the Asian Player of the Century by the IFFHS in 1999.

Cha was a soccer great because he charted the way for future South Korean and Asian stars, including his son, Cha Du-Ri, who played for Celtic (Scotland) and various German professional clubs, and now plays for FC Seoul. In 2013, Bayer Leverkusen signed up-and-coming South Korean international star Son Heung-min to a lucrative deal worth as much as US$33.3 million.[18] Leverkusen was Cha's former club and Son dreamed of being a European soccer star like Cha. After his signing, Son stated the following in relation to the legendary Cha: "It's an honor to see my name mentioned in the same sentence [as Cha]. But it's also a huge pressure. I know there's a lot of expectations on me, so I'll be sure to be ready for it."[19]

In addition, the Cha Bum-Kun Footballing Award was established by the South Korean legend in order to discover young talents and encourage the dreams of future South Korean stars. Michael Hudson is adamant that Cha's example inspired the dreams of countless contemporary Asian soccer stars:

> Even now, there's a Frankfurt band named Bum Khun Cha Youth and the Cha Bum Kun Award is given annually to South Korea's most promising school-boy footballer (previous recipients include Park Ji-sung and ex-Middlesbrough forward Lee Dong-guk). Together with Japan's Yasuhiko Okudera, who won the Bundesliga title with FC Köln in 1978, Cha was a true footballing pioneer, the first in a line of Asian players which today includes Hidetoshi Nakata, Lee Young-pyo, Keisuke Honda, Shunsuke Nakamura, Lee Chung-yong and Shinji Kagawa. All of them owe a debt to Cha Bum-kun.[20]

Wayne, a Manchester United fan from South Korea, also highlights Cha's impact on the soccer dreams of young Asians: "I might not be old enough to have seen him play live, but my dad and grandpa told me he was the greatest influence for the Asian football communities. He gave hopes to Asians about playing in Europe (or on top foreign teams) and especially their World Cup dreams."[21] He also points out that Park Ji-Sung took soccer lessons from Cha when he was about seven years old, thus inspiring his dreams of playing in Europe.[22] From 2005 to 2012, Park made 134 appearances and scored nineteen goals for Manchester United. In 2013, he played for Dutch side PSV Eindhoven, his first European club, from 2002 to 2005.

Roger Milla

Milla was a schemer, a brilliant dribbler, and a trickster with an eye for goal. His goal-scoring celebrations lit the world with joy! Roger Milla was born Albert Roger Mooh Miller on May 20, 1952. Milla impressed at the 1982 World Cup, as did Cameroon's entire team for its daring soccer and its defensive stability. Cameroon and Milla exited the tournament in the first round after three ties, a record equivalent to the 1982 World Cup champions Italy. Cameroon's tie against Italy was heroic. Thomas N'Kono was a genius in goal and Milla caused havoc up front throughout the match. N'Kono was a star for Barcelona club Espanyol (1982–1991) and a pioneer because he was one of the early Africans playing in Europe. He won two African *Ballon d'Or* awards in 1979 and 1982. Gianluigi Buffon, one of the representatives of chapter 1, was then only a child and was inspired to change from an outfield position to a goalkeeper after watching N'Kono's scintillating performances.[23] A 2006 World Cup winner with Italy, Gianluigi Buffon is clear about his boyhood idol: "It was watching Thomas N'Kono play that made me want to become a goalkeeper."[24] This is a tribute that touches the legendary Cameroonian goalkeeper deeply, and he labels the Juventus star's comments "a great honour."[25]

Milla was a great number 9, scoring for clubs in France such as Bastia, Saint-Étienne, and Montpellier (103 combined goals) from 1980 to 1989 with great regularity and also for his country at the advanced ages of thirty-eight and forty-two at the 1990 and 1994 World Cups. He was one of the first African players to be a major star on the international stage and began his brilliant career with Douala in his native Cameroon at the tender age of thirteen. He won the African Soccer Player of the Year playing for Tonnerre (Cameroon) in 1974. He played in three World Cups for the Cameroon national team in 1982, 1990, and 1994.

Milla's performance in 1982 was good, but at the 1990 World Cup he was spectacular as he scored four goals, the most memorable one against Colombia when he dispossessed the hot-dogging Colombian goalkeeper René Higuita 35 yards from goal and scored into an empty net. He helped Cameroon reach the quarterfinals and made all of Africa proud. When he came on in the second half with Cameroon down 1–0 against England in the quarterfinals, he set up one goal and scored another on a penalty. Cameroon lost 3–2 on a dubious penalty call, but it became the first African team to reach the World Cup quarterfinals. Milla showed hope to children and adults alike because of his daring performances, love for the game, beaming smile, and success even at an advanced age. When Milla scored at the age of forty-two against Russia in the 1994 World Cup, he broke his own record to become, at thirty-eight, the oldest player to score in World Cup history. This sealed the Milla legend forever and won him more supporters around the globe. Like Sánchez, Milla celebrated his goals with panache; his trademark dance around the corner post at the 1990 World Cup was imitated by numerous other African players. Coca-Cola liked the dance so much that they used it for the 2010 World Cup in South Africa! Milla was named one of the 125 greatest living soccer players of all time by Pelé. There will never be another Milla.

Milla was an inspiration for many children worldwide, especially African children. He paved the way for the likes of Nigerian superstar Jay-Jay Okocha, Ivorian international Didier Drogba, and Liberian international and AC Milan star George Weah, perhaps one of the greatest African players of all time. Samuel Eto'o, a Chelsea star, Cameroonian international, and the African Player of the Year winner a record four times (2003, 2004, 2005, and 2010), dreamed of being the new Roger Milla as a child:

In my childhood, my room was adorned with posters of football players who I wanted to look like. The largest poster that was above my bed was that of Roger Milla. I said in my dreams at the time, "if I have to look like a footballer, I should be like the great Roger." I even happened to write "Milla" with a marker on the back of my t-shirts, like many other children in the early 90s. [26]

IT ALL BEGINS IN CHILDHOOD

How many of us, as children, dreamed of becoming as good as Milla, Cha, or Sánchez? Or perhaps even better than the soccer idols of our respective nations? In childhood, our soccer dreams begin. As pointed out earlier, Manchester United teaches its young fans that they are entering the "theatre of dreams." Barcelona advertise themselves as "more than a club"; a soccer club dedicated to the cause of the Catalan people and social responsibility. [27] Young children are deeply affected by these messages and thus dream of representing Manchester United and Barcelona. Both clubs have famous soccer academies where for the first time they can live and breathe soccer, thus nurturing the dreams of tomorrow's stars.

Alfredo Di Stéfano won domestic titles in his native Argentina, as well as Colombia and Spain, thus playing internationally in three countries (Argentina, Spain, and Colombia), a dream that will never again materialize under today's FIFA rules, as pointed out in chapter 1. He was a superstar before the marketing overkill of Beckham, Messi, Neymar, and Cristiano Ronaldo. Di Stéfano's combination of dribbling ability, fakes, pace, passing skills, and lethal goal scoring made him one of the greatest soccer players of all time. He could audaciously state the following: "We are all footballers, and as such should be able to perform competently in all 11 positions." [28]

Born in Buenos Aires on June 4, 1926 to Italian immigrant parents, Alfredo Di Stéfano is perhaps the greatest center forward (number 9) in the history of the game. Twice named European Footballer of the Year, in 1957 and 1959, for his legendary performances with Spanish outfit Real Madrid, Di Stéfano had skill, pace, and exceptional stamina. He made his debut in 1944 with Argentinean giants River Plate. By 1947, he was Argentina's top scorer in the domestic league with twenty-seven goals and River became first division champions. In 1947, Di Stéfano played six times for Argentina and helped them win the South American Championship. Di Stéfano was then lured by the Millonarios in Colombia, where he won three league titles (1949, 1951, and 1952) and was the league's leading scorer twice (1951 and 1952). It was his move to Real Madrid in 1953, however, that catapulted Di Stéfano into a European and worldwide soccer idol. Di Stéfano played with some of the greatest stars of all time at Real Madrid, including Kopa, Gento, and Puskás. He spent an impressive eleven seasons at Real Madrid, led the league in scoring four consecutive seasons from 1956 to 1959, and guided the Madrid club to a whopping eight first division titles (1954–1955, 1957–1958, and 1961–1964), the Spanish Cup in 1962, an impressive five European Champions' Cups (1956–1960), and the first Intercontinental Cup in 1960. At the height of his club glories with Real Madrid, Di Stéfano also scored twenty-three goals for Spain from 1957 to 1961 and played in the 1962 World Cup, where his goal-scoring touch abandoned him for once. Di Stéfano retired in 1966, having scored 377 goals in 521 official club games.

As a young boy, Di Stéfano dreamed of being a soccer star because of an obscure yet talented Paraguayan who played for Independiente named Arsenio Erico (1915–1977). Erico remains the all-time highest goal scorer in the Argentine first division, with 295 goals, all of them scored for Independiente. He is considered the greatest Paraguayan soccer player of all time. In a 2007 interview Di Stéfano stated: "I wanted to wear the number 9 shirt, just like my hero, Arsenio."[29] He admired Erico because he was "a master goalscorer, a dancer, a genius for headers and back-heels. Erico didn't run; he glided. He was so elegant."[30]

Some soccer stars were told as children that they would never achieve their soccer dreams. Garrincha had polio and Elias Figueroa, my representative for chapter 2, was told by doctors that his physical activities would be severely restricted. They became two of the greatest soccer stars in the history of the game. In adulthood, the realization of those dreams is tested by trials and tribulations. Think of a Cha Bum-Kun or Roger Milla, from South Korea and Cameroon respectively, as they made long journeys from their countries of origins to seek fame and fortune in Germany and France. One needs mental strength in order to survive the changed foreign circumstances, as well as new climate, language, and culture. Many foreign players have not made it in Europe and returned home because they could not adapt to their new surroundings. An Argentinean legend, Juan Román Riquelme (b. 1978), was reportedly unhappy in his time with Barcelona, as he longed to return to the comfortable and popular surroundings of his native San Fernando neighborhood in Buenos Aires.

You, too, as the reader must remember your early childhood memories of soccer. Think of your dream players and your soccer hopes. What is beautiful is that those memories and those dreams never go away. They stay with you. They make you remember with tenderness, joy, and perhaps a tear the beauty of your childhood. The beauty of playing on the streets or fields for hours with your friends. The beauty of a time that was not heavy with the burden of time. The beauty of a time that was not consumed with work and its daily routines and responsibilities. Now as adults we go to the match, or watch a World Cup match on television, to forget real time, to enjoy our lives, and to recall with nostalgia the soccer of our childhood.

While some people have the privilege of playing soccer with a real ball, soccer boots, and a regular change of soccer kits, there are many people around the globe who do not have this privilege. It is true that soccer can be a great societal equalizer. It is the people's game. It is a universal game. It can unite people from diverse faiths, cultures, and nations. Yet billions of children come from humble origins and do not have the same opportunities as others did in their childhood. The good thing with soccer is that only one ball is needed—not all players need to have one in order to play the game.

The writer Albert Camus was one of those kids from humble origins in Algeria. Camus even called himself that "little poor child" from Algiers.[31] He dreamed of soccer glory. An Algerian university team player, Camus "had been playing goalkeeper since he was a child, because in that position your shoes don't wear out as fast. From a poor home, Camus couldn't afford the luxury of running the fields."[32] The life of the future Nobel Prize winner and soccer goalkeeper began in very difficult circumstances:

> A double haunting presence looms throughout all the books: that of Algeria, where Camus was born, and of his mother, Catherine. Before he was a year old, the infant Albert lost his father, an early settler in French Algeria, in the battle of the Marne. His mute and illiterate mother, and her extended family, raised her two sons in a small flat in Algiers with neither a lavatory nor running water. Alain Vircondelet writes movingly of the "minuscule life" in the apartment with nothing: "those white sheets, his mother's folded hands, a handkerchief and a little comb." Her purity and silent dignity marked her son, as he struggled to confront his own shame at such poverty—and his shame at being ashamed. "With those we love," he once said of her, "we have ceased to speak, and this is not silence."[33]

Lots of soccer players in Africa, Asia, and Latin America can relate to the humble origins of Albert Camus. The grinding poverty, the importance of faith, and the dream of a better life unites many children around the world. They can escape the misery of their social conditions, for 90 minutes at least. There are soccer players who have fortunately overcome their very humble beginnings. Those rags to riches stories can be an inspiration to all those children, even those who will remain poor in adulthood and never experience the joys of professional soccer or even a "normal life."

The English newspaper *The Guardian* ran a fascinating story in 2010 entitled the "Joy of Six: Footballers who have overcome humble beginnings."[34] The six soccer players in question are the following: Brazil's Garrincha (1933–1983), Uruguay's Hector Castro (1904–1960), Ireland's Paul McGrath (b. 1959), England's Ricky Otto (b. 1967), Cameroon's Lauren (b. 1977), and France's Steve Savidan (b. 1978).

Garrincha is the legend in this list of aforementioned soccer players. He is one of the greatest soccer stars of all time and a dribbling god. Garrincha made competent defenders seem like amateurs. Garrincha's skills were so impeccable that "four times in his career he scored direct from corners and in one famous match against Fiorentina he beat four defenders and the goal-keeper, stopped short of the line to wait for the defenders to catch up with him and beat them again before rolling the ball into the net."[35] Yet his life was tragic and sad. His greatest triumphs were overcoming polio and his very humble origins to win the World Cup for Brazil in 1958 and 1962. Garrincha, like Maradona, Ronaldo, Rivaldo (who endured malnutrition as a child), and other soccer legends, began life in poverty and even ended it in misery:

> The Little Bird was born into poverty with an alcoholic father and several birth defects: a deformed spine, and a right leg bent inwards and two inches longer than his left one, which was turned outwards. He began working in the local factory when he was 14, started drinking around the same time, and lost his virginity to a goat. He was married (not to a goat) and a father by the time he became a professional footballer at 19. . . . Not for nothing was he nicknamed *Alegria do Povo* (Joy of the People). Off the field his joy was riddled with agonies, largely because of his alcoholism. If he inherited that problem from his father, he inadvertently caused retribution by knocking the old man down when drunk at the wheel in 1959. Ten years later his mother-in-law was killed when he crashed into a truck. Garrincha died of cirrhosis of the liver at the age of 49. Perhaps it is more accurate to say his triumphs were amid adversity rather than over it.[36]

The Uruguayan writer Eduardo Galeano wrote about Garrincha even more elegantly in *Soccer in Sun and Shadow*:

> One of his many brothers baptized him Garrincha, the name of an ugly, useless little bird. When he started playing soccer, doctors made the sign of the cross. They predicted that this misshapen survivor of hunger and polio, dumb and lame, with the brain of an infant, a spinal column like an S and both legs bowed to the same side, would never be an athlete . . .
>
> When he played, the field became a circus ring, the ball a tame beast, the game an invitation to party. Like a child defending his pet, Garrincha wouldn't let go of the ball, and the ball and he would perform devilish tricks that had people dying of laughter. He would jump on her, she would hop on him, she would hide, he would escape, she would chase after him. In the process, the opposing players would crash into each other, their legs twisting around until they would fall, seasick, to the ground. Garrincha did his rascal's mischief at the edge of the field, along the right touchline, far from the center: raised in the shantytown suburbs, that is where he played.[37]

Other soccer players faced grinding poverty or great adversity before becoming professionals. At the age of thirteen, Hector Castro lost his right forearm while cutting wood with an electric saw. Castro began his career at the age of nineteen with the Montevideo-based Nacional. Known as *El Divino Manco* in Uruguay, Castro helped Uruguay to victory in the 1928 Olympics and scored the fourth goal in the first World Cup final, a 4–2 win over Argentina.

He scored eighteen goals in twenty-five appearances for Uruguay and was known for his ferocious desire to win. Known for "drinking, smoking, gambling and womanizing" off the pitch, Castro became a Nacional legend, guiding the club to four consecutive titles from 1940 to 1943 and another in 1952.[38]

Or here is Eduardo Galeano's description of another African-born superstar, the legendary Portuguese superstar Eusébio in *Soccer in Sun and Shadow*: "He was born to shine shoes, sell peanuts or pick pockets. As a child they called him 'Ninguem': no one, nobody. Son of a widowed mother, he played soccer from dawn to dusk with his many brothers in the empty lots of the shantytowns."[39]

Eusébio, a Portuguese legend at the 1966 World Cup with a tournament high of nine goals, was also a sensational number 9 and one of the greatest soccer stars of all time. He won the *Ballon d'Or* award in 1965 and was also a runner-up twice. He played for Benfica for fifteen years of his twenty-two-year career. He is Benfica's all-time top scorer with 638 goals in 614 official games: a sensational strike-rate of more than one goal a game! He finished his career with 733 goals in 745 professional matches. He led Benfica to eleven Primeira Liga titles, five Portuguese Cup trophies, and one European Cup title (1961–1962). Eusébio also helped Benfica to reach three European Cup finals in 1962–1963, 1964–1965, and 1967–1968. He was the European Cup top scorer in 1965, 1966, and 1968. He also won the Primeira Liga top scorer award seven times (a national record) in 1964, 1965, 1966, 1967, 1968, 1970, and 1973. In 1968, he became the first player to win the European Golden Boot award. He won the prestigious award again in 1973. Eusébio is undoubtedly one of the immortals of soccer history. The Mozambican-born Portuguese international scored forty-one goals for Portugal in sixty-four matches from 1961 to 1973. I got to see him play near the end of his career when he scored eighteen goals in only twenty-five matches for the Toronto Metros-Croatia in the 1975–1976 season. Eusébio was fast, energetic, and possessed a lethal finishing touch with his trusted right foot.

Eusébio was born to a poor family in Lourenco Marques, Mozambique on January 25, 1942. As a child, he quickly discovered his passion for soccer, playing daily on the streets of his hometown. For Eusébio, only soccer mattered as a boy. In a 2002 interview, Eusébio said the following: "I was the only child in the family who did not finish school. I was born for football. My mother used to tell me off because I would stop on the way to school to play football with my friends."[40]

Who has not dreamed of becoming as great as Pelé? In Pelé's farewell match between the New York Cosmos and Santos, he retired in front of the Cosmos faithful and his former Santos club. He played one half with each club and retired with the words "Love, love, love." The rabid supporters of Mexican club side León regularly sing about how they "love" the club "more each day." We learn this love for soccer, just like Pelé and the León fans, as children. This love for soccer often mirrors our love for life. Here is Eduardo Galeano's poetic description of Pelé in *Soccer in Sun and Shadow*:

> When Pelé ran hard he cut right through his opponents like a hot knife through butter. When he stopped, his opponents got lost in the labyrinths his legs embroidered. When he jumped, he climbed into the air as if there were a staircase. When he executed a free kick, his opponents in the wall wanted to turn around and face the net, so as not to miss the goal.
>
> He was born in a poor home in a far-off village, and he reached the summit of power and fortune where blacks were not allowed. . . . But those of us who were lucky enough to see him play received alms of an extraordinary beauty: moments so worthy of immortality that they make us believe immortality exists.[41]

Soccer players and clubs are more "professional" today. Professionals are hired by clubs to work on psychology, technique, fitness, and nutrition. Players take their jobs very seriously on and off the pitch and many now play more matches (league, cup, European, and international competitions). Players run on average more distance and faster than in the past: before the 1990s, players ran up to 8 km (4.9 miles) per game, whereas today they run 11–12 km (6.8–7.4 miles) and they run 2 percent faster than in the 1990s.[42]

"Players today must withstand the most difficult conditions. The pressure is immense, and the physical demands are higher than ever. Players push themselves to the limit, and have to be at top physical, physiological and mental shape,"[43] insisted the former Real Madrid defender Michel Salgado. Given that players can sometimes bankrupt the clubs that they play for with their expensive, even outlandish salaries, it makes sense that they are more prepared. The rule today is less drinking before and after matches and more attention to diet, exercise, weights, and personal coaches and even psychologists. As Dr. Greg Whyte, head of physiology at the English Institute of Sport explains, "The nature of play is more dynamic and mobile these days. The need for aerobic conditioning and speed is greater than strength."[44] Lior Many, who worked with Maccabi Haifa and the Israeli national team stated: "A healthy and balanced diet is a critical element in the professional athlete's lifestyle. Just a few years ago, a player who signed for a *Serie A* team could have had cookies for dinner. Those days are long gone—clubs are now well-educated about the importance of nutrition, and they can now help their players improve every facet of their professional life."

Winning and performance matter as they mean higher salaries for players and greater marketing opportunities. Matches have become tighter and more defensive, with more diving, rough play, fouls, and defensive tactics. This reduces the beauty of soccer. If you buy the best players, you often play better soccer and win titles. This means that only the teams with money often find success, and therefore very few clubs and national teams win titles. Soccer is predictable to the extent that it is dominated by the big clubs and key soccer nations. On the one hand, soccer will always produce a genius like Zinedine Zidane, even in the most commercial era in the history of soccer. On the other hand, Real Madrid buys the most famous and most expensive players today, just as it bought Puskás, Di Stéfano, Kopa, and Gento in another era.

The 1986 World Cup was for some the end of the era of romantic, attractive, and attacking soccer. The 1990 World Cup finals between West Germany and Argentina in Italy featured a cynical victory by the Germans courtesy of a solitary Andreas Brehme penalty. It was a far cry from the 1980s, with the technical wizardry of Brazilian stars Zico, Falcao, and Sócrates, or the extremely talented French midfield in 1986 consisting of Platini, Tigana, Giresse, and Fernandez, or the tremendous saves of the Cameroonian goalkeeper Thomas N'Kono. N'Kono seemed to make saves that were headed for the top corner of the net, as if he were picking apples from a tree. He inspired an Italian child, Gianluigi Buffon, to become the greatest goalkeeper of the 1990s and first decade of the twenty-first century. And the Cameroon team played attractive and less-than-naïve soccer, including its star striker Roger Milla. Milla was forty-two years old at the 1994 World Cup when he led Cameroon to a quarterfinal berth after stealing the ball from an amazed Colombian keeper Higuita in midfield. He even received a personal call from the president to come out of retirement!

All that is left are the sweet memories of these matches. There is no doubt that there are spectacular players today, whether Xavi, Iniesta, Neymar, Cristiano Ronaldo, Radamel Falcao, or Messi. But we are in another era with a different ethic and new value system. These players are certainly artists, but they do not have the characters of the players of the past, whether Sánchez, Milla, or Cha. There was more magic in soccer in the past, which appeals to one's inner child. The French and Brazilian teams of the 1980s may have lost, but they appealed to the inner child. Carlos Valderrama (b. 1961), the retired Colombian midfield general with his lion-like blond Afro hair, appealed to the inner child because he loved to play, to touch the ball, to spray the ball with his pin-point passes all over the field, to play the one-twos, or to caress the ball as if it was his lover. Valderrama played a record 111 times for his native Colombia, including being its captain at the 1994 World Cup. Winning is important, but playing with elegance and joy is also important. Thus, it was no accident that Argentinean fans clapped for Valderrama and the entire Colombian national team after they trounced Argentina 5–0 in Buenos Aires in a qualifying match for the 1994 World Cup.

Eduardo Galeano, in his *Soccer in Sun and Shadow*, is also adamant that soccer is changing because of its commercial imperatives and that it will be a less magical world for all the world's soccer fans and particularly the children:

> The history of football is a sad voyage from beauty to duty. When the sport became an industry, the beauty that blossoms from the joy of play got torn out by its very roots. In this fin de siècle world, professional football condemns all that is useless, and useless means not profitable. Nobody earns a thing from that crazy feeling that for a moment turns a man into a child playing with a balloon, like a cat with a ball of yarn; a ballet dancer who romps with a ball as light as a balloon or a ball of yarn, playing without even knowing he's playing, with no purpose or clock or referee. [45]

The soccer that most captivates millions of fans is daring, innovative, attractive, and free flowing. Thus, memories of the 1982 and 1986 World Cups are particularly fond because Falcao, Sócrates, Platini, and Tigana played as if the score was secondary and the style of the game itself was more important. They played to win, of course, but they also played for you and me and billions of soccer fans. They played as if there was "no purpose or clock or referee." Or more precisely, they played with the purpose of producing aesthetically attractive soccer. The gorgeous one touch, the clever give-and-go, the outlandish fake, the surprising back heel, the no-look pass, the involvement of the entire team in the attack, the short and attractive passing game, and spontaneous and inspired dribbling as if they were possessed by the gods.

There are players of such quality that they are forever remembered within their countries and even around the world: Di Stéfano, Gento, Cubilas, Milla, Weah, Maradona, Pelé, Garrincha, Falcao, Zico, Sócrates, Sánchez, Cruyff, Neeskens, Puskás, Kocsis, Eusébio, Beckenbauer, Džajić, Timoumi, Abedi Pele, Madjer, Assad, Belloumi, Cha, Müller, Best, Charlton, Baresi, Fachetti, Riva, Piola, Platini, Fontaine, Zidane, and van Basten. N'Kono, Yashin, Maier, Buffon, Casillas, Carrizo, Zamora, and Chilavert are their equivalents as goalkeepers. There are of course many more fantastic players as well. What made these players special was that they not only excelled at what they did, but they made us dream in childhood and long after as adults.

Young boys, but also young girls today, dream of becoming professional soccer players. Mia Hamm (b. 1972) is arguably the greatest number 9 in the history of the women's game. She is perhaps the best women's soccer player of all time and has made many young girls in the United States and around the world dream of becoming professional players. Tony Williams argues that there was a "Mia Ham effect" on young girls: "Mia Hamm had a great effect on the game's popularity. Girls who grew up in the 1990s and early 2000s tried to emulate Hamm, one of the world's more famous female athletes." [46] The "Mia Hamm effect" extended to the commercial impact of the game as a result of the American superstar:

In Atlanta at the 1996 Centennial Olympic Games, she led Team USA to gold in front of 80,000 fans. At that time, never in history had so many spectators come out to watch a women's sporting event. The Games highlighted female athletes as an equal to their male counterparts, and at the head of the table was Hamm. Hamm's team went on to dominate the world again, this time at the 1999 Women's World Cup, where Team USA won the championship in front of 40 million television viewers in this country alone. That same team was responsible for selling over 650,000 tickets that year, including sellouts at then-Giants Stadium and the Rose Bowl. Overall, Hamm has played a very large role in bringing women's soccer to a new playing level in this country. She was one of the 20 founding players for the Women's United Soccer Association (WUSA) that lasted. . . . Thanks to having Hamm as the league's marquee player, the WUSA even had games televised on national networks like TNT, CNNSI, ESPN2, and PAX TV. And when WUSA games weren't televised nationally, each of the eight teams had their games broadcasted on various local and regional sports channels. [47]

The now retired USA international and Washington Freedom star was so talented that she got many women and men hooked on watching women's soccer, or dreaming of becoming soccer stars. As CNN pointed out, Hamm's "winning style has garnered her legions of fans, including young girls throughout the United States who are flocking to soccer fields to imitate their idol." [48] Hamm discovered soccer as a baby, when the family moved to Italy, a soccer-mad country: "Mia was in a park in Italy playing, and the next thing they knew, she went darting across the green. And she was taking away a soccer ball from a kid that was 5 years old, and she was maybe 2," [49] said her sister Caroline Cruickshank.

At fifteen, Hamm became the youngest member of the U.S. national women's team. Hamm scored a whopping 158 international goals from 1987 until her retirement in 2004. She appeared internationally 275 times for the United States, more than any male player in history and second behind another U.S. legend, Kristine Lilly (352 caps). Ahmed Hassan, an active midfielder and winger with Zamalek SC and Egyptian international, holds the men's all-time record with 184 caps. The second most capped players in the history of men's soccer are retired internationals: Mexico's Luis Suárez and the Saudi Arabian goalkeeper Mohamed al-Deayea (tied with 178 caps). Given the bruising and punishing nature of soccer training and matches, the accomplishments of Hamm and Lilly are extraordinary and superhuman.

Hamm's soccer accolades are impressive. She was named the women's FIFA World Player of the Year in 2001 and 2002. Pelé listed her as one of FIFA's 125 best living players of all time. Women's Professional Soccer, a professional soccer league that started operations in 2009, included Hamm's silhouette in its logo. [50] Hamm was not the only great USA international of her generation. She was the key member of the "Fab Five"—along with Julie Foudy (highlighted in chapter 8 for her leadership skills), Kristine Lilly,

Brandi Chastain, and Joy Fawcett—that led the United States to an impressive two World Cup wins and two Olympic gold medals from 1991 to 2004.[51] The "Fab Five" inspired countless young girls and women in the United States to become professional soccer stars. One such star especially inspired by Hamm is the USA international May "Abby" Wambach, the 2012 FIFA World Player of the Year and the world record holder for international goals by men and women (162): "When I look in the mirror I don't see a person who's made the kind of impact that Mia Hamm made on the game. She's still my idol, the greatest player and the greatest team-mate. She achieved so much in so many different ways. What she did for women's soccer can't be measured."[52] Furthermore, Kristine Lilly, Tisha Venturini-Hoch, and Hamm created a soccer academy called Team First to allow future stars to dream of soccer greatness and "to basically help share with young girls our experiences and what we felt helped make us successful,"[53] states Hamm.

* * *

Soccer is both a "dream" and a "faith" born in childhood.[54] The best clubs or national teams are teams of "friends," an idea that we first learn in childhood.[55] Soccer is ultimately a dream, a dream that begins in childhood, and hopefully a dream that is never extinguished. Academies are special training programs set up by clubs to help them develop young players and nourish dreams, and in fact, all Premiership clubs in Britain have academies.[56]

Although perhaps too few, children have been rescued from crushing poverty and life's indignities as a result of the professional development programs of professional clubs, examples of how, at times, "soccer saves lives."[57] Recall that Rivaldo, Eusébio, McGrath, and countless other soccer stars were "saved" by the dream of playing professional soccer and eventually escaping the poverty of their childhood. A joint UNICEF and FIFA program called "Spaces of Hope" reaches out to poor children in violent slum areas in Brazilian cities such as Rio de Janeiro and São Paulo.[58] For Antonio Muller, schools for more children combined with soccer can nourish the dreams of future soccer professionals and non-players alike: "The schools belong to society. Society should move to promote opportunity for all Brazilians by putting soccer to work in its schools. For a few, it might turn out to be the dream come true of soccer stardom, but with a complete academic education, even for the many, economic opportunity will begin to expand."[59] The campaign "Professional Football against Hunger" was launched in 2008 at the Food and Agricultural Organization (FAO) headquarters in the presence of former Italian soccer star and FAO Goodwill Ambassador Roberto Baggio: "The implementation of the campaign represents an important milestone in the involvement of Professional Football in the global fight against hunger and poverty, which includes the 30 Member Leagues and Associate Members of European Professional Football Leagues representing more than 800 professional football clubs across Europe."[60]

Seen from a Freudian perspective, soccer is ultimately a series of dreams and attempts to fulfill dreams. The best soccer players such as Sánchez, Cha, and Milla inspire the soccer dreams of future generations of children. They leave us with their memories and those memories are the nuggets of gold that nourish our hearts and souls. Your childhood might be gone, but its memories live on. For soccer to be great and beautiful, we must never forget that it is a simple child's game that should give us joy. Victory, defeat, or draw, soccer is made up of billions of dreams of little boys and girls. It is the magic of dreams in childhood that gives soccer both its tragedy and ultimately its beauty.

Chapter Ten

Immortal Heroes?

Soccer and the Meaning of Life

Philosophy is the discipline concerned with how we acquire knowledge and wisdom, meaning, and the purpose of life. It can be defined as "the study of ideas about knowledge, truth, the nature and meaning of life"; as "a particular set of ideas about knowledge, truth, the nature and meaning of life"; or "a set of ideas about how to do something or how to live."[1] Philosophers from Plato to Nietzsche and Heidegger to Levinas have opined about knowledge, wisdom, spirituality, the human condition, immortality, and the meaning of life.

Plato (429–347 BCE) is "by any reckoning, one of the most dazzling writers in the Western literary tradition and one of the most penetrating, wide-ranging, and influential authors in the history of philosophy, as it is often conceived—a rigorous and systematic examination of ethical, political, metaphysical, and epistemological issues, armed with a distinctive method—can be called his invention."[2]

For the German philosopher Friedrich Nietzsche, a "re-evaluation of all values" was imperative in a modern age when "god was dead."[3] He attacks morality for its commitment to false claims about human agency and its negative impact on the distinctive norms and values of the highest types of human beings ("higher men"). Morality, argued Nietzsche, is beyond "good" and "evil," as well as a form of false consciousness imposed by society, limiting "higher" human beings.[4]

For the French philosopher Emmanuel Levinas, philosophy should primarily be concerned with the "calculation of happiness (utilitarianism)," "the cultivation of virtues (virtue ethics)," or the search for the "wisdom of love" rather than the quest for "love of wisdom" (that is, the literal Greek meaning of the word "philosophy").[5] Levinas insists that ethics and responsibility are shaped through the face-to-face experiences of the encounter with the Other. This encounter can possibly evoke a greater understanding of oneself, as well as empathy and tenderness with respect to the Other.

For Martin Heidegger, one of the towering German philosophical giants of the twentieth century and the author of *Being and Time* (1927), "Philosophy is metaphysics. Metaphysics thinks beings as a whole—the world, man, God—with respect to the belonging together of beings in Being."[6] Echoing Nietzsche's "talk about the end of philosophy," Heidegger argued that Western philosophy had lost its way and questioned what it was searching for.[7] As a result, truth had become unclear and we must return to the essence of Being. Heidegger thus called for a return to the practical as a way to reveal truth for humanity. He analyzes the notion of Being through themes such as mortality, care, anxiety, time, history, and death. Yet Heidegger joined the Nazi Party in 1933 and in a 1935 lecture described the "inner truth and greatness" of the Nazi movement, thus leading to one interpretation that for Heidegger Nazism was the embodiment of Being.

Other philosophers were also concerned with the relationship between philosophy and engagement with the world. Karl Marx declared in his "Theses on Feuerbach" in the first chapter of *The German Ideology* (1845) the following revolutionary philosophical claim: "The philosophers have only interpreted the world, in various ways; the point is to change it."[8] Marx argued that history was a titanic struggle between the bourgeoisie and proletariat, but made it clear that he sided with the proletariat in its desire to smash capitalism as an unethical economic system. Philosophers must thus play a role in helping to overthrow capitalism and erecting a more egalitarian, classless, and international communist order.

In short, philosophers have viewed the world from radically different perspectives, but those different perspectives can teach us about the relationship between philosophy and soccer. Had the aforementioned philosophers been alive, Plato might have called for the abolition of FIFA and its replacement by a Worldwide Soccer Republic ruled by philosopher-kings; Levinas might have encouraged us to have more empathy for our opponents; Heidegger might have seen soccer as embedded in universal Being; Nietzsche would have praised the heroic immortals of the game; and Marx would have completely changed the nationalistic and capitalist basis around which world soccer is structured. As Ethan Zohn, the winner of *Survivor: Africa* and co-founder of Grassroot Soccer who played professionally for the Hawaii Tsunami and Cape Cod Crusaders of the United Soccer Leagues and in Zimbabwe for Highlanders Football Club, stated in what appeared to echo a union of Heideggerian and Levinasian perspectives, "Soccer is part of the Being of billions of players fans and worldwide and thus allows you to know others:

Soccer is inside me—it's part of who I am. It's a window into lives all around the world."[9]

This chapter is about the relationships between soccer and philosophy (or the search for knowledge and wisdom), spirituality, immortality, the human condition, and the meaning of life. Philosophers allow us to reflect on soccer and the quest for knowledge (or wisdom), the spirituality of the game, immortality, the human condition, and the meaning of life.

Edited by Ted Richards, a lecturer in philosophy from the University of Tennessee, *Soccer and Philosophy: Beautiful Thoughts on the Beautiful Game* is an innovative edited collection of articles by a team of international philosophers, who use philosphers as diverse as Aristotle, Gadamer, and Wittgenstein in order to analyze soccer's universality and its specific rules, aesthetic players, the metaphysics of free kicks, the nature of fans, and the ethics of referees.[10] Steve Taylor connects soccer and sports in general to spirituality: "In fact it's possible to say that—depending on your definition of spirituality—the desire to experience spiritual well-being is one reason we play sports."[11] An integral part of the human condition is the drama of the game. Soccer is also related to the drama of life and the game. As Pete Davies, a British soccer writer, stated, "Soccer is not about justice. It's a drama—and criminally wrong decisions against you are part and parcel of that."[12] Soccer players have no choice about where they were born, their material circumstances at birth, or their physical traits. Despite his height of only five feet seven inches, the Argentinean-born Barcelona star Lionel Messi is arguably "the best sportsman alive."[13]

Soccer also teaches us about immortality. We will all die one day, but soccer players and especially exceptional players leave their mark on all future generations and are often seen as immortal heroes. Their accomplishments and their legacies often stand the test of time and are valorized by future generations. Through a reflection on soccer and spirituality, immortality, and the human condition, we might learn about the various meanings of life.

Examples of immortality in soccer abound with players, clubs, and fans. The former Manchester United great and Northern Ireland international George Best is such an immortal idol among his people that he had an international airport in Belfast named after him. Airports are usually named after famous politicians or generals (Pierre Trudeau in Montreal or Charles de Gaulle in Paris), or revered heroes of the nation (Benito Juárez in Mexico City), but not soccer players—except for George Best. The Belfast-born Best won the European Cup with Manchester United and was named the European Footballer of the Year in 1968. Northern Ireland's Football Association immortalized him by calling him the "greatest player to ever pull on the green shirt of Northern Ireland."[14]

Clubs in particular historical periods can also be immortalized. Founded in 1899, AC Milan is one of the most famous soccer clubs in history. Its website describes the period between 1986 and 1996 as "without a doubt the most prolific period, not only in terms of the number of trophies won, but in the excellent performances and exciting style of play."[15] Those AC Milan teams were known as "The Immortals" or "The Invincibles," as they took the game to new heights through Dutch legends Gullit, Van Basten, and Frank Rijkaard.[16] In the 1988–1989 season, Milan ruled Europe, lifting the Champions' Cup after beating Red Star Belgrade, Werder Bremen, Real Madrid in the semi-finals, and Steaua Bucharest in the finals. With over 100,000 spectators filling Barcelona's *Camp Nou* stadium, Milan were emphatic 4–0 winners in the finals. With Sacchi at the helm, the team won a league title, two Champions' Cups, two Intercontinental Cups, two European Super Cups, and one Italian League Super Cup.

Eduardo Galeano explains how the great Real Madrid teams of the 1950s and 1960s "embodied all the virtues of Immortal Spain, but it looked more like a Foreign Legion"[17]—the Spanish club won twelve La Liga titles in their glory days from 1953 to 1969. Those Real Madrid teams won five consecutive European Cups from 1955 to 1960 and included a dazzling array of "immortal" foreign talents: the Argentines Di Stéfano and Rial, the Frenchman Kopa, the Uruguayan Santamaria, and the Hungarians Puskás, Kocsis, and Kubala.[18] These Real Madrid sides also included Spanish "immortals" such as Gento and Del Sol. The Real side comprising Di Stéfano and Puskás that hammered Eintracht Frankfurt 7–3 in the 1960 European Cup final was according to a group of BBC soccer experts—"without equal" in soccer history.[19] In 1960, Real Madrid played "a kind of football we hadn't seen before. They had the whole package, and the star that shone brightest was Alfredo Di Stéfano," insisted soccer pundit Armfield.[20]

Helenio Herrera, the great former Inter Milan coach, insisted that the Argentine-born forward was the soccer immortal of all time: "Alfredo Di Stéfano was the greatest footballer of all time—far better even than Pelé. He was, simultaneously, the anchor in defence, the playmaker in midfield, and the most dangerous marksman in attack."[21] Soccer writer Richard Henshaw made this germane remark about the former Real Madrid giant: "Di Stéfano's ability to perform all tasks on the field elevated him above the stature of other great players."[22] Soccer analyst Keir Radnedge said the following about Di Stéfano: "No other player so effectively combined individual expertise with an all-embracing ability to organize a team to play to his command. He was 'total soccer' personified before the term had been invented. Di Stéfano remains to many of us the Greatest Footballer of All Time."[23] The former Real Madrid president Lorenzo Sanz expressed gratitude toward Di Stéfano: "We will never be able to thank him enough for all he has done for Real Madrid. Di Stéfano will always be in our hearts."[24] Perhaps the greatest praise for Di Stéfano came from his own countryman and another soccer immortal, Diego Maradona: "I don't know if I had been a better player than Pelé, but I can say without any doubt that Di Stéfano was better than Pelé. I am proud when one speaks of Di Stéfano. Pelé would have flopped had he played in Europe, whereas Alfredo has played very well throughout the world. I can say that Maradona could be worse than Pelé. But I emphasize Di Stéfano was better."[25]

Immortality can also be a concern for soccer fans. Who wants to think about having their organs removed after death? One famous Brazilian soccer club seems to have the answer to this question:

> Brazil has helped to remove that anxiety by giving soccer fans a compelling reason to sign a donation card: the ability to become "immortal fans" of their favorite soccer club, keeping their passion alive. Organ donor cards were distributed to fans of Sport Club Recife at the stadium, through a Facebook app or through the mail. The integrated campaign featured real patients on transplant waiting lists promising to be loyal fans, thus giving people a real connection and reason to donate. Having their hearts continue to beat for Sport Club Recife is a concept that hits close to home for many ardent fans. As one says in the case study video, "First God, second Sport Club Recife, third family, fourth work." By getting Sport Club Recife fans to feel they are helping their team by signing a donation card, the campaign succeeded in making people more at ease and even excited about becoming a donor. So much so that more than 51,000 organ donor cards have been distributed to date, and organ donations increased by 54 percent in one year.[26]

Remember how in earlier chapters I pointed to Albert Camus and Eduardo Galeano as writers who wrote about soccer and thus immortalized the game and some of its greatest characters and stars. I have more insights about the relationship between soccer and fine arts in chapter 11, especially how artists have immortalized the game, its players, and fans. It is the claim of this chapter that while soccer players are mere mortals, through their play on the pitch or their actions off the pitch, their legacies endure and can inspire billions of people across the world. They inspire not only the living, but also the unborn and therefore future generations of players and fans. Players can become immortals because of their performances, characters, and larger-than-life charisma. Clubs and fans can also seek to attain immortality. In teaching us about life, death, and immortality, soccer stars also teach us lessons about philosophy, the human condition, the quest for knowledge, spirituality, joy, tragedy, and the meaning of life.

JERSEY #10: THE IMMORTALS

Before I further discuss these aforementioned insights, I need to pick two number 10s, perhaps the greatest soccer immortals of all time.

The number 10 is the player that all fans really come to see when they pay for their tickets. He is a playmaker, a goalscorer, a trickster, a showman, and a charismatic leader that carries the entire team on his shoulders. He can become a soccer immortal. African national teams and clubs reserve the number 10 for their greatest player; a player who does magical things on the field. When we think of number 10, we immediately think of Pelé and Diego Maradona. The debate will always rage about which player was better and which player is more immortal. Some insist that Pelé had greater players around him. Others say that Maradona was better because soccer was slower and less physical in Pelé's days. Another view says that Pelé scored more goals, won more World Cups, and was a more complete (ethical) person on and off the field compared to Maradona. I will not judge between the two perspectives. They were different types of players playing in differing epochs. Both Maradona and Pelé were honored as joint FIFA Players of the Twentieth Century. Thus, I pick Maradona and Pelé as the greatest number 10s in the history of soccer. These two soccer stars are immortals like no other players that have played the game.

The "King of Soccer"

He was known as "the King," "the King Pelé," the "King of Soccer," or "the Black Pearl." Writing in *The Encyclopedia of World Soccer*, Richard Henshaw paid this fitting tribute to Pelé:

> The most celebrated player of all time and probably the best, though some Brazilians still believe Arthur Friedenreich has never been surpassed, and some Europeans would rank Alfedo Di Stéfano as his equal. Pelé's statistical record is staggering, but anyone who has ever seen him play will think first of genius as a stylist on the field on the field. It is probably true, as Brazilian observers have often pointed out, that Pelé would have become the world's most accomplished player at any position, but it was at inside left that he received all the accolades a player could possibly muster. The perfection of his physical attributes, moreover, has been miraculously paralleled by a gracious and engaging personality, as well as a strong desire to teach and lead, which have given him universal recognition as a genuine world idol.
>
> Memories focus on flashes of movement: body feints, dribbles in which his feet are an unnecessary luxury, dummies sold, headers taken over towering defenders, and widely arched shots around walls of players. In his first goal against Sweden in 1958, he pushed the ball over his shoulder with his thigh, pivoted, and fired a shot past the hapless goalkeeper. In 1961, against Fluminense at the Maracaña, he dribbled from his own penalty area past six oncom-

ing defenders and the goalkeeper—into the opponent's net. (This famous goal became immortalized as the *Gol de Placa*, or Commemorative Plate Goal.) Among his haunting, yet prophetic, near-misses was that quick shot in his World Cup debut against the USSR that hit the post and left the great Yashin beaten. Some have tried to explain Pelé's magical qualities in physiological terms: his well-placed center of gravity for the particular skills needed in the game, or his uncommon peripheral vision, or even some form of advanced neurological development. Pelé himself, however, simply points to God-given gifts for which he is very thankful.[27]

Here are three famous memories of Pelé: leaping higher than Italy's taller defender Fachetti and scoring with a magnificent header in the 1970 World Cup finals; comforted by the veteran goalkeeper Gilmar after breaking down with tears of joy when Brazil won its first World Cup in 1958 (he was only seventeen years old); and his retirement from the national team in 1971 in front of 130,000 screaming fans that implored him to "Stay! Stay! Stay!" There are many more memories, including his "Love, Love, Love!" retirement speech with the New York Cosmos in 1977. Or there was a special moment in the World Cup final against Italy in 1970 when Pelé held up the ball with such calm on Brazil's third goal against Italy in the finals, waited for the overlapping Carlos Alberto as if he had eyes in the back of his head, and fed him a delicate pass, thus culminating one of the best collective goals in the history of soccer. He assisted on three goals and scored another in Brazil's 4–1 final win against Italy. Or the famous photo where he made experienced defenders from Schalke 04 eat dirt with his breathtaking dribbling for Santos in Essen in 1963.

Pelé's statistical history is like no other player. With Santos, he won four São Paulo championships from 1958 to 1962, twice more in 1964 and 1965, and three in a row from 1967 to 1969. His goal-scoring tally is awe inspiring: 127 goals in 1959, 110 goals in 1961, 101 goals in 1965, and in the years in between an average of more than 70 goals per season. He was the scoring leader of the São Paulo league competition from 1957 to 1965, in 1969, and in 1973. In 1962 and 1963, he inspired Santos to win both the Copa Libertadores and Intercontinental Cup. European crowds in Lisbon and Milan sang his praises.

For the Brazilian national team, Pelé was even more heroic. He led Brazil to three World Cup triumphs in 1958, 1962, and 1970. Injuries in 1962 due to hacking and dirty tackling became a serious problem for Pelé, as they did at the 1966 World Cup where Bulgarian and Portuguese defenders harassed him brutally. Yet he holds the record for goals at the international level (ninety-seven) in only ninety-three appearances. He made a stunning 1,363 appearances for club and country, scoring 1,281 goals, second only to Arthur Friedenreich for the all-time record. He has a whopping ninety-two hat tricks to his record and a record seven international hat tricks. He was the scoring

leader in the South American Championship in 1959 and the Copa Libertadores in 1965. He was feted as the Latin American Footballer of the Year in
1973. He was voted the Best Player of the Twentieth Century. Pelé was
elected "Athlete of the Century" by the International Olympic Committee
and Reuters News Agency in 1999, as well as by the French newspaper
L'Équipe in 1981. Even in his final sojourn with the New York Cosmos from
1975 to 1977, Pelé could still play well and he scored fifty-five goals in only
105 appearances. A giant stadium in Maceio, *Estadio Rei Pelé* (King Pelé
Stadium), is named in his honor.

The accolades Pelé has received are like no other soccer player in history.
Franz Beckenbauer, a teammate of Pelé's with the New York Cosmos said
this about the Brazilian superstar: "Pelé is the greatest player of all time. He
reigned supreme for 20 years. All the others—Diego Maradona, Johan
Cruyff, Michel Platini—rank beneath him. There's no one to compare with
Pelé."[28] As a response to critics who might view Messi, Neymar, or Cristiano
Ronaldo as better than Pelé, Alfredo Di Stéfano, the Real Madrid legend
replied: "The best player ever? Pelé. Messi and Cristiano Ronaldo are both
great players with specific qualities, but Pelé was better."[29] The implication
here is that Pelé was more of a complete player than either the Argentinean
star Lionel Messi, or the Portuguese hero Cristano Ronaldo. Johan Cruyff, a
Dutch soccer legend, was philosophical about Pelé startling gifts: "Pelé was
the only footballer who surpassed the boundaries of logic."[30]

After his soccer career ended, Pelé became a Brazilian Extraordinary
Minister of Sports in 1995. He remains an icon promoting soccer as a commercial enterprise, various causes, and his own interests. Pelé seems ageless,
although he is now in his seventies. The Pelé brand has been handled by a
marketing firm, Legends 10, since 2012. He does lots of ambassadorial work
with the UN and UNESCO with respect to the environment and children. He
has sought to stamp out corruption in soccer, although this is a tough task as I
showed in chapter 6. He helped promote both the 2006 and 2010 World
Cups. In 1997, Pelé even received an honorary Knight Commander of the
Order of the British Empire award from Queen Elizabeth II. Years after his
greatest triumphs, he is still viewed as a soccer immortal by politicians, fans,
and administrators, all conscious of using his name in order to promote
soccer and their image. Yet some soccer fans in his own country harshly
criticized Pelé in 2013 when he urged anti-government protestors to get
behind the Brazilian national team in the Confederation Cup rather than
focus on politics.[31]

The Argentinean Legend

For many Argentineans, Diego Armando Maradona was better than Pelé. He
is a soccer immortal, legend, or even a god. Pelé played on great teams,

whereas it is argued that Maradona made great teams through his sheer genius. Younger fans with no frames of reference necessarily see him as the greatest in world history, as many today see Lionel Messi as the best in world history. They also forget about the accomplishments of Di Stéfano, which have forever sealed him among the immortals in soccer history.

Maradona is remembered for perhaps the greatest moment in soccer history. Byron Butler made these comments on the BBC during Maradona's stunning sixty-five-yard solo goal against England in the quarterfinal of the 1986 World Cup, which was voted the goal of the century and immortalized Maradona in soccer history:

> Maradona, turns like a little eel, he comes away from trouble, little squat man . . . comes inside Butcher and leaves him for dead, outside Fenwick and leaves him for dead, and puts the ball away . . . and that is why Maradona is the greatest player in the world.[32]

Despite Maradona's earlier "hand of God" goal, the second goal against England is the greatest goal in the history of the World Cup. Why is the goal so great? Maradona received the ball in his own half, did a majestic pirouette as he was being harassed by several players, ran more than half the length of the pitch, and made five England internationals (Peter Beardsley, Steve Hodge, Peter Reid, Terry Butcher, and Terry Fenwick) and goalkeeper Peter Shilton look like they were flies on the wall. We do not know if we will ever see a goal of this kind again.

Maradona was a genius at the 1986 World Cup and he single-handedly led his country to its second World Cup triumph after defeating West Germany 3–2 in an entertaining final. In the semi-final against Belgium, he scored on another stunning solo run. In the final, hounded by the German defenders with double and triple marking, he found a way to make space to set up Jorge Burruchaga for the winning goal. The 115,000 spectators at the Azteca Stadium went mad with joy. The soccer authorities responsible for the Azteca built a statue of Maradona scoring the "goal of the century," located at the entrance of the stadium. He is thus an immortal in Mexico too. Of Argentina's fourteen goals at the 1986 World Cup, Maradona scored or assisted on ten. Perhaps with the exception of France's Just Fontaine thirteen goals at the 1958 World Cup, there is no more dominating single performance in the history of a World Cup tournament.

If Maradona is a soccer immortal, he has also stirred his fair share of controversy. The "hand of God" goal was a shame for most soccer fans around the world, although some have justified it using unjustifiable arguments. Maradona has battled drugs and was sent home after a failed drug test after scoring an incredible, curling goal against Greece in the 1994 World Cup. His politically leftist leanings are obvious, including support for Fidel

Castro, Che Guevara, Hugo Chavez, and even the genocidal regime of the Islamic Republic of Iran. If one had to pick between Pelé and Maradona as role models, Pelé wins. If we narrow the Pelé-Maradona debate to talent, fans in polls unanimously pick Maradona, often because they did not see Pelé play.

Jorge Valdano, a former teammate of Maradona's on the 1986 World Cup-winning Argentinean squad, summed up the chasm between Maradona's public adoration (and accomplishments) and his personal struggles:

> He is someone many people want to emulate, a controversial figure, loved, hated, who stirs great upheaval, especially in Argentina. . . . Stressing his personal life is a mistake. Maradona has no peers inside the pitch, but he has turned his life into a show, and is now living a personal ordeal that should not be imitated. [33]

Writing in *The Houston Chronicle*, Jen Bensinger summarized for a North American audience the iconic status and religious-like veneration of Maradona in his native Argentina:

> To understand the gargantuan shadow Maradona casts over his soccer-mad homeland, one has to conjure up the athleticism of Michael Jordan, the power of Babe Ruth—and the human fallibility of Mike Tyson. Lump them together in a single barrel-chested man with shaggy black hair and you have El Diego, idol to the millions who call him D10S, a mashup of his playing number and the Spanish word for God. [34]

If Maradona was a "divine" and immortal soccer figure, his empirical numbers on soccer pitches are a "revelation" of his greatness. He was joint FIFA Player of the Twentieth Century with Pelé. He led Argentina as a captain to a second World Cup win in 1986 and in the 1990 World Cup to a runner-up finish. In his international career, he earned ninety-one caps and scored thirty-four goals, while dominating many of the matches in which he played. He started in a remarkable twenty-one consecutive matches for Argentina in four World Cups in 1982, 1986, 1990, and 1994. In twenty-one World Cup appearances, Maradona scored eight goals and added another eight assists. His five goals and five assists in 1986 were the most dominating World Cup performances in a single tournament. He is second behind the striker Gabriel Batistuta in goals for Argentina in World Cup finals.

Maradona twice broke world records for transfers. Maradona played for Argentinos Juniors, Boca Juniors, Barcelona, Napoli, Seville, and Newell's Old Boys. He is remembered fondly by all those clubs and their fans, although from 1993 to 1994 he made only five appearances for Argentinean club Newell's Old Boys and never scored. From 1976 to 1997 with his aforementioned club sides, Maradona scored 258 goals in 492 matches.

The Argentinean midfield general's trophy case for his various clubs is indeed impressive:

1. Boca Juniors: Metropolitano championship (1), 1981
2. Barcelona: *Copa del Rey* (1), 1983; Copa de la Liga (1), 1983; and *Supercopa de España* (1), 1983
3. Napoli: *Serie A* (2), 1987 and 1990; *Coppa Italia* (1), 1987; UEFA Cup (1), 1989; and *Supercoppa Italiana* (1), 1990

Maradona's individual honors are a testament to his soccer greatness:

1. Argentinean league Top Scorer: 1979, 1980, and 1981
2. World Player of the Year: 1979
3. Argentinean Football Writers' Player of the Year: 1979, 1980, 1981, and 1986
4. South American Footballer of the Year: 1979 and 1980
5. FIFA World Cup Golden Ball: 1986
6. FIFA World Cup All-Star Team: 1986 and 1990
7. FIFA World Cup Silver Boot: 1986
8. Argentinean Sports Writers' Sportsman of the Year: 1986
9. United Press International Athlete of the Year Award: 1986
10. Best Soccer Player in the World (*Onze d'Or*): 1986 and 1987
11. World Football Awards Player of the Year: 1986
12. Italian Serie A top scorer: 1987–1988
13. Golden Ball for services to soccer (*France Football*): 1996
14. Argentinean Sports Writers' Sportsman of the Century: 1999
15. FIFA Player of the Century: 2000
16. "FIFA Goal of the Century" (1986 [2–1] v. England; second goal): 2002
17. FIFA World Cup Dream Team: 2002
18. FIFA's 125 top living soccer players

In addition, Maradona's number 10 jersey was retired by Napoli in 2000. The Argentinean Senate honored him with the Domingo Faustino Sarmiento award for lifetime achievement. Yet more important than any of these collective and individual honors was the joy that Maradona gave Argentina and the world. In Napoli, there are still public and private soccer shrines dedicated to him. In his own country, he is probably just as revered—perhaps more—than any Catholic saint. Maradona is not only a soccer immortal, but perhaps the greatest player that ever played the game.

SOCCER IMMORTALS, THE HUMAN CONDITION, THE MEANING OF LIFE, AND SPIRITUALITY

Soccer has already created its share of immortals and not merely at the number 10 position. As previous chapters demonstrated, Chilavert, Buffon, Figueroa, Maldini, Andrade, Beckenbauer, Zidane, Cristiano Ronaldo, Beckham, Gerrard, Cha, and Hugo Sánchez are all immortals too. Some immortals are no longer with us, such as Matthias Sindelar, Giuseppe Meazza, and Ferenc Puskás, but their legacies live on in peoples' memories, street names, or names of stadiums. Some soccer stars are immortalized in bronze statues such as Bobby Moore, Duncan Edwards, Eusébio, and more recently Zinedine Zidane.

As we have shown, Maradona and Pelé are soccer immortals recognized for their on-field accomplishments by fans, critics, players, and coaches. The exploits of Maradona and Pelé, or Di Stéfano, will live for all time. There are immortals that are being created at this moment, such as Lionel Messi, Cristiano Ronaldo, Neymar, and Radamel Falcao. Maradona anointed Messi as his immortal successor.[35] Messi won the prestigious *Ballon d'Or* and FIFA World Player of the Year in 2009, as well as the FIFA *Ballon d'Or* in 2009, 2010, and 2011. He is in an elite list of only four soccer stars to win the *Ballon d'Or* three times. In the 2011–2012 season, he set the world record for goals with a staggering seventy-three goals. In that same season, he also scored a record fifty goals in Spain's La Liga. He scored a record five goals in one Champions League match in 2012. Messi has helped Barcelona win five La Liga trophies, two Copas del Rey, five Supercopas de España, three Champions League titles, two Super Cups, and two Club World Cups. If he ended his career tomorrow, Messi would still be one of the greatest number 10s in the history of the game. He is young, yet already a soccer immortal. When his career ends, we might better judge if he was Maradona's "second coming" and an equal to Maradona or Pelé.

We might debate whether Messi is a soccer immortal. Dividing soccer players between immortal and mortal is proabably part of the human condition. Another aspect of the human condition is related to the circumstances of our birth: poor or rich, place of birth, or physical stature. Those aforementioned factors might influence, but not fully determine, whether you become a soccer immortal. Messi is a case in point. Messi is rather short, but he did not allow his physical traits to stop him from becoming arguably the greatest player in the world today. Messi can thus inform us about soccer and the human condition because of his short stature:

> Put simply, there is no other team sport where size matters less. And while you do need stamina, you don't even need to be particularly quick. It is good in a team to have a mix, to have tall, strapping players as well as nimble, speedy

ones. But everyone can get a look in, with the possible exception of fatties—
though a few of those, notably the Brazilian Ronaldo in the later stages of his
career, have had the talent to continue to make the grade at the highest level.
Diego Maradona also played with a fair bit of spare blubber on him in his later
years but the point about him is that, beefy or lean, he was decidedly short.
Professional players average out at around 5'10" but Maradona was 5'5". . . .
His compatriot and rival Messi is barely taller. [36]

Two of Messi's "midfield lieutenants" with Barcelona are Andrés Iniesta and
Xavi Hernández. Their old and bitter rivals, Real Madrid, call the triumvarite
"the dwarves" in the Real Madrid locker room. [37] As one writer put it, "The
Real players are indeed giants, by comparison." [38] Using the Barcelona "immortals" as his examples, he concludes by stating that size is no obstacle to
soccer greatness: "All of which is to say that in almost every other team sport
in existence you'll know just by looking at your child's physique at the age
of 14 whether he's going to have any chance of making it as a professional;
in soccer, big dreams fit all sizes." [39] Like Messi, Iniesta and Xavi could have
lamented their short stature, but instead proved an important lesson with
respect to soccer and the human condition: talent, skill, and technical finesse
matter more than physical stature.

Ferenc Puskás (1927–2006) is undoubtedly one of the greatest soccer
legends of all time. Like Messi, he was short (five feet eight inches) yet
slightly rounder. Puskás did not allow his inherited physical attributes to
undermine his drive for soccer immortality. Thus, Puskás is an example of
both soccer immortality and a notion related to the human condition and
soccer, which argues that talent matters more than your biological or physical
traits. Puskás's goal-scoring record was nothing short of remarkable. He
scored eighty-four goals in eighty-five international matches for Hungary, as
well as 514 goals in 529 matches in the Hungarian and Spanish leagues.
Puskás was a terror for defenses and his almost one goal per match ratio is
astonishing, a rate that only Cristiano Ronaldo can match among contemporary players. Puskás was most known for his stunning performances with the
Hungarian national team in the early 1950s, especially the 6–3 drubbing of
England at Wembley and a 7–1 triumph against England in Budapest, as well
as Hungary's second place finish at the 1954 World Cup in Switzerland. He
also won a gold medal for Hungary at the 1952 Olympic Games.

When he joined Real Madrid in 1958, he was considered beyond his
prime and unfit, but Real Madrid president Santiago Bernabéu wanted to sign
him. He rewarded the Real Madrid president with 242 goals in 262 matches,
as well as the leading scorer titles in the Spanish league in 1960 (twenty-six),
1961 (twenty-seven), 1963 (twenty-six), and 1964 (ten). In this period, Real
Madrid was one of the best teams in Europe and the world, and as pointed
out earlier, can be considered one of the best club teams in soccer history.
With Di Stéfano as the center forward and Gento as outside left, as well as

the inside left Puskás, Real Madrid won five consecutive titles from 1960 to 1961 until 1964 to 1965. In Europe, Real Madrid and Puskás won three European Cups in 1959, 1960, and 1966. The Hungarian's most memorable moments were both with Real Madrid: four goals against Eintracht Frankfurt in the 1960 European Cup final and a hat trick against Benfica in the 1962 European Cup final. In total, Puskás won ten national championships (five Hungarian and five Spanish). He began his career with Kipest and Honved from 1943 to 1956, amassing 374 goals for the latter Budapest club in only 358 matches. He won eight scoring titles between his native Hungary and Spain.

There is no doubt that Puskás was the best of the gifted "Mighty Magyars" of the 1950s. He was a more complete player than the Hungarian legends Czibor, Bozsik, Kocsis, and Hidegkuti. At the 1954 World Cup final against Germany, he played with a hairline fracture and still scored. While in the opening round game against West Germany, Puskás scored and Hungary won 8–3, they lost 3–2 in the finals after a dramatic German fight back. He always scored, except in the 1962 World Cup when he played for his adopted country Spain. In four appearances for Spain from 1961 to 1962, Puskás never scored.

After retiring at the age of thirty-nine to a rapturous reception by the Real Madrid faithful, Puskás became a coach for thirteen different teams. His greatest coaching moment came in 1971 when he guided Panathinaikos to the European Cup final, where they lost 2–0 to AFC Ajax. Despite his defection in 1956 in the context of the Hungarian Revolution, he took charge of the Hungarian national team in 1993. As a sign of his immortal status, in 2002 the Népstadion in Budapest was renamed the Puskás Ferenc Stadion to honor the Hungarian great. In October 2009, FIFA inaugurated the introduction of the Puskás Award, to be presented to the player who has scored the "most beautiful goal" of the year. Puskás scored many lovely goals. He was short, stocky, and paunchy, yet technically gifted in front of goal. He hardly scored with his head or with his right foot, but he had great vision and a left foot that hardly ever failed him. His former teammates at Real Madrid speak of him not only as a gifted player with a sensational eye for goal, but also describe him as a team player.

In 2000, Puskás was diagnosed with Alzheimer's. He died from pneumonia in Budapest in 2006. He was the greatest Hungarian soccer player of all time and a world immortal. It is rare for soccer stars to be buried in a state funeral, but the legendary Puskás was. He was so revered by his compatriots that his coffin was moved from Puskás Ferenc Stadion to Heroes' Square for a military salute. As he began his career in the Kispest district of Budapest, a street was renamed after him in 2007 exactly on the one-year anniversary of his death. A statue was built in his honor of him teaching children how to play soccer. Hungary's former prime minister Ferenc Gyurcsany paid him the greatest honor and sealed him as an immortal for all of Hungary: "The best-known Hungarian of the 20th century is gone."[40] Thus, it was fitting that his former club Real Madrid gave him a moving and musically powerful pre-game tribute after his death in 2006.[41] The club's president Ramón Calderón was especially gracious:

> This is one of the saddest days for the Madrid fans, I can assure you that it is the most painful day since I took the presidency. He had many friends and was a man liked by everyone, admired as a professional and a person. I will remember his goals with much affection, he was the pichichi on four occasions. The Madrid fans in general, and those of my age in particular, will feel a great emptiness for the loss of one our childhood heroes. I want to send a big hug to all of his family and friends in these very painful moments.[42]

Soccer is also related to the human condition in that we cannot always win and game decisions by the referee are out of our control. "Typically dressed in funereal black, the referee offers living proof of the contradiction between the world as we would like it to be and the world as it is; of our tragic inability to control our lives (or deaths), however gifted we might be or however hard we try; of our unavoidable vulnerability to the slings and arrows of outrageous fortune,"[43] wrote John Carlin. Soccer analyst Vijay Murali compiled a list of the twenty-two worst refereeing decisions in soccer history because they played a "major role in the outcome of the game, and possibly the season as well."[44] Some of the worst decisions include the following: Spain was disallowed two perfectly legitimate goals against South Korea at the World Cup in 2002, Frank Lampard's incorrect no-goal call against Germany in the 2010 World Cup, and Thierry Henry's blatant hand-ball against Ireland, which led to a William Gallas goal in the crucial qualifying match against Ireland for the World Cup in 2010. Yet the worst decision ever by the referee cost one English team team a league title:

> Leeds United were in the midst of a title challenge when this inexplicable decision by Ray Tinkler cost them this game and ultimately, the title. The linesman signals West Brom player Colin Suggett offside and the Leeds defense stops dead, but Tinkler allows play to continue and Jeff Astle scores the goal. As a result, Leeds lost their title to Arsenal, leaving their manager and players devastated.[45]

There is a darker side to the human condition. Countless soccer players in Africa and Latin America are born into poverty (for example, Pelé) or malnutrition (Rivaldo, a key member of Brazil's World Cup-winning team in 2002). Rivaldo's physical appearance has left its scars from his difficult childhood: malnourishment caused bowleggedness and the loss of several teeth.[46] FIFA.com traced Rivaldo's improbable meteoric rise to soccer immortal status:

> Growing up as the son of a poor family in the Brazilian coastal town of Recife, Rivaldo was no stranger to hunger as a boy. At the age of 16 he lost his father, but despite all the hardships of his early years his talent has allowed him to carve out a successful career in world football. At the age of 27 a dream has come true for him; he has been selected as FIFA World Player 1999.[47]

Despite the extraordinary accomplishments of Pelé or Rivaldo, many soccer players born into poverty will remain in poverty. In 2013, 800 teenagers in Rio de Janeiro took part in the Favelas Cup, a tournament that includes players from eighty local shantytowns.[48] Major Brazilian clubs such as Botafogo, Vasco, Flamengo, and Fluminense all brought scouts to the tournament.[49] Professional soccer could be a ticket out of poverty for some, but ultimately for too few. Poverty has always been part of the human condition, and harsh capitalism without any social and health safety nets perpetuates this cycle.

According to one soccer commentator, soccer is still the most democratic sport in the world because you can be short and poor and still be successful:

> It does not matter how poor you are, how meagre your circumstances, you'll find the means to rustle up a game of soccer. Because you don't need any means. You can play on a street, on an empty lot or, as I have seen in Africa, on a field splattered with cow-dung. For "goalposts" you can use a couple of small rocks, or old shirts. You don't even need a ball, in the conventional sense of the word. You can play with rolled up plastic bags or, as I did as a child in Argentina, with rolled-up socks. It is in conditions such as these did Maradona and the likes of Cameroon's Samuel Eto'o, who played both for Real Madrid and Barcelona, have learned the beautiful game.[50]

All these reflections about the human condition and immortal soccer stars and clubs lead us to the view that soccer is not merely a game, as the legendary manager Shankly pointed out, but "much, much more than that." Our soccer heroes and their immortal exploits are reflections of the human condition. We are animals that breathe, eat, procreate, live, and die. Yet we are surely more than animals, as we search for meaning in our lives. Victor Frankl's famous book first published in 1946, *Man's Search for Meaning,* is still powerful today.[51] Here was a world-famous psychologist who survived the absolute horrors of the Nazi concentration camps, yet what is most profound about the book was that Frankl insisted that our final freedom is our given attitude in any situation in life. We cannot always choose our circumstances: the culture we are born into, our families, the political system we live under, or our economic conditions. In this respect, think back to chapter 2 and soccer players like Elias Figueroa who lived under military dictatorships. Yet we can choose to be freer through our attitude toward life. We can liberate ourselves by searching for meaning in the face of life's adversities. Frankl was truly inspirational and taught us not to sweat the small stuff in life. If a concentration camp survivor could be so heroic and a leader in his field, we could all try to do more in our lives.

Frankl was correct. Humans search for meaning. It is part of the human condition to ask questions such as: What is the meaning of my life? Why do I suffer? Where am I from? Where will I go when I die? Meaning can come from traditional religions, politics, human interactions, friendship, love, and even soccer. Meaning can be found in all aspects of our lives.

Arsène Wenger, the Arsenal soccer manager, embodies that positive attitude toward life even in the face of life's obstacles. "If you do not believe you can do it, then you have no chance at all,"[52] insisted Wenger with respect to soccer players. Or as the former Ireland international and Manchester United star Roy Keane stated: "Fail to prepare, prepare to fail."[53] The legendary manager Bill Shankly insisted, like Frankl, that attitude is what differentiates success from failure: "A lot of football success is in the mind. You must believe you are the best and then make sure that you are."[54]

Ethan Zohn, a former American professional player and cancer survivor, truly takes Frankl's philosophy to heart. He is a founder of Grassroot Soccer, a nonprofit organization that trains professional soccer players to teach African children a life skills curriculum, as well as HIV/AIDS prevention.[55] He co-wrote *Soccer World*, "a series of six books for young readers to explore the culture, history, science, math and geography of different nations in a compelling and meaningful way, through the sport of soccer."[56] One blogger was adamant that Zohn's positive attitude and accomplishments were an inspiration for us all:

> Ethan had to dig deep within to gain strength from his values, character, loved ones and the will to survive. He reiterates that everyone has the power to transcend any situation that is given to us. This power is etched deep within our being and we forget about this invaluable power and start feeling bad for ourselves when we are faced with challenges. Ethan has always reminded himself of this quote, "Never let a crisis go to waste because it is an opportunity to do some really important things."[57]

The Wannsee Conference was an infamous meeting of senior Nazi officials, held in the Berlin suburb of Wannsee on January 20, 1942. The conference organized by the German Nazi state was called by director of the *SS-Reichssicherheitshauptamt* (Reich Main Security Office; RSHA). *SS-Obergruppenführer* Reinhard Heydrich was entrusted with the gruesome task of ensuring the cooperation of administrative elites of various government departments in the implementation of the "final solution to the Jewish question." It was decided at Wannsee that most of the Jews of German-occupied

Europe would be deported to Poland and later exterminated. Soccer players were not spared from the Nazi's barbaric policy. In a far different context compared to Ethan Zohn, a disturbing video "Jewish Soccer Players in Nazis 1944 Propaganda Film" highlights how concentration camp victims were involved in a soccer match of great historical significance and tragedy:

> The players on this field are Jews, prisoners of the Theresienstadt Ghetto set up by the Nazis in 1941. They organized a soccer league and played each week, unaware that deportations to the death camps, to the gas chambers, awaited them. . . . Don't be fooled by the players' nice uniforms or the healthy, well-dressed adults and kids watching the game. This clip is part of a Nazi propaganda film that hoped to refute rumors that Hitler was systematically exterminating the Jews. . . . Nearly 160,000 Jews arrived at the ghetto, but 80% of them died. Almost 90,000 were sent east to the death camps. The Jews who played on the soccer league make up part of those statistics. Just days after filming the soccer sequence for the Nazi propaganda film, nearly all the players, spectators and those who helped the Nazis make the film were sent to Auschwitz and murdered. [58]

In *Kabul Girls Soccer Club: A Dream, Eight Girls, and a Journey Home*,[59] the Afghan-American Awista Ayub explains the power of soccer and life meaning in the face of an authoritarian state, oppression, and extreme poverty:

> Despite major restrictions on their liberties, Afghan women have made inroads in competitive sports such as boxing, martial arts and soccer. Hence it is an opportune time to have a closer look at an inspiring true story of an Afghan-American woman bringing eight Afghan teenagers to the United States for soccer camp and how playing soccer changed the lives of these girls. In the pages of *Kabul Girls Soccer Club*, Awista Ayub interweaves her own story as an Afghan-American, the girls' personal struggle to play soccer and hard-hitting realities like war, oppression, displacement and poverty. [60]

Our soccer immortals also provide us with meaning about "us" and "them." Most of us are soccer mortals. We will be neither soccer professionals, nor superstars such as Maradona or Pelé. Yet even if we cannot be soccer immortals, we might become immortals in what we do outside of the soccer pitch through our works, deeds, or words.

If we are really honest with ourselves, we will recognize that it is hard to be an immortal like Maradona or Pelé, on or off the field. We cannot be immortal gods like Aphrodite, Apollo, or Athena. We cannot be titans like Cronus, the leader of the Titans, who overthrew his father Uranus, only to be overthrown in turn by his son, Zeus. Perhaps we can be heroes like Odysseus, a king of Ithaca who played a key role in the Trojan War and whose adventures are the subject of Homer's *Odyssey*. Or could we be like Achilles, a hero of the Trojan War and a key character in Homer's *Iliad*? We might admit that even being a hero is a tough nut to crack for most of us.

The Epic of Gilgamesh is an ancient literary classic written more than 4,000 years ago. In one passage from the text, Siduri tells Gilgamesh to abandon his quest and instead focus on the joys of life as immortality was never really designed for mortals. She urges him to enjoy each moment here and now rather than pining for what he can never have:

> Who is the mortal who can live forever?
> The life of man is short.
> Only the gods can live forever.
> Therefore put on new clothes,
> a clean robe and a cloak tied with a sash,
> and wash the filth of the journey from your body.
> Eat and drink your fill of the food and drink men eat and drink.
> Let there be pleasure and dancing.[61]

I might also add to "let there be pleasure and dancing," "and enjoyment in soccer." Most of us can never attain immortality. Although soccer greats are heroes of their times who will eventually die, their exploits live forever. Most players are neither heroes nor immortals. Most soccer players, whether professionals or amateurs, will be forgotten, the memories of their soccer joys their greatest compensation. Yet a select group of soccer immortals such as Maradona and Pelé will be remembered when their playing days are over and even when they leave us.

For writers such as the anonymous author of *The Epic of Gilgamesh*, the quest for immortality is a part of the human condition, or an integral aspect of the human psyche. In death, we are surely all one and death is humanity's greatest fear. There is no escaping death, unless you are Aphrodite or Apollo. In life, what unites us is our common humanity. Yet what really divides us are our words, deeds, actions, and exploits. What divides Maradona from you and me is not our humanity, but the fact that he won the World Cup in 1986. He also won domestic titles with Napoli; he scored the greatest goal in the history of the game; he scored outlandish goals from near the half-way mark of the field; he could curl a free kick delicately into the top corner of the net, or break the mesh with a thunderous volley; he dictated and controlled the tempo of a match; he had the desire of a tiger; and he could pass the ball as if his left foot was kissed by providence. His records and titles are his own and also belong to his respective teams. They separate Maradona from the rest of us mortals.

If there were no immortal soccer stars like Maradona, then soccer would be less meaningful. There would be less drive and ambition, as well as little room for self-surpassing. There would be no geniuses, merely soccer players of equal merit. There would be no players kissed by the gods, as highlighted in chapter 5. Soccer is neither communism nor capitalism. It is neither socialism nor liberalism. It neither creates nor desires a world of equals. It is a world of hierarchy. Soccer has its ranks of immortals, mortal heroes, greats, and then all the rest. We seem to like it that way. It is unclear whether our soccer immortals always like it that way. Their immortality does not mean an escape from their alcoholism or drug addictions, as tragically shown by Garrincha or Maradona. Or by the gods of fate that take away soccer squads before their times such as Manchester United, Torino, or the Zambian national team. How much more of an immortal would Duncan Edwards have been had he not died in the Manchester United crash in 1958?

From soccer's immortals, as well as the game's joys and tragedies, we learn life lessons related to life, death, hierarchies, and the meaning of life. By examining the world through soccer, we gain knowledge and nourish the soul. Soccer is a terrain replete with possibilities for knowledge and spirituality.

It is true that we learned a lot in school, yet through soccer we can also examine the world and learn a lot. Through soccer, we learn about life, death, and immortality.

We can also learn about the importance of memories. We know that the memories of our childhood, whether the camaraderie of our own matches and the joy of watching key World Cup matches, will never be experienced again. This is both sweet and tinged with sadness. The matches come and go. We shall take our memories with us to our graves. Those memories are sometimes sweet and pleasurable, making us recall another time when we were younger and perhaps when soccer was different, attractive, and more audacious.

At other times, those memories are filled with pain. They reveal the cruelty of human beings. When Brazil lost the 1950 World Cup final to Uruguay on home soil, Brazil's goalkeeper Moacyr Barbosa (1921–2000) was blamed for letting in the "soft" game-winning goal scored by Alcides Ghiggia and was haunted by ghosts for the rest of his life. Although he won numerous domestic trophies and the *Copa América* with Brazil in 1949, he died penniless, sad, cursed, neglected, and a scapegoat. He lived the life of Job from the Old Testament: abandoned, attacked, disdained, bereft of friends and possessions, and crucified by an entire society of cruel inquisitors. Barbosa is forever identified with the curse of the *Maracanazo*, or "the Maracana blow," named after the stadium where Brazil lost the World Cup final to Uruguay. "The maximum punishment in Brazil is 30 years imprisonment, but I have been paying, for something I am not even responsible for, by now, for 50 years," stated Barbosa years after his goalkeeping blunder.[62] Barbosa was refused commentator roles on television and was barred from Brazilian national team training grounds. Barbosa is the ugly flip side of soccer's penchant for immortals. Immortals must perform and win. If they do not, they will be crucified and perhaps never be forgiven. Barbosa died of a heart attack in 2000. He should have been given some credit for his accomplishments—he took Brazil to the World Cup finals and won the Copa América. He was a decent keeper who wore no gloves and made the greatest blunder in soccer history. Was it fair that Barbosa was treated like a leper, despised by all? When he died, there was relief in Brazil. Some Brazilian immortals such as Sócrates get state recognition and others like Barbosa are ignored and cursed. When Sócrates died in 2011, Brazilian president Dilma Rousseff said Brazil lost "one of its most cherished sons."[63]

The sad tale of Moacyr Barbosa highlights the continuing seriousness of the game for soccer fans. Yet soccer can also offer us some insights about spirituality. Spirituality is the concept of an ultimate or an alleged reality, which is non-material and beyond the here and now. Spirituality is also the inner path of the heart and soul of all those soccer and non-soccer fans around the globe. It is an inner path that allows us to discover the essence of our beings. Or as Philip Sheldrake writes in *A Brief History of Spirituality*, spirituality is ultimately about "deepest values and meanings by which people live."[64] Those values can be forged on and off the soccer pitch. Soccer players and fans derive great meaning from the "world's game" and the "peoples' game." The deep values by which they live, from fair play to fighting to the end of a match with "hope in your heart," are reflected in their soccer exploits, joys, and tragedies.

A spiritual perspective on soccer was highlighted by the legendary Jamaican reggae singer Bob Marley: "Football is a part of I, keep you out of trouble. Discipline. Mek you run in the morningtime. When you run you clear out your head. The world wake up round you."[65] According to the psychologist Mihaly Csikszentmihalyi, sports like soccer allow us to be spiritually in the "flow" and thus assist our physical and mental well-being:

> Sports is important because it's one of the most readily available ways of generating the state of being he calls "flow." This is the state we experience when our attention is completely absorbed in an activity, and our awareness of our surroundings even of ourselves fades away. It's not the passive absorption of watching television or playing computer games, but the "active" absorption we experience when we fully concentrate and make powerful mental efforts—when we perform challenging, stimulating, creative activities like learning a foreign language or a musical instrument, painting or playing sports. "Flow" enables us to take control of our own consciousness, and step beyond the "psychic entropy" which is our normal state, when worries, desires and other kinds of chaotic "thought chatter" run through our minds. We experience an inner peace, and a sense of being more "energised" or alive than usual.[66]

His talent as a youngster earned him the nickname "Pele" "while learning to play on the red dirt streets" of his hometown.[67] A Namibian paper called him "the greatest star of Africa" and insisted that only the former AC Milan and

Liberian international George Weah and the Cameroonian legend Roger Milla could compare in skill to "Pele."[68] Abedi Pele was one of the trailblazers for African soccer players in Europe. He played with major clubs in France, Germany, Switzerland, Italy, Qatar, and the United Arab Emirates. His club sides included Lille and Marseille in France, Torino in Italy, 1860 Munich in Germany, and Zurich in Switzerland. In total, Pele scored 157 goals in 479 club matches in twenty years. These are great goal-scoring numbers for a man who was considered a playmaker, a distributor, and the brains of the teams he played with. Pele is an example of an African immortal who was recognized worldwide because of his tremendous accomplishments on the pitch.

Internationally, Pele never played in a World Cup, although two of his sons were on Ghana's roster for the 2010 World Cup. For Ghana, Pele netted thirty-three goals in sixty-seven matches from 1982 to 1998. Despite not making a World Cup competition, Pele was known throughout Africa and the world for his silky sweet skills and delicate left foot. He played in five African Cup of Nations' tournaments: 1982, 1992, 1994, 1996, and 1998. He was named to several FIFA all-star selections and captained the African all stars in their victory over their European counterparts in the Meridian Cup in 1997. In Italy, Pele won an award for best foreign player with Torino from 1995 to 1996. He won the France Football African Player of the Year award three consecutive times from 1991 to 1993, the only African player to accomplish this feat. He won the Golden Ball award for being the best player at the 1992 African Cup of Nations, when Ghana lost in the finals to the Ivory Coast. He guided Ghana to the African Cup of Nations' title ten years earlier in 1982.

His performance at the 1992 African Cup of Nations is one of the most outstanding displays by any player in world soccer history. The performances earned Pele a comparison with another soccer immortal, as "The African Maradona." His solo run goal against Congo in the quarterfinals was sublime and often evokes comparisons to Maradona's second goal against England in the 1986 World Cup. His stunning back header goal against Nigeria from the edge of the opponent's penalty box was pure genius.

It was no accident that Pele was the spokesperson for the South African World Cup bid, despite the fact that he is from Ghana rather than South Africa. This is because Pele is considered one of the best players in world history not to appear at a World Cup and arguably the best African player ever. Ghana awarded him the country's highest honor, the Order of the Volta, thus becoming the first Ghanaian sportsman to be honored with the award. To highlight the enduring immortal status of Pele, Kelechi Iheanacho, the star playmaker of Nigeria's U-17 World Cup title in 2013, is an Arsenal "target" and has evoked comparisons with two African immortals: the retired

Nigerian international Jay-Jay Okocha and Abedi Pele.[69] Yet the greatest praise for Pele as an African immortal came from an astute fan:

> Abedi Pele was way ahead of his time. . . . If he had become great during the internet era, the question of who is Africa's best wouldn't have been in doubt. Those of us who saw him play were wowed . . . his deft touches, flair and unimpeachable vision in the game of football is unrivaled on the continent. Abedi Ayew was both effective and efficient . . . he was a middle field general like no other in Africa's football . . . Abedi only scored important goals . . . and all were taken from the top drawer of world class football.[70]

In contrast to the "flow," soccer can, unfortunately, include grisly displays of racist ultra-nationalism (chapter 1), violent hooliganism, and chasing victory at all costs devoid of any values (chapter 6), and thus lapses into a trend that inhabits our world: de-spiritualization. So for example, in 2013 AEK Athens midfielder Giorgos Katidis was banned from any Greek national team for life after giving a Nazi salute while celebrating a goal in the Greek league. Greece's soccer federation said the player's gesture "is a deep insult to all victims of Nazi brutality."[71] This does not mean that we should demonize the game and all its participants and fans, as we sometimes witness in the North American press. The spiritual lesson of soccer is that it includes both deep value and meaning and also the demise of value and meaning. Sometimes meaning and the loss of meaning, or values and the lack of values, inhabit the same soccer player.

Diego Maradona is a case in point. Maradona has his leftist political leanings and that is a right of any soccer player as a citizen of a state (or states), or even as a member of an international society. This type of political engagement is lacking in a world where citizen participation is losing out to mere entertainment, money, and a narrow focus on our jobs and lives. The issue with Maradona is that he cheated and violated the soccer ethic of fair play when he was sanctioned for doping at the 1994 World Cup. He scored his infamous "hand of God" goal in 1986 and flouted the ethic of fair play. Camus would not have been proud. Maradona abused drugs and was certainly not a good role model for the millions of children that saw him as an immortal. Yet Maradona was simultaneously the greatest soccer star that the world has ever seen. New Maradonas have been announced since and none have arrived. Perhaps Messi. However, that remains to be seen. There is no one like Maradona. There may never be another like him. He is a gift for all of humanity. He is a treasure for the world. He is a soccer immortal. Yet he is a human being like you and me, both strong and weak, with all his warts and imperfections. Thus, soccer can also teach us about tolerance, the ability to humanize and empathize with players and people, and the ability to see reality from different perspectives.

Pelé, the only equal to Maradona in soccer history, has also reflected on soccer from both philosophical and spiritual perspectives. In his *My Life and the Beautiful Game*,[72] Pelé's epigraph tells it all spiritually and is worth quoting in full:

> I was born, grew,
> Because of this I am here,
> I pass by,
> I walk by,
> Not hurrying to arrive,
> I go much faster
> Than those who run
> Without thinking
> This is not our life
> Everything here is a game
> A passing thing,
> What matters is what I've done
> And what I'll leave behind
> Let it be an example
> For those that come
> I am leading who he comes
> But following he who has already gone by
> If he reached the end he has already rested
> I also will reach the end
> Because I want to rest
> There are many people
> With the will to fight
> Life is not just this
> Truth is farther beyond.

These words are touching and moving. They evoke joy, nostalgia, and sadness all merged into one. One day we will be no more. One day there will be no soccer, no soccer mortals, and no immortals for us. One day we will no longer go to the soccer stadiums, or see its array of people, colors, smells, foods, and souvenirs. One day there will be no soccer teammates. One day there will be no mother, father, brother, sister, wife, husband, girlfriend, friend, or stranger. One day there will be a truth beyond the pitch and this life, "farther beyond." For all the philosophical depth of a Plato, Nietzsche, Heidegger, Levinas, or Marx, or the poetic brilliance of a Garcia Lorca, Langston Hughes, or W. H. Auden, Pelé, a mere soccer player, has eloquently captured what most soccer players and fans have only vaguely thought about and felt.

We are born into a life where our circumstances are beyond our control. As Pelé writes, "Everything here is a game." The game is momentary, just like this life. Immortality can be gained through "what I've done" and "what I'll leave behind," insists Pelé. The Brazilian legend is clear that in life and in soccer, it is not always those who are the busiest, or the fastest, or the smartest, that are necessarily the most effective. "Not hurrying to arrive, I go much faster than those who run," states the Brazilian immortal. Pelé is conscious that there are future generations who we need to teach about the values of fair play, honesty, solidarity, tolerance, and justice. He insists that by teaching children about the positive values of soccer, we can serve as an "example for those that come." He is aware that he is merely a part of the golden historical chain of beings that is life that links all the generations of humanity, whether present, past, or future: "I am leading who he comes" and "But following he who has already gone by." Our road in life is long, sometimes hard and tough, with its share of trials and tribulations. Soccer is a joy and an antidote to the harshness of the lives of the many. We know that we must work hard on the pitch, or at whatever we do in life, because in the end we all "want to rest." Pelé ends with this acknowledgement: "There are many people" in this life, both past and present. Many people have that great "will to fight" in the face of obstacles on or off the pitch. Yet we all know that while the soccer game is important and meaningful, it ultimately teaches us that "Life is not just this" and "Truth is farther beyond."

Chapter Eleven

The Pitch as Canvas and Player as Artist

Soccer and Fine Arts

The great Soviet Russian composer Dmitri Shostakovich argued that soccer was a type of art for the people: "Football is the ballet of the masses."[1] Dmitry Shostakovich wrote three full-length ballet scores between 1925 and 1935. The Golden Age "revolves around the visit of a Soviet football team to a Western city (referred to as 'U-town') at the time of an industrial exhibition, only for its heroic sporting and social endeavours constantly to be undermined by hostile administrators, decadent artists and corrupt officials."[2]

In this final chapter, I examine the relationship between soccer and fine arts. The main fine arts were historically painting, sculpture, architecture, music, and poetry. Increasingly, theater and dance are added to the fine arts. Today, the fine arts also include film, photography, conceptual art, and printmaking. In this chapter, I will also include poetry, creative writing, and literature under the ambit of the fine arts.

The connections between soccer and fine arts are not readily apparent, but speaking to artists, writers, and soccer players one comes to the conclusion that soccer is akin to an art form; soccer players paint their canvases on the pitch through their subtle movements, and the best players are as memorable as the most famous artists, architects, singers, photographers, or writers in history. Soccer, like art, is based on the interpretations of the players, fans, and critics. The players that you might hate are the players I most admire. Like art, soccer has its aesthetic qualities, beyond merely winning or losing. Soccer, like art, is based on the interpretations and creativity of the players, fans, and critics. Coaches might also "encourage" creativity among players "by holding practice sessions where there is no coaching and only free play," insists Stan Baker, author of *Our Competition Is the World*.[3] Soccer stadiums have an aura of the theatrical with their rival teams, colorful hats and scarves, and unique banners. One soccer writer urges us to reject Orwell's war metaphor and see soccer "as an art, not a war."[4]

Given the diversity of art throughout human history from the bison on the wall of a cave in Lascaux, France, 50,000 years ago to the surrealism of Marc Chagall in the twentieth century, we all have differing artistic tastes and conceptions of beauty. For one renowned art critic, the majority of people "like to see in pictures what they would also like to see in reality."[5] Does this apply to soccer fans? Do they want to see artistic and innovative players, or merely players that are efficient and win without any aesthetic criteria? For artistic purists, art of the late twentieth and early twenty-first centuries is not really art, but E. H. Gombrich insists that this view is mistaken because you can "crush" an artist by telling them that what they are doing is "quite good in its own way, only it is not 'Art.'"[6] Later in the chapter I discuss a unique professional soccer player that is also an artist off the field. He has even had an art exhibition and perhaps been told that he should stick to soccer alone.

It is interesting to note that soccer is today ubiquitous around the world and hence it is not surprising that artists have painted soccer players, matches, and fans. In chapter 5, I highlighted the notion of soccer stars as gods playing in soccer temples and in chapter 10 I posited the relationship between soccer players and immortality. I pointed out that artists have erected statues in homage to great soccer players from Zinedine Zidane to Eusébio and Duncan Edwards to Bobby Moore.

A Mexican artist based in Querétaro, Manuel Mancilla has a large series of soccer paintings: "gods" and warriors playing old Aztec and Mayan ball games, internationally famous soccer stars such as Franz Beckenbauer (one of the representatives of chapter 5), and a unique reconceptualization of Albrecht Dürer's "Self-Portrait" wearing a German national team jersey.[7] Dürer (1471–1528) was a German painter, engraver, printmaker, and mathematician from Nuremberg. A native of Orizaba, Veracruz, Mancilla is no ordinary soccer artist. One of his most beautiful paintings is called "La chilena de Chac-mool," an ancient pre-Columbian figure performing the difficult "bicycle kick" maneuver. *Chilena* connotes bicycle kick, while *Chac-mool* refers to a form of pre-Columbian Mesoamerican sculpture showing a reclining figure with its head facing ninety degrees from the front, supporting itself on its elbows and holding a bowl or a disk upon its stomach. The figures first appeared in the Valley of Mexico among the Aztecs and the northern Yucatán Peninsula in the ninth century. When Mexico defeated Panama in a key World Cup qualifier at the fabled Azteca in 2013, the game-winning goal was scored through a spectacular Raúl Jiménez *chilena*. On the night of the goal, the artist Manuel Mancilla sent Raúl Jiménez the image of his "La chilena de Chac-mool" through Facebook and the Mexican star forward responded with a "like."[8]

Other Mancilla paintings include his "Juego de los dioses" (Game of the gods) and "Dioses del estadio" (Gods of the stadium), which view soccer as a secular religion. Another has the god Itzama holding a soccer ball, as he stoically looks to the future. Yet another painting has four Aztec figures having a ritual ceremony in honor of the ball. Recall that in chapter 5 I highlighted the purposes of games in the history of humanity, including the ancient notion that the game was a reflection of the struggle of the gods. Mancilla is obviously a lover of the game. While he gets his inspiration from the relationship between ancient and contemporary ball games such as soccer, he also paints more modern pieces. One of his works is titled "The Virgin of the Ball," with an angelic-like woman in a German national team uniform. Recall that in chapter 5 I highlighted the relationship between soccer and religion. For Mancilla, soccer is a secular religion and its practitioners and fans (including himself) experience the divine. Another painting entitled "Antonio Puerta" honors the Spanish soccer star killed on the pitch, which I mentioned in the introduction.

Brilliant photographs have immortalized the legends of world soccer and the game's touching moments. Songs are sung by supporters and have been sung in memory of great soccer stars from George Best to Pelé. Soccer stars have starred in famous films. Countless books and poems have been written about soccer. Architects outdo each other to build the best soccer stadiums and statues. When we enter soccer stadiums, there is elaborate choreography in the songs, banners, and gestures of the home and away fans. The brilliant colors and banners combine ritualistic and aesthetic elements; soccer as a pagan religion (chapter 5) and soccer as art. Soccer scarves and uniforms are an art in themselves, in part reflecting fashion trends of the epoch and commercial imperatives to sell jerseys (chapter 7). The jersey of the All Whites, representing New Zealand's national soccer team, plays on the All Blacks, the famous national rugby union team. The silver fern, a symbol of New Zealand, appears on the All Whites' jersey. Another unique jersey is the pink, black, and gray color combination of the Italian second division side *U.S. Città di Palermo*. The team is known as *Rosanero* ("The Pink-blacks") or *Aquile* ("The Eagles") because there is a lone eagle on the pink-black jersey.

JERSEY #11: SOCCER ARTISTS

The left-winger or wide midfielder position is that of the number 11. Typically, the left-winger has tremendous pace and runs all day. He is known for his fakes, trickery and guile, dribbling skills, crossing technique, and the ability to terrorize defenders and goalies with his goal-scoring instincts. The soccer website Football's Greatest neatly describes the evolving role of the number 11:

> The role of the winger, or wide midfielder, has changed considerably over the years. Originally the job was well-defined, and crucial to the team's creativity: stay close to the touchline, dribble past the full-back and float in a cross for the center-forward (as exemplified by Sir Stanley Matthews). The greatest wingers have always scored a healthy amount of goals too, sometimes a staggering amount given their position. The heyday of the traditional winger lasted until the 1960s. After that Alf Ramsey's 4-4-2 and the Italian *catenaccio* defence changed everything. . . . The 4-3-3 system, popular in the 1970s, had either only one winger in a lop-sided formation (i.e., Garrincha for Brazil in 1962 or Overmars for Arsenal in 1996/97) or two wingers who also had to take it in turns to come inside to support a lone striker when the opposite winger stayed wide. Now, with the modern variation of 4-3-3 the winger also has to drop back when needed to help the midfield (as used by Mourinho's Chelsea) . . .
>
> With the newly popular 4-2-3-1 though the traditional winger is making something of a return. Able to stay forward, these players are definitely forwards rather than midfielders and are often not required to track back (for example Ronaldinho, Neymar or Ronaldo). However, these new wingers are now more likely to cut inside and make runs into the box rather than hugging the touchline to put crosses in; the crossing job is often left for the full-back. These new wingers are often played on their "wrong" sides (i.e. right footed players on the left and vice versa) to reflect this new role (i.e., as in 2009/10 by Mancini at Manchester City or van Gaal at Bayern Munich with Robben and Ribery). Wingers are becoming important again in the game and scoring many goals themselves in addition to setting up chances for others, and this can be seen by the goal tallies of players like Cristiano Ronaldo and Lionel Messi (who began as a right winger before being moved to a more central position). Throughout all these changes wingers have been probably the most exciting players on the pitch, doing what they do best: moving the ball at pace and using their skill to dribble past opponents and creating goal-scoring chances. [9]

While there are numerous sensational number 11s in the history of the game, I selected the Stoke City winger (on loan to Barnsley in 2014), USA international, and artist "Brek" Shea (he actually paints and sells his abstract paintings) and the Brazilian international and Barcelona star Neymar. Shea best illustrates the links between soccer and art on and off the field. Neymar is a master artist with the ball on the field; a breathtaking dribbler; and a constant danger through his speed, trickery, improvisational skills, and excellent goal-scoring and passing abilities. Neymar has inspired numerous artists to create paintings of him.

Brek Shea

Dane Brekken "Brek" Shea was born on February 28, 1990, in College Station, Texas. A tall winger at six feet three inches, Shea is known for his pace, energy, work rate, and dribbling skills. He is a winger with Stoke City in the English Premier League, signed with the club in January 2013, and wears the number 11 for the English club. He joined the club for a fee of £2.5 million (about US$4 million), a fraction of the price Real Madrid paid for Gareth Bale in 2013. He is also a member of the USA national team, helping the nation win the CONCACAF championship in 2013 by scoring the winning goal in the finals against Panama. He has played with the national team since 2010 and scored two goals in twenty-three appearances.

Shea began his career with Major League Soccer club FC Dallas. From 2008 to 2012, Shea made ninety-eight appearances for the Texas team and scored nineteen goals. He helped Dallas reach the MLS Cup Playoffs in 2010 and 2011.

While Shea is an artist on the field, he is a genuine artist off the field. In January 2013, Shea and a number of colleagues launched the brand Left Foot Studio.[10] The site contains Shea's abstract art through different media: paintings, clothing, and longboards and skateboards. Shea paints often on his time off from duties to Stoke City and the USA national team. His studio is located at Left Foot Studio, in his garage, and the soccer star "most often paints the day after a game or on Mondays and Tuesdays before training picks back up."[11] In June 2011, Shea showed ten of his abstract pieces to the Controlled Chaos Art Show and Auction at NYLO Hotel in Plano, Texas, and in the process raised nearly $10,000 for the FC Dallas Foundation for disadvantaged youth through soccer.[12]

Shea revealed how a knee ligament injury in a Stoke City training match in Philadelphia in 2013 allowed him to focus on his art as therapy from the injury and the pressures of professional soccer:

> My hobby is painting; I wouldn't say I'm very good I just enjoy it. It keeps my mind off things and gives me something to do instead of getting into trouble or playing video games. It's a nice way to relax. There is no right or wrong, it's just opinions so I can do whatever I want. It's not like the pressure of winning Premier League matches. I've certainly been painting a lot lately while I've been injured. It keeps me busy, and the more I do it the better I get.[13]

Writing in *Sabotage Times* in 2011, Peter Karl called Shea "the American Gareth Bale," compared his creativity to the USA national team captain Clint Dempsey, and highlighted his artistic character on and off the field:

> Like Dempsey, the biggest draw about Shea is his creativity. But what sets Shea apart is his eccentricity on and off the pitch. Shea is a true lefty—

freethinking and inventive. He expresses himself through six tattoos, his own abstract art studio, and a medley of unconventional hairstyles, be it cornrows or faux hawks. His unique image is one of a truly edgy footballer that America has hardly been familiar with. So please, excuse us for the hype. But at 21, Brek Shea has become one of the brightest talents in American soccer. And he's far from a finished product.[14]

Neymar

In 2013, the Brazilian superstar Neymar signed with Barcelona. As another great star and teammate Lionel Messi is the number 10, Neymar was handed the number 11 jersey. Neymar da Silva Santos Júnior has already scored twenty-six goals in forty-two matches for the Brazilian national team and an impressive fifty-four goals in 103 appearances for Brazilian club side Santos from 2009 to 2013. Playing for Santos, Neymar won three *Campeonato Paulista* (2010, 2011, and 2012), one *Copa do Brasil* (2010), one *Copa Libertadores* (2011), and one *Recopa Sudamericana* (2012). He was also voted Best Forward of the *Campeonato Brasileiro Série A* three times (2010, 2011, and 2012), as well as Best Player of the Campeonato Paulista four times: 2010, 2011, 2012, and 2013. He won the FIFA Puskás Award in 2011 for the most outlandish and audacious goal of the year. The Puskás Award is recognition for the most artistic or aesthetically pleasing goal of the year.

At the tender age of nineteen, Neymar won the 2011 South American Footballer of the Year award. He also won the award in 2012. In 2013, he was the hero of Brazil's Confederation Cup victory on home soil where he scored four goals in the tournament. He won the tournament's Golden Ball for best player. He is destined to become one of the all-time great number 11s in the history of the game. He is flashy, fast, creative, and an incredible dribbler that is able to expertly whizz by numerous players. He can create countless chances for his teammates, score on outlandish volleys or solo runs, and set the tempo of an entire match through his mastery in midfield. He is only in his early twenties, but already a master painter on the soccer pitch.

Artists have taken note of Neymar's artistic skills on the pitch. One writer comically commented on a surrealistic portrait of Neymar:

> I may not completely understand this, but it's definitely interesting. The work of artist/designer Bruno Hamzagic, this Neymar portrait is exactly how I imagine Neymar looks to people who watch Neymar play while they're tripping on mushrooms. Not that I'm implying Bruno was tripping on mushrooms when he created this piece of art. Nothing is in the right place, but that's probably the point, right? Still, Bruno nailed the hair.[15]

Another artist was also moved by Neymar's skills and challenged by Neymar's "ever-changing hairstyles."[16] A new comic book was created in partnership with legendary Brazilian cartoonist Mauricio de Sousa. The Associated Press neatly described the comic book: "Neymar will be portrayed as a child with his own football-playing friends and his well-known Mohawk hair style. The first issue is called 'A boy with talent.'. . . The series will include Neymar's real-life family and friends and De Sousa sees it spreading beyond Brazil and to the rest of the world like his other footballer based comics."[17] Interestingly, other Brazilian players have become children's comic book characters, including Pelé, Ronaldinho, and Ronaldo.[18]

Another famous artist took note of Neymar. Aware that Neymar is an emerging global superstar, the world-renowned rapper, record producer, and entrepreneur Jay-Z was "reportedly interested in signing him to Roc Nation Sports" in 2013.[19] Jay-Z is launching his own sports agency, Roc Nation Sports, a sport management group, and it will work as partners with Creative Artists Agency.

SOCCER AS ART

Soccer players and non-players have been known to view the craft of soccer as an art. The retired and mercurial French international winger David Ginola said the following: "Football is a matter of creativity and imagination."[20] The brilliant and retired French international Lilian Thuram, a winner of the 1998 World Cup, said this about the relationship between soccer and art: "Footballers can be like artists when the mind and body are working as one. It is what Miles Davis does when he plays free jazz—everything pulls together into one intense moment that is beautiful."[21] Thuram had his greatest Miles Davis moments in the semi-finals of the 1998 World Cup against Croatia when he scored his only two international goals in a 2–1 victory. Even the feminist theorist Germaine Greer stated: "Football is an art."[22]

Tom Utley, a British journalist who writes for the *Daily Mail*, went further than Thuram, Ginola, and Greer in his assessment of soccer and art: "Football is only a game. That is the most outrageous nonsense of the lot. Football is a science, it's an art, it is war, ballet, drama, terror and joy all rolled into one."[23] Utley's assessment of soccer supports what *The World through Soccer* has shown, that although soccer is a simple game, it can inform us about art, politics, business, ethics, leadership, childhood dreams, immortality and the meaning of life, and the fine arts. The Arsenal manager Arséne Wenger could opine that soccer and art are essentially one:

> I believe the target of anything in life should be to do it so well that it becomes an art. When you read some books they are fantastic, the writer touches something in you that you know you would not have brought out of yourself. He makes you discover something interesting in your life. If you are living like an

animal, what is the point of living? What makes daily life interesting is that we
try to transform it to something that is close to art. And football is like that. [24]

The performances of some gifted soccer players can also be compared to
poetry. The website of AC Milan pays homage to one of its legends by
comparing his play to poetry: "The class and style of Gianni Rivera earned
the midfield playmaker the Golden Ball for the European Footballer of the
Year in 1969, earning this wonderful tribute: 'in a barren world of football,
Rivera is the only one to possess a sense of poetry.'"[25] Internationally, Rivera played for Italy sixty times and scored fourteen goals. He appeared in
four World Cups (1962, 1966, 1970, and 1974) and his greatest glory came
when Italy won its first European Soccer Championship in 1968.

Soccer stars have also been immortalized in song and literature. Cátulo
Castillo, the poet and composer of Argentine tango, dedicated a tango to
Arsenio Erico and said that the soccer star played with "the elegance of a
ballerina."[26] Castillo's tango contains this powerful line in memory of Erico:
"It will be a millennium before anyone replicates your heel or head
passes."[27] He was called the "Gardels of soccer," in homage to the tango
legend Carlos Gardels.[28] Arsenio Erico (1915–1977) was not Argentinean,
but a brilliant Paraguayan striker. He is the all-time highest goal scorer in the
Argentine first division, with 295 goals, almost all scored for Buenos Aires
club Independiente. He is considered the best Paraguayan soccer player of all
time, even better than José Luis Chilavert, one of the representatives of
chapter 1.

There are lots of songs in honor of the two greatest soccer immortals of
all time: Pelé and Maradona. One is called "Pelé Ou Maradona" by Caju and
Castanha, which tries to make a case for which is the greatest soccer player in
history. "O Rei, Pelé" by Jackson Do Pandeiro is a famous Brazilian song,
which pays homage to "The King of Soccer." There is a "Maradona" hip-hop
song by the German group The Business. Maradona's cult-like following at
Napoli led to an album by The Underachievers about the soccer star entitled
"Maradona è meglio 'e Pelè" (Maradona is better than Pelé). There is a
soccer song in homage to the diminutive former Scottish international Gordon Strachan called "Strachan" by The Hitchers. "George Best" is a song in
honor of the former Northern Ireland and Manchester United star. The U.S.
band Barcelona recorded a song called "Kasey Keller," after his heroic shut-
out performance against Brazil in the 1998 Gold Cup.

Coca-Cola's 2010 World Cup campaign song, Canadian K'Naan's "Wa-
vin' Flag," has become a worldwide hit.[29] K'Naan has also turned the song
into a book. The "guiding spirit" for both the book and song "Wavin' Flag" is
K'naan's grandfather, Haji Mohammad, a celebrated poet in his homeland
Somalia, "who could stop people fighting with a poem," insisted K'naan.[30]
The song highlights K'Naan's love of soccer well before fleeing Somalia's

civil war to Canada and was recorded at the *Centenario* in Montevideo, the site of Uruguay's World Cup triumph in 1930. The song is extremely catchy, yet also tells the story of the immigrant experience, its difficulties, and love of soccer embodied by the waving of national flags at World Cup competitions. The key refrain of the song is the following: "When I get older I will be stronger, They'll call me freedom, just like a wavin' flag."[31]

In addition, Shakira's "Waka Waka," the theme of the 2010 World Cup, remains on the list of most viewed YouTube videos of all time.[32] In June 2013, the music video for "Waka Waka" became the sixth most watched music video of all time on YouTube, with more than 500 million views. The song has sold more than four million copies worldwide, thus making it the best-selling and the fastest-selling World Cup anthem. The Spanish-language counterpart of "Waka Waka" was released simultaneously as "Esto es África" (This Is Africa). "Waka Waka" is based upon a traditional African soldiers' song named "Zamina mina (Zangaléwa)," a 1986 hit for Cameroonian group Golden Sounds and also a 1980s radio hit in Shakira's Colombian hometown Barranquilla. "Waka Waka" was performed by Shakira and Freshlyground (a South African group) at the 2010 FIFA World Cup Kick-Off concert in Soweto, South Africa, on June 10, 2010, as well as at the final on July 11, 2010. Shakira's soccer connections go beyond her native Colombia. She is married to the brilliant FC Barcelona and Spanish international defender Gerard Piqué.

The most famous melody associated with soccer in Brazil is "Na Cadência do Samba," or more popularly known as "Que bonito é" (How beautiful it is), which served as the theme tune for a popular radio station from the early 1960s to 1980s. It is a soft samba composed and written by Luis Bandeira, although the song was used by newsreel producer Carlos Niemeyer in an instrumental version. "Forward" was composed by Miguel Gustavo and used in the film of the same name for the 1970 World Cup. It is a harsh criticism of the military dictatorship's use of soccer to alienate people and to hide the horrors of the military regime's political repression. Recall that in chapter 2 I discussed the relationship between soccer and dictators, while in chapters 3 and 4 I pointed out that soccer and culture in general could be used to either support or challenge the ruling ideology.

Less than a week before demonstrators in the streets of Brazil began protesting the high costs of hosting the 2014 FIFA World Cup, among other grievances, Coca-Cola sent a more positive message about the international event out to Brazilian soccer fans, posting a video of one version of its new World Cup anthem on YouTube:

> The song teams regional techno-pop singer Gaby Amarantos, MTV Brazil's 2012 Artist of the Year, with samba big band Monobloco for a tribute to the game. The stadium friendly pop song backed by a Carnaval beat features

shouts of "*Gol*," calls for hand clapping, and the sound of a referee's whistle.[33]

Soccer fans have also contributed to immortalizing the game and its players through their supporters' songs.[34] They have been at the forefront of adding humor and the politically incorrect to soccer. Here is one of the oddest, but funniest, supporters' songs by USA national soccer team fans:

> I saw my mate the other day,
> He said to me he saw the white Pelé,
> So I asked, who is he?
> He goes by the name of Clint Dempsey,
> Clint Dempsey, Clint Dempsey,
> He goes by the name of Clint Dempsey.

Dempsey is a veritable superstar and captain with the USA national team. He currently plays with the Seattle Sounders FC. Dempsey is one of the representatives of chapter 8 because of his leadership skills. The song in question is funny because Dempsey looks nothing like Pelé, especially considering the differences in their skin colors. Moreover, if one has seen Dempsey and Pelé play, the gap is wide in terms of talent and style. Pelé is undoubtedly one of the greatest players of all time and he was an elegant striker. As pointed out in chapter 10, along with Maradona, Pelé is the greatest soccer immortal of all time. Dempsey is surely talented and a great leader, but gets many of his goals from hard work and tireless running.

Another song by the Sunderland faithful pays homage to their former manager Paolo di Canio in politically incorrect terms that would make feminists and most women wince with disbelief: "Paolo Di Canio. You are the love of my life Paolo Di Canio I'll let ya shag my wife, Paolo Di Canio." Shag is a colloquial term for sleeping with someone. In this case, it connotes Di Canio sleeping with the wife of a hardcore Sunderland fan. As the white English working classes have lost their power and status in a more neoliberal and anti-racist age, they now use the soccer stadium as one of the few places where they can express politically incorrect and sexist sentiments. Recall that in chapter 1 I pointed to Di Canio's neo-fascist worldview as a player and his smooth transition to a de-politicized and technocratic manager that merely gets results. As Di Canio saved Sunderland from relegation from the English Premier League in 2013, some of the hardcore fans were willing to overlook Di Canio's pro-fascist past.

Some supporters' songs borrow from local cultural traditions. There is a famous Mexican folk song that has been adopted by Mexican national team fans:

> *Ay, ay, ay, ay,*
> *Canta y no llores,*
> *Porque cantando se alegran,*

cielito lindo, los corazones.

The translation of this refrain is the following: "Ay, ay, ay, ay, sing and don't cry, because singing gladdens, pretty little heaven, the hearts." The song "Ceilito lindo" was popularized in 1882 by Quirino Mendoza y Cortés (1859–1957). It means "Lovely Sweet One." *Cielo* actually translates as sky or heaven, but it can also mean sweetheart. *Lindo* connotes cute, pretty, or lovely.

Hapoel Tel-Aviv, a famous club in Israel, is known for its vociferous fans and affinity with the trade-union movement and socialism. Yet there is one song that highlights the dark underbelly of some supporters' songs and the de-humanization of one's rivals:

> To any place I come to—I cause chaos,
> I go with Hapoel in bad times and good times,
> Beitar are illiterate and Maccabi are pigs,
> I will always love the Red Devils . . .

Yet there are also culturally beautiful moments with respect to supporters' songs. Parma FC in Italy was formed in 1913 as Verdi Foot Ball Club in honor of the centenary of famous opera composer Giuseppe Verdi (1813–1901). The Italian composer was born in the province of Parma in Italy. Parma fans have been known to even chant lines from Verdi's operas. Verdi's operas are known in popular culture throughout Italy and the world, including "La donna è mobile" from *Rigoletto*, "Libiamo ne' lieti calici" (The Drinking Song) from *La traviata*, "Va, pensiero" (The Chorus of the Hebrew Slaves) from *Nabucco*, and the "Grand March" from *Aida*.

Many supporters' songs have nationalistic and militaristic overtones. One Spanish national team supporters' song repeats the following refrain: "Gibraltar is Spanish! Gibraltar is Spanish! Gibraltar!" Gibraltar is located at the southern tip of Spain and has belonged to Britain since the Treaty of Utrecht in 1713, but many Spaniards claim it as their territory. An Anglo-Dutch force invaded Gibraltar and wrestled it from the Kingdom of Castile in 1704 during the War of the Spanish Succession. Recall that in chapter 1 I highlighted the linkages between soccer and nationalism. Moreover, in chapter 7 I introduced the concept of "marketing nationalism" in which FIFA includes more member "nations" than sovereign members of the United Nations. Despite the protestations of Spain and the aforementioned supporters' song, Gibraltar is one of the newest members of FIFA. Although Gibraltar has a miniscule population of about 30,000 people, in 2013 it gained the right to compete for qualifying for the UEFA European Championship in 2016.

Some supporters' songs are clearly ideological and militaristic. French national team fans chant the country's national anthem, *La Marseillaise*. *La Marseillaise* was originally known as "Chant de guerre pour l'Armée du Rhin" (War Song for the Army of the Rhine). It was written and composed

by Claude Joseph Rouget de Lisle in 1792. As a result of the French Revolution in 1789, the French National Convention adopted it as the new liberal
republic regime's anthem in 1795. The name Marseille in the song's title is in
reference to the first volunteers for war from Marseille who chanted the song.

Soccer has also been celebrated in literature. In a Ted Richards edited
work entitled *Soccer and Philosophy: Beautiful Thoughts on the Beautiful
Game*, Tim Elcombe compares Cristiano Ronaldo's on-field dribbling and
moves, as well as soccer technique in general, to poetry.[35] He asks whether
Ronaldo is a "modern Picasso."[36] Elcombe views Ronaldo's "magical play"
as akin to poetry in motion, which allows the spectators to connect to our
common humanity.[37]

David Peace, the English author of *Nineteen Seventy Four* (1999) and *The
Damned Utd* (2006), remembers his father comparing two English soccer
stars to artists: "My father used to say, 'If you want to know the artist, look at
the art.' He was usually talking about Stanley Matthews or Don Bradman
when he said it."[38] *The Damned Utd* is a novel based on Brian Clough's short
forty-four-day spell in 1974 as manager of Leeds United FC. Peace is a
supporter of Huddersfield Town, a key local rival of Leeds United, and the
team that Leeds United played in Clough's first and last games in charge of
the club. In the book, Peace tells the story of a man troubled by a fear of
failure and a hunger for success. He "offers a compelling insight into the
mind of a footballing genius, proud father and legendary drinker."[39] The
former soccer player and manager Johnny Giles successfully sued Peace for
The Damned Utd as to what he perceived were falsehoods in the book, and
Peace was ordered to remove from any future editions the references highlighted by Giles as damaging and untrue.[40] *The Damned Utd* has been made
into a film entitled "The Damned United," with actor Michael Sheen playing
Brian Clough.

In 1977, Nottingham Forest was promoted to England's top flight and the
following season won its first ever league title, making Clough one of four
managers to have won the English league with two different clubs. Under
Clough, Nottingham Forest won two consecutive European Cups (1979 and
1980) and two League Cups (1978 and 1979). When Nottingham Forest was
relegated from the Premier League in 1993, Clough retired from soccer.
Brian Clough and Peter Taylor, his assistant at Derby County and partner
during the Nottingham Forest glory days, are immortalized through the Brian
Clough and Peter Taylor Statue at Pride Park (the home of Derby County). In
the 1968–1969 season, Derby County was promoted to the First Division
under the Clough and Taylor partnership. Three years later, Derby County
was crowned champion of England for the first time in the club's history.
There is also a Brian Clough Statue in Nottingham paid for by his fans.
Another Brian Clough Statue can be found in Middlesbrough, as Clough
scored 197 goals for the club as a player from 1955 to 1961.

Camus, Nabokov, Dimitrijević, Galeano, and Villoro have all opined about soccer from distinctively literary lenses. These writers see soccer and the world poetically, aesthetically, spiritually, socially, and politically. They might differ in their assessments about soccer in the context of the wider world, but they all view soccer as a microcosm of the human condition, including its joys and tragedies. The Mexican writer Juan Villoro has used the soccer field (for example, his *God is Round*) to provide us with metaphors about life and the contemporary state and society in Mexico. "Soccer has much less to do with sporting triumphs than with the desire to form an emotional community,"[41] insisted Villoro in a *New York Times* interview in 2013. Carlos Fuentes, a god in Mexican letters, once told an interviewer asking him about soccer, "If you want to talk about soccer, go talk to Juan Villoro."[42]

The Uruguayan writer Eduardo Galeano, in his *Soccer in Sun and Shadow*, shows us how soccer is really about visceral *passions* formed early in life; how the commercialization of the game kills "fantasy" and "daring";[43] and the way the quality of soccer on the pitch is related to the political and economic events of the day. Galeano's romanticized version of soccer is the image of a group of boys kicking a ball in a dusty street, and then singing: "We lost, we won, either way we had fun."[44]

Vladimir Dimitrijević, the Skopje-born Swiss writer, like Galeano, longs for a more romantic, spontaneous, and adventurous soccer.[45] He criticizes modern soccer for its win-at-all-costs philosophy, its rapid commercialization, and the attendant "boring" and "predictable" matches where teams play "not to lose." He longs for the more spontaneous soccer of his ex-Yugoslavia; a soccer that was characterized by more liberty on the pitch and individual genius.

The academic world has also caught note of the relationship between soccer and literature. Birkbeck, University of London, recently held a prematch panel followed by the Champions League final on May 25, 2013, entitled "Literature and Football." The panel sought to discover the links between soccer and literature, such as: Can Zidane's head-butt teach us about Camus? What is Shakespeare implying when Kent calls Oswald a "base football player" (King Lear)? Why is Joey Barton like Ezra Pound?

It is a testament to literature and culture that Garcilaso de la Vega, one of the greatest Latin American writers of all time and the author of *The Royal Commentaries*,[46] has a soccer stadium named after him in the ancient Incan city of Cusco and a soccer club named in his honor, Real Garcilaso (Cusco-based). Founded only in 2009, in 2013 Real Garcilaso shocked the soccer world by reaching the quarterfinals of the Copa Libertadores (South American club championship) before bowing out to superior Colombian opponents. It says a lot about a culture that it names its soccer stadium after a literary hero and *mestizo* son of an Incan princess and Spanish conquistador.

Soccer has not only been immortalized in literature, but in photography and film as well.

The filmmakers Philippe Parreno and Douglas Gordon shot a ninety-minute documentary about the French superstar Zinedine Zidane during an entire match entitled *Zidane: A Portrait of the 21st Century Portrait.* In 2013, the film toured Sherbrooke, Quebec, as part of a National Gallery of Canada initiative:

> Spectators taking in the soccer matches at the Canada Summer Games—running to August 17 at a variety of Sherbrooke venues—can also get a completely different view of the sport at the Musee des beaux-arts de Sherbrooke. The downtown museum is hosting Zidane: A Portrait of the 21st Century, a video installation on tour from the National Gallery of Canada. Artists Douglas Gordon of Scotland and Philippe Parreno of France trained 17 cameras on French soccer star Zinedine Zidane during a match between Real Madrid and Villarreal on April 23, 2005, at Madrid's Santiago Bernabeu Stadium, aiming to capture his every gesture and expression. The result is "a radically different experience of both soccer and portraiture," says the museum.[47]

Escape to Victory is a 1981 film directed by John Huston that included a star-studded cast consisting of Sylvester Stallone, Michael Caine, and Max von Sidon. The film also included numerous professional soccer players: Bobby Moore, Osvaldo Audiles, Kazimierz Deyna, Paul Van Himst, Mike Summerbee, Hallvar Thoresen, and Pelé. Numerous Ipswich Town players such as John Wark, Russell Osman, Laurie Sivell, Robin Turner, and Kevin O'Callaghan were also part of the cast. The plot is based on a team of Allied prisoners of war coached and led by English captain John Colby (Michael Caine), a professional soccer player for West Ham United before the war, as they agree to play an exhibition match against a German team.

Or there is *Heleno*, the tragic story of Brazilian soccer legend Heleno de Frietas (1920–1959) directed by Brazilian filmmaker José Henrique Fonseca in 2012. Known as "Prince Cursed" for his tragic story, the Brazilian striker spent the majority of his career with Botafogo, scoring 209 goals for the club, mostly with his head. De Freitas scored nineteen goals in eighteen appearances for Brazil and was a member of the national team that finished runners-up in both the 1945 and 1946 Copa América. He was joint top goal scorer in the 1945 tournament. De Frietas died in 1959 at the age of thirty-nine in a sanatorium in Barbacena, Brazil. He was sadly known for his alcoholism, drug addiction, womanizing, and wife beating. De Freitas, like Barbosa, is the flip side of our love for soccer immortals, as I showed in chapter 10.

As I write these lines, I am glancing at a book of soccer photographs, a collaboration between the AS Roma fan and photographer Andrea Staccioli and Monica Maristain entitled *En el nombre del fútbol* (In the name of soccer).[48] The book has a number of wonderful texts about soccer by the

Mexican writer Juan Villoro, the former coach of Argentina's 1978 World Cup victory César Luis Menotti, and the esteemed soccer writer and scorer in Argentina's 1986 World Cup finals triumph against West Germany Jorge Valdano. Although there are photographs of international matches, the wonderful photographs are heavily focused on Roma and its immortal hero Francesco Totti, who has spent his entire career with AS Roma since 1992 and is a folk legend for the Roman club. He has scored well over 200 goals for Roma. Totti also endeared himself to the Italian national team and won the 2006 World Cup, shortly before his retirement from international soccer. The Italian midfield playmaker or lone striker has won a record five Italian Player of the Year awards and two Serie A Player of the Year awards. Pelé thought Totti was so talented that he named him in his list of the 125 greatest living soccer players of all time. As a result of his exceptional technical skills, ability to chip goalkeepers for outlandish goals, and his longevity with one club his entire career, Totti is one of the most loved Italian players of all time. This book of photographs and text immortalizes the lives of living soccer players for future generations.

Although not a major soccer fan, the Brazilian artist named Andréia Michels based in Forquilhinha, Santa Catarina, was moved to paint soccer paintings during the 2013 Confederations Cup in Brazil. One untitled painting plays on the Norwegian artist Edvard Munch's 1893 painting "The Scream," but in this case the scream is not the infinite scream of nature, but rather the anguished scream of a solitary figure and the screams of angry anti-government protesters during the Confederations Cup. [49]

There is also a famous soccer artist from Great Britain: Ben Mosley. Arthaus Galleries states the following about the artist:

> Ben Mosley is one of Britain's leading sports artists, his work capturing the emotional energy, overflowing passion and dynamic movement of athletic display in pieces that may be described as at once figurative, cubist and abstract expressionist. Commissioned by the biggest organisations within football, including the League Managers Association and the Professional Footballers Association, Wembley Stadium and Manchester United, his work can be found in many private collections throughout the UK, United States and Europe.
>
> In addition, Mosley is the first artist to ever paint a mural at the immortalized Wembley Stadium, as well as having a permanent collection of work on display in Club Wembley. His mural traces the history of Wembley from 1923–2013 and stretches over an area of 20m². [50]

Mosley's soccer art is known as "action painting—or, more broadly speaking, abstract expressionism—is a style of painting which artist Ben Mosley has used to powerful effect to capture the drama of sport." [51] Like his abstract expressionism predecessors, such as Wilem and Elaine de Kooning, Franz

Kline, and Lee Krasner, Mosley "values spontaneity and creates his images by stroking paint directly on to each canvas in a gestural, dynamic fashion."[52] His process is to create bonds between his art and the athletes, and thus effectively representing "the unfurling action and emotion."[53] The combination between soccer and abstract expressionism creates a colorful, dynamic, and moving take on "the beautiful game." Two of his famous paintings are related to Manchester United, with which he had a relationship to sell paintings for charity. "The Rooney vs. Man City" depicts Wayne Rooney's stunning overhead kick in the Manchester derby in 2011, while "Legends" features Denis Law, Denis Irwin, and Peter Schmeichel and was painted "live" during a dinner in London where the three United stars were guests of honor.[54] The Rooney painting was depicted from many different angles, argues Mosley, "due to the enormity of the goal. It was quite spectacular and I wanted the viewer to become engrossed by it."[55]

A Manchester United legend and former Welsh international, Ryan Giggs, has also been compared to a soccer artist for his on-field performances and depicted by artists. Alessandro Del Piero, a former Italian international legend who could score artistic, curling free kick goals with ease, could admit that he "cried twice" in his life "watching a football player": the first time was watching Maradona and the second time seeing Ryan Giggs.[56]

An artist named Felio Sotomayor was moved to depict Giggs in art as a result of his longevity, consistency, skills, and accomplishments:

> Ryan Giggs continues to dazzle us on the pitch with his soccer wizardry and with over 20 years of high level soccer experience, the term "seasoned veteran'" suits him well. His skill and consistency is unmatched and in the words of his coach Sir Alex Ferguson ". . . Ryan can leave the best defenders with twisted blood." This comment from the veteran coach inspired artist Felio Sotomayor to create an intricate vector illustration depicting the Manchester United winger in his element. The visual doubles-up as an infographic by creatively representing some of Gigg[s]'s major sporting achievements.[57]

Giggs is perhaps the most decorated player in English soccer history. He also holds the Manchester United club record for competitive appearances, having made his nine-hundredth appearance in 2012. With Manchester United, he has won an amazing thirteen Premier League titles, four FA Cup winner's medals, three League Cup winner's trophies, and two Champions League winner's medals. Giggs has captained Manchester United, particularly in the 2007–2008 season. As a result of these incredible achievements, the artist Heather Gail Harman had a two-year affiliation with Giggs, who she dubbed "the most decorated player in British football."[58] One of her paintings is a pastel entitled "Ryan Giggs" and it is set against the backdrop of Old Trafford (the home of Manchester United) at sunset.[59]

In chapter 10, I discussed the notion of how some soccer stars such as Bobby Moore, Eusébio, Duncan Edwards, and Zinedine Zidane have been immortalized through the works of artistic statues. One such statue is located in Hanley, England, one of six towns to join together to form the city of Stroke-on-Trent in 1910. The statue is of Sir Stanley Matthews, CBE (1915–2000), a veritable legend of English soccer and perhaps the greatest England has ever seen. The statue is revealing because it consists of Matthews with a soccer ball literally glued to his feet. Matthews was a dribbling sensation, one of the players that revolutionized the game with his dashing solo runs.

Matthews is the only player to have been knighted while still playing. He was the first winner of both the European Footballers of the Year and the Football Writers' Association Player of the Year awards. Known as "The Wizard of the Dribble" and "The Magician," Matthews played top flight soccer into his fifties. He was the oldest player to play in England's first division and the oldest player to represent the country. He played his final competitive game in 1985, at the age of seventy.

Matthews spent nineteen years with Stoke City from 1932 to 1947 and from 1961 to 1965. He helped Stoke to the Second Division title in 1932–1933 and 1962–1963. He spent fourteen years with Blackpool, where he became an FA Cup winner in 1953. Between 1937 and 1957 he won fifty-four caps for England, playing in the World Cup in 1950 and 1954.

NEYMAR AND SHEA: ARTISTS OF OUR TIMES

Neymar and Shea are the soccer artists of our times. They are soccer legends for their fans and they paint their canvases on the pitch through their fancy footwork, dribbling, passes, and goals. These soccer stars are united by an artistic desire for beauty, a struggle between liberty and determination, mimicry (with their own twist) of the idols of the past, a creative, interpretive capacity, and a dialogue with other soccer artists, their fans, and critics.[60] Like art, soccer has its standards of what is beautiful and ugly, its rules, and its limits. Great soccer stars, like gifted artists, transcend the limits of the possible. Our standards of great players, like great artists, vary based on individual preferences and interpretations. Yet we might try to neither lapse into a complete relativism, which insists that all players are equally artistic, nor a total romanticism in which our standards are so high that we only allow Maradona and Pelé to enter the hall of fame of universal soccer artistry.

Neymar is already a soccer star and time will tell whether he will be one of the greatest soccer artists of all time. Shea is at the start of his promising career and is an artist on the field and painter off the field.

In this chapter, I examined soccer through literature, song, photographs, films, painting, and statues. Sometimes one also senses that players such as Neymar and Shea are like well-trained ballerinas or gymnasts, who even get better with age. In fact, Mexican artist Manuel Mancilla has several paintings of gymnasts in their complicated poses with a soccer ball tied to their feet. Soccer is a sport. It is not the fine arts. Yet some soccer players become stars and are thus immortalized by their fans and future generations. They are akin to artists in their movements, strategies, discipline, hard work, vision, and commitment to an overarching ideal. The best soccer artists such as Neymar still have the popular touch of street soccer in their unpredictable, innovative, and unique styles. Neymar or Giggs are soccer's equivalents to Don Quixote or Breughel.

Shea will not be a Picasso or Dali, but his abstract paintings project a different idea of a soccer player as an artist and integral human being. Recall that in chapter 7 I highlighted the relationship between soccer, business, and marketing. Shea is in the business of professional soccer, but also in the art and assorted gear business. Through Left Foot Studio, Shea markets himself as a soccer star and as an artist. Shea's abstract art includes images of Albert Einstein and Bob Marley, two geniuses that the soccer star hopes to emulate. Indeed, one of his abstract pieces is entitled "Emulate."

Left Foot Studio also markets another professional soccer star, Lee Nguyen, a friend of Shea's who was born in Texas and, like Shea, played for the Dallas Texans in his youth. The team has produced numerous domestic and international soccer stars including Clint Dempsey and Omar Gonzalez (USA national team), the Honduran and FC Dallas attacking midfielder Ramón Fernando Núñez, the Texas-born Japanese midfielder Hirofumi Moriyasu, and the retired Venezuelan striker Alejandro Enrique Moreno Riera. Here is Nguyean's interesting biography:

> Lee grew up in Dallas and played for Dallas Texans, one of the nation's elite youth teams. A winger with creative dribbling skills, he was the only high school player to be named in the U.S. squad for the 2005 FIFA World Youth Championship and was named the 2004–05 Gatorade National Boy Soccer Player of the Year. Nguyen turned down an offer from Major League Soccer, choosing instead to accept an offer from PSV Eindhoven in Holland. He was the first professional soccer player of Vietnamese decent to play in Europe which boosted his fame within Vietnam. He eventually decided to go back to his roots and play in Vietnam for 3 years before returning to Major League Soccer where in 2012 he proved to be one of the New England Revolution's most valuable players.[61]

Shea and Lee have used their capital as soccer stars to sell various products, fashion gear, and even art. While Shea and Lee are artists on the field, they are also artists and businessmen beyond the pitch.

* * *

In conclusion, this chapter advances the idea that soccer players such as Shea and Neymar are the soccer artists of our times. I purposefully selected active players for this lesson because although people admire the immortal players of the past, they also want to see the latest player-artists and their theatrical performances. Books, films, songs, poems, and sculptures have paid tribute to the game, its great stars, and the fans. Shea created art as a soccer star, as well as off the field through his abstract paintings and gear designs. Yet soccer, like art, has its aesthetic standards. While we might disagree on whether Maradona or Pelé was a better player, or which star was more of an "artist" on the field, few people will dispute that these were two of the greatest soccer stars of all time.

Neymar is in an aesthetic league of his own when it comes to on-field soccer artistry, which Shea will unlikely ever match. Neymar is thus far more of an accomplished on-field artist compared to Shea, but both players are merely beginning their artistic output. Shea can still dream of improving his artistic talents for many years to come both on and off the field.

Conclusion

Soccer as "Life and Death" and "Much, Much More"

As *The World through Soccer* demonstrated, soccer is an important but underestimated global cultural phenomenon. If we examine the world through soccer, we learn lessons about politics, religion, ethics, marketing and business, leadership, childhood and dreams, immortality and the meaning of life, and fine arts. In the introduction, I highlighted how the Mexican philosopher Mauricio Beuchot coined the term analogic hermeneutics, which is a type of hermeneutics based upon interpretation, taking into account the plurality of aspects of meaning. *The World through Soccer* uses analogic hermeneutics to see soccer through different disciplines, interpretations, and meanings.

Recall that in the introduction I quoted Bill Shankly, the legendary Scottish manager of Liverpool. Like Shankly, I argued that soccer is "much, much more important" than "life and death." In the previous eleven chapters, I advanced two main ideas: 1) how soccer is intricately connected to life and death; and 2) how soccer is more important than life and death because it teaches us invaluable lessons about all realms of existence, from politics and religion to ethics and the meaning of life. The first proposition was especially obvious for soccer players living under the ambit of authoritarian and totalitarian regimes (chapter 2), or for players that died on the pitch (introduction). The second proposition was demonstrated in relation to all the previous chapters, especially in chapter 10 when I discussed soccer, immortality, and the meaning of life.

The World through Soccer highlighted eleven lessons of soccer. In the conclusion, I attempt to link all those chapters (lessons) together. Recall that the eleven lessons are related to the following themes and players:

Lesson 1. Soccer and nationalism (José Luis Chilavert—Paraguay and Gianluigi Buffon—Italy).

Lesson 2. Soccer and authoritarian and totalitarian regimes (Elias Figueroa—Chile).

Lesson 3. Soccer, ideological hegemony, and "class warfare" (Paolo Maldini—Italy and Salvador Mariona—El Salvador).

Lesson 4. Soccer and social transformation (José Leandro Andrade—Uruguay, Cesc Fàbregas—Spain, Tom Huddlestone—England, and Patrick Vieira—France).

Lesson 5. Soccer as a secular (pagan) religion (Franz Beckenbauer—West Germany and Zinedine Zidane—France).

Lesson 6. Soccer and ethics (Igor Netto—USSR and John Terry—England).

Lesson 7. Soccer, business, and marketing (Cristiano Ronaldo—Portugal and David Beckham—England)

Lesson 8. Soccer as a leadership opportunity (Xavi—Spain, Steven Gerrard—England, and Clint Dempsey—USA)

Lesson 9. Soccer as a childhood dream (Roger Milla—Cameroon, Hugo Sánchez—Mexico, and Cha Bum-Kun—South Korea)

Lesson 10. Soccer and immortality (Pelé—Brazil and Diego Maradona—Argentina)

Lesson 11. Soccer and fine arts (Brek Shea—USA and Neymar—Brazil)

I have chosen a retired number eleven from the former Yugoslavia, Dragan Džajić, in order to help summarize the eleven chapters.

THE "BALKAN MIRACLE"

Dragan Džajić (b. 1946) was a sensational left winger. He had a brilliant left foot, scored a healthy amount of goals, demonstrated great creativity, and was a brilliant crosser of the ball into the dangerous goal area. His dribbling skills left defenders dazed. His close control of the ball was as good as any player in the game. He was a master of the *pedalada*, a complicated step over move that allows you to beat defenders. He could juggle the ball with his head as players chased him down without success. He could effortlessly use the *sombrero* technique: flicking, juggling, or scooping the ball over a defender's head and still maintaining possession, or going around the defender. His curling free kick goals were the stuff of dreams. One soccer website insisted that Džajić was "a left winger blessed with demonic dribbling skills, brilliant ball control, speed, a great cross, a superb free kick, and a sharp eye for the goal."[1] Another website was even more generous in describing the technical class of the Yugoslavian master:

Slender, with a long step, elegant in his movement, incomprehensibly fast and with a fine dribbling and shooting technique. . . . Even though he preferred his left foot, he was a complete football player of a world class calibre. He knew how to trick the opponent in full speed, to wait for him to step on the "wrong foot," leave him behind helpless and sprint towards goal. He would then shoot or, which he did more often, cross the ball masterfully, bringing despairing fear into the opponent's defense. He was known for incomparable free kicks that he often turned into goals.[2]

Džajić was born on May 30, 1946, in Ub, Serbia, in the former Socialist Federal Republic of Yugoslavia (1943–1992). He is considered one of the greatest Serbian soccer players to emerge from the former Yugoslavia and one of the greatest players to ever wear the Yugoslavian national team jersey. Džajić played in an epoch of Yugoslavian soccer, which was marked by greater "spontaneity" and "liberty."[3] Looking back at old Red Star Belgrade or Yugoslavian national team film reels, it was obvious that Džajić was fast, technical, a dashing dribbler, a sensational passer and crosser of the ball, and a brilliant free kick artist. In 2011, the soccer website Goal.com named Džajić in "the greatest European Championship XI of all time."[4] The choice of Džajić might surprise the reader, but that is because we are accustomed to focus on European players, and largely European players from Western Europe. As Džajić was from the former Yugoslavia in Central and Eastern Europe, he got far less international recognition than he deserved. One might reflect on whether professional soccer, like other realms of culture, imbues us with what Antonio Gramsci called "common sense," which privileges more powerful nations and classes above less powerful ones (chapter 3).

Džajić was not only a Yugoslavian hero, but one of the greatest soccer players of all time. Pelé clearly recognized the supreme talent of the Yugoslavian legend: "Džajić is the Balkan miracle—a real wizard. I'm just sorry he's not Brazilian because I've never seen such a natural footballer."[5] Returning from a match between a World Team and Brazil in 1968, Florian Albert, the Hungarian international and the European Footballer of the Year in 1967, pointed out that only the Yugoslavian superstar really dominated and impressed the Brazilians: "We played very well Amancio, Overath, Beckenbauer, Marzolini and me, but we still owe something to the Brazilians. The only one among us that conquered the Brazilians entirely was Dragan Džajic."[6] In his native Serbia, Dragan Džajić remains a veritable soccer icon. A poll taken in the last decade showed that 97 percent of the population remembered the name of the former FK Crvena Zvezda (Red Star Belgrade) and Yugoslavia player.[7]

In almost 600 appearances for Red Star Belgrade from 1961 to 1975 and 1977 to 1978, Dragan Džajić scored 287 goals. He made his debut for the Belgrade-based club at the tender age of seventeen. He led Red Star Belgrade to five domestic titles (1963–1964, 1967–1968, 1968–1969, 1969–1970, and

1972–1973) and four Yugoslavian Cups (1963–1964, 1967–1968, 1969–1970, and 1970–1971). In the 1970–1971 season, Red Star Belgrade reached the semi-finals of the European Champion Clubs' Cup, the top continental club competition. Red Star beat Panathinaikos FC 4–1 in the first leg in Belgrade, but Džajić was suspended for the return leg in Athens and the Greek side won 3–0 to go through to the finals on away goals.

Internationally, Džajić was also a Yugoslavian national team star. He was only eighteen when he joined the national team. He participated in the 1974 World Cup in West Germany, where he helped Yugoslavia draw Brazil. He scored one goal in a record 9–0 victory against Zaire. In the second round, Yugoslavia lost three games in a row and was eliminated from the World Cup. Džajić's greatest soccer moments, however, came at the European Nations' tournament in 1968 in Italy. He was voted UEFA European Player of the Tournament. He was also the tournament's top scorer. His most famous international match was the 1968 European Championship semi-final against England. In the eighty-seventh minute, he delicately lobbed the brilliant English goalkeeper Gordon Banks, thus giving Yugoslavia a 1–0 victory. The British press delightfully called him "the magic Dragan."[8] He went on to score in the final against Italy (a 1–1 draw in the first match), but the Italians prevailed 2–0 in the replay final match.

As a result of these performances, Džajić was third in the *Ballon d'Or* voting in 1968. The legendary sweeper Franz Beckenbauer would later argue that Džajić, not George Best, should have won the trophy.[9] From 1964 until 1978, Džajić would earn eighty-five caps, the most in the history of the Yugoslavian national team, and score twenty-three goals for his country. In 2004, to celebrate the Union of European Football Association's fiftieth anniversary, each of its member associations was asked by UEFA to choose one of its own players as the most outstanding player of the past fifty years (1954–2003). The fifty-two players were known as the Golden Players. Džajić was selected as Yugoslavia's Golden Player.

Džajić retired in 1978 from both Red Star Belgrade and the Yugoslavian national team. He was only thirty-two. From 1975 to 1977, he played for SC Bastia in France, scoring thirty-one times in fifty-six matches for the Corsican side. He is considered one of the greatest players in the history of both SC Bastia and Red Star Belgrade.

In 1979, Džajić remained in the Red Star Belgrade organization as a technical director. From 1998, he was the club's president, but he resigned the post in 2004.

In 2011, a trial started in which Džajić was charged with fraud. It was reported that he might have pocketed money from the sale of four players when he was the Red Star Belgrade president. Džajić pleaded not guilty to the charges, which could have landed him and two other defendants twelve years in jail. Džajić denied any wrongdoing, saying to the court: "I always conducted my work within the limits of the law and I did not take anybody's money."[10] These charges surprised some of the Red Star faithful. Džajić is remembered mostly for his exceptional technical skills and his kind and easy-going nature. Recall that in chapter 6 I discussed the growing ethical problems in soccer, some of which are related to the rapid global commercialization of the game (chapter 7).

In 2012, Serbian president Tomislav Nikolić decided to exempt Dragan Džajić from criminal liability. Some critics suggested that the charges were political. Others asked whether more powerful people pinned the charges against Džajić. With or without the corruption charges, Džajić was nearly an untouchable god in Serbia because of his soccer talents and accomplishments. He was a Red Star legend for all time. On December 19, 2012, Dragan Džajić was elected as Red Star president for a third time, thus enhancing his leadership skills (chapter 8). He also suggested that he would help the club get out of debt and open up its commercial opportunities (chapter 7). Remember that soccer clubs are in the business of business and they make vast profits from player sales to other clubs. Another set of issues for Red Star and Džajić is whether they can resist attempts to privatize the club and sell it to foreigners, thus further cementing soccer as a transnational industry and arguably undermining nationalist sentiments (chapters 7 and 1).

Džajić summed up his career, his time with Red Star Belgrade, and suggested that there was a more ethical type of soccer in the past (chapter 6):

> It was a different kind of football back then. The game was fairer and today it is much more difficult to dribble. But I was lucky to play for *Zvezda* [Red Star]. They were a very strong club in a first-class league—one of the top five in Europe at the time. The stadiums were always full and every match was a huge challenge. But I always felt an inner strength, particularly when going towards the opposition goal. I loved it.[11]

WHY DRAGAN DŽAJIĆ?

Dragan Džajić was one of the greatest number 11s of all time and he best allows us to summarize the eleven lessons highlighted in *The World through Soccer*. At this juncture, I underscore chapter-by-chapter how Dragan Džajić helps us to synthesize our eleven lessons of soccer.

Lesson One: Soccer and Competing Nationalist Visions

Remember that Paraguay's goalkeeper José Luis Chilavert and Gianluigi Buffon are the representatives of lesson one because the former scored for and "saved the nation," while the latter "saved the nation," especially when Italy won the 2006 World Cup. I posited that Chilavert and Buffon both represented a nationalist ethos, but Buffon embodied an ultra-nationalist and neo-fascist ethos. I pointed to some soccer players that were virulently ultra-nationalist, even to the point of collaborating with Nazism. I called those players and their supporters ethnic nationalists in contrast to more inclusive civic nationalists. In any case, the reality is that the eleven named starting players on the field represent the unity of the nation, but also its diversity in ideological, ethnic, regional, religious, and cultural terms. Some national soccer teams like the USA embody a merit-based multicultural ethos where whites, blacks, Hispanics, Jews, Italians, and others are selected for the national team. In France, it was hoped that after winning the 1998 World Cup, the white-Basque-black-Berber-Arab unity of the national team would lead to a democratization and greater inclusiveness of French society and government. Markovits and Rensmann allowed us to see how soccer simultaneously promotes nationalist exclusiveness, as well as more inclusive cosmopolitan forms of national belonging that privilege merit, winning, and a colorless ethos.

Dragan Džajić played for his country, the former Yugoslavia, and led it to great heights, nearly winning the 1968 European Nations' trophy. Today Yugoslavia is no longer a nation-state. It has split up into numerous new states as a result of the rise of national independence movements and the civil war from 1992 to 1995. Slovenia, Croatia, Bosnia-Herzegovina, Macedonia, Serbia, and Montenegro are the new independent states erected out of the ashes of the destruction of Yugoslavia. Interestingly, the old Yugoslavian national teams were more ethnically inclusive than the new national teams, which are keen to disproportionately represent members of the titular majority groups. All this begs the question whether Yugoslavia was held together as a result of Tito's imposed socialist "unity and brotherhood," or a sense of genuine patriotism and socialist idealism among ordinary Yugoslavians. Yugoslavia was unique because it never asked if you were a Muslim, Catholic, or Orthodox Christian, whether you were a Bosnian, Croat, or Serb. Yet some Yugoslavians complained of the dampening of ethnic consciousness and discrimination against their respective ethnic groups.

Citizens of various countries ask themselves what type of nation and state they want. Soccer fans of various states ask themselves: How can we truly represent both the unity and diversity of the nation? For some rabid ultra-nationalists, a Balotelli should not be on the Italian national team because he is Jewish and African. For those with more inclusive visions of Italy, Italy is a nation of all its citizens, irrespective of their cultural, ethnic, religious, or linguistic origins. Markovits and Rensmann argue that in sporting contests our visions of the nation are becoming more cosmopolitan because we want to see the best players and winners, regardless of their countries of origins.

Lesson Two: Soccer and Authoritarian/Totalitarian Regimes

Recall that Chile's Elias Figueroa, a retired soccer star and supporter of the Pinochet military junta in the 1970s and 1980s, is the representative of lesson two. Figueroa received great honors during and after his playing days because he tacitly and even openly supported the Pinochet regime as a savior of the nation against communist internationalism. Some of his more outspoken or pro-communist (or pro-liberal) teammates and their families were not as fortunate as Figueroa. They were tortured by the military junta.

Dragan Džajić lived most of his playing life (save for a few years in France) under the ambit of an authoritarian, socialist regime dominated by the Yugoslavian Communist Party. Yugoslavia was neither Nazi Germany nor fascist Italy. It was different from Franco's Spain, or the authoritarian military regime of Pinochet's Chile. Yet as the Yugoslavian dissident Milovan Đilas pointed out back in 1957, the "new class of oppressors" included the Communist Party officials, replacing the capitalist "oppressors" of liberal societies.[12] There were appalling Yugoslavian prison camps for dissidents, intellectuals, and perceived opponents of the regime.

Marshal Josip Broz Tito (1892–1980) was a Yugoslav revolutionary and statesman that led the socialist state as its first president from 1953 until his death in 1980. While he was a unique and charismatic figure and was seen as charting a non-aligned foreign policy, Tito was accused of stamping out ethnic consciousness and promoting authoritarianism. Yet given the civil war and ethnic cleansing of the 1990s, many Yugoslavians look back with nostalgia to the socialist system, its high levels of education, decent employment record, the ability of citizens to travel, and the regime's lack of ethnic consciousness.

Lesson Three: Soccer, Ideological Hegemony, and "Class Warfare"

Recall that lesson three was about ideological hegemony and "class warfare." Remember that Italy's Paolo Maldini (AC Milan) and El Salvador's Salvador Mariona (Alianza FC) are the representatives of lesson three. AC Milan is one of the wealthiest clubs in the world and it is owned by the former Italian prime minister and media mogul Silvio Berlusconi. Berlusconi's and Maldini's AC Milan played a key role in creating ideological consensus through soccer and even in the political realm as a result of the creation of Berlusconi's *Forza Italia!* (a ruling political party created in 1994 and named after a nationalist Italian soccer chant).

Dragan Džajić's main club team, Red Star Belgrade, led the struggle for socialist ideological hegemony by proudly displaying the communist "red star" on its jerseys. Remember that following Gramsci, soccer is a part of the struggle for ideological hegemony in any society, whether in socialist or liberal societies. Maldini reinforced liberal capitalist ideological hegemony through his club AC Milan and the Italian national team, while Dragan Džajić contributed to the molding of socialist ideological hegemony through Red Star Belgrade and the Yugoslavian national team.

Whether this attempt to mold ideological hegemony works or not is an interesting question. Gramsci pointed out that the course of history depends on the country, the constellation of hegemonic and counter-hegemonic forces in civil society, and the interaction of material interests, dominant ideas, and political, military, and "strategic" powers.[13] It is also true that ideological hegemony only functions for the short term because ideologies have their summers of success and winters of despair when the ideology loses its patrons, supporters, and energy (for example, the Bolshevik Revolution in 1917 and the official disintegration of the communist Soviet Union in 1991).[14] If ideological consensus cannot be molded through culture or soccer, the "repressive state apparatus" can be used as with the Soccer War between Honduras and El Salvador in 1969. In this respect, Salvador Mariona was a symbol of the Soccer War as the captain of El Salvador's national team at the 1970 World Cup.

Lesson Four: Soccer and Social Transformation

Dragan Džajić was one of the greatest soccer players of all time. He was from a socialist state in the Balkans. His scintillating performances in Yugoslavia, France, and in international matches arguably helped to transform mentalities about his country and the Balkans.

By becoming a world soccer icon from a country outside of the traditional powers in Western Europe and South America, he likely opened up doors for other soccer players in the former Yugoslavia, the Balkans, and Eastern Europe. Like Uruguay's José Leandro Andrade (one of the representatives of lesson four) who opened doors for black players in Uruguay and South America, Džajić was a pioneer for future generations of Yugoslavian and East European soccer players. Yugoslavian players became soccer exports because of their skills and Džajić played an important role in this phenomenon. Think of successful Serb soccer players abroad: Dejan Petković in Brazil, Siniša Mihajlović in Italy, or Nemanja Vidić in England. Did a Stoichkov (Bulgaria) or Hagi (Romania) also benefit from the pioneering legacy of Džajić? When Džajić was a club director for Red Star Belgrade, he signed a Croatian legend from Dinamo Zagreb in 1987, Robert Prosinečki, who later played for Real Madrid and the Croatian national team that finished third at the 1998 World Cup. "It was obvious we had a classy player on our hands, and I initiated the contract proceedings right away," which took less than five minutes because the club did not have to pay a transfer fee to Zagreb, stated Džajić.[15]

In lesson four, I selected four players: Vieira, Fàbregas, Huddlestone, and Andrade. The very presence of minority players on the soccer field and the participation of three contemporary players in anti-racism campaigns (Vieira, Fàbregas, and Huddlestone) helped to change the world by changing the consciousness of other players, fans, clubs, and soccer administrators. Andrade was engaging in anti-racism work long before it was fashionable because he was a black Uruguayan playing for his country abroad in the 1920s and 1930s.

Lesson Five: Soccer as a Pagan (Secular) Religion

Like the retired West German international Franz Beckenbauer and French star Zinedine Zidane, the representatives of lesson five, Džajić was a soccer god in Yugoslavia. He remains a soccer legend for many younger people in Serbia today. Zidane and Beckenbauer are still idols for millions of fans who saw them play. Going to the soccer temple, Red Star Stadium (*Marakana*) (it mimics the name of another soccer "cathedral" in Brazil), to see Džajić play was like a religious experience for his legions of fans. As one fan put it, "He was aware that he could make opponents on the pitch disappear like with a magic stick, he could direct horrendous crosses and often threaten the goal directly even from a corner kick!"[16] For those of you who saw Džajić, Beckenbauer, or Zidane play in their respective soccer cathedrals around the world, you watched god-kissed players. New soccer gods like Neymar or Messi have been declared. In the face of those soccer gods, most of us mere mortals can only tilt our eyes and heads toward the heavens in awe.

Lesson Six: Soccer and Ethics

The representative of lesson six is the former Soviet Union national team star Igor Netto. John Terry, the Chelsea star and former England international, is the anti-ethical choice for the lesson because of his numerous unethical actions on and off the field. In chapter 6, I used the insights of French existentialist writer Albert Camus, a former goalkeeper in Algeria, to help us understand how soccer can teach us lessons about morals and ethics.

Igor Netto was a fair play man long before the introduction of the FIFA Fair Play Award. In the midst of the 1962 World Cup, the most important soccer tournament in the world, Netto went to the referee that awarded the Soviet Union a goal to tell him that it was not a goal. In contemporary soccer with its excessive commercialization and win-at-all-costs philosophy, few players might follow Netto's example. In lesson six, I also argued that FIFA corruption, game fixing, diving on the field, and drugs are real problems in the game today. Remember that there were allegations of corruption leveled against Džajić when he was the president of Red Star Belgrade. It is true that allegations do not prove guilt, but doubts will continue to swirl in some people's minds, just like they do for Gianluigi Buffon after he was cleared of betting and fixing matches (while his club Juventus faced severe sanctions and was demoted to the lower leagues of Italian professional soccer). Džajić could rightly argue that his pardon made him innocent and he said the following to *Blic*, a Serbian daily tabloid, after a board meeting with Red Star: "I spoke with people from the club, the desire to return was not disputed, I wanted to help, because everything that I previously experienced with the club cannot be forgotten. I followed, listened to and read what happened at the meeting, I wanted to come back but nothing happened and life goes on. I remain available and in this case I can only wish Red Star better days."[17] This comment was made in 2011 and his patience paid off as he was elected Red Star president for a third time in 2012.

Lesson Seven: Soccer, Business, and Marketing

The representatives of lesson seven are the retired English superstar David Beckham and the contemporary Portuguese international Cristiano Ronaldo. Ronaldo and Beckham turned themselves, their clubs, companies, advertisers, the Portuguese and English national teams, and soccer in general into major business and marketing opportunities. As Red Star president Džajić in his third term, many fans put faith in the soccer legend to restore financial sanity, growth, and prestige (for example, domestic and European titles) for the famous club.

In addition, one can make the argument that Džajić was under-marketed because of the epoch he played in and the fact that he came from the less than glamorous socialist state of Yugoslavia. Had he been from Western Europe, Džajić would have probably had the fame of Johan Cruyff or Michel Platini. As the website 4DFoot astutely points out, the Yugoslavian great was a "forgotten footballer": "Džajić shares the fate of many brilliant players who plied their trade in an era when not every great footballer ended up in the limelight of Spain, Italy or England. Remaining in their own country, their careers began, developed, peaked, declined and ended—and the world barely took notice."[18] Naveed Tariq was even more concise with respect to Džajić: "Widely unknown outside his native Serbia, but widely hailed as a national legend within it."[19] Tariq argued that along with Brian Clough, Nándor Hidegkuti, Josef Bican, and John Charles, Džajić was one of the top five "forgotten footballers" of all time.[20]

After he became president of Red Star in 2012, Džajić was "expected to undertake complete control over the club," while "a set of financial solutions has also been prepared" in 2013.[21] Red Star was cash strapped and Džajić was keen to implement "numerous changes" on the "difficult" road toward financial stability for the club.[22]

Also, remember that in lesson seven I introduced the concept of "marketing nationalism," whereby FIFA makes vast profits from each national team match. As Yugoslavia is now split up into six sovereign states, FIFA now makes even more profits, while making people from older and newer nations alike feel proud of their national colors. For FIFA, nationalism is viewed in pragmatic terms related to corporate imperatives. World Cup competitions and an array of FIFA companies ensure that FIFA's profits surpass the majority of the sovereign states of the world.

Lesson Eight: Soccer as a Leadership Opportunity

Xavi (Spain), Steven Gerrard (England), and Clint Dempsey (United States) are the representatives of lesson eight. The USA national team captain Clint Dempsey was a leader on and off the field. He overcame a difficult working-class background and the loss of his athlete sister as a youth, but still became a superstar in the English Premier League and with the USA national team as its captain. Xavi was the brains and the technical and tactical leader of Spain's World Cup title in 2010 and European Championship victories in 2008 and 2012. Gerrard is the inspirational leader of Liverpool and England, but also a player that has overcome personal adversity to perform like a giant (especially when Liverpool won the Champions League finals against AC Milan 4–3, coming back from a 3–0 halftime deficit).

Similarly, Džajić was a soccer leader with both Red Star Belgrade and Yugoslavia, in his time at Bastia SC in France, and an administrative leader as the president of Red Star Belgrade three times. Great leaders excel on the pitch and try to improve themselves off the pitch. They do more than they can, or we can, imagine. They surpass their own expectations, as well as those expectations of their admiring fans. Džajić's might save the fancied Belgrade club, but if not the legend of the player always remains. Yet the club will test his leadership skills because of its dire financial situation in 2013: "The former Yugoslavia winger, who was Red Star's technical director when they won Europe's premier club competition in 1991, sent an open letter to Serbia's sports minister Alisa Maric asking her to allocate a loan in order to save 'a fallen giant from going under.'"[23] While the board failed to make any major signings, Džajić could appeal to the history of the fabled Serbian club as he sought out state funds to rescue the team: "With 25 league titles, 24 national cups, one European Cup and a World Club Cup trophy in our cabinet, Red Star is one of Serbia's biggest brands and a name that still merits respect across the world."[24]

Lesson Nine: Soccer as a Childhood Dream

Remember that the representatives of lesson nine are three players from different soccer regions of the world: Roger Milla (Cameroon), Cha Bum-Kun (South Korea), and Hugo Sánchez (Mexico). Around the world, soccer is a dream for players, fans, journalists, referees, and administrators. This dream begins in childhood. Who as a young soccer player in Yugoslavia did not dream of becoming as good as Džajić? One Serbian website points out that if you take *Ljutice Bogdana* street, you will arrive to the Serbian Marakana (the Red Star stadium), which is a "theatre of dreams" for future stars: "Sportsmanship simply breaths out of this street, along which many new kids on the block train hard on Red Star's courts, dreaming of the fame of their predecessors like Rajko Mitić, Dragoslav Šekularac, Dragan Džajić, Vladimir Petrović, and Dragan Stojković."[25]

For professional soccer stars such as the representatives of lesson nine, dreaming began early in childhood. Those players, unlike most of us, were lucky enough to become world-renowned soccer heroes. Years after, in retirement from our amateur or professional careers, all that remains are our memories: the memories of our bitter defeats and our exhilarating victories. The memories of a "beautiful game."

Lesson Ten: Soccer and Immortality

The representatives of lesson ten are arguably the two greatest soccer players of all time: Pelé and Diego Maradona. Retired soccer players can become soccer immortals for generations. There are soccer immortals in respective countries, continents, or even the world. Retiring soccer jerseys becomes another way of attaining immortality. The greatest players attain the highest levels of immortality. In teaching us about immortality, soccer teaches us about the meaning of life. The meaning of life can be found in the game itself, but also beyond this world outside the pitch.

Džajić is a Serbian and Yugoslavian soccer immortal, an immortal among the great number 11s in soccer history, and a world soccer immortal. As one fan stated, "There is only one and unique Dragan Džajić! That's why he lasts in football [in the way he played and in our memories] as long as he does."[26] His former club Red Star Belgrade calls him one of the "five immortals" in the club's history, an honor only shared with Rajko Mitić, Dragoslav Šekularac, Vladimir Petrović, and Dragan Stojković.[27] Or the legendary sweeper Bobby Moore could question the suggestion of manager Harry Redknapp that Alan Groves was "the best winger he had ever clapped eyes on": "Is he as good as Dragan Džajić?" replied Moore.[28] Few of us mere soccer mortals can hope to attain such immortality. In this chapter, I posited the idea that soccer is certainly an egalitarian game in that it is played by all people from all cultures, faith, nations, and sexes. It is the world's most popular sport. Yet soccer is not egalitarian in the sense that it produces immortal heroes and scapegoats. In life, as in death, a Džajić, a Pelé, a Maradona, or a Messi are valorized far more than other professional soccer players.

Lesson Eleven: Soccer Players as Artists

In this chapter, I examined the way fine arts (that is, painting, statues, photographs, architecture, literature, poetry, songs, and music) all pay or paid homage to soccer and its stars. The representatives of lesson eleven are the Brazilian star Neymar and the USA's Brek Shea. Shea is an American abstract painter and professional soccer player. These two players share a number of traits: left-footed, disciplined, technically gifted, fast, inspirational, improvisational, and artistic in their passing and goal-scoring abilities. In short, they are soccer "artists"; their canvas being the soccer pitch. Yet it can be convincingly argued that Neymar is far more of an on-field soccer artist than Shea. Shea is the more accomplished artist off the field.

Džajić was a Serbian and Yugoslavian soccer artist. He was also left-footed, like the two representatives of chapter 11. He was like a performance artist, with each performance leaving you hungry for more. He was "the Balkan miracle" touched by providence and gifted like the finest painters in history. All that is left of his art are stories, memories, allegories, tales, photographs, YouTube videos, and songs in homage to the Balkan immortal. One commentator was adamant that Džajić was an artist during the European Championship match against England in 1968:

> On 5th of June 1968 in Florence, in a match against the overconfident England led by Bobby Moore, Dragan Džajić proved in a way that football can be an art. He fooled his direct opponent Wilson in his run, then he put the hardly beatable English captain Moore onto his knees in the 16 yard box, and to top it all, tricking the stationery and dizzy keeper Banks, who saw the ball only after it was in the net at the junction of the goal post and the cross bar. [29]

Džajić allows us to better understand how soccer is a simple and universal game that informs us about the joys of life and death's tragedies, as well as politics, religion, ethics, business and marketing, leadership, childhood dreams, immortality and life meaning, and the fine arts.

* * *

The World through Soccer is intended to be an educational book. The hope is that you might use the book in the classroom in order to learn about different disciplines through "the beautiful game," or to use it for your personal edification. If there was a lesson number twelve, I would dedicate it to the soccer fans, the so-called twelfth player. In the Japanese soccer tradition,

almost all the professional clubs have retired the number 12 for their supporters. Numerous clubs around the world from CF Monterrey and Parma to FC
Seoul and Red Star Belgrade have retired the number 12 jersey in honor of
their fans. I agree with the Argentinean writer Martín Caparrós, who insists
that soccer provides its fans with "a space for savage happiness."[30] Contrary
to the insights of chapter 3 with respect to ideological hegemony, soccer is
not, as Terry Eagleton pointed out, merely the "crack cocaine" of the masses.

In addition, recall that in the introduction I highlighted players that have
died on the field and in chapter 2 soccer professionals killed by authoritarian
regimes. In 2009, German national team goalkeeper Robert Enke, who was
battling depression, committed suicide by leaping in front of an express train
near Hannover. In 2011, former Nigerian international defender Uche Okafor
(a participant at the 1994 and 1998 World Cups) committed suicide at his
Dallas-area home. Famous plane crashes decimated soccer teams such as
Manchester United's "Busby Babes" in 1958. Coming back to Turin on a
foggy day on May 4, 1949, from an exhibition match in Lisbon, a plane
carrying the Torino FC team crashed into a hill overlooking Turin. Most of
the talented Zambian national squad, which came within one crucial match of
qualifying for the 1994 World Cup (Morocco qualified instead), was killed
on its way to a match in Senegal in 1993. The Zambian squad was believed
to be one of Africa's most promising national outfits in decades. All these
examples of soccer deaths remind us, as the legendary Pelé pointed out in
chapter 10, that "Life is not just this, Truth is farther beyond." The meanings
of life can be found through soccer, but also beyond the game.

Yet despite the soccer tragedies and the demise of ethics in soccer (chapter 6), the Hungarian legend Ferenc Puskás could say the following about
soccer: "I will write my life as a footballer as if it were a love story, for who
shall say it is not? It began with my great love of football and it will end the
same way."[31] As with love, in soccer we learn life lessons about "everything
that is done under the sun." We learn to appreciate that soccer is "a matter of
life and death," but surely also "much, much more than that."

Appendix

Here are my eleven best soccer players, as well as my second team, selected from each of the eleven chapters and conclusion of *The World through Soccer*:

FIRST TEAM

1. Gianluigi Buffon—Italy
2. Elias Figueroa—Chile
3. Paolo Maldini—Italy
4. José Leandro Andrade—Uruguay
5. Zinedine Zidane—France
6. Igor Netto—USSR
7. Cristiano Ronaldo—Portugal
8. Steven Gerrard—England
9. Hugo Sánchez—Mexico
10. Pelé—Brazil
11. Dragan Džajić—Yugoslavia

SECOND TEAM

1. José Luis Félix Chilavert—Paraguay
2. Djalma Santos—Brazil
3. Salvador Mariona—El Salvador
4. Francesc "Cesc" Fàbregas Soler—Spain
5. Franz Beckenbauer—Germany
6. John Terry—England

7. David Beckham—England
8. Xavi—Spain
9. Roger Milla—Cameroon
10. Diego Maradona—Argentina
11. Neymar—Brazil

Notes

INTRODUCTION

1. See, for example, Tamir Bar-On, *Rethinking the French New Right: Alternatives to Modernity* (Abingdon, UK: Routledge, 2013) and *Where Have All the Fascists Gone?* (Aldershot, UK: Ashgate, 2007).

2. Jack Bell, "Soccer: NOTEBOOK," *New York Times*, 13 February 2001, http://www.nytimes.com/2001/02/13/sports/soccer-notebook-us-coach-in-england-to-scout.html (12 May 2011).

3. Simon Ingle, "FootofGod.com forced to close," *The Guardian*, 15 February 2001, http://www.guardian.co.uk/football/2001/feb/15/newsstory.sport8 (12 May 2011).

4. Cahal Milmo, "Fifa shows red card to football fanatics' website," *The Independent*, 17 February 2001, http://www.independent.co.uk/sport/football/news-and-comment/fifa-shows-red-card-to-football-fanatics-website-692194.html (16 May 2011).

5. Sam Green, "Foot of God gets the boot," *Soccer America*, 1503, 28 May 2001, 52–53.

6. Ibid., 53.

7. Pelé (with Robert L. Fish), *My Life and the Beautiful Game: The Autobiography of Pelé* (New York: Warner Books, 1977), 12.

8. Maria Mackay, "Football the New Religion, Warn Brazilian Academics," *Christian Today*, 12 July 2006, http://www.christiantoday.com/article/football.the.new.religion.warn.brazilian.academics/6900.htm (12 May 2011).

9. Tim Vickery, "The 'Hand of God' Church," *BBC Online Network*, 4 November 2002, http://news.bbc.co.uk/sport2/hi/football/2396503.stm (15 May 2011).

10. Bill Shankly, "Own words," *Bill Shankly*, http://www.shankly.com/article/2517 (12 May 2011).

11. Juanita Darling, "In Memory of Slain Soccer Player, Boys Set Their Goals," *Los Angeles Times*, 17 July 1998, http://articles.latimes.com/1998/jul/17/news/mn-4559 (12 May 2011).

12. BBC, "Lightning kills football team," *BBC Online Network*, 28 October 1998, http://news.bbc.co.uk/2/hi/africa/203137.stm (12 May 2011).

13. Living in Peru, "New revelations about plane crash killing Peruvian football team 19 years ago," *Living in Peru*, 11 October 2006, http://www.livinginperu.com/news/2562 (12 May 2011).

14. Richard Henshaw, *The Encyclopedia of World Soccer* (Washington, D.C.: New Republic Books, 1979), 628.

15. Ibid.

16. The Mexican philosopher Mauricio Beuchot coined the term analogic hermeneutics, which is a type of hermeneutics based upon interpretation, taking into account the plurality of aspects of meaning. A colleague, Fernando Arriaga, made me aware that *The World through Soccer* uses analogic hermeneutics to see soccer through different disciplines and meanings. See Beuchot's *Hermenéutica analógica. Aplicaciones en América Latina* (Bogotá: El Búho, 2003).

17. Quoted from The English Standard Version (2001) in Biblos, "Eclessiastes 1:14," *Biblos*, http://bible.cc/ecclesiastes/1-14.htm (13 May 2011).

18. Ibid.

19. Eduardo Galeano, *El fútbol a sol y sombra* (Madrid: Siglo XXI, 2006).

20. Jean Baudrillard, *The Perfect Crime* (London: Verso, 1996).

21. Vladimir Nabokov, *Speak, Memory: An Autobiography Revisited* (New York: Vintage, 1989).

22. See, for example, Juan Villoro's, *Dios es redondo* (México, D.F.: Editorial Planeta, 2006) and *Los once de la tribu* (México, D.F.: Nuevo Siglo, 1995); Angel Cappa, *La intimidad del fútbol* (San-Sebastian: Tercera Prensa Hirrugarren, 1996); Martín Caparrós and Juan Villoro, *Ida y Vuelta: una correspondencia sobre fútbol* (México, D.F.: Seix Barral, 2012); *Foreign Affairs En Español*, "El imperio del fútbol," 6, no. 3 (Julio–Septiembre 2006): 121–196.

23. See, for example, Aaron Beacom, "Sport in International Relations: A Case For Cross-Disciplinary Investigation," *The Sports Historian* 20, no. 2 (November 2000): 1–23; Aaron Beacom and R. Levermore, eds., *Sport and International Development* (Basingstoke, UK: Palgrave Macmillan, 2009); International Review for the Sociology of Sport, "Archive of All Online Issues," *International Review of the Sociology of Sport*, http://irs.sagepub.com/content/by/year (13 May 2011).

24. See, for example, A. Kruger and J. Riordan, *The International Politics of Sport in the Twentieth Century* (New York: Routledge, 1999); David Winter, *Brilliant Orange: The Neurotic Genius of Dutch Football* (New York: Bloomsbury Publishing, 2000); and Gabriel Kuhn, *Football vs. the State: Tackling Football and Radical Politics* (Oakland: PM Press, 2011).

25. Peter Alegi and Chris Bolsmann, eds., *South Africa and the Global Game: Football, Apartheid and Beyond* (London: Routledge, 2010).

26. See, for example, Diego Maradona, *Maradona: The Autobiography of Soccer's Greatest and Most Controversial Star* (New York: Skyhorse Publishing, 2007); Patrick Barclay, *Football—Bloody Hell!: The Biography of Alex Ferguson* (London: Yellow Jersey, 2011); Bill Buford, *Among the Thugs: The Experience, and the Seduction, of Crowd Violence* (New York: W. W. Norton and Company, 1992); and Jay Allan, *Bloody Casuals: Diary of a Football Hooligan* (Ellon: Famedram Publishers, 1989).

27. Franklin Foer, *How Soccer Explains the World: An Unlikely Theory of Globalization* (New York: HarperCollins, 2004).

28. Eric Dunning and Norbert Elias, *Sport and Leisure and the Civilizing Process* (Oxford: Basil Blackwell, 1986).

29. Laurent Dubois, *Soccer Empire: The World Cup and the Future of France* (Berkeley: University of California Press, 2010) and Kuhn, *Football vs. the State*.

30. Enrique Ghersi and Andrés Roemer, eds., *¿Por qué amamos el fútbol? Un enfoque de política pública* (México, D.F.: Miguel Ángel Porrúa, 2008).

31. Ferran Soriano, *La pelota no entra por azar* (México, D.F.: Santillana, 2012).

32. I owe this organizational framework to Christen Karniski of Scarecrow Press.

33. Tamir Bar-On, "The Ambiguities of Football, Politics, Culture, and Social Transformation in Latin America," *Sociological Research Online* 2, no. 4 (1997), http://www.socresonline.org.uk/socresonline/2/4/2.html (12 May 2011).

34. Maurice Biriotti Del Burgo, "Don't Stop the Carnival: Football in the Societies of Latin America," in Stephen Wagg, ed., *Giving the Game Away: Football, Politics and Culture on Five Continents* (London: St. Martin's Press, 1995), 69.

35. Ibid.

36. Vedad Kusturica, personal communication with the author (an FK Sarajevo fan), Toronto, 22 June 2009.

37. Bar-On, *Where Have All the Fascists Gone?*, 1.

38. Marshall McLuhan, *Understanding Media: The Extensions of Man* (New York: McGraw-Hill, 1964), 209–216.

39. Ibid., 209.

40. Quoted in Albert Camus Society of the UK, "Albert Camus and football," *The Albert Camus Society of the UK*, http://www.camus-society.com/camus-football.html (13 May 2011).

41. I was born in the city of Beersheba. Hapoel Tel-Aviv FC is a famous Israeli club. I lived in Toronto for most of my life. I played with a Bosnian side FK Sarajevo in Toronto. Since 2009 I have lived in Querétaro. Liverpool FC was the club I adored as a boy.

42. Victor Andrade de Melo and Francisco Pinheiro, eds., *A Bola ao Ritmo de Fado e Samba—100 anos de relações luso-brasileiras no futebol* (Porto, Portugal: Edições Afrontamento, 2013).

43. ABC News, "Game of Soccer Gets Nobel Peace Nomination," *ABC News*, 23 January 2001, http://abcnews.go.com/International/story?id=81640&page=1 (12 November 2012).

44. Ibid.

1. SAVING THE NATION

1. Hans Kohn, *The Idea of Nationalism: A Study in Its Origins and Background* (New Brunswick, NJ: Transaction Publishers, 2008), 18–19.

2. Ibid., 18.

3. Ibid., 19.

4. George Orwell, "The Sporting Spirit," *Tribune*, December 1945, http://orwell.ru/library/articles/spirit/english/e_spirit (22 July 2013).

5. Quoted in Simon Kuper, *Football Against the Enemy* (London: Phoenix 1995), 138.

6. Nahal Toosi, "Afghanistan wins 1st international soccer title," *Associated Press*, 11 September 2013, http://news.yahoo.com/afghanistan-wins-1st-international-soccer-title-181455598--spt.html (14 September 2013).

7. Ibid.

8. Gary Armstrong and Alberto Testa, "The Ultras: The Extreme Right in Contemporary Italian Football," in Andrea Mammone, Emmanuel Godin, and Brian Jenkins, eds., *Varieties of Right-Wing Extremism in Europe* (London: Routledge, 2013), 265.

9. Kohn, *The Idea of Nationalism: A Study in Its Origins and Background*, 574.

10. Ibid.

11. Craig Calhoun, "Introduction to the Transaction Edition," in Hans Kohn, *The Idea of Nationalism: A Study in Its Origins and Background*, xii.

12. Vladimir Nabokov, *Speak, Memory: An Autobiography Revisited* (New York: Vintage Books 1989).

13. FIFA, "They said it: Jose Luis Chilavert," *FIFA*, 2010, http://www.fifa.com/newscentre/features/news/newsid=1306860/index.html (27 October 2012).

14. Ibid.

15. El Sol, "Chilavert negó un golpe de estado en Paraguay y criticó a Cristina y Rousseff," *El Sol Diario Online*, 23 June 2012, http://elsolonline.com/noticias/view/138430/chilavert-nego-un-golpe-de-estado-en-paraguay-y-critico-a-cristina-y-rousseff (22 July 2013).

16. Ibid.

17. ABC, "Argentina, Uruguay y Brasil apuñalaron al Paraguay," *ABC*, 5 July 2012, http://www.abc.com.py/nacionales/chilavert-argentina-uruguay-y-brasil-apunalaron-a-paraguay-422808.html (22 July 2013).

18. Jon Brodkin, "Buffon in trouble for choosing the wrong number at Parma," *The Guardian*, 9 September 2000, http://www.guardian.co.uk/football/2000/sep/09/newsstory.sport1 (14 July 2013).

19. See, for example, Ze'ev Sternhell (with Mario Sznajder and Maia Asheri), *The Birth of Fascist Ideology: From Cultural Rebellion to Political Revolution*), trans. David Maisel (Princeton, NJ: Princeton University Press, 1995).

20. Tamir Bar-On, *Where Have All the Fascists Gone?* (Aldershot, UK: Ashgate), 1.

21. Richard Conway, "Miners' Di Canio protest 'will only end with Sunderland campaign support,'" *BBC Online Network*, 6 April 2013, http://www.bbc.co.uk/news/uk-england-tyne-22049080 (15 July 2013).

22. Ibid.

23. Bar-On, *Where Have All the Fascists Gone?*, 2.

24. Armstrong and Testa, "The Ultras: The Extreme Right in Contemporary Italian Football," 266.

25. Bar-On, *Where Have All the Fascists Gone?*, 1–2.

26. Umberto Eco, "Eternal Fascism: Fourteen Ways of Looking at a Blackshirt," *New York Review of Books*, 22 June 1995, 12–15.

27. Bar-On, *Where Have All the Fascists Gone?*, 2.

28. Stanley G. Payne, *A History of Fascism: 1914–1945* (London: UCL Press, 1995), 7.

29. Bar-On, *Where Have All the Fascists Gone?*, 2.

30. Armstrong and Testa, "The Ultras: The Extreme Right in Contemporary Italian Football," 267.

31. The words are from French neo-fascist author Maurice Bardèche (1907–1998). See his *Qu'est-ce que le fascisme?* (Paris: Les Sept Couleurs, 1961), 175–176.

32. Tamir Bar-On, *Rethinking the French New Right: Alternatives to Modernity* (Abingdon, UK: Routledge, 2013).

33. Paul Doyle, "The forgotten story of . . . the France football captain who murdered for Hitler," *The Guardian*, 16 November 2009, http://www.guardian.co.uk/sport/blog/2009/nov/16/france (12 May 2012).

34. Simon Wiesenthal Centre, "Wiesenthal Centre Welcomes Estonian Historical Commission Findings Which Confirm Holocaust Crimes of Evald Mikson," *Simon Wiesenthal Centre*, 21 June 2001, http://www.wiesenthal.com/site/apps/s/content.asp?c=lsKWLbPJLnF&b=4442915&ct=5853153 (12 May 2012).

35. Jews in Sports, "Hirsch, Julius," *Jews in Sports*, 2011, http://www.jewsinsports.org/profile.asp?sport=soccer&ID=102 (12 May 2012).

36. Maurice Biriotti Del Burgo, "Don't Stop the Carnival: Football in the Societies of Latin America," in Stephen Wagg, ed., *Giving the Game Away: Football, Politics and Culture on Five Continents* (London: St. Martin's Press, 1995), 60.

37. Benedict Anderson, *Imagined Communities: Reflections on the Origin and Spread of Nationalism* (London: Verso, 1983).

38. Eric Hobsbawm, *Nations and Nationalism Since 1780: Programme, Myth, Reality* (Cambridge, UK: Cambridge University Press, 1990), 143.

39. José Vales, "Argentina: mas que un deporte, herramienta política," *Foreign Affairs En Español* 6, no. 3 (Julio–Septiembre 2006): 161.

40. Andrei S. Markovits and Lars Rensmann, *Gaming the World: How Sports Are Reshaping Global Politics and Culture* (Princeton, NJ: Princeton University Press, 2010), 12, 31.

41. Richard Henshaw, *The Encyclopedia of World Soccer* (Washington, D.C.: New Republic Books, 1979), 774.

42. Manuel Gameros, "Las goles de la FIFA," *Foreign Affairs En Español* 6, no. 3 (Julio–Septiembre 2006): 124.

43. Colombia Reports, "Thousands pay tribute to Colombia's Miguel Calero in Mexico," *Colombia Reports*, 5 December 2012, http://colombiareports.com/colombia-news/sports/27297-thousands-pay-tribute-to-colombia-miguel-calero-in-mexico.html (5 December 2012).

44. Footy-Boots, "Rene Higuita Delighted with Victory," *Footy-Boots*, 24 July 2008, http://www.footy-boots.com/rene-higuita-interview-4649/ (22 July 2013).

45. Phil Shaw, "Schmeichel slices into fixture," *The Independent*, 16 February 1998.

46. Eduardo Galeano, *El fútbol a sol y sombra* (Madrid: Siglo XXI, 2006).

47. Kofi A. Annan, "How We Envy the World Cup," *United Nations*, June 2006, http://www.un.org/sport2005/newsroom/worldcup.pdf (15 July 2013).

48. Pablo Alabarces, "Fútbol y patria," *Foreign Affairs En Español* 6, no. 3 (Julio–Septiembre 2006): 194.

49. Biriotti Del Burgo, "Don't Stop the Carnival: Football in the Societies of Latin America," 61.

50. Quoted in *Latin America and the Caribbean*, ed. C. Veliz (London: Anthony Blond, 1968), 743.

51. Markovits and Rensmann, *Gaming the World: How Sports Are Reshaping Global Politics and Culture*, 33.

52. Ofer Aderet, "WATCH: Hungarian soccer fans disrupt Israeli anthem with anti-Semitic slurs," *Haaretz*, 19 August 2012, http://www.haaretz.com/jewish-world/jewish-world-news/watch-hungarian-soccer-fans-disrupt-israeli-anthem-with-anti-semitic-slurs-1.459251 (27 October 2012).

53. Armstrong and Testa, "The Ultras: The Extreme Right in Contemporary Italian Football," 268.

54. Ibid.

55. Pablo Alabarces, "Fútbol y patria," 191.

56. Laurent Dubois, *Soccer Empire: The World Cup and the Future of France* (Berkeley: University of California Press, 2010), 169.

57. Gameros, "Las goles de la FIFA," 124.

58. Tamir Sorek, *Arab Soccer in a Jewish State: The Integrative Enclave* (Cambridge, UK: Cambridge University Press, 2007).

59. Martin Johnes, "We Hate England! We Hate England? National Identity and Anti-Englishness in Welsh Soccer Fan Culture," *Cycnos* 25, no. 2 (2008), http://revel.unice.fr/cycnos/index.html?id=6224 (27 October 2012).

60. Tamir Sorek, "Arab Football in Israel as an 'Integrative Enclave,'" *Ethnic and Racial Studies* 26, no. 2 (May 2003): 431.

61. Ibid.

62. Joseph Arbena, "Sport and the Promotion of Nationalism in Latin America: A Preliminary Interpretation," *Studies in Latin American Popular Culture* 11 (1992): 146–148.

63. Ibid., 146.

64. Brian Glanville, *The Story of the World Cup* (London: Faber and Faber, 1993), 201.

65. My translation. Fausto Pretelin Muñoz de Cote, "El imperio global de fútbol," *Foreign Affairs En Español* 6, no. 3 (Julio–Septiembre 2006): 132.

66. Jim Hoagland, "The Game of Nations," *Washington Post*, 9 July 1998, 19 (A).

67. Ibid.

68. Ibid.

69. Luxury Player, "Gianluigi Buffon, Piazzale Loreto and an uncomfortable relationship with history," *Luxury Player*, 2 July 2011, http://luxuryplayer.wordpress.com/2011/07/02/gianluigi-buffon-piazzale-loreto-and-an-uncomfortable-relationship-with-history/ (15 November 2012).

70. Quoted in León Krauze, "México y Estados Unidos: identidad y fútbol," *Foreign Affairs En Español* 6, no. 3 (Julio–Septiembre 2006): 147.

71. FIFA, "They said it: Jose Luis Chilavert."

72. Krauze, "México y Estados Unidos: identidad y fútbol," 148.

73. Michael Minkenberg, "Viadrina Summer University 2012," *Kuwi*, http://www.kuwi.europa-uni.de/de/studium/summeruniversity/detailed_programme/cc1_minkenberg/index.html (21 August 2012).

74. Annan, "How We Envy the World Cup."

75. Kohn, *The Idea of Nationalism: A Study in Its Origins and Background*, 574.

76. Annan, "How We Envy the World Cup."

2. "BELIEVE, OBEY, AND FIGHT"

1. Andrei S. Markovits and Lars Rensmann, *Gaming the World: How Sports Are Reshaping Global Politics and Culture* (Princeton, NJ: Princeton University Press, 2010), 8.

2. Eduardo Galeano, *Soccer in Sun and Shadow*, trans. Mark Fried (London: Verso, 2003), 35.

3. See, for example, Joseph L. Arbena, ed., *Sport and Society in Latin America: Diffusion, Dependency and the Rise of Mass Culture* (Westport, CT: Greenwood Press, 1988) and Joseph L. Arbena, "Sport and the Promotion of Nationalism in Latin America: A Preliminary Interpretation," *Studies in Latin American Popular Culture*, no. 11 (1992): 146–148.

4. FIFA, "Figueroa, Chile's defensive commander," *FIFA*, 2012, http://www.fifa.com/classicfootball/players/player=49415/index.html (23 July 2013).

5. Ibid.

6. The Clinic Online, "Los 100 rostros del Sí," *The Clinic*, http://www.theclinic.cl/2012/07/30/los-100-rostros-del-si/ (25 November 2013).

7. Diego Bastarrica, "Los futboleros que 'querían' ser los albaceas en el testamento de Pinochet," *Ferplei*, 25 abril 2012, http://www.ferplei.com/2012/04/los-futboleros-que-querian-ser-los-albaceas-en-el-testamento-de-pinochet/ (25 November 2013).

8. Miguel Ángel Iara, "Caszely, el goleador que plantó cara a Pinochet," *Marca*, 2011, http://www.marca.com/reportajes/2011/12/el_poder_del_balon/2012/03/27/seccion_01/13328 81843.html (25 November 2013).

9. Ibid.

10. Lamula, "El fútbol chileno y Pinochet: El goleador Carlos Caszely fue incómodo para la dictadura militar," *Lamula*, 9 November 2013, http://lamula.pe/2013/09/11/el-futbol-chileno-y-pinochet/albertoniquen/ (25 November 2013).

11. Lorena Venegas and Alfredo Peña, "A 25 años del plebiscito del 88 que derrotó a Pinochet: Los 100 rostros que estuvieron en la campaña del Sí," *Cambio21*, 4 October 2013, http://www.cambio21.cl/cambio21/site/artic/20131002/pags/20131002180358.html (25 November 2013).

12. Ibid.

13. Ibid.

14. Ibid.

15. FIFA, "Figueroa, Chile's defensive commander."

16. Leander Schaerlaeckens, "Chasing Gaetjens," *ESPN*, 26 February 2010, http://soccernet.espn.go.com/world-cup/story/_/id/4937012/ce/us/real-story-1950-world-cup-hero?cc=3888&ver=global (24 October 2012).

17. John R. Tunis, "Los Dictadores Descubren El Deporte," *Foreign Affairs En Español* 6, no. 3 (Julio–Septiembre 2006): 235–245. Originally published in *Foreign Affairs* (July–August 1936).

18. Ibid., 236.

19. Ibid., 239.

20. Ibid., 240.

21. Paul Doyle and Tom Lutz, "Joy of Six: Footballers who have overcome humble beginnings," *The Guardian*, 3 September 2010, http://www.guardian.co.uk/sport/blog/2010/sep/03/joy-six-footballers-humble-beginnings (12 October 2012).

22. Duncan Shaw, "The Politics of 'Futbol,'" *History Today* 35, no. 8 (1985), http://www.historytoday.com/duncan-shaw/politics-futbol (22 August 2012).

23. Ibid.

24. Ibid.

25. Ibid.

26. Andrew Jennings, *Foul! The Secret World of FIFA: Bribes, Vote-Rigging and Ticket Scandals* (London: Harper Collins, 2006), ix.

27. El País, "La larga carrera de un hombre polifacético," *El País*, 21 April 2010, http://deportes.elpais.com/deportes/2010/04/21/actualidad/1271834520_850215.html (23 July 2013).

28. Shaw, "The Politics of 'Futbol.'"

29. Ibid.

30. Ibid.

31. Ibid.

32. Manuel Gameros, "Las goles de la FIFA," *Foreign Affairs En Español* 6, no. 3 (Julio–Septiembre 2006): 124.

33. Ryszard Kapuściński, *The Soccer War*, trans. William Brand (London: Granta, 1990), 159.

34. Markovits and Rensmann, *Gaming the World: How Sports Are Reshaping Global Politics and Culture*, 8.

35. Kapuściński, *The Soccer War*, 166.

36. Blog Cuscatlán, "Alianza F.C. Entre Los 10 Mejores," 9 October 2009, http://cuxcatla.blogspot.mx/2009/10/alianza-fc-entre-los-10-mejores.html (23 July 2013).

37. Janet Lever, "Sport in a Fractured Society: Brazil under Military Rule," in Joseph L. Arbena, ed., *Sport and Society in Latin America: Diffusion, Dependency and the Rise of Mass Culture* (Westport, CT: Greenwood Press 1988), 85–96.

38. David Goldblatt, *The Ball Is Round: A Global History of Soccer* (New York: Penguin, 2008), 266.

39. Fausto Pretelin Muñoz de Cote, "El imperio global de fútbol," *Foreign Affairs En Español* 6, no. 3 (Julio–Septiembre 2006): 137

40. Stefan Szymanski and Andrew Zimbalist, *National Pastime: How Americans Play Baseball and the Rest of the World Plays Soccer* (Washington, D.C.: The Brookings Institution, 2005), 73–74.

41. Brian Glanville, *The Story of the World Cup* (London: Faber and Faber, 1993), 211.

42. Juan J. Linz, *Totalitarian and Authoritarian Regimes* (Boulder, CO: Lynne Rienner, 2000).

43. Emilio Gentile, *Politics as Religion*, trans. George Staunton (Princeton, NJ: Princeton University Press, 2006).

44. A. J. Gregor, *Italian Fascism and Developmental Dictatorship* (Princeton, NJ: Princeton University Press, 1979).

45. Pretelin Muñoz de Cote, "El imperio global de fútbol," 134–135.

46. Ibid., 135.

47. Juan Villoro, *Los once de la tribu* (México, D.F.: Nuevo Siglo, 1995).

48. José Vales, "Argentina: mas que un deporte, herramienta política," *Foreign Affairs En Español* 6, no. 3 (Julio–Septiembre 2006): 159.

49. Legends of the Game, "Johan Cruyff," *Legends of the Game*, http://legendsofthega.me/beta/cruyff/index.html (16 November 2012).

50. Ángel Iara, "Caszely, el goleador que plantó cara a Pinochet."

51. Ibid.

52. La nación, "Hasta temas políticos aborda la biografía de Elías Figueroa," *Nación*, 27 May 2005, http://www.lanacion.cl/noticias/site/artic/20050526/pags/20050526210233.html (27 August 2012).

53. Ibid.

54. El Mostrador, "Ivo Basay: "Pinochet fue un hombre necesario en cierto momento de la historia de Chile," *Elmostrador*, 5 October 2011, http://www.elmostrador.cl/noticias/pais/2011/10/05/ivo-basay-pinochet-fue-un-hombre-necesario-en-cierto-momento-de-la-historia-de-chile/ (28 October 2012).

55. Aleksandr I. Solzhenitsyn, *The Gulag Archipelago 1918–1956: An Experiment in Literary Investigation*, trans. Thomas P. Whitney (New York: Harper and Row, 1974).

56. Sebastian Leiva Rodriquez, "Entrevista a Elías Figueroa Branden," *Fundacion Asciende*, 2010, http://www.fundacionasciende.com/publicaciones-de-fundacion-asciende/entrevistas/196-entrevista-a-elias-figueroa-branden (27 August 2012).

57. Ibid.

58. My translation. Rodrigo Ogalde, "Elías Figueroa está interesado en ser candidato a diputado por San Antonio," *soysanantonio*, 7 March 2013, http://www.soychile.cl/San-Antonio/Politica/2013/03/07/159096/Elias-Figueroa-esta-interesado-en-ser-candidato-a-diputado-por-San-Antonio.aspx (25 November 2013).

59. Baljit Singh Grewal, "Johan Galtung: Positive and Negative Peace," 30 August 2003, http://www.activeforpeace.org/no/fred/Positive_Negative_Peace.pdf (7 September 2013).

60. Mark Bisson, "ChangeFIFA Urges Federations to Back South American Legend's Challenge to Blatter Presidency," *World Football Insider*, 29 March 2011, http://www.worldfootballinsider.com/Story.aspx?id=34235 (28 October 2012).

61. Rodolfo Arredondo Sánchez, "Elías Figueroa baja candidatura a la FIFA por falta de apoyo," *Suite 101*, 31 March 2011, http://suite101.net/article/elias-figueroa-baja-candidatura-a-la-fifa-por-falta-de-apoyo-a46773 (16 November 2012).

3. WINNING HEARTS AND MINDS

1. Karl Marx and Friedrich Engels, *The Communist Manifesto* (Moscow: Progress Publishers, [1848] 1977).

2. Quoted in Lawrence H. Simon, ed., "Introduction," *Karl Marx: Selected Writings* (Indianapolis: Hacket Publishing Company, Inc., 1994), xviii.

3. Ibid.

4. Mark Rupert, "Marxism," in Martin Griffiths, ed., *International Relations Theory for the 21st Century* (London: Routledge, 2007), 40.

5. Ibid.

6. Antonio Gramsci, *Selections from the Prison Notebooks*, ed. and trans. by Quentin Hoare and Geoffrey Nowell Smith (London: Lawrence and Wishart, 1971).

7. Ibid., 367.

8. Ibid., 433.

9. Ibid., 625.

10. FIFA, "World Football: Salvador Mariona," *FIFA*, 2013, http://www.fifa.com/worldfootball/statisticsandrecords/players/player=53654/ (26 July 2013).

11. Fausto Pretelin Muñoz de Cote, "El imperio global de fútbol," *Foreign Affairs En Español* 6, no. 3 (Julio–Septiembre 2006): 136.

12. José Ortega y Gasset, *The Revolt of the Masses* (original in Spanish first published in 1930) (New York: W. W. Norton and Company, 1993).

13. Gerhard Vinnai, *El fútbol como ideología* (México, D.F.: Siglo XXI, 2003).

14. James Procter, *Stuart Hall* (London: Routledge, 2004), 2.

15. Patrick Hutchison, "Breaking Boundaries: Football and Colonialism in the British Empire," *Student Pulse* 1, no. 11 (2009), http://www.studentpulse.com/articles/64/breaking-boundaries-football-and-colonialism-in-the-british-empire (26 July 2013).

16. FIFA, "Pachuca: cradle of football to Hall of Fame," *FIFA*, 10 July 2011, http://www.fifa.com/worldfootball/news/newsid=1472823.html (26 July 2013).

17. Maurice Biriotti Del Burgo, "Don't Stop the Carnival: Football in the Societies of Latin America," in Stephen Wagg, ed., *Giving the Game Away: Football, Politics and Culture on Five Continents* (London: St. Martin's Press, 1995), 54.

18. Ibid., 65–66.

19. Jean Baudrillard, *The Perfect Crime* (London: Verso, 1996).

20. Gabriel Kuhn, *Football vs. the State: Tackling Football and Radical Politics* (Oakland, CA: PM Press, 2011), 19.

21. Ibid., 20.

22. Maurice Biriotti Del Burgo, "Don't Stop the Carnival: Football in the Societies of Latin America," 55.

23. See William H. Durham, *Scarcity and Survival in Central America: Ecological Origins of the Football War* (Stanford: Stanford University Press, 1979).

24. Ryszard Kapuściński, *The Soccer War*, trans. William Brand (London: Granta, 1990), 182.

25. Cuscatla, "LA GUERRA DEL FÚTBOL 1969," *Cuscatla*, http://www.cuscatla.com/la_guerra.htm (3 December 2013).

26. Pedro Lemus, "A 44 años de la primera vez," *El Blog*, 8 October 2013, http://www.elblog.com/deportes/a-44-anos-de-la-primera-vez.html (3 December 2013).

27. My translation. O. Arriola and C. Peñate, "'Pipo' Rodríguez, Deportista Destacado," *La Prensa Grafica*, 18 October 2013, http://www.laprensagrafica.com/2013/10/18/pipo-rodriguez-deportista-destacado (3 December 2013).

28. YouTube, "Salvador Mariona en La Kaliente," 20 October 2011, *YouTube*, http://www.youtube.com/watch?v=mcivFSvWPGg (3 December 2013).

29. Cuscatla, "LA GUERRA DEL FÚTBOL 1969," *Cuscatla*, http://www.cuscatla.com/la_guerra.htm (3 December 2013).

30. See, for example, George Friedman, *The Next 100 Years: A Forecast for the 21st Century* (New York: Anchor Books, 2010).

31. David Sobek, "Rallying Around the Podesta: Testing Diversionary Theory Across Time," *Journal of Peace Research* 44, no. 1 (2007): 29–45.

32. Jack Bell, "Philosophy Football," *New York Times Soccer Blog*, 30 April 2010, http://goal.blogs.nytimes.com/2010/04/30/philosophy-football/ (20 September 2012).

33. Quoted in Eduardo Galeano, *Soccer in Sun and Shadow*, trans. Mark Fried (London: Verso, 2003), 34.

34. Quoted in Working Class Ballet, "Football Quotes," *Working Class Ballet*, http://workingclassballet.wordpress.com/theres-some-people-on-the-pitch-football-quotes/ (16 September 2013).

35. Theodor Adorno and Max Horkheimer, *Dialectic of Enlightenment* (New York: Continuum, 1993), quoted in Theodor Adorno and Max Horkheimer, "The Culture Industry: Enlightenment as Mass Deception," *Dialectic of Enlightenment* (1944), http://www.marxists.org/reference/archive/adorno/1944/culture-industry.htm (25 September 2013).

36. Ibid.

37. Rupert, "Marxism," 40.

38. Stephen Gill, *Power and Resistance in the New World Order*, second edition (Basingstoke: Palgrave Macmillan, 2008), 14.

39. Steve Hellerman and Andrei Markovits, *Offside: Soccer and American Exceptionalism* (Princeton, NJ: Princeton University Press, 2001), 10.

40. Ibid.

41. Adorno and Horkheimer, *Dialectic of Enlightenment*, in "The Culture Industry: Enlightenment as Mass Deception."

42. Louis Althusser, "Ideology and Ideological State Apparatuses," in *Lenin and Philosophy and other Essays* (New York: Monthly Review Press, 1970), 121–176.

43. Ibid.

44. Alan G. Ingham, "The Sportification Process: A Biographical Analysis Framed by the Work of Marx, Weber, Durkheim and Freud," in R. Giulianotti, ed., *Sport and Modern Social Theorists* (New York: Palgrave Macmillan, 2004), 26–27.

45. Ibid., 27.

46. Ibid., 26.

47. Andrei S. Markovits and Lars Rensmann, *Gaming the World: How Sports Are Reshaping Global Politics and Culture* (Princeton, NJ: Princeton University Press, 2010), 9.

48. Terry Eagleton, "Football: a dear friend to capitalism," *The Guardian*, 15 June 2010, http://www.guardian.co.uk/commentisfree/2010/jun/15/football-socialism-crack-cocaine-people (2 September 2012).

49. Ibid.

50. Ibid.

51. Ibid.

52. Matt Lawless, "Fifa president Sepp Blatter 'alarmed' over foreign influx and demands level playing field," *The Telegraph*, 7 October 2008, http://www.telegraph.co.uk/sport/football/competitions/premier-league/3150222/Fifa-president-Sepp-Blatter-alarmed-over-foreign-ownership-influx-and-demands-level-playing-field-Football.html (2 September 2012).

53. Ibid.

54. Forbes, "Soccer Team Valuations," *Forbes*, 29 September 2010, http://www.forbes.com/2010/04/21/soccer-value-teams-business-sports-soccer-10-wealth_land.html (2 September 2012).

55. Bell, "Philosophy Football."

4. "ONE BALL CAN CHANGE THE WORLD"

1. Show Racism the Red Card, *Website of Show Racism the Red Card*, 2013, http://www.srtrc.org/ (26 July 2013).

2. Ibid.

3. Kick It Out, "About Kick It Out," *Kick It Out*, http://www.kickitout.org/2.php (19 September 2012).

4. Ibid.

5. England Football Online, "England's 70 Black Players," *England Football Online*, 2012, http://www.englandfootballonline.com/TeamBlack/Black.html (19 September 2012).

6. Kick It Out, "About Kick It Out."

7. Ibid.

8. Eduardo Galeano, *Soccer in Sun and Shadow*, trans. Mark Fried (London: Verso, 2003), 47.

9. Ibid.

10. Ibid., 39.

11. Hans Ulrich Gumbrecht, *In Praise of Athletic Beauty* (Cambridge, MA: Harvard University Press, 2006), 249–251.

12. Eduardo Galeano, *El fútbol a sol y sombra* (Madrid: Siglo XXI, 2006), 51–54.

13. Espacio Latino, "José Leandro Andrade," *Espacio Latino*, http://letras-uruguay.espaciolatino.com/abalos_m/c/andrade.htm (26 July 2013).

14. Galeano, *Soccer in Sun and Shadow*, 47.

15. Alex Bellos, *Futebol: The Brazilian Way of Life* (London: Bloomsbury, 2002), 10.

16. Philip O'Connor, "Anti-homophobia rainbow campaign hit by controversy," *Reuters*, 19 September 2013, http://news.yahoo.com/anti-homophobia-rainbow-campaign-hit-controversy-012935851--sow.html (21 September 2013).

17. Ibid.

18. Chris Greenberg, "Robbie Rogers, Openly Gay Soccer Player, Makes Historic L.A. Galaxy Debut," *The Huffington Post*, 27 May 2013, http://www.huffingtonpost.com/2013/05/27/gay-soccer-player-robbie-rogers-debut_n_3341036.html?utm_hp_ref=robbie-rogers (29 August 2013).

19. Franklin Foer, *How Soccer Explains the World: An Unlikely Theory of Globalization* (New York: HarperCollins, 2004).

20. Bradford Plumer, "How Soccer Explains the World," *Mother Jones*, 4 August 2004, http://www.motherjones.com/politics/2004/08/how-soccer-explains-world (12 September 2012).

21. Ibid.

22. Ibid.

23. Andrei S. Markovits and Lars Rensmann, *Gaming the World: How Sports Are Reshaping Global Politics and Culture* (Princeton, NJ: Princeton University Press, 2010), 1.

24. Ibid., 2.

25. Ibid.

26. Ibid.

27. Ibid., 3.

28. Ibid., 12–13.

29. Emilio Gentile, *Politics as Religion*, trans. George Staunton (Princeton, NJ: Princeton University Press, 2006).

30. Simon Hattenstone, "Racism in football: putting the boot in," *The Guardian*, 13 July 2012, http://www.guardian.co.uk/football/2012/jul/13/racism-football-premier-league-campbell (12 September 2012).

31. Ibid.

32. Anthony Clavane, *Does Your Rabbi Know You're Here?: The Story of English Football's Forgotten Tribe* (London: Quercus, 2012).

33. Ibid.

34. Hattenstone, "Racism in football: putting the boot in."

35. Ibid.
36. Ibid.
37. David Winter, *Brilliant Orange: The Neurotic Genius of Dutch Football* (New York: Bloomsbury Publishing, 2000).
38. Stephen Wagg, ed., *Giving the Game Away: Football, Politics and Culture on Five Continents* (Leicester, UK: Leicester University Press, 1995), 115–117.
39. Matt Fleming, "Black players should ignore racist chants, says Rijkaard," *The Independent*, 31 October 2006, http://www.independent.co.uk/sport/football/european/black-players-should-ignore-racist-chants-says-rijkaard-422294.html (26 July 2013).
40. Haaretz, "British soccer body deems 'yid' anti-Semitic slur," *Haaretz*, 12 September 2013, http://www.haaretz.com/jewish-world/jewish-world-news/1.546665 (14 September 2013).
41. Ibid.
42. Markovits and Rensmann, *Gaming the World: How Sports are Reshaping Global Politics and Culture*, 40.
43. Ibid.
44. Ibid.
45. Patrick Camiller and Pierre-Andre Taguieff, *Rising from the Muck: The New Anti-Semitism in Europe* (Chicago: Ivan R. Dee, 2004).
46. BBC, "Netherlands Islam Freedom: Profile of Geert Wilders," *BBC Online Network*, 23 June 2011, http://www.bbc.co.uk/news/world-europe-11443211 (27 July 2013).
47. Sarah L. De Lange, "Radical Right-Wing Populist Parties in Office—A Cross-National Comparison," in Uwe Backes and Patrick Moreau, eds., *The Extreme Right in Europe: Current Trends and Perspectives*, (Göttingen: Vandenhoeck and Ruprecht, 2012), 173, 192.
48. See, for example, Lilian Thuram's *Fondation Lilian Thuram*, http://www.thuram.org/ (27 July 2013).
49. Jonathan Long and Karl Spracklen, "Positioning Anti-Racism in Sport and Sport in Anti-Racism," in Jonathan Long and Karl Spracklen, eds. *Sport and Challenges to Racism*, (London: Palgrave Macmillan, 2010), 9.
50. Ibid.
51. Ibid.
52. BBC, "Brazil football legend Sócrates dies at 57," *BBC Online Network*, 4 December 2011, http://www.bbc.co.uk/sport/0/football/16017071 (27 July 2013).
53. Ibid.
54. Matthew Shirts, "Sócrates, Corinthians and Question of Democracy," in Joseph Arbena, ed., *Sport and Society in Latin America* (Westport, CT: Greenwood Press, 1988), 100.
55. Ibid.
56. Maurice Biriotti Del Burgo, "Don't Stop the Carnival: Football in the Societies of Latin America," in Stephen Wagg, ed., *Giving the Game Away: Football, Politics and Culture on Five Continents* (London: St. Martin's Press, 1995), 69.
57. Manuel Vázquez Montalbán, *Un Polaco en la corte del Rey Juan Carlos* (Madrid: Alfaguara, 1996).
58. Homeless World Cup, "Homeless World Cup Mexico City 2012," *Homeless World Cup*, 2012, http://www.homelessworldcup.org/ (13 September 2012).
59. Ibid.
60. Ibid.
61. Ibid.
62. FC Barcelona, "Legends: Paulino Alcántara," *FC Barcelona*, 2012, http://www.fcbarcelona.com/club/history/detail/card/paulino-alcantara (31 October 2012).
63. Markovits and Rensmann, *Gaming the World: How Sports Are Reshaping Global Politics and Culture*, 32.
64. Galeano, *Soccer in Sun and Shadow*, 34.
65. Markovits and Rensmann, *Gaming the World: How Sports Are Reshaping Global Politics and Culture*, 32.
66. Ibid.
67. Ibid.

5. GODS AND THEIR SHRINES

1. See, for example, section 108 in Friedrich Nietzsche, *The Gay Science: With a Prelude in Rhymes and an Appendix of Songs by Friedrich Nietzsche*, trans. Walter Kaufmann (New York: Vintage Books, 1974).

2. Ibid., section 125.

3. Juan Villoro, *Dios es redondo* (México, D.F.: Editorial Planeta, 2006).

4. Quoted in Thomas Pitts, "A Philosopher's Guide to Football," *The False Nine*, 13 July 2012, http://www.thefalsenine.co.uk/2012/07/13/a-philosophers-guide-to-football/ (28 July 2013).

5. Quoted in Philosophy Football, *Philosophy football quotations*, http://www.philosophyfootball.com/quotations.php (28 July 2013).

6. Eduardo Galeano, *Soccer in Sun and Shadow*, trans. Mark Fried (London: Verso, 2003).

7. Thilo Thielke, "They'll Put a Spell on You: The Witchdoctors of African Football," *Spiegel Online International*, 11 June 2010, http://www.spiegel.de/international/zeitgeist/they-ll-put-a-spell-on-you-the-witchdoctors-of-african-football-a-699704.html (26 November 2013).

8. Ibid.

9. Jeremy Wilson, "United not the greatest test of faith for Primus," *The Guardian*, 27 January 2007, http://www.guardian.co.uk/football/2007/jan/27/newsstory.sport3 (28 July 2013).

10. Desmond Morris, *The Soccer Tribe* (London: Jonathan Cape, 1981).

11. FIFA, "Bale: I want to help Real win Champions League," *FIFA*, 2 September 2013, http://www.fifa.com/worldfootball/clubfootball/news/news-id=2166551.html?intcmp=fifacom_hp_module_news (2 September 2013).

12. FIFA, "Pele—I was there," *FIFA*, http://www.fifa.com/classicfootball/players/player=63869/quotes.html (10 August 2013).

13. Vladimir Dimitrijević, *La vida es un balón redondo*, trans. Antonio Castilla Cerezo (México, D.F.: Sexto Piso, 2010), 19.

14. Ibid., 18.

15. Ibid., 24–27.

16. Christoph Biermann, "Franz is a god, and Jurgen a mere mortal," *The Observer*, 26 March 2006.

17. BBC, "Zidane: Le football God," *BBC Online Network*, n.d., http://news.bbc.co.uk/sportacademy/hi/sa/football/features/newsid_3749000/3749667.stm (12 October 2013).

18. World Soccer, "The Greatest Team Ever," *World Soccer*, Summer 2013, 41–53.

19. Biermann, "Franz is a god, and Jurgen a mere mortal."

20. International Federation of Football History and Statistics (IFFHS), *IFFHS*, 2012, http://www.iffhs.de/?31748d16 (8 October 2012).

21. SoccerWay, "Henry hails 'God Zidane,'" *SoccerWay*, 5 August 2005, http://br.soccerway.com/news/2005/august/5/henry-hails-god-zidane/ (12 October 2013).

22. Laurent Dubois, *Soccer Empire: The World Cup and the Future of France* (Berkeley: University of California Press, 2010).

23. Soccer News, "Zidane is the best player ever, says Beckham," *Soccer News*, 13 July 2008, http://www.soccernews.com/zidane-is-the-best-player-ever-says-beckham/4033/date (16 September 2012).

24. Ibid.

25. Jon Stevenson, "Zidane's lasting legacy," *BBC Sport*, 2010, http://news.bbc.co.uk/sport2/hi/football/world_cup_2006/teams/france/5147908.stmdate (16 September 2012).

26. Andrew Anthony, "Zizou Top," *The Guardian*, 2 July 2000, http://www.guardian.co.uk/football/2000/jul/02/euro2000.sport2 (16 September 2012).

27. Jean-Sébastien Stehli et al., "Zidane: Icône malgré lui," *L'Express*, 8 June 2006, http://web.archive.org/web/20071014204041/http://lexpress.fr/mag/sports/dossier/mondial-2006/dossier.asp?ida=438679&p=3 (16 September 2012).

28. Jason Burt, "Brazil 0 France 1: Zidane regains mastery to tame Brazil," *The Independent*, 3 July 2006, http://www.independent.co.uk/sport/football/international/brazil-0-france-1-zidane-regains-mastery-to-tame-brazil-406473.html (12 October 2013).

29. Ibid.

30. Patrick Barclay, "Zidane has the measure of true greatness," *The Telegraph*, 27 August 2000.

31. Jules Delay, "Zidane the greatest of all time," *Nouse*, 29 January 2013, http://www.nouse.co.uk/2013/01/29/zidane-the-greatest-of-all-time/ (28 July 2013).

32. Emilio Gentile, *Politics as Religion*, trans. George Staunton (Princeton, NJ: Princeton University Press, 2006).

33. Alan G. Ingham, "The Sportification Process: A Biographical Analysis Framed by the Work of Marx, Weber, Durkheim and Freud," in R. Giulianotti, ed., *Sport and Modern Social Theorists* (New York: Palgrave Macmillan, 2004), 27.

34. Marshall McLuhan, *Understanding Media: The Extensions of Man* (New York: McGraw-Hill, 1964), 207–216.

35. Ibid., 209.

36. Ibid.

37. Ibid.

38. Ibid., 211.

39. Juan Villoro in *Ida y Vuelta: una correspondencia sobre fútbol*, Martín Caparrós and Juan Villoro (México, D.F.: Seix Barral, 2012), 133.

40. Chris Mann, "The 10 Largest Football Stadiums in the World," *Soccer Lens*, 2009, http://soccerlens.com/largest-football-stadiums/36427/ (16 September 2012).

41. Ibid.

42. Tony Mason, *Passion of the People?: Football in South America* (London: Verso, 1995), 78.

43. Frommer's, "Maracanã Stadium," *Frommer's*, 2013, http://www.frommers.com/destinations/rio-de-janeiro/attractions/212698 (26 November 2013).

44. Connie Watson, "Modernizing Brazil bulldozes its slums and soccer's shrine," *CBC News*, 10 April 2012, http://www.cbc.ca/news/world/modernizing-brazil-bulldozes-its-slums-and-soccer-s-shrine-1.1141696 (26 November 2013).

45. Jane Lasky, "England ties Brazil at Maracana in a soccer match that almost didn't happen," *Examiner*, 2 June 2013, http://www.examiner.com/article/england-ties-brazil-at-maracana-a-soccer-match-that-almost-didn-t-happen (26 November 2013).

46. Martín Caparrós in *Ida y Vuelta: una correspondencia sobre fútbol*, 156.

47. IMDb, "Reviews & Ratings for Zidane: A 21st Century Portrait," *IMDb*, 12 April 2007, http://www.imdb.com/title/tt0478337/reviews (12 October 2013).

48. Robert K. Merton, "Introduction" in Gustave Le Bon, *The Crowd: A Study of the Popular Mind* (New York: The Viking Press, 1960), ix–xi.

49. McLuhan, *Understanding Media: The Extensions of Man*, 209–216.

50. Eloy Caloca Lafont, *Ocio y civilización* (Querétaro, México: Tres Editores, 2013), 56.

51. John Bale, *Sport, Space and the City* (London: Routledge, 1993), 6.

52. Christian Derbaix, Alain Decrop, and Olivier Cabossart, "Colors and Scarves: the Symbolic Consumption of Material Possessions By Soccer Fans," *NA—Advances in Consumer Research* 29 (2002), 511.

53. Ibid.

54. Ibid., 518.

55. Christopher Gaffney and Gilmar Mascarenhasa, "The Soccer Stadium as a Disciplinary Space," International Michel Foucault Seminar, Universidade Federal de Santa Catarina Florianopolis, Brazil, September 21–24, 2004.

56. Football Italia, "Klopp: 'Napoli a mystical experience,'" *Football Italia*, 17 September 2013, http://www.football-italia.net/39605/klopp-napoli-mystical-experience (26 November 2013).

57. Yelp, "Camp Nou: Danielle F.," *Yelp*, 14 March 2013, http://www.yelp.com/biz/camp-nou-barcelona (26 November 2013).

58. FIFA, "Schumacher: Football is like a religion in Turkey," *FIFA*, 23 November 2012, http://www.fifa.com/u20worldcup/news/newsid=1943797/ (27 November 2013).

59. Stretford End "Chants: We'll Never Die," *Stretford-End*, 2013, http://www.stretford-end.com/chants/ (28 November 2013).

60. Marca, "Zidane: 'No soy un Dios, sólo soy un futbolista,'" *Marca*, 25 December 2003, http://archivo.marca.com/primeras/03/12/1226.html (12 October 2013).

61. Enrique Ghersi and Andrés Roemer, eds., *¿Por qué amamos el fútbol? Un enfoque de política pública* (México, D.F.: Miguel Ángel Porrúa, 2008), 31–32.

6. PLAYING FAIR

1. Colin Allen and Wendell Wallach, *Moral Robots: Teaching Machines Right from Wrong* (New York: Oxford University Press, 2008).

2. David Korten, *When Corporations Rule the World* (West Hartford, CT: Kumarian, 1995).

3. Declan Hill, *Juego sucio: Fútbol y crimen organizado*, trans. Concha Cardeñoso Sáenz de Miera and Francisco López Martín (Barcelona: Alba, 2010).

4. Yahoo!Sports, "El Salvador ban 14 internationals for life for fixing," *Reuters*, 20 September 2013, http://sports.yahoo.com/news/el-salvador-ban-14-internationals-life-match-fixing-211930119--sow.html (23 September 2013).

5. George Orwell, "The Sporting Spirit," *Tribune*, December 1945, http://orwell.ru/library/articles/spirit/english/e_spirit (22 July 2013).

6. Robert Conquest, *The Great Terror: A Reassessment* (Oxford: Oxford University Press, 2007), xvi.

7. World Football Legends, "Igor Netto," *World Football Legends UK*, 2012, http://www.world-football-legends.co.uk/index.php/urs/115-netto-igor (25 October 2012).

8. Pes Stats Database, "Igor Netto," *Pes Stats Database*, 2012, http://pesstatsdatabase.com/viewtopic.php?f=182&t=9435 (25 October 2012).

9. Ibid.

10. Bruce Henderson, "There is Fair Play in Soccer," *OSA*, n.d., http://www.ssra.ca/there_is_fair_play_in_soccer.htm (25 October 2012).

11. Rankopedia, "Best Russian-Soviet Soccer Player Ever," *Rankopedia*, 2011, http://www.rankopedia.com/Best-Russian/Soviet-soccer-Player-ever/Step1/14794/.htm (25 October 2012).

12. BBC, "Ronaldinho regains FifPro crown," *BBC Online Network*, 6 November 2006, http://news.bbc.co.uk/sport2/hi/football/internationals/5414328.stm (6 November 2013).

13. Jonathan Clegg and Bruce Orwall, "Last Taboo in English Football: Playing Footsie With Mate's Mate," *The Wall Street Journal*, 4 February 2010, http://online.wsj.com/news/articles/SB10001424052748704259304575043212033975040 (6 November 2013).

14. Ibid.

15. BBC, "Summary of the reasons for John Terry's FA ban," *BBC Online Network*, 5 October 2012, http://www.bbc.co.uk/sport/0/football/19845841 (6 November 2013).

16. BBC, "John Terry fights FA charge over Anton Ferdinand," *BBC Online Network*, 3 August 2012, http://www.bbc.co.uk/sport/0/football/19021184 (6 November 2013).

17. Peter Singer, "Ethics," *Encyclopædia Britannica*, 1985, 627–648, http://www.utilitarian.net/singer/by/1985----.htm (23 September 2012).

18. Andrew Jennings, *Foul! The Secret World of FIFA: Bribes, Vote-Rigging and Ticket Scandals* (London: Harper Collins, 2006).

19. The Guardian Blog, "From the Vault: Remembering the life and football of Bobby Moore," *The Guardian Blog*, 22 February 2013, http://www.theguardian.com/sport/blog/2013/feb/22/vault-remembering-life-football-bobby-moore (30 July 2013).

20. Rory Smith, "World Cup 2010: Top 50 World Cup moments," *The Telegraph* 25 June 2010, http://www.telegraph.co.uk/sport/football/competitions/world-cup-2010/6151657/World-Cup-2010-Top-50-World-Cup-moments.html (30 July 2013).

21. BBC, "Hero: The Bobby Moore Story," *BBC Online Network*, 12 June 2010, http://www.bbc.co.uk/programmes/b0074r86 (30 July 2013).

22. FIFA, "Bobby MOORE England's captain incomparable," *FIFA*, 2012, http://www.fifa.com/classicfootball/players/player=174780/index.html (16 November 2012).

23. Ibid.

24. Ibid.

25. Ibid.

26. Ibid.

27. Albert Camus Society of the UK, "Albert Camus and football," *The Albert Camus Society of the UK*, http://www.camus-society.com/camus-football.html (13 May 2011).

28. Ibid.

29. Ibid.

30. CNN, "Pope: Football a moral guide," *CNN*, 10 January 2008, http://edition.cnn.com/2008/WORLD/europe/01/10/pope.football/index.html (26 September 2012).

31. Jim White, "Albert Camus: thinker, goalkeeper," *The Telegraph*, 6 January 2010, http://www.telegraph.co.uk/culture/books/6941924/Albert-Camus-thinker-goalkeeper.html (23 September 2012).

32. Ibid.

33. ESPN, "Statue of Zidane's WC head-butt unveiled," *ESPN Soccer*, 26 September 2012, http://soccernet.espn.go.com/news/story/_/id/1171942/paris-museum-erects-statue-of-head-butting-zidane?cc=3888 (27 September 2012).

34. Ibid.

35. Mark Ogden, "Thierry Henry admits to handball that defeated Ireland in World Cup play-off," *The Telegraph*, 19 November 2009, http://www.telegraph.co.uk/sport/football/teams/republic-of-ireland/6599687/Thierry-Henry-admits-to-handball-that-defeated-Ireland-in-World-Cup-play-off.html (23 September 2011).

36. Ibid.

37. Ibid.

38. Ibid.

39. Ibid.

40. Ibid.

41. Ibid.

42. Peter Singer, "Why is cheating OK in football?" *The Guardian*, 29 June 2010, http://www.guardian.co.uk/commentisfree/2010/jun/29/cheating-football-germany-goalkeeper (25 September 2012).

43. Ibid.

44. Miles Chambers, "Klose handball confession draws praise from FIFA president Sepp Blatter," *Goal*, 27 September 2012, http://sports.yahoo.com/news/klose-handball-confession-draws-praise-170500776--sow.html (27 September 2012).

45. Ibid.

46. Hedwig Kröner and Shane Stokes, "Spanish soccer clubs linked to Fuentes?" *Cycling News*, 8 December 2006, http://autobus.cyclingnews.com/news.php?id=news/2006/dec06/dec08news (6 November 2013).

47. The Independent, "Football: Xavier hit with 18-month ban for steroid use," *The Independent*, 24 November 2005.

48. Peter Singer, "Is Doping Wrong?" *Project Syndicate*, 14 August 2007, http://www.project-syndicate.org/commentary/is-doping-wrong- (23 September 2012).

49. Ibid.

50. BBC, "Caf's Hayatou and Anouma accused of taking Qatar bribes," *BBC Online Network*, 11 May 2011, http://www.bbc.co.uk/sport/0/football/13345669 (25 September 2012).

51. Pete Pattisson, "At 16, Ganesh got a job in Qatar. Two months later he was dead," *The Guardian*, 25 September 2013, http://www.theguardian.com/global-development/2013/sep/25/qatar-nepalese-workers-poverty-camps (27 September 2013).

52. Paul Darby, *Africa, Football and FIFA: Politics, Colonialism and Resistance* (London: Frank Cass, 2002), 110.

53. CNN, "Ethics scandal hurts soccer, Visa and other sponsors warn," *CNN*, 31 May 2011, http://edition.cnn.com/2011/SPORT/football/05/31/soccer.fifa.corruption/index.html (23 September 2012).
54. Ibid.
55. Ibid.
56. Ibid.
57. Mirror Football, "Australia senator calls for FIFA 'red card,'" *Mirror Football*, 30 May 2011, http://www.mirrorfootball.co.uk/news/Australia-senator-Nick-Xenophon-calls-for-FIFA-red-card-after-latest-corruption-scandal-article742679.html (25 September 2012).
58. The Australian, "IOC's Dick Pound says FIFA not transparent," *The Australian*, 4 October 2011, http://www.theaustralian.com.au/sport/iocs-dick-pound-says-fifa-not-transparent/story-e6frg7mf-1226157992722 (30 July 2013).
59. Hill, *Juego sucio: Fútbol y crimen organizado*.
60. Ibid.
61. John Barnes, "Racist abuse of Yaya Touré is a smokescreen, real problem is at home," *The Guardian*, 4 November 2013, http://www.theguardian.com/football/2013/nov/04/racist-abuse-yaya-toure-john-barnes (7 November 2013).
62. Ibid.
63. Ibid.

7. THE BUSINESS OF BUSINESS

1. Calvin Coolidge, "The Press Under a Free Government," Address to the American Society of Newspaper Editors, 17 January 1925, Washington, D.C., Calvin Coolidge Memorial Foundation.
2. Andrei S. Markovits and Lars Rensmann, *Gaming the World: How Sports Are Reshaping Global Politics and Culture* (Princeton, NJ: Princeton University Press, 2010), 32–33.
3. Ibid., 37.
4. Ben Rycroft, "Beckham attracted media, but MLS has driven its own growth," *CBC Sports*, 3 December 2012, http://www.cbc.ca/sports/soccer/opinion/2012/12/beckham-attracted-media-attention-but-mls-drove-the-growth.html (5 December 2012).
5. Premier Soccer Stats, "All Time Player Records," *Premier Soccer Stats*, 2012, http://www.premiersoccerstats.com/Records.cfm?DOrderby=Ass&DYearby=All%20Seasons (27 September 2012).
6. Nick Harris, "Ferguson will never talk to the BBC again," *The Independent*, 6 September 2007, http://www.independent.co.uk/sport/football/news-and-comment/ferguson-will-never-talk-to-the-bbc-again-401487.html (27 September 2012).
7. Martin Hardy, "End of his Galaxy quest: Where now for David Beckham?" *The Independent*, 21 November 2012, http://www.independent.co.uk/sport/football/news-and-comment/end-of-his-galaxy-quest-where-now-for-david-beckham-8329694.html (31 July 2013).
8. Alex Ferguson (with Paul Hayward), *Alex Ferguson: My Autobiography* (London: Hodder and Stoughton Ltd., 2013).
9. Irish Examiner, "Beckham: I can't hold grudge against Fergie," *Irish Examiner*, 31 October 2013, http://www.irishexaminer.com/breakingnews/sport/beckham-i-cant-hold-grudge-against-fergie-611748.html (6 November 2013).
10. Ibid.
11. David Beckham, *David Beckham's Website*, 2012, http://www.davidbeckham.com/ (28 September 2012).
12. Associated Press, "Beckham set to invade America," *ESPN Soccer*, 12 January 2007, http://sports.espn.go.com/espn/wire?section=soccer&id=2728604 (28 September 2012).
13. The Sunday Times, "Britain's rich list—David and Victoria Beckham," *The Sunday Times*, 26 April 2009.

14. Sam Wallace, "Beckham rejected Milan and Inter to take Galaxy millions," *The Independent*, 12 January 2007, http://www.independent.co.uk/sport/football/european/beckham-rejected-milan-and-inter-to-take-galaxy-millions-431736.html (28 September 2012).

15. Ibid.

16. Luca Caioli, *Ronaldo: The Obsession for Perfection* (London: Icon, 2012).

17. Ceroacero, "Ronaldo makes history scoring against every La Liga team," *Ceroacero*, 13 May 2012, http://www.ceroacero.es/noticia.php?id=63858 (5 December 2012).

18. Sammy Said, "Cristiano Ronaldo Net Worth," *The Richest*, 2013, http://www.therichest.com/celebnetworth/athletes/footballer/cristiano-ronaldo-net-worth/ (6 November 2013).

19. Ibid.

20. Ibid.

21. Ibid.

22. Jason Chester, "Ronaldo emulates David Beckham as he launches his debut underwear range in spectacular fashion," *Mail Online*, 31 October 2013, http://www.dailymail.co.uk/tvshowbiz/article-2481755/Cristiano-Ronaldo-attempts-outdo-David-Beckham-underwear-range.html (6 November 2013).

23. Ibid.

24. Kofi A. Annan, "How We Envy the World Cup," *United Nations*, June 2006, http://www.un.org/sport2005/newsroom/worldcup.pdf (15 July 2013).

25. Manuel Gameros, "Las goles de la FIFA," *Foreign Affairs En Español* 6, no. 3 (Julio–Septiembre 2006), 126.

26. Ibid.

27. Ibid.

28. Ibid., 127.

29. Brian Glanville, *The Story of the World Cup* (London: Faber and Faber, 1993), 45.

30. Markovits and Rensmann, *Gaming the World: How Sports Are Reshaping Global Politics and Culture*, 38–39.

31. FIFA, "2006 FIFA World Cup broadcast wider, longer and farther than ever before," *FIFA*, 6 February 2007, http://www.fifa.com/aboutfifa/organisation/marketing/news/newsid=111247/index.html (29 September 2012).

32. Gameros, "Las goles de la FIFA," 128.

33. Mark Wheeler, "Hosting World Cup would draw revenue like 12 Super Bowls," *The City Paper* (Nashville), 13 June 2010, http://nashvillecitypaper.com/content/city-news/hosting-world-cup-would-draw-revenue-12-super-bowls (29 September 2012).

34. Peter Pedroncelli, "World Cup 2010: FIFA Revenue Tops A Billion Dollars For The First Time," *Goal*, 22 March 2010, http://www.goal.com/en-us/news/1786/fifa/2010/03/22/1844168/world-cup-2010-fifa-revenue-tops-a-billion-dollars-for-the-first- (29 September 2012).

35. Adidas, "2010 FIFA World Cup already sales success for adidas," *Adidas Group*, 21 June 2010, http://www.adidas-group.com/en/pressroom/archive/2010/21June2010.aspx (29 September 2012).

36. Ibid.

37. David Richard, "Mexico's World Cup qualifying chances in 'Crisis' mode," *USA Today*, 11 September 2013, http://www.usatoday.com/story/sports/soccer/worldcup/2013/09/11/mexico-world-cup-qualifying/2802243/ (6 November 2013).

38. Bryan Preston, "Mexican TV Announcer Goes on Epic PRO-AMERICA Rant After the U.S. Saves Mexico's World Cup Hopes," *PJ Media*, 16 October 2013, http://pjmedia.com/tatler/2013/10/16/mexican-tv-announcer-goes-on-epic-pro-america-rant-after-the-us-saves-mexicos-world-cup-hopes/ (6 November 2013).

39. Simon Zekaria, "Soccer Still the Main Event for Advertisers," *The Wall Street Journal*, 17 September 2012, http://online.wsj.com/article/SB10000872396390444450004578000021105998576.html (29 September 2012).

40. Ibid.

41. Ibid.

42. Gameros, "Las goles de la FIFA," 127.

43. Ibid.
44. Alan G. Ingham, "The Sportification Process: A Biographical Analysis Framed by the Work of Marx, Weber, Durkheim and Freud," in R. Giulianotti, ed., *Sport and Modern Social Theorists* (New York: Palgrave Macmillan, 2004), 17–18.
45. Richard Williams, "Football's short-team loan system is in dire need of reformation," *The Guardian*, 22 February 2011, http://www.theguardian.com/football/blog/2011/feb/22/football-loans-richard-williams (6 November 2013).
46. The Richest, "Richest Football Clubs 2012—World's Most Valuable Football Teams," *Forbes*, 20 April 2012, http://www.therichest.org/sports/richest-football-clubs/ (28 September 2012).
47. Fausto Pretelin Muñoz de Cote, "El imperio global de fútbol," *Foreign Affairs En Español* 6, no. 3 (Julio–Septiembre 2006), 138.
48. Goal, "Paris Saint-Germain seal Cavani signing," *Goal*, 26 July 2013, http://www.goal.com/en/news/11/transfer-zone/2013/07/16/4114477/breaking-news-paris-saint-germain-seal-cavani-signing?ICID=HP_BN_1 (30 August 2013).
49. FIFA, "Bale: I want to help Real win Champions League," *FIFA*, 2 September 2013, http://www.fifa.com/worldfootball/clubfootball/news/newsid=2166551.html?intcmp=fifacom_hp_module_news (2 September 2013).
50. BBC, "Ronaldo agrees six-year Real deal," *BBC Online Network*, 26 June 2009, http://news.bbc.co.uk/sport2/hi/football/teams/m/man_utd/8121951.stm (28 September 2012).
51. Ibid.
52. IBN Live, "Messi tops rich list ahead of Beckham," *IBN Live*, 23 March 2012, http://ibnlive.in.com/news/messi-tops-rich-list-ahead-of-beckham/242045-5-21.html (28 September 2012).
53. Ibid.
54. Press TV, "Cruyff: Ronaldo, United's best ever," *Press TV*, 2 April 2008, http://edition.presstv.ir/detail/49967.html (28 September 2012).
55. Soccernet, "Cristiano Ronaldo," *Soccernet.espn*, 2012, http://soccernet.espn.go.com/player/_/id/22774/cristiano-dos-santos-aveiro-ronaldo?cc=3888 (28 September 2012).
56. Alex Ferguson (with Paul Hayward), *Alex Ferguson: My Autobiography*.
57. YouTube, "The CR7 Shop," http://www.youtube.com/watch?v=J_FdylBD_mc (31 July 2013).
58. Forbes, "The World's Most Powerful Celebrities," *Forbes*, 2012, http://www.forbes.com/celebrities/#p_4_s_a0_All%20categories (28 September 2012).
59. The Guardian, "If Messi is best on planet, Ronaldo is best in universe—José Mourinho," *The Guardian*, 12 October 2012, http://www.guardian.co.uk/football/2012/oct/12/messi-ronaldo-mourinho-ballon-dor (31 July 2013).
60. Forbes, "The World's Most Powerful Celebrities."
61. Simon Moon, "Beckham the worldwide brand," *Mail Online*, 8 June 2006, http://www.thisismoney.co.uk/money/news/article-1599337/Beckham-the-worldwide-brand.html (31 July 2013).
62. Ibid.
63. Ibid.
64. Mark Simpson, "Meet the metrosexual," *Salon*, 22 July 2002, http://www.salon.com/2002/07/22/metrosexual/ (31 July 2013).
65. Ibid.
66. David Beckham, *David Beckham: My Side* (New York: HarperCollins Willow, 2003).
67. The David Beckham Brand, "The David Beckham Brand," *ICMR*, 2003, http://www.icmrindia.org/casestudies/catalogue/Marketing/MKTG077.htm (28 September 2012).
68. Ibid., 1.
69. Ibid.
70. Ibid.
71. John May, "The best and worst of a legend," *BBC Online Network*, 25 November 2005, http://news.bbc.co.uk/sport2/hi/football/4312792.stm (29 September 2012).

72. Sean Hotchkiss, "Your Morning Shot: George Best," *GQ*, 29 November 2011, http://www.gq.com/style/blogs/the-gq-eye/2011/11/your-morning-shot-george-best.html (7 November 2013).

73. Ibid.

74. Wynton Rufer, "Wynton Rufer Soccer School of Excellence," *Wynton Rufer's Website*, 2012, http://www.wynrs.co.nz/ (21 October 2012).

75. John McManus, "Been There, Done That, Bought the T-Shirt: Besiktas Fans and the Commodification of Football in Turkey," *International Journal of Middle East Studies*, 45 (2013), 10–11.

76. My translation. Ferran Soriano, *La pelota no entra por azar* (México, D.F.: Santillana, 2012), 53–57.

77. Carlos Monsiváis, *Los rituales del caos* (México, D.F.: Ediciones Era, 2001), 31.

78. Ingham, "The Sportification Process: A Biographical Analysis Framed by the Work of Marx, Weber, Durkheim and Freud," 27.

8. LEADING BY EXAMPLE

1. Jorge Valdano, *Los 11 Poderes Del Líder* (México, D.F.: Connecta, 2013).

2. Veronica Bishop, "What is Leadership?" pp. 8–31, *McGraw-Hill UK*, http://mcgraw-hill.co.uk/openup/chapters/9780335225330.pdf (12 November 2012).

3. Valdano, *Los 11 Poderes Del Líder*, 23–181.

4. Peter Northouse in Steve Rowe, "What is Leadership?" pp. 1–28, *Sagepub*, 2007, http://www.corwin.com/upm-data/15104_Rowe_Chapter_01.pdf (3 October 2012).

5. Center for Ethical Leadership, "Ethical Leadership Definition," *Center for Ethical Leadership*, http://ethicalleadership.org/about-us/philosophies-definitions/ethical-leadership (3 October 2012).

6. Valdano, *Los 11 Poderes Del Líder*, 29–30.

7. Kate Hairopoulos, "Quite a trip for U.S. midfielder," *The Dallas Morning News*, 8 June 2006.

8. Alex Labidou, "Clint Dempsey: Not much has changed since becoming U.S. captain," *Goal.com*, 6 June 2013, http://sports.yahoo.com/news/clint-dempsey-not-much-changed-214800971--sow.html (7 November 2013).

9. Ibid.

10. Ibid.

11. Daily Mail, "Zidane: Forget Ronaldo and Messi, the best player in the world is Liverpool star Gerrard," *Mail Online*, 14 March 2009, http://www.dailymail.co.uk/sport/football/article-1161649/Zidane-Forget-Ronaldo-Messi-best-player-world-Liverpool-star-Gerrard.html (7 November 2013).

12. Valdano, *Los 11 Poderes Del Líder*, 136–137.

13. Ibid., 163.

14. Sid Lowe, "I'm a romantic, says Xavi, heartbeat of Barcelona and Spain," *The Guardian*, 10 February 2011.

15. Valdano, *Los 11 Poderes Del Líder*, 169–170.

16. Emily Benammar, "Liverpool's Steven Gerrard hailed as world's best player by Zinedine Zidane," *The Telegraph*, 13 March 2009, http://www.telegraph.co.uk/sport/football/teams/liverpool/4984191/Liverpools-Steven-Gerrard-hailed-as-worlds-best-player-by-Zinedine-Zidane.html (2 August 2013).

17. Steve Busfield, "Steven Gerrard—the one man tracking back in our World XI?" *The Guardian*, 24 October 2010, http://www.theguardian.com/football/series/the-greatest-xi (2 August 2013).

18. My translation. Valdano, *Los 11 Poderes Del Líder*, 11.

19. Henry Winter (with Steven Gerrard), *My Autobiography* (London: Bantam, 2007).

20. Phil Scraton, *Hillsborough: The Truth* (Edinburgh: Mainstream Publishing Company, 2009), 11.

21. Daily Mail Online, "Steven Gerrard's bedside visit to 10-year-old boy he knocked down in car," *Mail Online*, 3 October 2007, http://www.dailymail.co.uk/news/article-485083/Steven-Gerrards-bedside-visit-10-year-old-boy-knocked-car.html (2 August 2013).

22. Sounders FC, "Sounders FC Signs Clint Dempsey," *Sounders FC*, 3 August 2013, http://www.soundersfc.com/News/Articles/2013/08-August/Sounders-FC-Signs-USA-International-Clint-Dempsey.aspx (14 September 2013). In 2014, the Sounders loaned Dempsey to Fulham.

23. Joshua Mayers, "Clint Dempsey's journey from humble beginnings has shaped his game and character," *Sounders FC Blog*, 24 August 2013, http://seattletimes.com/html/sounders/2021683347_sounders25xml.html (8 November 2013).

24. Ibid.

25. Clint Dempsey, "Clint Dempsey 'Don't Tread,'" *YouTube*, 2009, http://www.youtube.com/watch?v=h1eu7opg6UE (14 September 2014).

26. Joshua Mayers, "More quotes and pictures from a story on Clint Dempsey's roots," *Sounders FC Blog*, 27 August 2013, http://blogs.seattletimes.com/soundersfc/2013/08/27/more-quotes-and-pictures-from-a-story-on-clint-dempseys-roots/ (8 November 2013).

27. Ibid.

28. John D. Halloran, "Why Clint Dempsey Is Ready to Be the Leader for USMNT," *Bleacher Report*, 20 June 2013, http://bleacherreport.com/articles/1679157-why-clint-dempsey-is-ready-to-be-the-leader-for-usmnt (8 November 2013).

29. Ibid.

30. Jeremiah Oshan, "Seattle Sounders players are excited to welcome Clint Dempsey to the team," *MLSsoccer.com*, 4 August 2013, http://m.mlssoccer.com/news/article/2013/08/04/seattle-sounders-players-are-excited-welcome-clint-dempsey-team (8 November 2013).

31. Sam Borden, "Dempsey Named U.S. Captain," *The New York Times Soccer Blog*, 20 March 2013, http://goal.blogs.nytimes.com/2013/03/20/dempsey-named-u-s-captain/?_r=0 (8 November 2013).

32. This Is Announcements, "Donald Simpson Bell VC: Obituary," *This Is Announcements*, 29 September 2008. http://www.thisisannouncements.co.uk/5860367 (2 August 2013).

33. Gay Life, "The Hidden History of Justin Fashanu," *About*, http://gaylife.about.com/od/gaycelebrityprofiles/ig/Gay-Celebrity-Profiles/Justin-Fashanu.-6_L.htm (2 August 2013)

34. July Foudy Sports Leadership Academy, *July Foudy Sport Leadership Academy*, http://www.juliefoudyleadership.com/ (4 October 2012).

35. Mike Lewis, "FIFA holds meeting on notorious Robben Island," *MLSSOCCER*, 23 January 2010, http://m.mlssoccer.com/news/article/fifa-holds-meeting-notorious-robben-island (2 August 2013).

36. Junaid Ahmed, "More than just a Game," *Filmex (Pty) Ltd.*, 2005, http://www.morethanjustagame.co.za/downloads/MTJAG_presskit.pdf (4 October 2012).

37. Ibid., 8–9.

38. Lewis, "FIFA holds meeting on notorious Robben Island."

39. Ferran Soriano, *La pelota no entra por azar* (México, D.F.: Santillana, 2012), 177; 196–197.

40. Simon Austin, "Fergie v. Strachan," *BBC Sport*, 12 September 2006, http://news.bbc.co.uk/sport2/hi/football/europe/5335578.stm (4 October 2006).

41. Metro, "Frank Lampard: Jose Mourinho is the best, he made me the player I am today," *Metro*, 20 May 2013, http://metro.co.uk/2013/05/20/frank-lampard-jose-mourinho-is-the-best-he-made-the-player-i-am-today-3801802/ (8 November 2013).

42. Ibid.

43. Wallace Immen, "Leadership lessons from the pitch," *The Globe and Mail*, 22 June 2010, http://www.theglobeandmail.com/report-on-business/careers/career-advice/leadership-lessons-from-the-soccer-pitch/article4322608/ (5 October 2012).

44. Valdano, *Los 11 Poderes Del Líder*, 87–88.

45. Paul Hayward, "World Cup 2010: France quit on the job to signal end of Domenech era," *The Guardian*, 18 June 2010, http://www.theguardian.com/football/blog/2010/jun/18/raymond-domenech-france-world-cup-2010 (2 August 2013).

46. Israel Ojoko, "FIFA take Confed Cup positives despite Brazil protest," *Futaa*, 2013, http://www.futaa.com/football/article/fifa-take-confed-cup-positives-despite-brazil-protest (16 July 2013).

47. Zac Wassink, "MLS Sets Attendance Records in 2012: Is it All Really Great News for the League?" *Yahoo! Sports*, 21 December 2012, http://sports.yahoo.com/news/mls-sets-attendance-records-2012-really-great-news-154000159--mls.html (2 August 2013).

48. James Mirtle, "It's all about the leadership for women's soccer team in London," *The Globe and Mail*, 11 July 2012, http://www.theglobeandmail.com/sports/olympics/its-all-about-the-leadership-for-womens-soccer-team-in-london/article4408958/ (5 October 2012).

49. Valdano, *Los 11 Poderes Del Líder*, 88.

50. My translation. Valdano, *Los 11 Poderes Del Líder*, 88.

9. DREAMING OF WEMBLEY OR ANFIELD

1. Sigmund Freud, *The Interpretation of Dreams* (trans. A. A. Brill) (New York: Macmillan Company, 1913).

2. Carl Gustav Jung, *Psychology of the Unconscious* (Mineola, NY: Dover Publications, 2003), quoted in Notable Quotes, "Carl Jung Quotes," http://www.notable-quotes.com/j/jung_carl.html (9 November 2013).

3. Philosophy Football, "Philosophy football quotations," http://www.philosophy football.com/quotations.php (6 August 2013).

4. My translation. Jorge Valdano, *Los 11 Poderes Del Líder* (México, D.F.: Connecta, 2013), 37.

5. Philosophy Football, "Philosophy football quotations."

6. Stephen Gill, *Power and Resistance in the New World Order*, second edition (Basingstoke: Palgrave Macmillan, 2008), 2–3.

7. Eduardo Galeano, *Soccer in Sun and Shadow*, trans. Mark Fried (London: Verso, 2003), 46.

8. Ibid., 45.

9. Joseph Nye, *Soft Power: The Means to Success in World Politics* (New York: Public Affairs, 2004).

10. Football's Greatest, "Shirt number 9," *Football's Greatest*, http://footballsgreatest.weebly.com/centre-forwards.html (6 October 2012).

11. Valdano, *Los 11 Poderes Del Líder*, 168–169.

12. Grahame L. Jones, "Leap of faith," *The Los Angeles Times*, 28 March 2007.

13. Ivan Orozco, "Mexico's Jimenez looks forward to Gold Cup, future," *Concacaf*, 7 July 2013, http://www.concacaf.com/article/mexicos-jimenez-looks-forward-to-gold-cup-future (9 November 2013).

14. Ibid.

15. Kevin Baxter, "Hernandez is playing a long game," *The Los Angeles Times*, 17 August 2013.

16. El País, "Inaugurada en México la calle Hugo Sánchez," *El País*, 1 September 2007, http://deportes.elpais.com/deportes/2007/09/01/actualidad/1188631312_850215.html (6 August 2013).

17. SOS Children's Villages Canada, "Mexico: Hugo Sanchez," *SOS Children's Villages*, 2006, http://www.soschildrensvillages.ca/about-us/international-partners/friends-worldwide/fifa-ambassadors-america/pages/mexico-hugo-sanchez.aspx (9 November 2013).

18. Steve Han, "Korean Soccer Star Spurns EPL, Signs With German Club," *KoreAm*, 14 June 2013, http://iamkoream.com/korean-soccer-star-spurns-epl-signs-with-german-club/ (9 November 2013).

19. Ibid.

20. Michael Hudson, "The Legend of Cha Bum Kun," *IBWM*, 31 January 2011, http://inbedwithmaradona.com/journal/2011/1/31/the-legend-of-cha-bum-kun.html (9 November 2013).

21. Footy Tube, "Forums Korea Republic: Korea Republic Chat," n.d., http://www.footytube.com/forums/korea-republic/korea-republic-chat-1875/3/ (9 November 2013).

22. Ibid.

23. "Asd Perticata Calcio: I Campioni—Gianluigi Buffon," *Perticata Calcio*, n.d., http://www.asdperticata.it/i_campioni.html (9 November 2013).

24. FIFA, "Nkono, the acrobatic pioneer," *FIFA*, 5 August 2008, http://www.fifa.com/worldfootball/news/newsid=838436.html (9 November 2013).

25. Ibid.

26. Nexdim Empire, "Samuel Eto's's Letter to Roger Milla," 1 June 2010, http://nexdimempire.com/samuel-etoos-letter-to-roger-milla.html/ (9 November 2013).

27. Ferran Soriano, *La pelota no entra por azar* (México, D.F.: Santillana, 2012), 74.

28. Adam Crafton, "REVEALED: The greatest XI in the history of football . . . and there's no room for Ronaldo, Eusebio and Best," *Mail Online*, 2 July 2013, http://www.dailymail.co.uk/sport/football/article-2353806/Greatest-XI-history-football.html (9 November 2013).

29. Jorge Barraza, "Erico," in Peter Lambert and Andrew Nickson, eds., *The Paraguay Reader: History, Culture, Politics* (Durham, NC: Duke University Press, 2012), 447.

30. Ibid.

31. The Economist, "Prince of the absurd: In search of the real Camus," *The Economist*, 7 January 2010.

32. Eduardo Galeano, *Soccer in Sun and Shadow*, quoted in Christopher George, "Camus Played in Goal for Algeria," *Football Poets*, 2005, http://www.footballpoets.org/p.asp?Id=10655 (9 November 2013).

33. The Economist, "Prince of the absurd: In search of the real Camus."

34. Paul Doyle and Tom Lutz, "Joy of Six: Footballers who have overcome humble beginnings," *The Guardian*, 3 September 2010, http://www.guardian.co.uk/sport/blog/2010/sep/03/joy-six-footballers-humble-beginnings (12 October 2012).

35. Ibid.

36. Ibid.

37. Galeano, *Soccer in Sun and Shadow*, 103–104.

38. Doyle and Lutz, "Joy of Six: Footballers who have overcome humble beginnings."

39. Galeano, *Soccer in Sun and Shadow*, 125.

40. Gary Armstrong, "The Migration of the Black Panther: An Interview with Eusebio of Mozambique and Portugal," in Gary Armstrong and Richard Giulianotti, eds., *Football in Africa* (Hampshire: Palgrave Macmillan, 2004), 254.

41. Galeano, *Soccer in Sun and Shadow*, 133.

42. Ouriel Daskal, "Can Professional Football Be More Professional?" *Soccer Issue*, n.d., http://www.soccerissue.com/2013/05/05/can-professional-football-be-more-professional/ (9 November 2013).

43. Ibid.

44. BBC, "How fit are footballers?" *BBC Sport*, n.d., http://news.bbc.co.uk/sportacademy/hi/sa/football/features/newsid_3710000/3710063.stm (9 November 2013).

45. Eduardo Galeano, *Soccer in Sun and Shadow*, quoted in *The Classical*, "Anxiety is Freedom: The Opacity of Football," *The Classical*, May 22, 2012, http://theclassical.org/articles/anxiety-is-freedom (20 September 2013).

46. Tony Williams, "The Mia Hamm Effect," *American Athlete*, n.d., http://www.americanathletemag.com/ArticleView/tabid/156/ArticleID/271/The-Mia-Hamm-Effect.aspx (9 November 2013).

47. Ibid.

48. CNN, "Soccer star raising goals in women's sports," *CNN*, n.d., http://www.cnn.com/CNN/Programs/people/shows/hamm/profile.html (9 November 2013).

49. Ibid.

50. USA Today, "Hamm's imprint made on new women's soccer league," *USA Today*, 18 January 2008, http://usatoday30.usatoday.com/sports/soccer/2008-01-18-hamm-silhouette-logo_N.htm (8 October 2012).

51. Ibid.

52. FIFA, "Wambach: Mia's still my idol," *FIFA*, 15 July 2013, http://www.fifa.com/womensworldcup/news/newsid=2135505/ (9 November 2013).

53. Mike Woitalla, "Mia Hamm's advice for girls, parents and coaches," *Soccer America*, 11 April 2012, http://www.socceramerica.com/article/46323/mia-hamms-advice-for-girls-parents-and-coaches.html (9 November 2013).

54. Vladimir Dimitrijević, *La vida es un balón redondo*, trans. Antonio Castilla Cerezo (México, D.F.: Sexto Piso, 2010), 43.

55. Ibid., 44.

56. Paul Holder, "Life at a football academy," *BBC Online Network*, n.d., http://news.bbc.co.uk/sport2/hi/football/get_involved/4207962.stm (9 November 2013).

57. My translation, quoted in Enrique Ghersi and Andrés Roemer, eds., *¿Por qué amamos el fútbol? Un enfoque de política pública* (México, D.F.: Miguel Ángel Porrúa, 2008), 69–83.

58. UNICEF, "Spaces of hope," n.d., http://www.unicef.org/football/world/brazil.html (9 November 2013).

59. Antonio J. Muller, "Use of Brazilian Soccer to Improve Children's School Experience," *The Sport Journal*, n.d., http://www.thesportjournal.org/article/soccer-culture-brazil (9 November 2013).

60. European Professional Football Leagues, "Professional Football Against Hunger," *EPFL*, 2008, http://www.epfl-europeanleagues.com/social_responsibility.htm (9 November 2013).

10. IMMORTAL HEROES?

1. Merriam-Webster, "Philosophy," http://www.merriam-webster.com/dictionary/philosophy (13 November 2013).

2. Stanford Encyclopedia of Philosophy, "Plato," *Stanford Encyclopedia of Philosophy*, http://plato.stanford.edu/entries/plato/ (13 November 2013).

3. Friedrich Nietzsche, *On the Genealogy of Morals*, trans. and ed. Douglas Smith (Oxford: Oxford World's Classics, 1996).

4. Friedrich Nietzsche, *Beyond Good and Evil*, trans. Walter Kaufmann (New York: Random House, 1966).

5. Stanford Encyclopedia of Philosophy, "Emmanuel Levinas," *Stanford Encyclopedia of Philosophy*, http://plato.stanford.edu/entries/levinas/ (13 November 2013).

6. Martin Heidegger, *Basic Writings*, ed. David Farrell Krell (New York: HarperCollins, 1993), 432.

7. Ibid., 432–433.

8. Karl Marx, "Theses on Fuerbach," in *Selected Writings of Karl Marx*, ed. Lawrence H. Simon (Indianapolis: Hacket Publishing Co., 1994), 101.

9. Quoted in Open Court Publishing, "Soccer and Philosophy Beautiful Thoughts on the Beautiful Game," *Open Court Book*, http://www.opencourtbooks.com/books_n/soccer.htm (14 November 2013).

10. Ted Richards, *Soccer and Philosophy: Beautiful Thoughts on the Beautiful Game* (Chicago: Open Court Publishing, 2010).

11. Steve Taylor, "Spirituality: The Hidden Side of Sports," *New Renaissance*, vol. 11, no. 1, Issue 36 (Spring 2002), http://www.ru.org/sports/spirituality-the-hidden-side-of-sports.html (13 November 2013).

12. Quoted in John Carlin, "The Greatest Game: Why the World Loves Soccer, and America Doesn't," *SBNation*, 16 November 2012, http://www.sbnation.com/longform/2012/11/16/3650028/lionel-messi-european-soccer (13 November 2013).

13. Ibid.

14. The Official Website of the Irish Football Association, "Profile of George Best," http://www.irishfa.com/international/squad-profiles/profile/341/legends-of-the-game/george-best/ (13 November 2013)

15. A.C. Milan, "A.C. Milan: The Most Successful Club," n.d., http://www.acmilan.com/en/club/history (10 November 2013).

16. Ibid.

17. Eduardo Galeano, *Soccer in Sun and Shadow*, trans. Mark Fried (London: Verso, 2003), 37.

18. Ibid., 37.

19. Jonathan Stevenson, "Real Madrid 1960: The greatest club side of all time," *BBC Online*, 23 May 2011, http://www.bbc.co.uk/blogs/jonathanstevenson/2011/05/the_greatest_club_side_of_all.html(10 November 2013).

20. Ibid.

21. Oocities, "What they Said: Di Sefano," *Oocities*, n.d., http://www.oocities.org/colosseum/bleachers/7429/DiStefano8.htm (10 November 2013).

22. Ibid.

23. Ibid.

24. Ibid.

25. Ibid.

26. Sarah Siegel, "Brazilian soccer club drives organ donations with 'immortal fan' concept," *JWT Anxiety Index*, 24 June 2013, http://anxietyindex.com/2013/06/brazilian-soccer-club-drives-organ-donations-with-immortal-fan-concept/ (10 November 2013).

27. Richard Henshaw, *The Encyclopedia of World Soccer* (Washington, D.C.: New Republic Books, 1979), 564.

28. FIFA, "Pele—I was there," *FIFA*, http://www.fifa.com/classicfootball/players/player=63869/quotes.html (10 August 2013).

29. YouTube, "Alfredo Di Stéfano: 'Pelé is the best player of all time, better than Messi and Ronaldo,'" *YouTube*, http://www.youtube.com/watch?v=y13irjInPno (10 August 2013).

30. FIFA, "What they said about Pele," *FIFA*, 23 October 2010, http://www.fifa.com/world-football/news/newsid=1321917.html (10 August 2013).

31. Euronews, "Pelé draws criticism for calls for Brazil to 'forget' protests," *Euronews*, 20 June 2013, http://www.euronews.com/2013/06/20/pele-draws-criticism-for-calls-for-brazil-to-forget-protests/ (10 August 2013).

32. John Motson, *Motson's World Cup Extravaganza: Football's Greatest Drama 1930–2006* (London: Anova Books, 2006), 103.

33. Jorge Valdano, "Jorge Valdano Entrevista," *La Revista*, 5 October 1997, http://www.elmundo.es/larevista/num103/textos/valdano1.html (23 October 2012).

34. Jen Bensinger, "Maradona puts his Legacy on the Line at the World Cup," *The Houston Chronicle*, 8 June 2010.

35. Sportsnet, "Maradona anoints Messi as his successor," *Sportsnet*, 25 March 2010, http://www.sportsnet.ca/soccer/maradona-messi-0/ (10 August 2013).

36. John Carlin, "The Greatest Game: Why the World Loves Soccer, and America Doesn't."

37. Ibid.

38. Ibid.

39. Ibid.

40. The Guardian, "Ferenc Puskas dies aged 79," *The Guardian*, 17 November 2006, http://www.theguardian.com/football/2006/nov/17/newsstory.sport6 (10 August 2013).

41. See YouTube, "Ferenc Puskas Tribute," http://www.youtube.com/watch?v=9oEt4zQZ9Jg (10 August 2013).

42. The Guardian, "Ferenc Puskas dies aged 79."

43. John Carlin, "The Greatest Game: Why the World Loves Soccer, and America Doesn't."

44. Vijay Murali, "Top 22 Worst Refereeing Decisions in World Football History," *Bleacher Report*, 30 October 2011, http://bleacherreport.com/articles/915954-top-22-worst-refereeing-decisions-in-world-football-history (14 November 2013).

45. Ibid.

46. FIFA, "Rivaldo: In the name of the father," *FIFA*, 1 February 2000, http://www.fifa.com/ballondor/archive/edition=1999901999/news/newsid=74934/index.html (13 November 2013).

47. Ibid.

48. Javier Tovar, "Is Soccer The Ticket Out Of Rio Poverty?" *Agence France Presse*, 2 February 2013, http://www.huffingtonpost.com/2013/02/02/soccer-football-rio-poverty_n_2606935.html (13 November 2013).

49. Ibid.

50. John Carlin, "The Greatest Game: Why the World Loves Soccer, and America Doesn't."

51. Victor Frankl, *Man's Search for Meaning* (New York: Washington Square Press, 1985).

52. Football Soccer Focus, "Imagine Being Able To Perform Consistently At Your Peak Potential Every Day of Your Professional Career," http://www.footballsoccerfocus.com/football-mindset/ (14 November 2013).

53. Ibid.

54. Ibid.

55. Ethan Zohn, "About Ethan Zohn," *Ethan Zohn's Website*, http://www.ezohn.com/about/ (14 November 2013).

56. Ibid.

57. Vinya Sankaran Vasu, "Ethan Zohn: Using Soccer To Change The World," *Service Space*, 7 December 2012, http://www.servicespace.org/blog/view.php?id=12388 (14 November 2013).

58. Jewish News One, Jewish Soccer Players in Nazis 1944 Propaganda Film, 16 July 2012, http://jn1.tv/video/jewish-week?media_id=39253 (13 November 2013).

59. Awista Ayub, *Kabul Girls Soccer Club: A Dream, Eight Girls, and a Journey Home* (New York: HarperCollins, 2009).

60. Hollings Center, "Good Reads—Kabul Girls Soccer Club Awista Ayub Review and author interview by Sanem Güner," http://www.hollingscenter.org/good-reads-kabul-girls-soccer-club (14 November 2013).

61. Anonymous, *The Epic of Gilgamesh: An English Verison with an Introduction*, trans. N. K. Sandars (London: Penguin, 1972), 57.

62. Carlo Garganese, "Top 10 World Cup Goalkeeping Blunders," *Goal*, 27 October 2009, http://www.goal.com/en/news/2377/top-10/2009/10/27/1587400/top-10-world-cup-goalkeeping-blunders (15 October 2012).

63. Associated Press, "Ex-Brazil captain Socrates dies at 57," *ESPN*, 4 December 2011, http://espn.go.com/sports/soccer/news/_/id/7314686/socrates-brazil-captain-1982-world-cup-dies-57 (13 November 2013).

64. Philip Sheldrake, *A Brief History of Spirituality* (Oxford, UK: Blackwell, 2007), 1–2.

65. Quoted in Jack Bell, "Philosophy Football," *New York Times Soccer Blog*, 30 April 2010, http://goal.blogs.nytimes.com/2010/04/30/philosophy-football/?_r=0 (20 September 2012).

66. Quoted in Steve Taylor "Spirituality: The Hidden Side of Sports."

67. FIFA, "Ghana's brightest Black Star," *FIFA.com*, n.d., http://www.fifa.com/classicfootball/players/player=161081/ (10 November 2013).

68. The Namibian, "Abedi Pele in Namibia today," *The Namibian*, 15 November 2007, http://www.namibian.com.na/indexx.php?archive_id=37932&page_type=archive_story_detail&page=3915 (10 November 2013).

69. The Guardian Nigeria, "Arsenal target, Iheanacho, joint candidate for successor to Abedi Pele, Okocha," *The Guardian*, 30 October 2013, http://www.worldwww.ngrguardiannews.com/index.php/home-sp-955664465/137206-arsenal-target-iheanacho-joint-candidate-for-successor-to-abedi-pele-okocha (10 November 2013).

70. The Top Tens, "Best African Soccer Players: Abedi Pele," n.d., http://www.thetoptens.com/best-african-soccer-players/ (11 November 2013).

71. CBS News, "Greek soccer player gets life ban for Nazi salute," 17 March 2013, http://www.cbsnews.com/8301-202_162-57574753/greek-soccer-player-gets-life-ban-for-nazi-salute/.

72. Pelé (with Robert L. Fish), *My Life and the Beautiful Game: The Autobiography of Pelé* (New York: Warner Books, 1977), "Epigraph."

11. THE PITCH AS CANVAS AND PLAYER AS ARTIST

1. Quoted in Good Reads, "Quotes About Soccer," 2013, http://www.goodreads.com/quotes/tag/soccer (11 November 2013).

2. Naxos, "SHOSTAKOVICH: Golden Age (The), Op. 22," *Naxos*, http://www.naxos.com/catalogue/item.asp?item_code=8.570217-18 (11 November 2013).

3. Mike Woitalla, "View the Game as an Art, not a War (Book Review)," *Soccer America's Youth Soccer Insider*, 18 February 2013, http://www.socceramerica.com/article/50388/view-the-game-as-an-art-not-a-war-book-review.html (10 November 2013).

4. Ibid.

5. E. H. Gombrich, *The Story of Art* (London: Phaidon, 2006), 21.

6. Ibid., 21.

7. Manuel Mancilla, "Manuel Mancilla Artista plástico," *Manuel Mancilla*, http://www.manuelmancilla.com/index.swf (19 September 2013).

8. Author's e-mail conversation with Manuel Mancilla, 16 October 2013.

9. Football's Greatest, "Shirt number 11," *Football's Greatest*, http://footballsgreatest.weebly.com/left-wingers.html (13 August 13).

10. Left Foot Studio, http://www.leftfootstudio.com/LFS.html (13 August 2013).

11. Robert Casner, "FCD Notebook," *MLSsoccer*, 27 June 2011, http://www.mlssoccer.com/news/article/2011/06/27/fcd-notebook-loyd-notches-first-goal-front-family (13 August 2013).

12. Ibid.

13. The Sentinel, "Stoke City: Shea reveals his abstract way to ease injury pain," 19 September 2013, http://www.stokesentinel.co.uk/Stoke-City-Shea-reveals-abstract-way-ease-injury/story-19815709-detail/story.html (10 November 2013).

14. Peter Karl, "Everything Arsenal Fans Need To Know About Brek Shea, The American Gareth Bale," *Sabotage Times*, 12 November 2011, http://sabotagetimes.com/reportage/everything-arsenal-fans-need-to-know-about-brek-shea-the-american-gareth-bale/ (10 November 2013).

15. Sean Davis, "Here's a Surrealist Portrait Of Neymar That Will Definitely Infiltrate Your Dreams," *KCKRS*, 27 September 2013, http://www.kckrs.com/heres-a-surrealist-portrait-of-neymar-that-will-definitely-infiltrate-your-dreams/ (20 November 2013).

16. Brooks Peck, "Neymar becomes a comic book character, frustrates artist with his hair," *Dirty Tackle*, 19 April 2013, http://sports.yahoo.com/blogs/soccer-dirty-tackle/neymar-becomes-comic-book-character-frustrates-artist-hair-041118168--sow.html (20 November 2013).

17. Ibid.

18. Ibid.

19. Chris Yuscavage, "Jay-Z Reportedly Wants to Sign Soccer Phenom Neymar to Roc Nation Sports," *Complex Sports*, 7 May 2013, http://www.complex.com/sports/2013/05/jay-z-reportedly-wants-to-sign-soccer-phenom-neymar-to-roc-nation-sports (20 November 2013).

20. Quoted in Philosophy Football, "Philosophyfootball.com quotations," http://www.philosophyfootball.com/quotations.php (13 August 2013).

21. Ibid.

22. Ibid.

23. Ibid.

24. Quoted in Pete Gill, "Our Favourite 60 Arsene Wenger Quotes," *Football365*, 22 October 2009, http://www.football365.com/f365-features/5643990/Our-Favourite-60-Arsene-Wenger-Quotes (13 August 2013).

25. A.C. Milan, "A.C. Milan: The Most Successful Club," n.d., http://www.acmilan.com/en/club/history (11 November 2013).

26. Armando Almada Roche, "Arsenio Erico, el Gardel del fútbol," *ABC* (Paraguay), 8 July 2012, http://www.abc.com.py/edicion-impresa/suplementos/cultural/arsenio-erico-el-gardel-del-futbol-423290.html (13 August 2013).

27. My translation. Ibid.

28. Ibid.

29. Greg Quill, "The story behind K'naan's 'Wavin' Flag,'" *Toronto Star*, 27 September 2012, http://www.thestar.com/entertainment/books/2012/09/27/the_story_behind_knaans_wavin_flag.html (13 August 2013).

30. Ibid.

31. Lyrics to K'naan's "Wavin' Flag," composed by Philip Lawrence, Keinan Warsame, Bruno Mars, Jean Daval, William Adams, David Guetta, and Nik Van De Wall, available at: http://www.metrolyrics.com/wavin-flag-lyrics-knaan.html.

32. PR Newswire, "Waka Waka (This Time For Africa) From Shakira's Forthcoming New Album Sale el Sol/The Sun Comes Out—Makes World Cup and YouTube History," http://www.prnewswire.com/news-releases/waka-waka-this-time-for-africa-from-shakiras-forthcoming-new-album-sale-el-solthe-sun-comes-out----makes-world-cup-and-youtube-history-101996118.html (13 August 2013).

33. Judy Cantor-Navas, "First Official 2014 World Cup Song Released by Coca-Cola in Brazil," *Billboardbiz*, 25 June 2013, http://www.billboard.com/biz/articles/news/1568148/first-official-2014-world-cup-song-released-by-coca-cola-in-brazil (15 September 2013).

34. For the lyrics of thousands of clubs and national teams around the world, see the website FanChants: http://fanchants.com/ (19 August 2013).

35. Tim Elcombe, "Is Ronaldo a Modern Picasso," in Ted Richards, ed., *Soccer and Philosophy: Beautiful Thoughts on the Beautiful Game* (Chicago: Carus Publishing, 2010), 161–171.

36. Ibid., 161–171.

37. Ibid., 164.

38. Quoted in Good Reads, "Quotes About Soccer," *Good Reads*, 2013, http://www.goodreads.com/quotes/tag/soccer (11 November 2013).

39. The Guardian, "The genius of the life of Brian," *The Observer*, 31 December 2006, http://www.theguardian.com/books/2006/dec/31/sportandleisure.features (11 November 2013).

40. The Independent, "Publish and be Damned: Giles fights back for Revie and Clough," 13 November 2010, http://www.independent.co.uk/sport/football/news-and-comment/publish-and-be-damned-giles-fights-back-for-revie-and-clough-2132719.html (11 November 2013).

41. Randal C. Archibold, "Mexican Writer Mines the Soccer Field for Metaphor," *The New York Times*, 25 October 2013, http://www.nytimes.com/2013/10/26/world/americas/mexican-writer-mines-the-soccer-field-for-metaphors.html?_r=0 (21 November 2013).

42. Ibid.

43. Eduardo Galeano, *Soccer in Sun and Shadow*, trans. Mark Fried (London: Verso, 2003), 2.

44. Ibid., "Epigraph."

45. Vladimir Dimitrijević, *La vida es un balón redondo*, trans. Antonio Castilla Cerezo (México, D.F.: Sexto Piso, 2010), 55.

46. Garcilaso De la Vega, *The Incas: The Royal Commentaries of the Inca Garcilaso de la Vega*, trans. Marie Jolas and ed. Alain Gheerbrant (Lima, Peru: PeruBook, 2004).

47. The Canadian Press, "Soccer star Zidane profiled in Quebec museum exhibit," *Herald*, 2 August 2013, http://thechronicleherald.ca/travel/1145803-soccer-star-zidane-profiled-in-quebec-museum-exhibit (10 November 2013).

48. Monica Maristain and Andrea Staccioli, *En el nombre del fútbol* (México, D.F.: Ediciones B, 2005).

49. E-mail conversations with the artist throughout 2013.

50. Art Haus Galleries, "Ben Mosley," http://arthausgalleries.co.uk/artist/Ben-Mosley (13 August 2013).

51. Johnny Weeks, "Beautiful Games: action paintings by Ben Mosley," *The Guardian*, 10 April 2013, http://www.theguardian.com/sport/gallery/2013/apr/10/painting-art (21 November 2013).

52. Ibid.

53. Ibid.

54. Adam Marshall, "Feature: A work of art," *Manchester United*, 26 March 2013, http://www.manutd.com/en/Fanzone/News-And-Blogs/2013/Mar/artist-ben-mosley-describes-work-for-the-manchester-united-foundation.aspx (21 November 2013).

55. Ibid.

56. Jake Watson, "The Welshman makes his 900th appearance for the Old Trafford outfit against Norwich and Goal.com have compiled the greatest soundbites on English football's most decorated player," *Goal*, 26 February 2012, http://www.goal.com/en-gb/news/2896/premier-league/2012/02/26/2924348/he-gives-players-twisted-blood-ryan-giggs-manchester-united (10 November 2013).

57. John Thairu, "Wizard of the Wing: Ryan Giggs Vector Art by Felio Sotomayor," *A Sporting Life*, 13 September 2012, http://www.asportinglife.com/ryan-giggs-vector-art-felio-sotomayor/ (10 November 2011).

58. Heather Gail Harman Fine Art, "Ryan Giggs," http://www.heatherharmanfineart.com/lg_view_multi.php?aid=2120263#.UoEUX2yFDIU (11 November 2013).

59. Ibid.

60. Mauricio Beuchot, *Perfiles esenciales de la hermenéutica* (México: Fondo de Cultura Económica, 2008), 59–74.

61. Left Foot Studio, "Lee Nguyen Bio."

CONCLUSION

1. 4DFoot, "Forgotten Footballers~Dragan Dzajic," 28 February 2013, http://www.4dfoot.com/2013/02/28/forgotten-footballers-dragan-dzajic/ (11 November 2013).

2. PCS Forum, "Dragan Džajić," 9 December 2011, http://pcsd.forumfree.it/?t=59220511 (11 November 2013).

3. Vladimir Dimitrijević, *La vida es un balón redondo*, trans. Antonio Castilla Cerezo (México, D.F.: Sexto Piso, 2010), 55.

4. Goal, "The greatest European Championship XI of all time—featuring Zidane, Van Basten & Maldini," *Goal*, 29 November 2011, http://www.goal.com/en/news/1717/editorial/2011/11/29/2776856/the-greatest-european-championship-xi-of-all-time-featuring (5 November 2012).

5. Aleksandar Bošković, "Why Serbia loves 'the magic Dragan,'" *Football Association of Serbia (FIFA)*, 3 February 2011, http://www.uefa.com/memberassociations/association=srb/news/newsid=250229.html (5 November 2012).

6. PCS Forum, "Dragan Džajić."

7. Bošković, "Why Serbia loves 'the magic Dragan.'"

8. Ibid.

9. 4DFoot, "Forgotten Footballers~Dragan Dzajic."

10. Sapa-dpa, "Serbian legend goes on corruption trial," *Times Live*, 31 January 2011, http://www.timeslive.co.za/sport/soccer/2011/01/31/serbian-legend-goes-on-corruption-trial (23 September 2013).

11. Bošković, "Why Serbia loves 'the magic Dragan.'"

12. Milovan Đilas, *The New Class: An Analysis of the Communist System* (New York: Harcourt Brace Jovanovich, 1957).

13. Antonio Gramsci, *Selections from the Prison Notebooks*, ed. and trans. by Quentin Hoare and Geoffrey Nowell Smith (London: Lawrence and Wishart, 1971).

14. Tamir Bar-On, "Understanding Political Conversion and Mimetic Rivalry," *Totalitarian Movements and Political Religions* 10, no. 3 (December 2009): 241–264.

15. The Tireless Midfielder, "#97: Robert Prosinečki," 30 May 2012, http://tirelessmidfielder.wordpress.com/page/3/ (12 November 2013).

16. PCS Forum, "Dragan Džajić."

17. Igor Velimirović, "Džajić: Hteo sam da se vratim u Zvezdu, ali me nisu ni zvali!," *Blic*, 18 December 2011, http://sport.blic.rs/Fudbal/Domaci-fudbal/207451/Dzajic-Hteo-sam-da-se-vratim-u-Zvezdu-ali-me-nisu-ni-zvali (12 November 2013).

18. 4DFoot, "Forgotten Footballers~Dragan Dzajic."

19. Naveed Tariq, "The 5 Greatest Footballers You've Never Heard Of," *Bleacher Report*, 7 July 2009, http://bleacherreport.com/articles/213877-the-5-greatest-footballers-youve-never-heard-of/page/3 (12 November 2013).

20. Ibid.

21. Miljan Milošević, "Dzajic to take everything in his hands," *Blic*, 25 October 2013, http://english.blic.rs/Sports/9986/Dzajic-to-take-everything-in-his-hands (12 November 2013).

22. Ibid.

23. Zoran Milosavljevic, "Soccer-Red Star on brink of administration, says club president," *Reuters*, 27 June 2013, http://uk.reuters.com/article/2013/06/27/soccer-serbia-redstar-idUKL3N0F33H020130627 (12 November 2013).

24. Ibid.

25. Serbia, "Belgrade Sports Route," *Serbia*, 27 June 2012, http://www.serbia.com/belgrade-sports-route/ (12 November 2013).

26. PCS Forum, "Dragan Džajić."

27. FC Crvena Zvezda, "Dragan Džajić," 2011–2013, http://www.crvenazvezdafk.com/en/istorija/zvezdine-zvezde/dragan-dzajic.html (12 November 2013).

28. Neil Meldrum, "Redknapp's autobiography: 'Bournemouth always had a way of bringing you down to earth,'" *Southern Daily Echo*, 11 October 2013, http://www.dailyecho.co.uk/news/10732133.Redknapp_s_autobiography___Bournemouth_always_had_a_way_of_bringing_you_down_to_earth_/?ref=rc (11 November 2013).

29. PCS Forum, "Dragan Džajić."

30. My translation. Martín Caparrós in Martín Caparrós and Juan Villoro, *Ida y Vuelta: una correspondencia sobre fútbol* (México, D.F.: Seix Barral, 2012), 25.

31. Ferenc Puskás, quoted in *Philosophy Football*, "Philosophy football quotations," 2013, http://www.philosophyfootball.com/quotations.php (13 August 2013).

Bibliography

4DFoot. "Forgotten Footballers ~ Dragan Dzajic." 28 February 2013. http://www.4dfoot.com/2013/02/28/forgotten-footballers-dragan-dzajic/ (11 November 2013).

ABC. "Argentina, Uruguay y Brasil apuñalaron al Paraguay." 5 July 2012. http://www.abc.com.py/nacionales/chilavert-argentina-uruguay-y-brasil-apunalaron-a-paraguay-422808.html (22 July 2013).

ABC News. "Game of Soccer Gets Nobel Peace Nomination." 23 January 2001. http://abcnews.go.com/International/story?id=81640&page=1 (12 November 2012).

A.C. Milan. "A.C. Milan: The Most Successful Club." N.d., http://www.acmilan.com/en/club/history (10 November 2013).

Aderet, Ofer. "WATCH: Hungarian soccer fans disrupt Israeli anthem with anti-Semitic slurs." *Haaretz.* 19 August 2012. http://www.haaretz.com/jewish-world/jewish-world-news/watch-hungarian-soccer-fans-disrupt-israeli-anthem-with-anti-semitic-slurs-1.459251 (27 October 2012).

Adidas. "2010 FIFA World Cup already sales success for adidas." *Adidas Group.* 21 June 2010. http://www.adidas-group.com/en/pressroom/archive/2010/21June2010.aspx (29 September 2012).

Adorno, Theodor and Max Horkheimer. "The Culture Industry: Enlightenment as Mass Deception," *Dialectic of Enlightenment.* 1944. http://www.marxists.org/reference/archive/adorno/1944/culture-industry.htm (25 September 2013).

Ahmed, Junaid. "More than just a Game." *Filmex (Pty) Ltd.* 2005. http://www.morethanjustagame.co.za/downloads/MTJAG_presskit.pdf (4 October 2012).

Alabarces, Pablo "Fútbol y patria." *Foreign Affairs En Español* 6, no. 3 (2006): 187–196.

Albert Camus Society of the UK. "Albert Camus and football." 2011. http://www.camus-society.com/camus-football.html (13 May 2011).

Albigol. "Arsenio Pastor 'Saltarín Rojo' Erico Martínez." 2012. http://www.albigol.com/albigol_v3/template_eins.php?lang=en&sekt=helden4&kat=2&id=1 (18 November 2012).

Alegi, Peter and Chris Bolsmann, eds. *South Africa and the Global Game: Football, Apartheid and Beyond.* London: Routledge, 2010.

Allan, Jay. *Bloody Casuals: Diary of a Football Hooligan.* Ellon: Famedram Publishers, 1989.

Allen, Colin and Wendell Wallach. *Moral Robots: Teaching Machines Right from Wrong.* New York: Oxford University Press, 2008.

Almada Roche, Armando. "Arsenio Erico, el Gardel del fútbol." *ABC* (Paraguay). 8 July 2012. http://www.abc.com.py/edicion-impresa/suplementos/cultural/arsenio-erico-el-gardel-del-futbol-423290.html (13 August 2013).

Althusser, Louis. "Ideology and Ideological State Apparatuses." In *Lenin and Philosophy and other Essays,* 121–176. New York: Monthly Review Press, 1970.

Anderson, Benedict. *Imagined Communities: Reflections on the Origin and Spread of Nationalism*. London: Verso, 1983.

Andrade de Melo, Victor and Francisco Pinheiro, eds. *A Bola ao Ritmo de Fado e Samba—100 anos de relações luso-brasileiras no futebol* (*The ball to the Rhythm of Fado and Samba: 100 years of Luso-Brazilian relations in soccer*). Porto, Portugal: Edições Afrontamento, 2013.

Annan, Kofi A. "How We Envy the World Cup." *United Nations*. June 2006. http://www.un.org/sport2005/newsroom/worldcup.pdf (15 July 2013).

Anonymous. *The Epic of Gilgamesh: An English Version with an Introduction*. Translated by Nancy K. Sandars. London: Penguin, 1972.

Anthony, Andrew. "Zizou Top." *The Guardian*. 2 July 2000. http://www.guardian.co.uk/football/2000/jul/02/euro2000.sport2 (16 September 2012).

Arbena, Joseph, ed. "Sport and the Promotion of Nationalism in Latin America: A Preliminary Interpretation." *Studies in Latin American Popular Culture* no. 11 (1992): 146–148.

———. *Sport and Society in Latin America: Diffusion, Dependency and the Rise of Mass Culture*. Westport, CT: Greenwood Press, 1988.

Archibold, Randal C. "Mexican Writer Mines the Soccer Field for Metaphor." *New York Times*. 25 October 2013. http://www.nytimes.com/2013/10/26/world/americas/mexican-writer-mines-the-soccer-field-for-metaphors.html?_r=0 (21 November 2013).

Armstrong, Gary. "The Migration of the Black Panther: An Interview with Eusebio of Mozambique and Portugal." In *Football in Africa*, edited by Gary Armstrong and Richard Giulianotti. Hampshire: Palgrave Macmillan, 2004.

Armstrong, Gary and Alberto Testa. "The Ultras: The Extreme Right in Contemporary Italian Football." In *Varieties of Right-Wing Extremism in Europe*, edited by Andrea Mammone, Emmanuel Godin, and Brian Jenkins. London: Routledge, 2012.

Arredondo, Rodolfo. "Elías Figueroa baja candidatura a la FIFA por falta de apoyo." *Suite 101*. 31 March 2011. http://suite101.net/article/elias-figueroa-baja-candidatura-a-la-fifa-por-falta-de-apoyo-a46773 (16 November 2012).

Arriola, O. and C. Peñate. "'Pipo' Rodríguez, Deportista Destacado." *La Prensa Gráfica*. 18 October 2013. http://www.laprensagrafica.com/2013/10/18/pipo-rodriguez-deportista-destacado (3 December 2013).

Art Haus Galleries. "Ben Mosley." http://arthausgalleries.co.uk/artist/Ben-Mosley (13 August 2013).

"Asd Perticata Calcio: I Campioni—Gianluigi Buffon." *Perticata Calcio*. N.d., http://www.asdperticata.it/i_campioni.html (9 November 2013).

Asian Football Confederation. *AFC*. 2004. http://www.the-afc.com/en/ (10 August 2013).

Associated Press. "Beckham set to invade America." *ESPN Sport*. 12 January 2007. http://sports.espn.go.com/espn/wire?section=soccer&id=2728604 (28 September 2012).

———. "Ex-Brazil captain Socrates dies at 57. " *ESPN*. 4 December 2011. http://espn.go.com/sports/soccer/news/_/id/7314686/socrates-brazil-captain-1982-world-cup-dies-57 (13 November 2013).

Austin, Simon. "Fergie v. Strachan." *BBC Sport*. 12 September 2006. http://news.bbc.co.uk/sport2/hi/football/europe/5335578.stm (4 October 2006).

Ayub, Awista. *Kabul Girls Soccer Club: A Dream, Eight Girls, and a Journey Home*. New York: HarperCollins, 2009.

Bale, John. *Sport, Space and the City*. London: Routledge, 1993.

Barclay, Patrick. *Football—Bloody Hell!: The Biography of Alex Ferguson*. London: Yellow Jersey, 2011.

———. "Zidane has the measure of true greatness." *The Telegraph*, 27 August 2000.

Bardèche, Maurice. *Qu'est-ce que le fascisme?* Paris: Les Sept Couleurs, 1961.

Barnes, John. "Racist abuse of Yaya Touré is a smokescreen, real problem is at home." *The Guardian*. 4 November 2013. http://www.theguardian.com/football/2013/nov/04/racist-abuse-yaya-toure-john-barnes (7 November 2013).

Bar-On, Tamir. *Rethinking the French New Right: Alternatives to Modernity*. Abingdon, UK: Routledge, 2013.

———. "The Ambiguities of Football, Politics, Culture, and Social Transformation in Latin America." *Sociological Research Online* 2, no. 4. 1997. http://www.socresonline.org.uk/socresonline/2/4/2.html (12 May 2011).

———. "Understanding Political Conversion and Mimetic Rivalry." *Totalitarian Movements and Political Religions* 10, no. 3 (December 2009): 241–264.

———. *Where Have All the Fascists Gone?* Aldershot, UK: Ashgate, 2007.

Barraza, Jorge. "Erico." *The Paraguay Reader: History, Culture, Politics.* Edited by Peter Lambert and Andrew Nickson. Durham, NC: Duke University Press, 2012.

Bastarrica, Diego. "Los futboleros que 'querían' ser los albaceas en el testamento de Pinochet." *Ferplei.* 25 April 2012. http://www.ferplei.com/2012/04/los-futboleros-que-querian-ser-los-albaceas-en-el-testamento-de-pinochet/ (25 November 2013).

Baudrillard, Jean. *The Perfect Crime.* London: Verso, 1996.

Baxter, Kevin. "Hernandez is playing a long game." *The Los Angeles Times.* 17 August 2013.

BBC. "Brazil football legend Sócrates dies at 57." *BBC Online Network.* 4 December 2011. http://www.bbc.co.uk/sport/0/football/16017071 (27 July 2013).

———. "Caf's Hayatou and Anouma accused of taking Qatar bribes." *BBC Online Network.* 11 May 2011. http://www.bbc.co.uk/sport/0/football/13345669 (25 September 2012).

———. "Gareth Bale joins Real Madrid from Spurs in £85m world record deal." *BBC Online Network.* 1 September 2013. http://www.bbc.co.uk/sport/0/football/23538218 (1 September 2013).

———. "Hero: The Bobby Moore Story." *BBC Online Network.* 12 June 2010. http://www.bbc.co.uk/programmes/b0074r86 (30 July 2013).

———. "How fit are footballers?" *BBC Sport.* N.d. http://news.bbc.co.uk/sportacademy/hi/sa/football/features/newsid_3710000/3710063.stm (9 November 2013).

———. "John Terry fights FA charge over Anton Ferdinand." *BBC Online Network.* 3 August 2012. http://www.bbc.co.uk/sport/0/football/19021184 (6 November 2013).

———. "Lightning kills football team." *BBC Online Network.* 28 October 1998. http://news.bbc.co.uk/2/hi/africa/203137.stm (12 May 2011).

———. "Netherlands Islam Freedom: Profile of Geert Wilders." *BBC Online Network.* 23 June 2011. http://www.bbc.co.uk/news/world-europe-11443211 (27 July 2013).

———. "OBE honour for United hero Giggs." *BBC Online Network.* 11 December 2007. http://news.bbc.co.uk/2/hi/uk_news/england/manchester/7138518.stm (13 August 2013).

———. "Ronaldo agrees six-year Real deal." *BBC Online Network.* 26 June 2009. http://news.bbc.co.uk/sport2/hi/football/teams/m/man_utd/8121951.stm (28 September 2012).

———. "Ronaldinho regains FifPro crown." *BBC Online Network,* 6 November 2006. http://news.bbc.co.uk/sport2/hi/football/internationals/5414328.stm (6 November 2013).

———. "Summary of the reasons for John Terry's FA ban." *BBC Online Network.* 5 October 2012. http://www.bbc.co.uk/sport/0/football/19845841 (6 November 2013).

———. "Zidane: Le football God," *BBC Online Network.* N.d. http://news.bbc.co.uk/sportacademy/hi/sa/football/features/newsid_3749000/3749667.stm (12 October 2013).

Beacom, Aaron. "Sport in International Relations: A Case for Cross-Disciplinary Investigation." *The Sports Historian* 20, no. 2 (November 2000): 1–23.

Beacom, Aaron and R. Levermore, eds. *Sport and International Development.* Basingstoke: Palgrave Macmillan, 2009.

Beckham, David. *David Beckham: My Side.* New York: HarperCollins Willow, 2003.

———. *David Beckham's Website.* 2012. http://www.davidbeckham.com/ (28 September 2012).

Bell, Jack. "Philosophy Football." *New York Times Soccer Blog.* 30 April 2010. http://goal.blogs.nytimes.com/2010/04/30/philosophy-football/ (20 September 2012).

———. "Soccer: NOTEBOOK." *New York Times.* 13 February 2001. http://www.nytimes.com/2001/02/13/sports/soccer-notebook-us-coach-in-england-to-scout.html (12 May 2011).

Bellos, Alex. *Futebol: The Brazilian Way of Life.* London: Bloomsbury, 2002.

Ben Mosley Art. *Ben Mosley.* 2013. http://www.benmosleyart.com/ (13 August 2013).

Benammar, Emily. "Liverpool's Steven Gerrard hailed as world's best player by Zinedine Zidane." *The Telegraph.* 13 March 2009. http://www.telegraph.co.uk/sport/football/teams/

liverpool/4984191/Liverpools-Steven-Gerrard-hailed-as-worlds-best-player-by-Zinedine-Zidane.html (2 August 2013).

Bensinger, Jen. "Maradona puts his Legacy on the Line at the World Cup." *The Houston Chronicle*, 8 June 2010.

Beuchot, Mauricio. *Hermenéutica analógica: Aplicaciones en América Latina*. Bogotá: El Búho, 2003.

————. *Perfiles esenciales de la hermenéutica*. México: Fondo de Cultura Económica, 2008.

Biblos. "Eclessiastes 1:14." *Biblos*. 2011. http://bible.cc/ecclesiastes/1-14.htm (13 May 2011).

Biermann, Christoph. "Franz is a god, and Jurgen a mere mortal." *The Observer*, 26 March 2006.

Biriotti, Maurice. "Don't Stop the Carnival: Football in the Societies of Latin America." In *Giving the Game Away: Football, Politics and Culture on Five Continents*, edited by Stephen Wagg. London: St. Martin's Press, 1995.

Bishop, Veronica. "What Is Leadership?" *McGraw-Hill UK*. http://mcgraw-.hill.co.uk/openup/chapters/9780335225330.pdf (12 November 2012).

Bisson, Mark. "ChangeFIFA Urges Federations to Back South American Legend's Challenge to Blatter Presidency." *World Football Insider*. 29 March 2011. http://www.worldfootballinsider.com/Story.aspx?id=34235 (28 October 2012).

Blog Cuscatlán. "Alianza F.C. Entre Los 10 Mejores." 9 October 2009. http://cuxcatla.blogspot.mx/2009/10/alianza-fc-entre-los-10-mejores.html (23 July 2013).

Bloomfield, Steve. *Africa United: Soccer, Passion, Politics, and the First World Cup in Africa*. New York: Harper Collins, 2010.

Borden, Sam. "Dempsey Named U.S. Captain." *New York Times Soccer Blog*, 20 March 2013. http://goal.blogs.nytimes.com/2013/03/20/dempsey-named-u-s-captain/?_r=0 (8 November 2013).

Bošković, Aleksandar. "Why Serbia loves 'the magic Dragan.'" *Football Association of Serbia (FIFA)*. 3 February 2011. http://www.uefa.com/memberassociations/association=srb/news/newsid=250229.html (5 November 2012).

Brodkin, Jon. "Buffon in trouble for choosing the wrong number at Parma." *The Guardian*. 9 September 2000. http://www.guardian.co.uk/football/2000/sep/09/newsstory.sport1 (14 July 2013).

Buford, Bill. *Among the Thugs: The Experience, and the Seduction, of Crowd Violence*. New York: W. W. Norton and Company, 1992.

Burt, Jason. "Brazil 0 France 1: Zidane regains mastery to tame Brazil." *The Independent*. 3 July 2006, http://www.independent.co.uk/sport/football/international/brazil-0-france-1-zidane-regains-mastery-to-tame-brazil-406473.html (12 October 2013).

Busfield, Steve. "Steven Gerrard—the one man tracking back in our World XI?" *The Guardian*. 24 October 2010. http://www.theguardian.com/football/series/the-greatest-xi (2 August 2013).

Caioli, Luca. *Ronaldo: The Obsession for Perfection*. London: Icon, 2012.

Caloca Lafont, Eloy. *Ocio y civilización*. Querétaro, México: Tres Editores, 2013.

Camiller, Patrick and Pierre-André Taguieff. *Rising from the Muck: The New Anti-Semitism in Europe*. Chicago: Ivan R. Dee, 2004.

Cantor-Navas, Judy. "First Official 2014 World Cup Song Released by Coca-Cola in Brazil." *Billboardbiz*. 25 June 2013. http://www.billboard.com/biz/articles/news/1568148/first-official-2014-world-cup-song-released-by-coca-cola-in-brazil (15 September 2013).

Caparrós, Martín and Juan Villoro. *Ida y Vuelta: una correspondencia sobre fútbol*. México, D.F.: Seix Barral, 2012.

Cappa, Angel. *La intimidad del fútbol*. San-Sebastian: Tercera Prensa Hirrugarren, 1996.

Carlin, John. "The Greatest Game: Why the World Loves Soccer, and America Doesn't." *SBNation*. 16 November 2012. http://www.sbnation.com/longform/2012/11/16/3650028/lionel-messi-european-soccer (13 November 2013).

Carlisle, Jeff. "Don't Tread on Clint." *ESPN Soccer net*. 7 February 2006.

Casner, Robert. "FCD Notebook." *MLSsoccer*. 27 June 2011. http://www.mlssoccer.com/news/article/2011/06/27/fcd-notebook-loyd-notches-first-goal-front-family (13 August 2013).

CBS News. "Greek soccer player gets life ban for Nazi salute." 17 March 2013. http://www.cbsnews.com/8301-202_162-57574753/greek-soccer-player-gets-life-ban-for-nazi-salute/ (13 August 2013).

Center for Ethical Leadership. "Ethical Leadership Definition." *Center for Ethical Leadership.* 2012. http://ethicalleadership.org/about-us/philosophies-definitions/ethical-leadership (3 October 2012).

Ceroacero. "Ronaldo makes history scoring against every La Liga team." *Ceroacero.* 13 May 2012. http://www.ceroacero.es/noticia.php?id=63858 (5 December 2012).

Chambers, Miles. "Klose handball confession draws praise from FIFA president Sepp Blatter." *Goal.* 27 September 2012. http://sports.yahoo.com/news/klose-handball-confession-draws-praise-170500776--sow.html (27 September 2012).

Chester, Jason. "Ronaldo emulates David Beckham as he launches his debut underwear range in spectacular fashion." *Mail Online.* 31 October 2013. http://www.dailymail.co.uk/tvshowbiz/article-2481755/Cristiano-Ronaldo-attempts-outdo-David-Beckham-underwear-range.html (6 November 2013).

Chicago Fire. "Chicago Fire Player Biographies." *Chicago Fire.* 2012. http://www.chicagofire.com/players/bio.jsp?player=blanco_c&playerId=bla435579&statType=current&team=t100 (22 October 2012).

Christopher, George. "Camus Played in Goal for Algeria." *Football Poets.* 2005. http://www.footballpoets.org/p.asp?Id=10655 (9 November 2013).

Clavane, Anthony. *Does Your Rabbi Know You're Here?: The Story of English Football's Forgotten Tribe.* London: Quercus, 2012.

Clegg, Jonathan and Bruce Orwall. "Last Taboo in English Football: Playing Footsie With Mate's Mate." *The Wall Street Journal.* 4 February 2010. http://online.wsj.com/news/articles/SB10001424052748704259304575043212033975040 (6 November 2013).

CNN. "Ethics scandal hurts soccer, Visa and other sponsors warn." *CNN.* 31 May 2011. http://edition.cnn.com/2011/SPORT/football/05/31/soccer.fifa.corruption/index.html (23 September 2012).

———. "Pope: Football a moral guide." *CNN.* 10 January 2008. http://edition.cnn.com/2008/WORLD/europe/01/10/pope.football/index.html (26 September 2012).

———. "Soccer star raising goals in women's sports." *CNN.* N.d. http://www.cnn.com/CNN/Programs/people/shows/hamm/profile.html (9 November 2013).

Collett, Mike. "Edwards had everything but time on his side." *Reuters.* 1 February 2008. http://www.reuters.com/article/2008/02/02/us-soccer-england-munich-edwards-idUSL2719728120080202?feedType=RSS&feedName=inDepthNews (24 September 2012).

Colombia Reports. "Thousands pay tribute to Colombia's Miguel Calero in Mexico." *Colombia Reports.* 5 December 2012. http://colombiareports.com/colombia-news/sports/27297-thousands-pay-tribute-to-colombia-miguel-calero-in-mexico.html (5 December 2012).

Conquest, Robert. *The Great Terror: A Reassessment.* Oxford: Oxford University Press, 2007.

Conway, Richard. "Miners' Di Canio protest 'will only end with Sunderland campaign support.'" *BBC Online Network.* 6 April 2013. http://www.bbc.co.uk/news/uk-england-tyne-22049080 (15 July 2013).

Coolidge, Calvin. "The Press Under a Free Government." Address to the American Society of Newspaper Editors, Washington, D.C., Calvin Coolidge Memorial Foundation, 17 January 1925.

Crafton, Adam. "REVEALED: The greatest XI in the history of football . . . and there's no room for Ronaldo, Eusebio and Best." *Mail Online.* 2 July 2013. http://www.dailymail.co.uk/sport/football/article-2353806/Greatest-XI-history-football.html (9 November 2013).

Crolley, Liz and Vic Duke. *Football, Nationality, and the State.* Harlow, England: Longman, 1996.

Cuscatla. "LA GUERRA DEL FÚTBOL 1969." *Cuscatla.* http://www.cuscatla.com/la_guerra.htm (3 December 2013).

Daily Mail. "Zidane: Forget Ronaldo and Messi, the best player in the world is Liverpool star Gerrard." *Mail Online,* 14 March 2009. http://www.dailymail.co.uk/sport/football/article-

1161649/Zidane-Forget-Ronaldo-Messi-best-player-world-Liverpool-star-Gerrard.html (7 November 2013).

Daily Mail Online. "Steven Gerrard's bedside visit to 10-year-old boy he knocked down in car." *Daily Mail*. 3 October 2007. http://www.dailymail.co.uk/news/article-485083/Steven-Gerrards-bedside-visit-10-year-old-boy-knocked-car.html (2 August 2013).

Daily Observer. "Sports profile: Abédi Pelé, a football legend." *The Daily Observer*. 18 June 2008. http://observer.gm/africa/gambia/article/2008/6/18/sports-profile (24 September 2013).

Darby, Paul. *Africa, Football and FIFA: Politics, Colonialism and Resistance*. London: Frank Cass, 2002.

Darling, Juanita. "In Memory of Slain Soccer Player, Boys Set Their Goals." *Los Angeles Times*. 17 July 1998. http://articles.latimes.com/1998/jul/17/news/mn-4559 (12 May 2011).

Daskal, Ouriel. "Can Professional Football Be More Professional?" *Soccer Issue*. N.d. http://www.soccerissue.com/2013/05/05/can-professional-football-be-more-professional/ (9 November 2013).

Davis, Sean. "Here's a Surrealist Portrait Of Neymar That Will Definitely Infiltrate Your Dreams." *KCKRS*. 27 September 2013. http://www.kckrs.com/heres-a-surrealist-portrait-of-neymar-that-will-definitely-infiltrate-your-dreams/ (20 November 2013).

De Lange, Sarah L. "Radical Right-Wing Populist Parties in Office—A Cross-National Comparison." In *The Extreme Right in Europe: Current Trends and Perspectives*, edited by Uwe Backes and Patrick Moreau, 171–194. Göttingen: Vandenhoeck and Ruprecht, 2012.

De la Vega, Garcilaso. *The Incas: The Royal Commentaries of the Inca Garcilaso de la Vega*. Translated by Marie Jolas and edited by Alain Gheerbrant. Lima, Peru: PeruBook, 2004.

Delay, Jules. "Zidane the greatest of all time." *Nouse*. 29 January 2013. http://www.nouse.co.uk/2013/01/29/zidane-the-greatest-of-all-time/ (28 July 2013).

Del Burgo, Maurice Biriotti. "Don't Stop the Carnival: Football in the Societies of Latin America." In *Giving the Game Away: Football, Politics and Culture on Five Continents*, edited by Stephen Wagg. London: St. Martin's Press, 1995.

Dempsey, Clint. "Don't Tread." *YouTube*. 2009. http://www.youtube.com/watch?v=h1eu7opg6UE (14 September 2014).

Derbaix, Christian, Alain Decrop, and Olivier Cabossart. "Colors and Scarves: the Symbolic Consumption of Material Possessions By Soccer Fans." *NA—Advances in Consumer Research* 29 (2002).

Dickinson, Matt. "Tragedy of the golden boy whose talent knew no bounds." *The Times*. London, 1 February 2008.

Đilas, Milovan. *The New Class: An Analysis of the Communist System*. New York: Harcourt Brace Jovanovich, 1957.

Dimitrijević, Vladimir. *La vida es un balón redondo*. Translated by Antonio Castilla. México, D.F.: Sexto Piso, 2010.

Doyle, Paul. "The forgotten story of . . . the France football captain who murdered for Hitler." *The Guardian*. 16 November 2009. http://www.guardian.co.uk/sport/blog/2009/nov/16/france (12 May 2001).

Doyle, Paul and Tom Lutz. "Joy of Six: Footballers who have overcome humble beginnings." *The Guardian*. 3 September 2010. http://www.guardian.co.uk/sport/blog/2010/sep/03/joy-six-footballers-humble-beginnings (12 October 2012).

Dubois, Laurent. *Soccer Empire: The World Cup and the Future of France*. Berkeley: University of California Press, 2010.

Dunning, Eric and Elias Norbert. *Sport and Leisure and the Civilizing Process*. Oxford: Basil Blackwell, 1986.

Dura-Villa, Victor. "Why Playing Beautifully Is Morally Better." In *Soccer and Philosophy: Beautiful Thoughts on the Beautiful Game*, edited by Ted Richards. Chicago: Carus Publishing, 2010.

Durham, William H. *Scarcity and Survival in Central America: Ecological Origins of the Football War*. Stanford: Stanford University Press, 1979.

Eagleton, Terry. "Football: a dear friend to capitalism." *The Guardian.* 15 June 2010. http://www.guardian.co.uk/commentisfree/2010/jun/15/football-socialism-crack-cocaine-people (2 September 2012).

Eco, Umberto. "Eternal Fascism: Fourteen Ways of Looking at a Blackshirt." *New York Review of Books* (22 June 1995): 12–15.

Elcombe, Tim. "Is Ronaldo a Modern Picasso." In *Soccer and Philosophy: Beautiful Thoughts on the Beautiful Game*, edited by Ted Richards. Chicago: Carus Publishing, 2010.

El Mostrador. "Ivo Basay: 'Pinochet fue un hombre necesario en cierto momento de la historia de Chile.'" *Elmostrador.* 5 October 2011. http://www.elmostrador.cl/noticias/pais/2011/10/05/ivo-basay-pinochet-fue-un-hombre-necesario-en-cierto-momento-de-la-historia-de-chile/ (28 October 2012).

El País. "Inaugurada en México la calle Hugo Sánchez." *El País.* 1 September 2007. http://deportes.elpais.com/deportes/2007/09/01/actualidad/1188631312_850215.html (6 August 2013).

———. "La larga carrera de un hombre polifacético." *El País.* 21 April 2010. http://deportes.elpais.com/deportes/2010/04/21/actualidad/1271834520_850215.html (23 July 2013).

Elsey, Brenda. *Citizens and Sportsmen: Fútbol and Politics in Twentieth-Century Chile.* Austin: University of Texas Press, 2011.

El Sol. "Chilavert negó un golpe de estado en Paraguay y criticó a Cristina y Rousseff." *El Sol Diario.* 23 June 2012. http://elsolonline.com/noticias/view/138430/chilavert-nego-un-golpe-de-estado-en-paraguay-y-critico-a-cristina-y-rousseff (22 July 2013).

England Football Online. "England's 70 Black Players." *England Football Online.* 2012. http://www.englandfootballonline.com/TeamBlack/Black.html (19 September 2012).

Espacio Latino. "José Leandro Andrade." *Espacio Latino.* http://letras-uruguay.espaciolatino.com/abalos_m/c/andrade.htm (26 July 2013).

ESPN. "Statue of Zidane's WC head-butt unveiled." *ESPN Soccer.* 26 September 2012. http://soccernet.espn.go.com/news/story/_/id/1171942/paris-museum-erects-statue-of-head-butting-zidane?cc=3888 (27 September 2012).

Euronews. "Pelé draws criticism for calls for Brazil to 'forget' protests." *Euronews.* June 20 2013. http://www.euronews.com/2013/06/20/pele-draws-criticism-for-calls-for-brazil-to-forget-protests/ (10 August 2013).

European Professional Football Leagues. "Professional Football Against Hunger." *EPFL.* 2008. http://www.epfl-europeanleagues.com/social_responsibility.htm (9 November 2013).

FanChants. *Web site of Fan Chants.* http://fanchants.com/ (19 August 2013).

FC Barcelona. "Legends: Paulino Alcántara." *FC Barcelona.* 2012. http://www.fcbarcelona.com/club/history/detail/card/paulino-alcantara (31 October 2012).

FC Crvena Zvezda. "Dragan Džajić." 2011–2013. http://www.crvenazvezdafk.com/en/istorija/zvezdine-zvezde/dragan-dzajic.html (12 November 2013).

Ferguson, Alex (with Paul Hayward). *Alex Ferguson: My Autobiography.* London: Hodder and Stoughton Ltd., 2013.

FIFA. "2006 FIFA World Cup broadcast wider, longer and farther than ever before." *FIFA.* 6 February 2007. http://www.fifa.com/aboutfifa/organisation/marketing/news/newsid=111247/index.html (29 September 2012).

———. "Bale: I want to help Real win Champions League." *FIFA.* 2 September 2013. http://www.fifa.com/worldfootball/clubfootball/news/newsid=2166551.html?intcmp=fifacom_hp_module_news (2 September 2013).

———. "Bobby Moore England's captain incomparable." *FIFA.* 2012. http://www.fifa.com/classicfootball/players/player=174780/index.html (16 November 2012).

———. "Figueroa, Chile's defensive commander." *FIFA.* 2012. http://www.fifa.com/classicfootball/players/player=49415/index.html (23 July 2013).

———. "Ghana's brightest Black Star." *FIFA.* N.d. http://www.fifa.com/classicfootball/players/player=161081/ (10 November 2013).

———. "Korea Republic's wild horse." *FIFA.* N.d. http://www.fifa.com/classicfootball/players/do-you-remember/newsid=1089023/index.html (14 September 2013).

———. "Nkono, the acrobatic pioneer." *FIFA.* 5 August 2008. http://www.fifa.com/worldfootball/news/newsid=838436.html (9 November 2013).

———. "Pachuca: Cradle of football to Hall of Fame." *FIFA.* 10 July 2011. http://www.fifa.com/worldfootball/news/newsid=1472823.html (26 July 2013).

———. "Pele—I was there." *FIFA.* N.d. http://www.fifa.com/classicfootball/players/player=63869/quotes.html (10 August 2013).

———. "Rivaldo: In the name of the father." *FIFA.* 1 February 2000. http://www.fifa.com/ballondor/archive/edition=1999901999/news/newsid=74934/index.html (13 November 2013).

———. "Schumacher: Football is like a religion in Turkey." *FIFA.* 23 November 2012. http://www.fifa.com/u20worldcup/news/newsid=1943797/ (27 November 2013).

———. "The wounded 'Little Bird' who soared for Brazil." *FIFA.* N.d. http://www.fifa.com/classicfootball/players/player=63868/index.html (31 July 2013).

———. "They said it: Jose Luis Chilavert." *FIFA.* 2010. http://www.fifa.com/newscentre/features/news/newsid=1306860/index.html (27 October 2012).

———. "Wambach: Mia's still my idol." *FIFA.* 15 July 2013. http://www.fifa.com/womensworldcup/news/newsid=2135505/ (9 November 2013).

———. "What they said about Pele." *FIFA.* 23 October 2010. *FIFA.* 23 October 2010. http://www.fifa.com/worldfootball/news/newsid=1321917.html (10 August 2013).

———. "World Football: Salvador Mariona." *FIFA.* 2013. http://www.fifa.com/worldfootball/statisticsandrecords/players/player=53654/ (26 July 2013).

Fleming, Matt. "Black players should ignore racist chants, says Rijkaard." *The Independent.* 31 October 2006. http://www.independent.co.uk/sport/football/european/black-players-should-ignore-racist-chants-says-rijkaard-422294.html (26 July 2013).

Foer, Franklin. *How Soccer Explains the World: An Unlikely Theory of Globalization.* New York: HarperCollins, 2004.

Fondation Lilian Thuram. *Fondation Lilian Thuram.* 2013. http://www.thuram.org/ (27 July 2013).

Football Soccer Focus. "Imagine Being Able To Perform Consistently At Your Peak Potential Every Day of Your Professional Career." http://www.footballsoccerfocus.com/football-mindset/ (14 November 2013).

Football's Greatest. "Shirt number 9." *Football's Greatest.* 2012. http://footballsgreatest.weebly.com/centre-forwards.html (6 October 2009).

———. "Shirt number 11." *Football's Greatest.* 2012. http://footballsgreatest.weebly.com/left-wingers.html (13 August 13).

Football Italia. "Klopp: 'Napoli a mystical experience.'" *Football Italia.* 17 September 2013. http://www.football-italia.net/39605/klopp-napoli-mystical-experience (26 November 2013).

Footy-Boots. "Rene Higuita Delighted with Victory." *Footy-boots.* 24 July 2008. http://www.footy-boots.com/rene-higuita-interview-4649/ (22 July 2013).

Footy Tube. "Forums Korea Republic: Korea Republic Chat." N.d. http://www.footytube.com/forums/korea-republic/korea-republic-chat-1875/3/ (9 November 2013).

Forbes. "Soccer Team Valuations." *Forbes.* 29 September 2010. http://www.forbes.com/2010/04/21/soccer-value-teams-business-sports-soccer-10-wealth_land.html (2 September 2012).

———. "The World's Most Powerful Celebrities." *Forbes.* 2012. http://www.forbes.com/celebrities/#p_4_s_a0_All%20categories (28 September 2012).

Foreign Affairs En Español. "El imperio del fútbol." 6, no. 3 (Julio–Septiembre 2006): 121–196.

Frank, Victor. *Man's Search for Meaning.* New York: Washington Square Press, 1985.

Freud, Sigmund. *The Interpretation of Dreams.* Translated by A. A. Brill. New York: Macmillan Company, 1913.

Friedman, George. *The Next 100 Years: A Forecast for the 21st Century.* New York: Anchor Books, 2010.

Frommer's. "Maracanã Stadium." *Frommer's.* 2013. http://www.frommers.com/destinations/rio-de-janeiro/attractions/212698 (26 November 2013).

Gaffney, Christopher and Gilmar Mascarenhasa. "The Soccer Stadium as a Disciplinary Space." Presented at the International Michel Foucault Seminar, Universidade Federal De Santa Catarina, Florianopolis, Brasil, September 21–24, 2004.

Galeano, Eduardo. *El fútbol a sol y sombra*. Madrid: Siglo XXI, 2006.

———. *Soccer in Sun and Shadow*. Translated by Mark Fried. London: Verso, 2003.

Gameros, Manuel. "Las goles de la FIFA." *Foreign Affairs En Español* 6, no. 3. (Julio–Septiembre 2006): 121–131.

Garganese, Carlo. "Top 10 World Cup Goalkeeping Blunders." *Goal*. 27 October 2009. http://www.goal.com/en/news/2377/top-10/2009/10/27/1587400/top-10-world-cup-goalkeeping-blunders (15 October 2012).

Gay Life. "The Hidden History of Justin Fashanu." *About*. http://gaylife.about.com/od/gaycelebrityprofiles/ig/Gay-Celebrity-Profiles/Justin-Fashanu.-6_L.htm (2 August 2013)

Gentile, Emilio. *Politics as Religion*. Translated by George Staunton. Princeton, NJ: Princeton University Press, 2006.

Ghersi, Enrique and Andrés Roemer, eds. *¿Por qué amamos el fútbol? Un enfoque de política pública*. México, D.F.: Miguel Ángel Porrúa, 2008.

Gill, Pete. "Our Favourite 60 Arsene Wenger Quotes." *Football365*. 22 October 2009. http://www.football365.com/f365-features/5643990/Our-Favourite-60-Arsene-Wenger-Quotes (13 August 2013).

Gill, Stephen. *Power and Resistance in the New World Order*, second edition. Basingstoke: Palgrave Macmillan, 2008.

Glanville, Brian. *The Story of the World Cup*. London: Faber and Faber, 1993.

Goal. "Paris Saint-Germain seal Cavani signing." *Goal*. 26 July 2013. http://www.goal.com/en/news/11/transfer-zone/2013/07/16/4114477/breaking-news-paris-saint-germain-seal-cavani-signing?ICID=HP_BN_1 (30 August 2013).

———. "The greatest European Championship XI of all time—featuring Zidane, Van Basten & Maldini." *Goal*. 29 November 2011. http://www.goal.com/en/news/1717/editorial/2011/11/29/2776856/the-greatest-european-championship-xi-of-all-time-featuring (5 November 2012).

Goldblatt, David. *The Ball Is Round: A Global History of Soccer*. New York: Penguin, 2008.

Gombrich, E. H. *The Story of Art*. London: Phaidon, 2006.

Good Reads. "Quotes About Soccer." *Good Reads*. 2013. http://www.goodreads.com/quotes/tag/soccer (11 November 2013).

Gramsci, Antonio. *Selections from the Prison Notebooks*. Edited and translated by Quentin Hoare and Geoffrey Nowell Smith. London: Lawrence and Wishart, 1971.

Green, Sam. "Foot of God gets the boot." *Soccer America* 1503, 28 May 2001. http://www.la84foundation.org/SportsLibrary/SoccerAmerica/2001/sa1503aa.pdf (12 May 2011).

Greenberg, Chris. "Robbie Rogers, Openly Gay Soccer Player, Makes Historic L.A. Galaxy Debut." *The Huffington Post*. 27 May 2013. http://www.huffingtonpost.com/2013/05/27/gay-soccer-player-robbie-rogers-debut_n_3341036.html?utm_hp_ref=robbie-rogers (29 August 2013).

Gregor, A. J. *Italian Fascism and Developmental Dictatorship*. Princeton, NJ: Princeton University Press, 1979.

Grewal, Baljit Singh. "Johan Galtung: Positive and Negative Peace." 30 August 2003. http://www.activeforpeace.org/no/fred/Positive_Negative_Peace.pdf (7 September 2013).

Gumbrecht, Hans Ulrich. *In Praise of Athletic Beauty*. Cambridge, MA: Harvard University Press, 2006.

Haaretz. "British soccer body deems 'yid' anti-Semitic slur." *Haaretz*. 12 September 2013. http://www.haaretz.com/jewish-world/jewish-world-news/1.546665 (14 September 2013).

Hairopoulos, Kate. "Quite a trip for U.S. midfielder." *The Dallas Morning News*, 8 June 2006.

Halloran, John D. "Why Clint Dempsey Is Ready to Be the Leader for USMNT." *Bleacher Report*, 20 June 2013. http://bleacherreport.com/articles/1679157-why-clint-dempsey-is-ready-to-be-the-leader-for-usmnt (8 November 2013).

Han, Steve. "Korean Soccer Star Spurns EPL, Signs With German Club." *KoreAm*. 14 June 2013. http://iamkoream.com/korean-soccer-star-spurns-epl-signs-with-german-club/ (9 November 2013).

Hardy, Martin. "End of his Galaxy quest: Where now for David Beckham?" *The Independent.* 21 November 2012. http://www.independent.co.uk/sport/football/news-and-comment/end-of-his-galaxy-quest-where-now-for-david-beckham-8329694.html (31 July 2013).

Harris, Nick. "Ferguson will never talk to the BBC again." *The Independent.* 6 September 2007. http://www.independent.co.uk/sport/football/news-and-comment/ferguson-will-never-talk-to-the-bbc-again-401487.html (27 September 2012).

Hattenstone, Simon. "Racism in football: Putting the boot in." *The Guardian.* 13 July 2012. http://www.guardian.co.uk/football/2012/jul/13/racism-football-premier-league-campbell (12 September 2012).

Hayward, Paul. "World Cup 2010: France quit on the job to signal end of Domenech era." *The Guardian.* 18 June 2010. http://www.theguardian.com/football/blog/2010/jun/18/raymond-domenech-france-world-cup-2010 (2 August 2013).

Heather Gail Harman Fine Art. "Ryan Giggs." http://www.heatherharmanfineart.com/lg_view_multi.php?aid=2120263#.UoEUX2yFDIU (11 November 2013).

Hellerman, Steve and Andrei Markovits. *Offside: Soccer and American Exceptionalism.* Princeton, NJ: Princeton University Press, 2001.

Heidegger, Martin. *Basic Writings.* Edited by David Farrell Krell. New York: HarperCollins, 1993.

Henderson, Bruce. "There is Fair Play in Soccer." *OSA.* N.d. http://www.ssra.ca/there_is_fair_play_in_soccer.htm (25 October 2012).

Henshaw, Richard. *The Encyclopedia of World Soccer.* Washington, DC: New Republic Books, 1979.

Hill, Declan. *Juego sucio: Fútbol y crimen organizado.* Translated by Concha Cardeñoso Sáenz de Miera and Francisco López Martín. Barcelona: Alba, 2010.

Hoagland, Jim. "The Game of Nations." *Washington Post.* 9 July 1998.

Hobsbawm, Eric. *Nations and Nationalism since 1780: Programme, Myth, Reality.* Cambridge, UK: Cambridge University Press, 1990.

Holder, Paul. "Life at a football academy." *BBC Online Network.* N.d. http://news.bbc.co.uk/sport2/hi/football/get_involved/4207962.stm (9 November 2013).

Hollings Center. "Good Reads—Kabul Girls Soccer Club Awista Ayub Review and author interview by Sanem Güner." *Hollings Center.* http://www.hollingscenter.org/good-reads-kabul-girls-soccer-club (14 November 2013).

Homeless World Cup. "Homeless World Cup Mexico City 2012." *Homeless World Cup.* 2012. http://www.homelessworldcup.org/ (13 September 2012).

Hotchkiss, Sean. "Your Morning Shot: George Best." *GQ.* 29 November 2011. http://www.gq.com/style/blogs/the-gq-eye/2011/11/your-morning-shot-george-best.html (7 November 2013).

Hudson, Michael. "The Legend of Cha Bum Kun." *IBWM.* 31 January 2011. http://inbedwith-maradona.com/journal/2011/1/31/the-legend-of-cha-bum-kun.html (9 November 2013).

Huizinga, Johan. *Homo ludens: el juego y la cultura.* Translated by Eugenio Ímaz. México, D.F.: Fondo de Cultura Económica, 2005.

Hutchison, Patrick. "Breaking Boundaries: Football and Colonialism in the British Empire." *Student Pulse* 1, no. 11. 2009. http://www.studentpulse.com/articles/64/breaking-boundaries-football-and-colonialism-in-the-british-empire (26 July 2013).

Iara, Miguel Ángel. "Caszely, el goleador que plantó cara a Pinochet." *Marca.* 2011. http://www.marca.com/reportajes/2011/12/el_poder_del_balon/2012/03/27/seccion_01/1332881843.html (25 November 2013).

IBN Live. "Messi tops rich list ahead of Beckham." *IBN Live.* 23 March 2012. http://ibnlive.in.com/news/messi-tops-rich-list-ahead-of-beckham/242045-5-21.html (28 September 2012).

IMDb. "Reviews & Ratings for Zidane: A 21st Century Portrait." *IMDb.* 12 April 2007. http://www.imdb.com/title/tt0478337/reviews (12 October 2013).

Immen, Wallace. "Leadership lessons from the pitch." *The Globe and Mail.* 22 June 2010. http://www.theglobeandmail.com/report-on-business/careers/career-advice/leadership-lessons-from-the-soccer-pitch/article4322608/ (5 October 2012).

Ingham, Alan G. "The Sportification Process: A Biographical Analysis Framed by the Work of Marx, Weber, Durkheim and Freud." In *Sport and Modern Social Theorists*, edited by R. Giulianotti, 11–32. New York: Palgrave Macmillan, 2004.

Ingle, Simon. "FootofGod.com forced to close." *The Guardian*. 15 February 2001. http://www.guardian.co.uk/football/2001/feb/15/newsstory.sport8 (12 May 2011).

International Federation of Football History and Statistics (IFFHS). *IFFHS*. 2012. http://www.iffhs.de/?31748d16 (8 October 2012).

International Review for the Sociology of Sport. "Archive of All Online Issues." *International Review of the Sociology of Sport*. 2011. http://irs.sagepub.com/content/by/year (13 May 2011).

Irish Examiner. "Beckham: I can't hold grudge against Fergie." *Irish Examiner*, 31 October 2013. http://www.irishexaminer.com/breakingnews/sport/beckham-i-cant-hold-grudge-against-fergie-611748.html (6 November 2013).

Jennings, Andrew. *Foul! The Secret World of FIFA: Bribes, Vote-Rigging and Ticket Scandals*. London: Harper Collins, 2006.

Jewish News One. "Jewish Soccer Players in Nazis 1944 Propaganda Film." 16 July 2012. http://jn1.tv/video/jewish-week?media_id=39253 (13 November 2013).

Jews in Sports. "Hirsch, Julius." *Jews in Sport*. 2011. http://www.jewsinsports.org/profile.asp?sport=soccer&ID=102 (12 May 2011).

Johnes, Martin. "We Hate England! We Hate England? National Identity and Anti-Englishness in Welsh Soccer Fan Culture." *Cycnos* 25, no. 2. 2008. http://revel.unice.fr/cycnos/index.html?id=6224 (27 October 2012).

Jones, Grahame L. "Leap of faith." *The Los Angeles Times*. 28 March 2007.

July Foudy Sports Leadership Academy. *July Foudy Sports Leadership Academy*. 2012. http://www.juliefoudyleadership.com/ (4 October 2012).

Jung, Carl Gustav. *Psychology of the Unconscious*. Mineola, New York: Dover Publications, 2003.

Kapuściński, Ryszard. *The Soccer War*. Translated by William Brand. London: Granta, 1990.

Karl, Peter. "Everything Arsenal Fans Need To Know About Brek Shea, The American Gareth Bale." *Sabotage Times*. 12 November 2011. http://sabotagetimes.com/reportage/everything-arsenal-fans-need-to-know-about-brek-shea-the-american-gareth-bale/ (10 November 2013).

Kaufmann, Alexander C. "How Brazil's 'Heleno' Resurrected 'Prince Cursed.'" *The Wrap*. 13 November 2012. http://www.thewrap.com/movies/article/how-brazils-oscar-entry-heleno-resurrected-prince-cursed-64761 (11 November 2013).

Kick It Out. "About Kick It Out." *Kick It Out*. 2012. http://www.kickitout.org/2.php (19 September 2012).

K'naan, Philip Lawrence, Keinan Warsame, Bruno Mars, Jean Daval, William Adams, David Guetta, and Nik Van De Wall. "Wavin' Flag Lyrics." *Metro Lyrics*. http://www.metrolyrics.com/wavin-flag-lyrics-knaan.html (13 August 2013).

Kohn, Hans. *The Idea of Nationalism: A Study in Its Origins and Backgrounds*. New Brunswick, NJ: Transaction Publishers, 2008.

Korten, David. *When Corporations Rule the World*. West Hartford, CT: Kumarian, 1995.

Krauze, León. "México y Estados Unidos: identidad y fútbol." *Foreign Affairs En Español* 6, no. 3 (Julio–Septiembre 2006): 147–151.

Kröner, Hedwig and Shane Stokes, "Spanish soccer clubs linked to Fuentes?" *Cycling News*, 8 December 2006. http://autobus.cyclingnews.com/news.php?id=news/2006/dec06/dec08 news (6 November 2013).

Kruger, A. and J. Riordan. *The International Politics of Sport in the Twentieth Century*. New York: Routledge, 1999.

Kuhn, Gabriel. *Football vs. the State: Tackling Football and Radical Politics*. Oakland: PM Press, 2011.

Kuper, Simon. *Football against the Enemy*. London: Phoenix, 1995.

———. *Soccer against the Enemy: How the World's Most Popular Sport Starts and Fuels Revolutions and Keeps Dictators in Power*. New York: Nation Books, 2006.

Kusturica, Vedad. Personal communication with author about FK Sarajevo. Toronto, 22 June 2009.

Labidou, Alex. "Clint Dempsey: Not much has changed since becoming U.S. captain." *Goal.com*, 6 June 2013. http://sports.yahoo.com/news/clint-dempsey-not-much-changed-214800971--sow.html (7 November 2013).

Lacey, Josh. "Lost boys." *The Guardian.* 14 August 2004. http://www.guardian.co.uk/books/2004/aug/14/featuresreviews.guardianreview2 (17 November 2012).

Lamula. "El fútbol chileno y Pinochet: El goleador Carlos Caszely fue incómodo para la dictadura militar." *Lamula.* 9 November 2013. http://lamula.pe/2013/09/11/el-futbol-chileno-y-pinochet/albertoniquen/ (25 November 2013).

La nación. "Hasta temas políticos aborda la biografía de Elías Figueroa." *Nación.* 27 May 2005. http://www.lanacion.cl/noticias/site/artic/20050526/pags/20050526210233.html (27 August 2012).

Lasky, Jane. "England ties Brazil at Maracana in a soccer match that almost didn't happen." *Examiner.* 2 June 2013. http://www.examiner.com/article/england-ties-brazil-at-maracana-a-soccer-match-that-almost-didn-t-happen (26 November 2013).

Lawless, Matt. "Fifa president Sepp Blatter 'alarmed' over foreign influx and demands level playing field." *The Telegraph.* 7 October 2008. http://www.telegraph.co.uk/sport/football/competitions/premier-league/3150222/Fifa-president-Sepp-Blatter-alarmed-over-foreign-ownership-influx-and-demands-level-playing-field-Football.html (2 September 2012).

Left Foot Studio. "Lee Nguyen Bio." *Left Foot Studio.* http://www.leftfootstudio.com/LeeNguyen.html (13 August 2013).

Legends of the Game. "Johan Cruyff." *Legends of the Game.* 2012. http://legendsofthega.me/beta/cruyff/index.html (16 November 2012).

Lemus, Pedro. "A 44 años de la primera vez." *El Blog.* 8 October 2013. http://www.elblog.com/deportes/a-44-anos-de-la-primera-vez.html (3 December 2013).

Lever, Janet. "Sport in a Fractured Society: Brazil under Military Rule." In *Sport and Society in Latin America: Diffusion, Dependency and the Rise of Mass Culture,* edited by Joseph L. Arbena, 85–96. Westport, CT: Greenwood Press, 1988.

Lewis, Mike. "FIFA holds meeting on notorious Robben Island." *MLSsoccer.* 23 January 2010. http://m.mlssoccer.com/news/article/fifa-holds-meeting-notorious-robben-island (2 August 2013).

Linz, Juan J. *Totalitarian and Authoritarian Regimes.* Boulder, CO: Lynne Rienner, 2000.

Liverpool FC. *Liverpool FC.* 2011. http://www.liverpoolfc.com/ (12 November 2012).

Living in Peru. "New revelations about plane crash killing Peruvian football team 19 years ago." *Living in Peru.* 11 October 2006. http://www.livinginperu.com/news/2562 (12 May 2001).

Long, Jonathan and Karl Spracklen. "Positioning Anti-Racism in Sport and Sport in Anti-Racism." In *Sport and Challenges to Racism,* edited by Jonathan Long and Karl Spracklen, 3–18. London: Palgrave Macmillan, 2010.

Lorenz, Konrad. *On Aggression.* Translated by Marjorie Latzke. London: Methuen Publishing, 1966.

Lowe, Sid. "I'm a romantic, says Xavi, heartbeat of Barcelona and Spain." *The Guardian,* 10 February 2011.

Luxury Player. "Gianluigi Buffon, Piazzale Loreto and an uncomfortable relationship with history." *Luxury Player.* 2 July 2011. http://luxuryplayer.wordpress.com/2011/07/02/gianluigi-buffon-piazzale-loreto-and-an-uncomfortable-relationship-with-history/ (15 November 2012).

Mackay, Maria. "Football the New Religion, Warn Brazilian Academics." *Christian Today.* 12 July 2006. http://www.christiantoday.com/article/football.the.new.religion.warn.brazilian.academics/6900.htm (12 May 2011).

Madison, Mike. "World Cup Intermezzo: Reflections on Law, Football, Ethics, and Technology." *Madisonian.* 1 July 2010. http://madisonian.net/2010/07/01/world-cup-intermezzo-reflections-on-law-football-ethics-and-technology/ (23 September 2012).

Mann, Chris. "The 10 Largest Football Stadiums in the World." *Soccer Lens.* 2009. http://soccerlens.com/largest-football-stadiums/36427/ (16 September 2012).

Mancilla, Manuel. "Manuel Mancilla Artista plástico." *Manuel Mancilla.* http://www. manuelmancilla.com/index.swf (19 September 2013).
Maradona, Diego. *Maradona: The Autobiography of Soccer's Greatest and Most Controversial Star.* New York: Skyhorse Publishing, 2007.
Marca. "Zidane: 'No soy un Dios, sólo soy un futbolista.'" *Marca.* 25 December 2003, http:// archivo.marca.com/primeras/03/12/1226.html (12 October 2013).
Maristain, Monica and Andrea Staccioli. *En el nombre del fútbol.* México, D.F.: Ediciones B, 2005.
Markovits, Andrei S. and Lars Rensmann. *Gaming the World: How Sports Are Reshaping Global Politics and Culture.* Princeton, NJ: Princeton University Press, 2010.
Marshall, Adam. "Feature: A work of art." *Manchester United.* 26 March 2013. http:// www.manutd.com/en/Fanzone/News-And-Blogs/2013/Mar/artist-ben-mosley-describes-work-for-the-manchester-united-foundation.aspx (21 November 2013).
Martin, Simon. *Football and Fascism: The National Game under Mussolini.* Oxford: Berg, 2004.
Marx, Karl. "Theses on Feuerbach." In *Selected Writing of Karl Marx*, edited by Lawrence H. Simon, 101. Indianapolis: Hacket Publishing Co., 1994.
Marx, Karl, and Friedrich Engels. *The Communist Manifesto.* Moscow: Progress Publishers, [1848] 1977.
Mason, Tony. *Passion of the People?: Football in South America.* London: Verso, 1995.
Matthews, Stanley and Les Scott. *The Way It Was.* London: Headline, 2000.
May, John. "The best and worst of a legend." *BBC Online Network.* 25 November 2005. http:// news.bbc.co.uk/sport2/hi/football/4312792.stm (29 September 2012).
Mayers, Joshua. "Clint Dempsey's journey from humble beginnings has shaped his game and character." *Sounders FC Blog*, 24 August 2013. http://seattletimes.com/html/sounders/ 2021683347_sounders25xml.html (8 November 2013).
———. "More quotes and pictures from a story on Clint Dempsey's roots." *Sounders FC Blog*, 27 August 2013. http://blogs.seattletimes.com/soundersfc/2013/08/27/more-quotes-and-pic-tures-from-a-story-on-clint-dempseys-roots/ (8 November 2013).
McLuhan, Marshall. *Understanding Media: The Extensions of Man.* New York: McGraw-Hill, 1964.
McManus, John. "Been There, Done That, Bought the T-Shirt: Besiktas Fans and the Commod-ification of Football in Turkey." *International Journal of Middle East Studies*, 45 (2013), 3–24.
Meldrum, Neil. "Redknapp's autobiography: 'Bournemouth always had a way of bringing you down to earth.'" *Southern Daily Echo.* 11 October 2013. http://www.dailyecho.co.uk/news/ 10732133.Redknapp_s_autobiography_Bournemouth_always_had_a_way_of_ bringing_you_down_to_earth_/?ref=rc (11 November 2013).
Merriam-Webster. "Philosophy." 2013. http://www.merriam-webster.com/dictionary/philoso-phy (13 November 2013).
Merton, Robert K. "Introduction." In *The Crowd: A Study of the Popular Mind,* by Gustave Le Bon. New York: The Viking Press, 1960.
Metcalfe, Nick. "Ryan Giggs voted greatest ever Manchester United player—Welsh wizard tops poll ahead of legends Eric Cantona and George Best." *Daily Mail*, 1 February 2011.
Metro. "Frank Lampard: Jose Mourinho is the best, he made me the player I am today." *Metro*, 20 May 2013. http://metro.co.uk/2013/05/20/frank-lampard-jose-mourinho-is-the-best-he-made-me-the-player-i-am-today-3801802/ (8 November 2013).
Mhaskar, Akshay. "The Bizarre History of Football Shirt Numbers." *Football Speak.* 5 April 2012. http://footballspeak.com/post/2012/04/05/The-Number-Game.aspx (28 October 2012).
Milmo, Cahal. "Fifa shows red card to football fanatics' website." *The Independent.* 17 Febru-ary 2001. http://www.independent.co.uk/sport/football/news-and-comment/fifa-shows-red-card-to-football-fanatics-website-692194.html (16 May 2011).
Milosavljevic, Zoran. "Soccer-Red Star on brink of administration, says club president." *Reuters.* 27 June 2013. http://uk.reuters.com/article/2013/06/27/soccer-serbia-redstar-idUKL3N0F33H020130627 (12 November 2013).

Milošević, Miljan. "Dzajic to take everything in his hands." *Blic.* 25 October 2013. http://english.blic.rs/Sports/9986/Dzajic-to-take-everything-in-his-hands (12 November 2013).

Minister, Stephen. "What's Wrong with Negative Soccer?" In *Soccer and Philosophy: Beautiful Thoughts on the Beautiful.* Edited by Ted Richards. Chicago: Carus Publishing, 2010.

Minkenberg, Michael. "Viadrina Summer University 2012." *Kuwi.* 2012. http://www.kuwi.europa-uni.de/de/studium/summeruniversity/detailed_programme/cc1_minkenberg/index.html (21 August 2012).

Mirror Football. "Australia senator calls for FIFA 'red card.'" *Mirror Football.* 30 May 2011. http://www.mirrorfootball.co.uk/news/Australia-senator-Nick-Xenophon-calls-for-FIFA-red-card-after-latest-corruption-scandal-article742679.html (25 September 2012).

Mirtle, James. "It's all about the leadership for women's soccer team in London." *The Globe and Mail.* 11 July 2012. http://www.theglobeandmail.com/sports/olympics/its-all-about-the-leadership-for-womens-soccer-team-in-london/article4408958/ (5 October 2012).

Monsiváis, Carlos. *Los rituales del caos.* México, D.F.: Ediciones Era, 2001.

Montalban, Manuel Vazquez. *Un Polaco en la corte del Rey Juan Carlos.* Madrid: Alfaguara, 1996.

Moon, Simon. "Beckham the worldwide brand." *Mail Online.* 8 June 2006. http://www.thisismoney.co.uk/money/news/article-1599337/Beckham-the-worldwide-brand.html (31 July 2013).

Morris, Desmond. *The Soccer Tribe.* London: Jonathan Cape, 1981.

Motson, John. *Motson's World Cup Extravaganza: Football's Greatest Drama 1930–2006.* London: Anova Books, 2006.

Muller, Antonio J. "Use of Brazilian Soccer to Improve Children's School Experience." *Sport Journal.* N.d. http://www.thesportjournal.org/article/soccer-culture-brazil (9 November 2013).

Mullock, Simon. "Dietmar Hamann urges Man City fans to behave for minute's silence." *Daily Mirror,* 10 February 2008.

Murali, Vijay. "Top 22 Worst Refereeing Decisions in World Football History." *Bleacher Report.* 30 October 2011. http://bleacherreport.com/articles/915954-top-22-worst-refereeing-decisions-in-world-football-history (14 November 2013).

Nabokov, Vladimir. *Speak, Memory: An Autobiography Revisited.* New York: Vintage Books, 1989.

Naxos. "Shostakovich: Golden Age (The), Op. 22." *Naxos.* N.d. http://www.naxos.com/catalogue/item.asp?item_code=8.570217-18 (11 November 2013).

Nexdim Empire. "Samuel Eto'o's Letter to Roger Milla." *Nexdim Empire.* 1 June 2010. http://nexdimempire.com/samuel-etoos-letter-to-roger-milla.html/ (9 November 2013).

Nietzsche, Friedrich. *Beyond Good and Evil.* Translated by Walter Kaufmann. New York: Random House, 1966.

———. *On the Genealogy of Morals.* Translated and edited by Douglas Smith. Oxford: Oxford World's Classics, 1996.

———. *The Gay Science: With a Prelude in Rhymes and an Appendix of Songs by Friedrich Nietzsche.* Translated by Walker Kaufmann. New York: Vintage Books, 1974.

Nilton Santos. *The Website of Nilton Santos.* 2013. http://www.niltonsantos.com.br/page/index.asp (26 July 2013).

Northcroft, Jonathan. "Lost in time—Manchester United's 1958 Busby Babes." *The Times* (London). 14 February 2008. http://www.thesundaytimes.co.uk/sto/sport/football/Premiership/article79873.ece (24 June 2012).

Notable Quotes. "Carl Jung Quotes." 2013. http://www.notable-quotes.com/j/jung_carl.html (9 November 2013).

Nye, Joseph. *Soft Power: The Means to Success in World Politics.* New York: Public Affairs, 2004.

Observer. "Sports profile: Abédi Pelé, a football legend." *The Daily Observer.* 18 June 2008. http://observer.gm/africa/gambia/article/2008/6/18/sports-profile (10 November 2013).

O'Connor, Philip. "Anti-homophobia rainbow campaign hit by controversy." Reuters. 19 September 2013. http://news.yahoo.com/anti-homophobia-rainbow-campaign-hit-controversy-012935851-sow.html (21 September 2013).

Ogalde, Rodrigo. "Elías Figueroa está interesado en ser candidato a diputado por San Antonio." *Soy Chile*. 7 March 2013. http://www.soychile.cl/San-Antonio/Politica/2013/03/07/159096/Elias-Figueroa-esta-interesado-en-ser-candidato-a-diputado-por-San-Antonio.aspx (25 November 2013).

Ogden, Mark. "Thierry Henry admits to handball that defeated Ireland in World Cup play-off." *The Telegraph*. 19 November 2009. http://www.telegraph.co.uk/sport/football/teams/republic-of-ireland/6599687/Thierry-Henry-admits-to-handball-that-defeated-Ireland-in-World-Cup-play-off.html (23 September 2009).

Ojoko, Israel. "FIFA take Confed Cup positives despite Brazil protest." *Futaa*. 2013. http://www.futaa.com/football/article/fifa-take-confed-cup-positives-despite-brazil-protest (16 July 2013).

Onze. *Onze Mondial*. 2011. http://www.onzemondial.com/ (13 May 2011).

Oocities. "What they Said: Di Sefano." *Oocities*. N.d. http://www.oocities.org/colosseum/bleachers/7429/DiStefano8.htm (10 November 2013).

Open Court Publishing. "Soccer and Philosophy Beautiful Thoughts on the Beautiful Game." *Open Court Book*. 2013. http://www.opencourtbooks.com/books_n/soccer.htm (14 November 2013).

Orozco, Ivan. "Mexico's Jimenez looks forward to Gold Cup, future." *Concacaf*. 7 July 2013. http://www.concacaf.com/article/mexicos-jimenez-looks-forward-to-gold-cup-future (9 November 2013).

Ortega y Gasset, José. *The Revolt of the Masses*. New York: W. W. Norton and Company, 1993.

Orwell, George. "The Sporting Spirit." *Tribune*. December 1945. http://orwell.ru/library/articles/spirit/english/e_spirit (22 July 2013).

Oshan, Jeremiah. "Seattle Sounders players are excited to welcome Clint Dempsey to the team." *MLSsoccer.com*, 4 August 2013. http://m.mlssoccer.com/news/article/2013/08/04/seattle-sounders-players-are-excited-welcome-clint-dempsey-team (8 November 2013).

Pattisson, Pete. "At 16, Ganesh got a job in Qatar. Two months later he was dead." *The Guardian*. 25 September 2013. http://www.theguardian.com/global-development/2013/sep/25/qatar-nepalese-workers-poverty-camps (27 September 2013).

Payne, Stanley G. *A History of Fascism: 1914–1945*. London: UCL Press, 1995.

PCS Forum. "Dragan Džajić." 9 December 2011. http://pcsd.forumfree.it/?t=59220511 (11 November 2013).

Peck, Brooks. "Neymar becomes a comic book character, frustrates artist with his hair." *Dirty Tackle*. 19 April 2013. http://sports.yahoo.com/blogs/soccer-dirty-tackle/neymar-becomes-comic-book-character-frustrates-artist-hair-041118168-sow.html (20 November 2013).

Pedroncelli, Peter. "World Cup 2010: FIFA Revenue Tops A Billion Dollars For The First Time." *Goal*. 22 March 2010. http://www.goal.com/en-us/news/1786/fifa/2010/03/22/1844168/world-cup-2010-fifa-revenue-tops-a-billion-dollars-for-the-first- (29 September 2012).

Pelé (with Robert L. Fish). *My Life and the Beautiful Game: The Autobiography of Pelé*. New York: Warner Books, 1977.

Peñaloza, Pedro Jose and Hector Larios Proa. "El fútbol es un sueño." *Foreign Affairs En Español* 6, no. 3 (July–September 2006): 175–181.

Perryman, Mark. *Philosophy Football: Eleven Great Thinkers Play It Deep*. London: Penguin, 1997.

Pes Stats Database. "Igor Netto." *Pes Stats Database*. 2012. http://pesstatsdatabase.com/viewtopic.php?f=182&t=9435 (25 October 2012).

Philosophy Football. "Goalkeeper." 2013. http://www.philosophyfootball.com/view_item.php?pid=242 (14 February 2014).

———. "Philosophy football quotations." 2013. http://www.philosophyfootball.com/quotations.php (28 July 2013).

Pitts, Thomas. "A Philosopher's Guide to Football." *The False Nine*. 13 July 2012, http://www.thefalsenine.co.uk/2012/07/13/a-philosophers-guide-to-football/ (28 July 2013).

Plumer, Bradford. "How Soccer Explains the World." *Mother Jones*. 4 August 2004. http://www.motherjones.com/politics/2004/08/how-soccer-explains-world (12 September 2012).

Premier Soccer Stats. "All Time Player Records." *Premier Soccer Stats.* 2012. http://www.premiersoccerstats.com/Records.cfm?DOrderby=Ass&DYearby=All%20Seasons (27 September 2012).

Press TV. "Cruyff: Ronaldo, United's best ever." *Press TV.* 2 April 2008. http://edition.presstv.ir/detail/49967.html (28 September 2012).

Preston, Bryan. "Mexican TV Announcer Goes on Epic PRO-AMERICA Rant After the US Saves Mexico's World Cup Hopes." *PJ Media.* 16 October 2013. http://pjmedia.com/tatler/2013/10/16/mexican-tv-announcer-goes-on-epic-pro-america-rant-after-the-us-saves-mexicos-world-cup-hopes/ (6 November 2013).

Pretelin Muñoz de Cote, Fausto. "El imperio global de fútbol." *Foreign Affairs En Español* 6, no. 3 (July–September 2006): 132–146.

PR Newswire. "Waka Waka (This Time For Africa) From Shakira's Forthcoming New Album Sale el Sol/The Sun Comes Out—Makes World Cup and YouTube History." http://www.prnewswire.com/news-releases/waka-waka-this-time-for-africa-from-shakiras-forthcoming-new-album-sale-el-solthe-sun-comes-out-makes-world-cup-and-youtube-history-101996118.html (13 August 2013).

Procter, James. *Stuart Hall.* London: Routledge, 2004.

Quill, Greg. "The story behind K'naan's 'Wavin' Flag.'" *Toronto Star.* 27 September 2012. http://www.thestar.com/entertainment/books/2012/09/27/the_story_behind_knaans_wavin_flag.html (13 August 2013).

Rankopedia. "Best Russian-Soviet Soccer Player Ever." *Rankopedia.* 2011. http://www.rankopedia.com/Best-Russian/Soviet-soccer-Player-ever/Step1/14794/.htm (25 October 2012).

Richard, David. "Mexico's World Cup qualifying chances in 'Crisis' mode." *USA Today.* 11 September 2013. http://www.usatoday.com/story/sports/soccer/worldcup/2013/09/11/mexico-world-cup-qualifying/2802243/ (6 November 2013).

Richards, Ted. *Soccer and Philosophy: Beautiful Thoughts on the Beautiful Game.* Chicago: Open Court Publishing, 2010.

Rodriquez, Sebastian Leiva. "Entrevista a Elías Figueroa Branden." *Fundacion Asciende.* 2012. http://www.fundacionasciende.com/publicaciones-de-fundacion-asciende/entrevistas/196-entrevista-a-elias-figueroa-branden (27 August 2012).

Ronaldo, Cristiano. *Cristiano Ronaldo.* 2013. http://www.cristianoronaldoofficial.com/ (31 July 2013).

Rowe, Steve. "What is Leadership?" *Sagepub.* 2007. http://www.corwin.com/upm-data/15104_Rowe_Chapter_01.pdf (3 October 2012).

Rufer, Wynton. "Wynton Rufer Soccer School of Excellence." *Wynton Rufer's Website.* 2012. http://www.wynrs.co.nz/ (21 October 2012).

Rupert, Mark. "Marxism." In *International Relations Theory for the 21st Century,* edited by Martin Griffiths, 35–46. London: Routledge, 2007.

Rycroft, Ben. "Beckham attracted media, but MLS has driven its own growth." *CBC Sports.* 3 December 2012. http://www.cbc.ca/sports/soccer/opinion/2012/12/beckham-attracted-media-attention-but-mls-drove-the-growth.html (5 December 2012).

Said, Sammy. "Cristiano Ronaldo Net Worth." *The Richest.* 2013. http://www.therichest.com/celebnetworth/athletes/footballer/cristiano-ronaldo-net-worth/ (6 November 2013).

Sankaran Vasu, Vinya. "Ethan Zohn: Using Soccer to Change the World." *Service Space.* 7 December 2012. http://www.servicespace.org/blog/view.php?id=12388 (14 November 2013).

Sapa-dpa. "Serbian legend goes on corruption trial." *Times Live.* 31 January 2011. http://www.timeslive.co.za/sport/soccer/2011/01/31/serbian-legend-goes-on-corruption-trial (23 September 2013).

Schaerlaeckens, Leander. "Chasing Gaetjens." *ESPN.* 26 February 2010. http://soccernet.espn.go.com/world-cup/story/_/id/4937012/ce/us/real-story-1950-world-cup-hero?cc=3888&ver=global (24 October 2012).

Scraton, Phil. *Hillsborough: The Truth.* Edinburgh: Mainstream Publishing Company, 2009.

Serbia. "Belgrade Sports Route." *Serbia.* 27 June 2012. http://www.serbia.com/belgrade-sports-route/ (12 November 2013).

Shankly, Bill. "Own words." *Bill Shankly's Website.* 2011. http://www.shankly.com/article/2517 (12 May 2011).

Shaw, Duncan. "The Politics of 'Futbol.'" *History Today* 35, no. 8. 1985. http://www.historytoday.com/duncan-shaw/politics-futbol (22 August 2012).

Shaw, Phil. "Schmeichel slices into fixture." *The Independent,* 16 February 1998.

Sheldrake, Philip. *A Brief History of Spirituality.* Oxford, UK: Blackwell, 2007.

Shirts, Matthew. "Socrates, Corinthians and Question of Democracy." In *Sport and Society in Latin America,* edited by Joseph Arbena. Westport, CT: Greenwood Press, 1988.

Show Racism the Red Card. *Website of Show Racism the Red Card.* 2013. http://www.srtrc.org/ (26 July 2013).

Siegel, Sarah. "Brazilian soccer club drives organ donations with 'immortal fan' concept." *JWT Anxiety Index.* 24 June 2013. http://anxietyindex.com/2013/06/brazilian-soccer-club-drives-organ-donations-with-immortal-fan-concept/ (10 November 2013).

Simon, Laurence H., ed. *Karl Marx: Selected Writings.* Indianapolis: Hacket Publishing Company, Inc., 1994.

Simon Wiesenthal Centre. "Wiesenthal Centre Welcomes Estonian Historical Commission Findings Which Confirm Holocaust Crimes of Evald Mikson." *Simon Wiesenthal Centre.* 21 June 2001. http://www.wiesenthal.com/site/apps/s/content.asp?c=lsKWLbPJLnF&b=4442915&ct=5853153 (12 May 2001).

Simpson, Mark. "Meet the metrosexual." *Salon.* 22 July 2002. http://www.salon.com/2002/07/22/metrosexual/ (31 July 2013).

Singer, Peter. "Ethics." *Encyclopædia Britannica.* http://www.utilitarian.net/singer/by/1985.htm (23 September 2012).

———. "Is Doping Wrong?" *Project Syndicate.* 14 August 2007. http://www.project-syndicate.org/commentary/is-doping-wrong (23 September 2012).

———. "Why is cheating OK in football?" *The Guardian.* 29 June 2010. http://www.guardian.co.uk/commentisfree/2010/jun/29/cheating-football-germany-goalkeeper (25 September 2012).

Smith, Rory. "World Cup 2010: Top 50 World Cup moments." *The Telegraph.* 25 June 2010, http://www.telegraph.co.uk/sport/football/competitions/world-cup-2010/6151657/World-Cup-2010-Top-50-World-Cup-moments.html (30 July 2013).

Sobek, David "Rallying around the Podesta: Testing Diversionary Theory across Time." *Journal of Peace Research* 44, no. 1. (2007): 29–45.

Soccernet. "Cristiano Ronaldo." *Soccernet.espn.* 2012. http://soccernet.espn.go.com/player/_/id/22774/cristiano-dos-santos-aveiro-ronaldo?cc=3888 (28 September 2012).

Soccer News. "Zidane is the best player ever, says Beckham." *Soccer News.* 13 July 2008. http://www.soccernews.com/zidane-is-the-best-player-ever-says-beckham/4033/date (16 September 2012).

SoccerWay. "Henry hails 'God Zidane,'" *SoccerWay.* 5 August 2005, http://br.soccerway.com/news/2005/august/5/henry-hails-god-zidane/ (12 October 2013).

Solzhenitsyn, Aleksandr I. *The Gulag Archipelago 1918–1956: An Experiment in Literary Investigation.* Translated by Thomas P. Whitney. New York: Harper and Row, 1974.

SOS Children's Villages Canada. "Mexico: Hugo Sanchez." *SOS Children's Villages.* 2006. http://www.soschildrensvillages.ca/about-us/international-partners/friends-worldwide/fifa-ambassadors-america/pages/mexico-hugo-sanchez.aspx (9 November 2013).

Sorek, Tamir. *Arab Soccer in a Jewish State: The Integrative Enclave.* Cambridge, UK: Cambridge University Press, 2007.

———. "Arab football in Israel as an 'integrative enclave.'" *Ethnic and Racial Studies* 26, no. 2 (May 2003): 422–450.

Soriano, Ferran. *La pelota no entra por azar.* México, D.F.: Santillana, 2012.

Sounders FC. "Sounders FC Signs Clint Dempsey." *Sounders FC.* 3 August 2013. http://www.soundersfc.com/News/Articles/2013/08-August/Sounders-FC-Signs-USA-International-Clint-Dempsey.aspx (14 September 2013).

Sportsnet. "Maradona anoints Messi as his successor." *Sportsnet.* 25 March 2010. http://www.sportsnet.ca/soccer/maradona-messi-0/ (10 August 2013).

Stanford Encyclopedia of Philosophy. "Emmanuel Levinas." *Stanford Encyclopedia of Philosophy.* http://plato.stanford.edu/entries/levinas/ (13 November 2013).
———. "Plato." *Stanford Encyclopedia of Philosophy.* http://plato.stanford.edu/entries/plato/ (13 November 2013).
Stehli, Jean-Sébastien et al. "Zidane: Icône malgré lui." *L'Express.* 8 June 2006. http://web.archive.org/web/20071014204041/http://lexpress.fr/mag/sports/dossier/mondial-2006/dossier.asp?ida=438679&p=3 (16 September 2012).
Sternhell, Ze'ev (with Mario Sznajder and Maia Asheri). *The Birth of Fascist Ideology: From Cultural Rebellion to Political Revolution.* Translated by David Maisel. Princeton, NJ: Princeton University Press, 1995.
Stevenson, Jon. "Zidane's lasting legacy." *BBC Sport.* 2010. http://news.bbc.co.uk/sport2/hi/football/world_cup_2006/teams/france/5147908.stmdate (16 September 2012).
Stevenson, Jonathan. "Real Madrid 1960: the greatest club side of all time." *BBC Online Network.* 23 May 2011. http://www.bbc.co.uk/blogs/jonathanstevenson/2011/05/the_greatest_club_side_of_all.html (10 November 2013).
Stretford End. "Chants: We'll Never Die." *Stretford-End.* 2013. http://www.stretford-end.com/chants/ (28 November 2013).
Szymanski, Stefan and Andrew Zimbalist. *National Pastime: How Americans Play Baseball and the Rest of the World Plays Soccer.* Washington: The Brookings Institution, 2005.
Tariq, Naveed. "The 5 Greatest Footballers You've Never Heard Of." *Bleacher Report.* 7 July 2009. http://bleacherreport.com/articles/213877-the-5-greatest-footballers-youve-never-heard-of/page/3 (12 November 2013).
Taylor, Steve. "Spirituality: The Hidden Side of Sports." *New Renaissance* 11, no. 1, issue 36 (Spring 2002). http://www.ru.org/sports/spirituality-the-hidden-side-of-sports.html (13 November 2013).
Thairu, John. "Wizard of the Wing: Ryan Giggs Vector Art by Felio Sotomayor." *A Sporting Life.* 13 September 2012. http://www.asportinglife.com/ryan-giggs-vector-art-felio-sotomayor/ (13 November 2013).
The Australian. "IOC's Dick Pound says FIFA not transparent." *The Australian.* 4 October 2011. http://www.theaustralian.com.au/sport/iocs-dick-pound-says-fifa-not-transparent/story-e6frg7mf-1226157922722 (30 July 2013).
The Canadian Press. "Soccer star Zidane profiled in Quebec museum exhibit." *Herald.* 2 August 2013. http://thechronicleherald.ca/travel/1145803-soccer-star-zidane-profiled-in-quebec-museum-exhibit (10 November 2013).
The Classical. "Anxiety is Freedom: The Opacity of Football." *The Classical.* 22 May 2012, http://theclassical.org/articles/anxiety-is-freedom (20 September 2013).
The Clinic Online. "Los 100 rostros del Sí." *The Clinic.* http://www.theclinic.cl/2012/07/30/los-100-rostros-del-si/ (25 November 2013).
The CR7 Shop. 2013. http://www.youtube.com/watch?v=J_FdylBD_mc (31 July 2013).
The David Beckham Brand. "The David Beckham Brand." *ICMR.* 2003. http://www.icmrindia.org/casestudies/catalogue/Marketing/MKTG077.htm (28 September 2012).
The Economist. "Prince of the absurd: In search of the real Camus." *The Economist.* 7 January 2010.
The Guardian. "Cameroon's Samuel Eto'o named in World Cup squad despite threat to quit." *The Guardian.* 29 May 2010. http://www.theguardian.com/football/2010/may/29/cameroon-samuel-etoo-world-cup (9 November 2013).
———. "Ferenc Puskas dies aged 79." *The Guardian.* 17 November 2006. http://www.theguardian.com/football/2006/nov/17/newsstory.sport6 (10 August 2013).
———. "If Messi is best on planet, Ronaldo is best in universe—José Mourinho." *The Guardian.* 12 October 2012. http://www.guardian.co.uk/football/2012/oct/12/messi-ronaldo-mourinho-ballon-dor (31 July 2013).
———. "The genius of the life of Brian." *The Observer.* 31 December 2006. http://www.theguardian.com/books/2006/dec/31/sportandleisure.features (11 November 2013).
The Guardian Blog. "From the Vault: Remembering the life and football of Bobby Moore." *The Guardian Blog.* 22 February 2013. http://www.theguardian.com/sport/blog/2013/feb/22/vault-remembering-life-football-bobby-moore (30 July 2013).

The Guardian Nigéria. "Arsenal target, Iheanacho, joint candidate for successor to Abedi Pele, Okocha." *The Guardian*. 30 October 2013. http://www.worldwww.ngrguardiannews.com/ index.php/home-sp-955664465/137206-arsenal-target-iheanacho-joint-candidate-for-successor-to-abedi-pele-okocha (10 November 2013).

The Independent. "Football: Xavier hit with 18-month ban for steroid use." *The Independent*. 24 November 2005.

———. "Publish and be Damned: Giles fights back for Revie and Clough." 13 November 2010. http://www.independent.co.uk/sport/football/news-and-comment/publish-and-be-damned-giles-fights-back-for-revie-and-clough-2132719.html (10 November 2013).

The Namibian. "Abedi Pele in Namibia today." *The Namibian*. 15 November 2007. http:// www.namibian.com.na/indexx.php?archive_id=37932&page_type=archive_story_detail& page=3915 (10 November 2013).

The New York Times. "Amsterdam Journal; A Dutch Soccer Riddle: Jewish Regalia Without Jews." *New York Times*, 28 March 2005.

The Official Website of the Irish Football Association. "Profile of George Best." http:// www.irishfa.com/international/squad-profiles/profile/341/legends-of-the-game/george-best/ (13 November 2013).

The Richest. "Richest Football Clubs 2012—World's Most Valuable Football Teams." *Forbes*. 20 April 2012. http://www.therichest.org/sports/richest-football-clubs/ (28 September 2012).

The Sentinel. "Stoke City: Shea reveals his abstract way to ease injury pain." 19 September 2013. http://www.stokesentinel.co.uk/Stoke-City-Shea-reveals-abstract-way-ease-injury/ story-19815709-detail/story.html (10 November 2013).

The Sunday Times. "Britain's rich list—David and Victoria Beckham." *The Sunday Times*. 26 April 2009.

The Tireless Midfielder. "#97: Robert Prosinečki." 30 May 2012. http://tirelessmidfielder.wordpress.com/page/3/ (12 November 2013).

The Top Tens. "Best African Soccer Players: Abedi Pele." N.d. http://www.thetoptens.com/ best-african-soccer-players/ (11 November 2013).

Thielke, Thilo. "They'll Put a Spell on You: The Witchdoctors of African Football." *Spiegel Online International*. 11 June 2010. http://www.spiegel.de/international/zeitgeist/they-ll-put-a-spell-on-you-the-witchdoctors-of-african-football-a-699704.html (26 November 2013).

This Is Announcements. "Donald Simpson Bell VC: Obituary." *This Is Announcements*. 29 September 2008. http://www.thisisannouncements.co.uk/5860367 (2 August 2013).

Toosi, Nahal. "Afghanistan wins 1st international soccer title." *Associated Press*. 11 September 2013. http://news.yahoo.com/afghanistan-wins-1st-international-soccer-title-181455598-spt.html (14 September 2013).

Tovar, Javier. "Is Soccer The Ticket Out Of Rio Poverty?" *Agence France Presse*. 2 February 2013. http://www.huffingtonpost.com/2013/02/02/soccer-football-rio-poverty_n_2606935.html (13 November 2013).

Trial Football. "Mourinho: Spurs Fullback Bale Better than Chelsea's Cole." *Trial Football*. 3 July 2009. http://www.tribalfootball.com/articles/mourinho-spurs-fullback-bale-better-chelseas-cole-254674#.UiOdoz86ZoE (1 September 2013).

Tunis, John R. "Los Dictadores Descubren El Deporte." *Foreign Affairs En Español* 6 no. 3 (July–September 2006): 235–245. Originally published in *Foreign Affairs* (July–August 1936).

UNICEF. "Spaces of hope." *Unicef*. N.d. http://www.unicef.org/football/world/brazil.html (9 November 2013).

USA Today. "Hamm's imprint made on new women's soccer league." *USA Today*. 18 January 2008. http://usatoday30.usatoday.com/sports/soccer/2008-01-18-hamm-silhouette-logo_N.htm (8 October 2012).

Valdano, Jorge. "Jorge Valdano Entrevista." *La Revista*. 5 October 1997. http:// www.elmundo.es/larevista/num103/textos/valdano1.html (23 October 2012).

———. *Los 11 poderes del líder*. México, D.F.: Connecta, 2013.

Vales, José. "Argentina: más que un deporte, herramienta política." *Foreign Affairs En Español* 6, no. 3 (Julio–Septiembre, 2006): 152–165.

Velimirović, Igor. "Džajić: Hteo sam da se vratim u Zvezdu, ali me nisu ni zvali!" *Blic*. 18 December 2011. http://sport.blic.rs/Fudbal/Domaci-fudbal/207451/Dzajic-Hteo-sam-da-se-vratim-u-Zvezdu-ali-me-nisu-ni-zvali (12 November 2013).

Veliz, C., ed. *Latin America and the Caribbean*. London: Anthony Blond, 1968.

Venegas, Lorena and Alfredo Peña. "A 25 años del plebiscito del 88 que derrotó a Pinochet: Los 100 rostros que estuvieron en la campaña del Sí." *Cambio21*. 4 October 2013. http://www.cambio21.cl/cambio21/site/artic/20131002/pags/20131002180358.html (25 November 2013).

Vickery, Tim. "The 'Hand of God' Church." *BBC Online Network*. 4 November 2002. http://news.bbc.co.uk/sport2/hi/football/2396503.stm (15 May 2011).

Villoro, Juan. *Dios es Redondo*. México, D.F: Editorial Planeta, 2006.

———. *Los once de la tribu*. México, D.F.: Nuevo Siglo, 1995.

Vinnai, Gerhard. *El fútbol como ideología*. México, D.F: Siglo XXI, 2003.

———. *Football Mania*. London: Ocean Books, 1973.

Virilio, Paul. *Popular Defense and Ecological Struggles*. New York: Semiotexte, 1990.

Wagg, Stephen, ed. *Giving the Game Away: Football, Politics and Culture on Five Continents*. Leicester, UK: Leicester University Press, 1995.

Wallace, Sam. "Beckham rejected Milan and Inter to take Galaxy millions." *The Independent*. 12 January 2007. http://www.independent.co.uk/sport/football/european/beckham-rejected-milan-and-inter-to-take-galaxy-millions-431736.html (28 September 2012).

Wassink, Zac. "MLS Sets Attendance Records in 2012: Is it All Really Great News for the League?" *Yahoo! Sports*. 21 December 2012. http://sports.yahoo.com/news/mls-sets-attendance-records-2012-really-great-news-154000159--mls.html (2 August 2013).

Watson, Connie. "Modernizing Brazil bulldozes its slums and soccer's shrine." *CBC News*. 10 April 2012. http://www.cbc.ca/news/world/modernizing-brazil-bulldozes-its-slums-and-soccer-s-shrine-1.1141696 (26 November 2013).

Watson, Jake. "The Welshman makes his 900th appearance for the Old Trafford outfit against Norwich and Goal.com have compiled the greatest soundbites on English football's most decorated player." *Goal*. 26 February 2012. http://www.goal.com/en-gb/news/2896/premier-league/2012/02/26/2924348/he-gives-players-twisted-blood-ryan-giggs-manchester-united (10 November 2013).

Weeks, Johnny. "Beautiful Games: Action Paintings by Ben Mosley." *The Guardian*, 10 April 2013. http://www.theguardian.com/sport/gallery/2013/apr/10/painting-art (21 November 2013).

Wheeler, Mark. "Hosting World Cup would draw revenue like 12 Super Bowls." *The City Paper* (Nashville). 13 June 2010. http://nashvillecitypaper.com/content/city-news/hosting-world-cup-would-draw-revenue-12-super-bowls (29 September 2012).

White, Jim. "Albert Camus: thinker, goalkeeper." *The Telegraph*. 6 January 2010. http://www.telegraph.co.uk/culture/books/6941924/Albert-Camus-thinker-goalkeeper.html (23 September 2012).

Williams, Richard. "Football's short-team loan system is in dire need of reformation," *The Guardian*, 22 February 2011, http://www.theguardian.com/football/blog/2011/feb/22/football-loans-richard-williams (6 November 2013).

———. "Ryan Giggs, Stanley Matthews and the art of growing old gracefully." *The Guardian*. 27 February 2012. http://www.theguardian.com/football/blog/2012/feb/27/ryan-giggs-stanley-matthews (10 November 2013).

Williams, Tony. "The Mia Hamm Effect." *American Athlete*. N.d. http://www.americanathletemag.com/ArticleView/tabid/156/ArticleID/271/The-Mia-Hamm-Effect.aspx (9 November 2013).

Wilson, Jeremy. "United not the greatest test of faith for Primus." *The Guardian*. 27 January 2007. http://www.guardian.co.uk/football/2007/jan/27/newsstory.sport3 (28 July 2013).

Winter, David. *Brilliant Orange: The Neurotic Genius of Dutch Football*. New York: Bloomsbury Publishing, 2000.

Winter, Henry and Steven Gerrard. *My Autobiography*. London: Bantam, 2007.

Woitalla, Mike. "Mia Hamm's advice for girls, parents and coaches." *Soccer America*. 11 April 2012. http://www.socceramerica.com/article/46323/mia-hamms-advice-for-girls-parents-and-coaches.html (9 November 2013).

———. "View the Game as an Art, not a War (Book Review)." *Soccer America's Youth Soccer Insider*. 18 February 2013. http://www.socceramerica.com/article/50388/view-the-game-as-an-art-not-a-war-book-review.html (10 November 2013).

Working Class Ballet. "Football Quotes." http://workingclassballet.wordpress.com/theres-some-people-on-the-pitch-football-quotes/ (16 September 2013).

World Football Legends. "Igor Netto." *World Football Legends UK*. 2012. http://www.world-football-legends.co.uk/index.php/urs/115-netto-igor (25 October 2012).

World Soccer. "The Greatest Team Ever." Summer 2013: 41–53.

Yahoo!Sports. "El Salvador ban 14 internationals for life for fixing." *Reuters*. 20 September 2013, http://sports.yahoo.com/news/el-salvador-ban-14-internationals-life-match-fixing-211930119-sow.html (23 September 2013).

Yelp. "Camp Nou: Danielle F." 14 March 2013. http://www.yelp.com/biz/camp-nou-barcelona (26 November 2013).

YoSoyFutbol. "El arco de la vida." 12 May 2008. http://yosoyfutbol.com/noticias_detalle.php?articles_id=14 (29 October 2012).

YouTube. "Alfredo Di Stéfano: Pelé is the best player of all time, better than Messi and Ronaldo." http://www.youtube.com/watch?v=y13irjlnPno (10 August 2013).

———. "Ferenc Puskas Tribute." http://www.youtube.com/watch?v=9oEt4zQZ9Jg (10 August 2013).

———. "Salvador Mariona en La Kaliente." *YouTube*. 20 October 2011. http://www.youtube.com/watch?v=mcivFSvWPGg (3 December 2013).

———. "The CR7 Shop." http://www.youtube.com/watch?v=J_FdylBD_mc (31 July 2013).

———. "Tribute to Puerta, Feher, Foe, O'Donnell, Rasmus Green." 2012. http://www.youtube.com/watch?v=oyY1ETgGRx4 (29 September 2008).

Yuscavage, Chris. "Jay-Z Reportedly Wants to Sign Soccer Phenom Neymar to Roc Nation Sports." *Complex Sports*. 7 May 2013. http://www.complex.com/sports/2013/05/jay-z-reportedly-wants-to-sign-soccer-phenom-neymar-to-roc-nation-sports (20 November 2013).

Zekaria, Simon. "Soccer Still the Main Event for Advertisers." *Wall Street Journal*. 17 September 2012. http://online.wsj.com/article/SB10000872396390444450004578000021105998576.html (29 September 2012).

Zohn, Ethan. "About Ethan Zohn." *Ethan Zohn's Website*. http://www.ezohn.com/about/ (14 November 2013).

Index

About the Author

Tamir Bar-On was born in Beersheba, Israel. He immigrated to Toronto, Canada, with his family in 1974. He is a full professor in the Department of International Relations and Humanities at the *Tecnológico de Monterrey*, Campus Querétaro, in Mexico. He received his BA and MA from York University (Toronto, Canada) and his PhD in political science from McGill University (Montreal, Canada). He was a postdoctoral fellow at DePaul University. Bar-On previously taught political science at the University of Toronto, University of Windsor, Royal Military College of Canada, and Wilfrid Laurier University, in Canada. Bar-On is the author of *Where Have All the Fascists Gone?* (2007) and *Rethinking the French New Right: Alternatives to Modernity* (2013). *The World through Soccer* is his third book.

CPSIA information can be obtained at www.ICGtesting.com
Printed in the USA
BVOW04*2013270414

351670BV00003B/5/P